MAO

5

Story and Art by
Rumiko Takahashi

Characters

TAISHO ERA

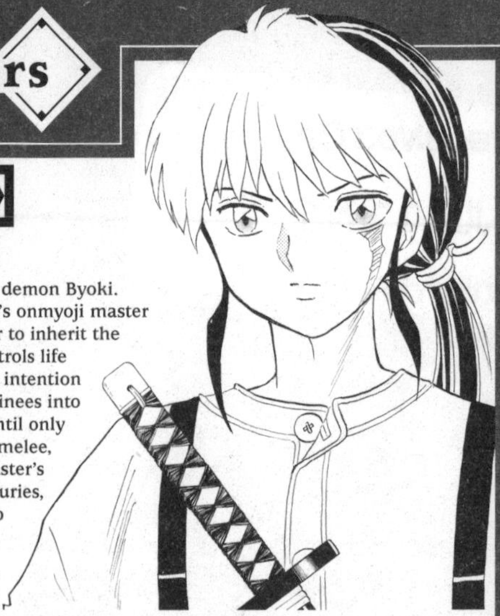

MAO

An exorcist cursed by the cat demon Byoki. Nine hundred years ago, Mao's onmyoji master proclaimed Mao his successor to inherit the Taizanfukun spell, which controls life spans. In reality, the master's intention was to goad the other five trainees into killing Mao and each other until only one survived. In the ensuing melee, Mao might have killed his master's daughter, Sana. For nine centuries, Mao has searched for Byoki to uncover the truth and purge his curse.

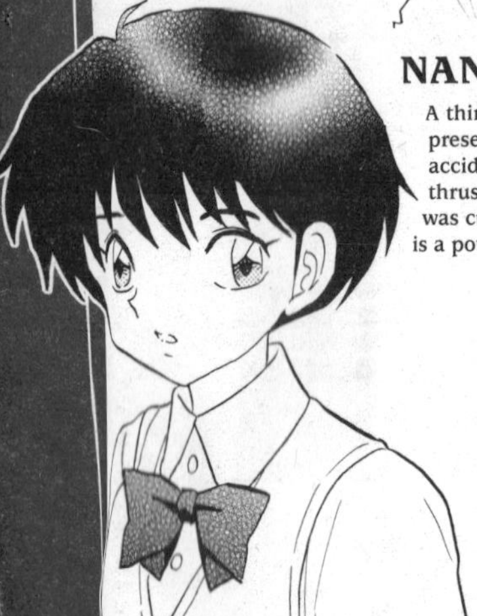

NANOKA KIBA

A third-year middle school student living in the present day. As a child, she was involved in a car accident that killed her parents and temporarily thrust her into the Taisho era. There, her body was cursed by Byoki. Nanoka's body, like Mao's, is a potential vessel that Byoki seeks to inhabit.

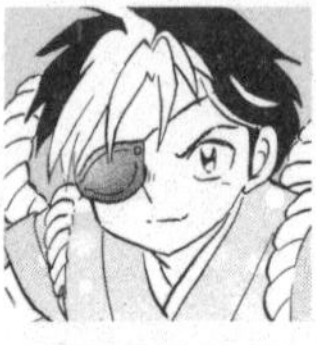

HYAKKA

Mao's senior student apprentice. Wields fire spells.

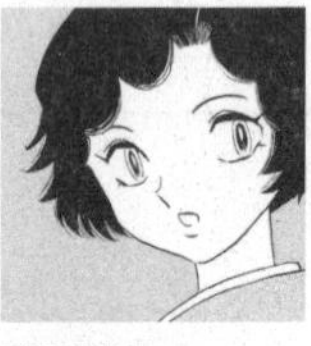

TENKO

Mao's informant, an ayakashi who works at Milk House.

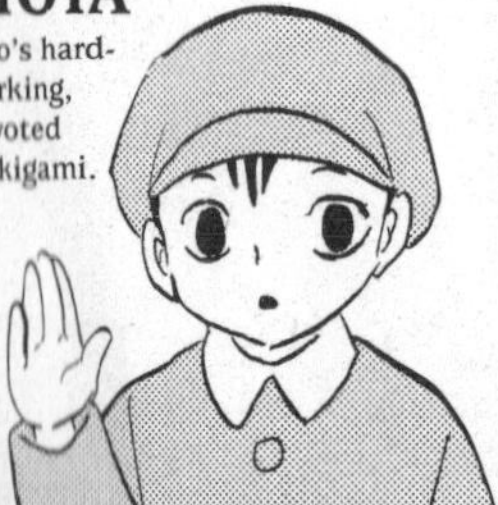

OTOYA

Mao's hard-working, devoted shikigami.

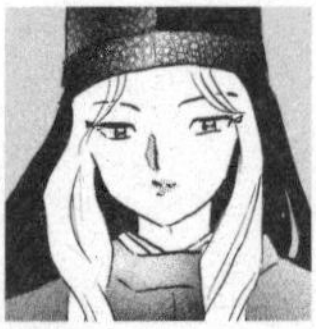

SHIRANUI

An exorcist who claims to be a member of the Goku clan. Keeps sending assassins after Mao.

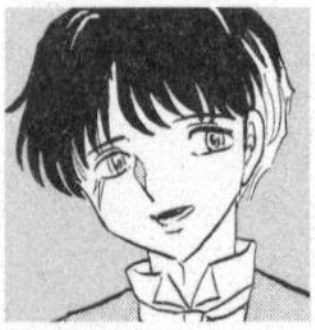

KAMON (KUCHINAWA)

Mao's senior student apprentice. Wields tree spells.

PRESENT DAY

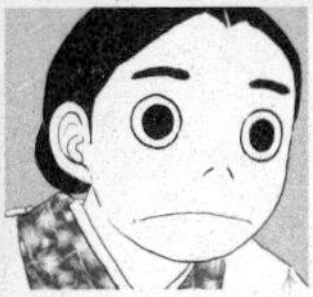

UOZUMI

Mao's shikigami and the housekeeper living in Nanoka's home.

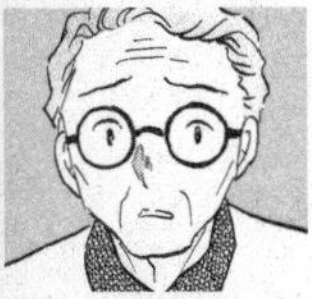

NANOKA'S GRANDFATHER

He was on his deathbed at the time of Nanoka's accident, but it seems his life is being extended by Byoki.

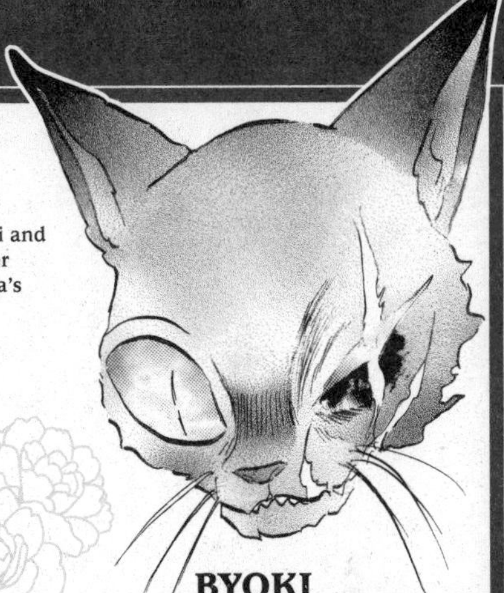

BYOKI

The kodoku cat who cursed Mao and Nanoka. Survives by possessing human bodies. After eating the forbidden scroll containing the Taizanfukun spell, he gained the ability to use it to control life spans.

HEIAN PERIOD

HOUSE OF GOKO

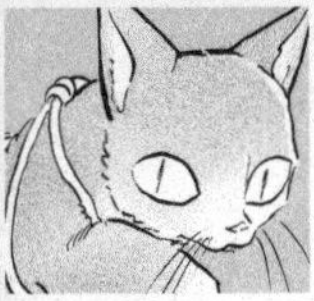

HAIMARU

Sana's beloved cat who only liked her and Mao.

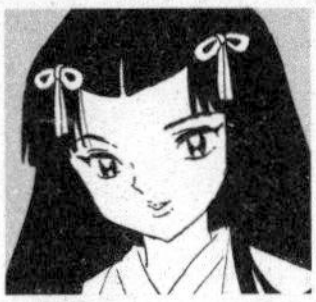

SANA

The master's daughter. Betrothed to Mao by her father.

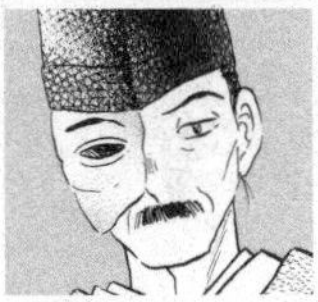

MASTER

The head of the Goko clan and Mao's former master. Wields forbidden spells and attempted to sacrifice Mao for his own ends.

Story thus far...

When Nanoka Kiba was seven years old, she was orphaned in a violent accident. Now she is a third-year student in middle school. One day she passes the spot where the accident occurred and is miraculously transported to the Taisho Era. There she meets an exorcist named Mao. When they realize they have both been cursed by Byoki, a cat demon, they join forces to find him and free themselves.

Mao is reunited with Hyakka and Kamon, two of his fellow apprentices who survived the succession ceremony. But moments later he is attacked by assassins and critically wounded. Fortunately, Nanoka is able to magically save him with her blood. They then learn that the man sending the assassins is Shiranui, an exorcist claiming to be affiliated with the Goko clan...

CONTENTS

Chapter 1:
Masago

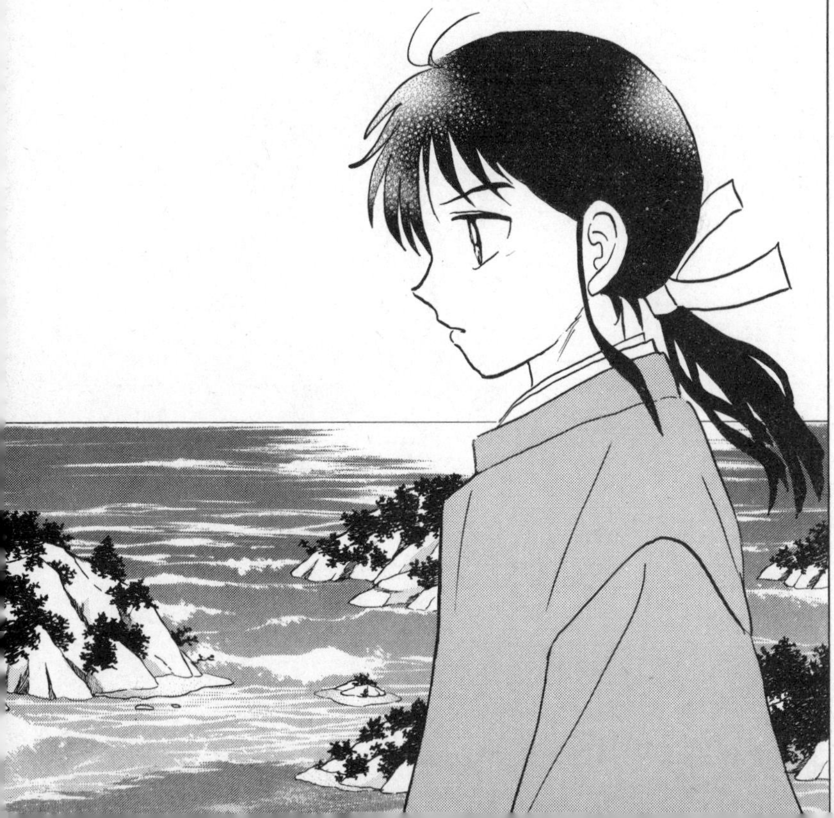

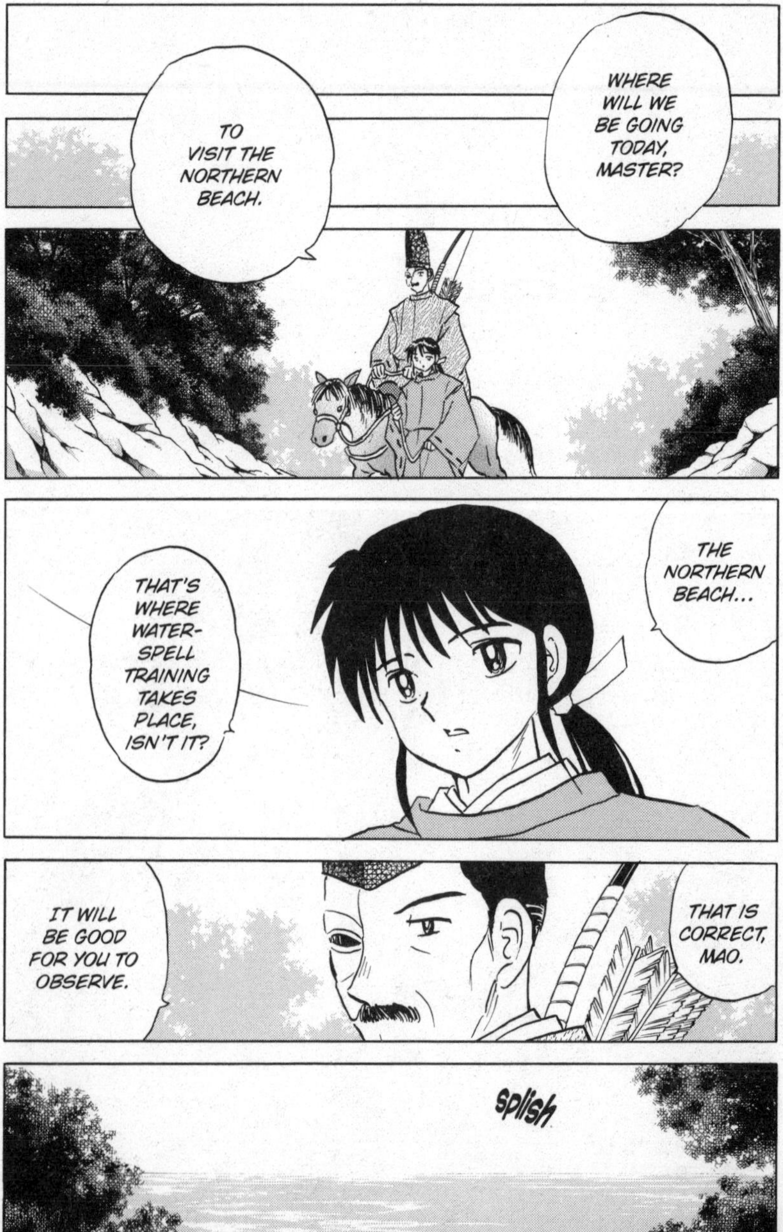
WHERE WILL WE BE GOING TODAY, MASTER?
TO VISIT THE NORTHERN BEACH.
THE NORTHERN BEACH...
THAT'S WHERE WATER-SPELL TRAINING TAKES PLACE, ISN'T IT?
THAT IS CORRECT, MAO.
IT WILL BE GOOD FOR YOU TO OBSERVE.
splish

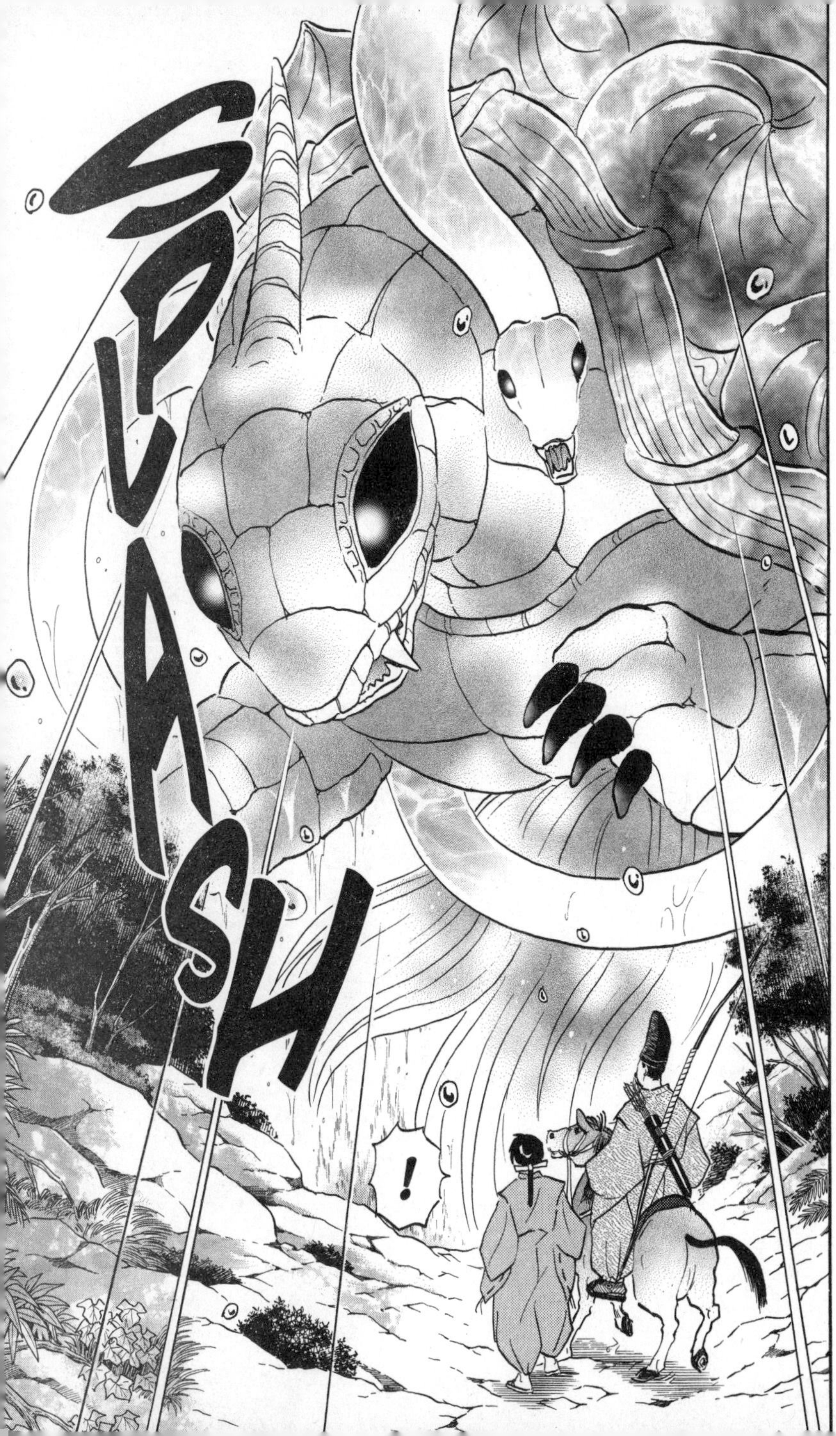
SPLASH
!

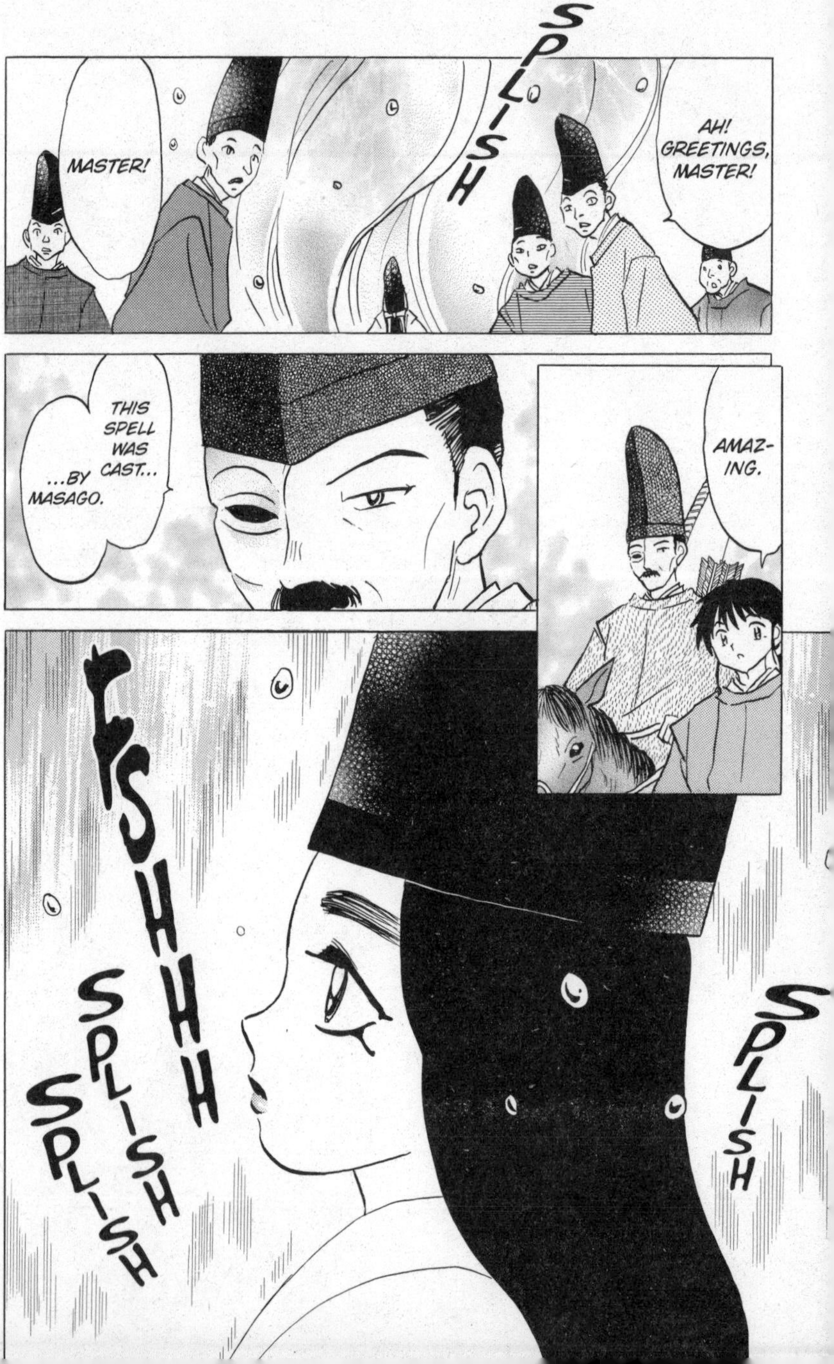
SPLISH
AH! GREETINGS, MASTER!
MASTER!
AMAZ-ING.
THIS SPELL WAS CAST...
...BY MASAGO.
SPLISH
FSHHH
SPLISH
SPLISH

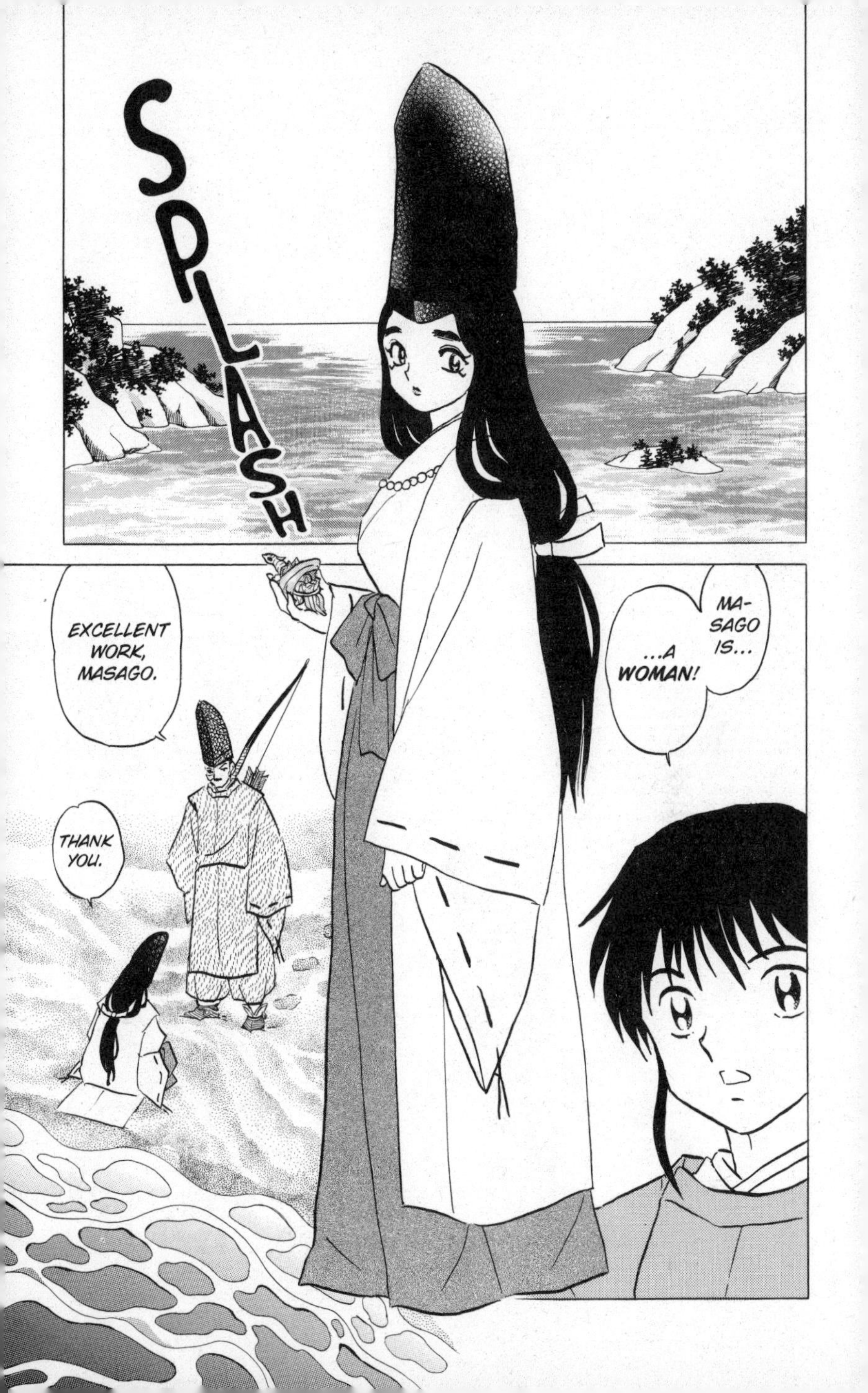
SPLASH
MASAGO IS... ...A WOMAN!
EXCELLENT WORK, MASAGO.
THANK YOU.

I HAVEN'T SEEN YOU AROUND BEFORE.
YOUR NAME IS... MAO?
YES. I JUST ARRIVED AT THE COMPOUND.
JUST AR-RIVED?
AND YET THE MASTER KEEPS YOU BY HIS SIDE AND ALLOWS YOU TO WITNESS OUR SECRETS...
splish
YOU HAD BETTER FLEE.
EX-CUSE ME?
THE LONGER YOU TARRY HERE, THE MORE DANGER YOU PUT YOURSELF IN.
YOU FOOL!
SMACK

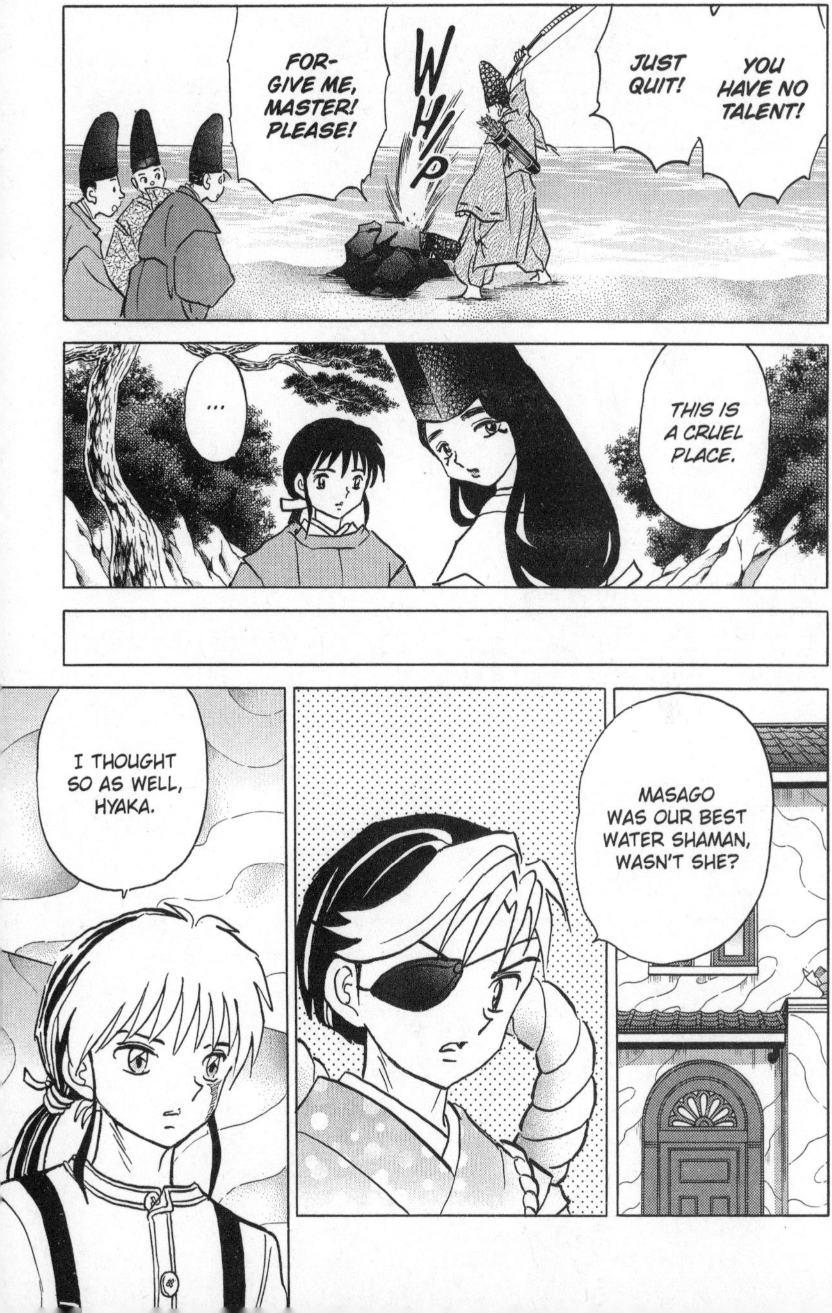
YOU HAVE NO TALENT!
JUST QUIT!
WHIP
FOR-GIVE ME, MASTER! PLEASE!
THIS IS A CRUEL PLACE.
...
MASAGO WAS OUR BEST WATER SHAMAN, WASN'T SHE?
I THOUGHT SO AS WELL, HYAKA.

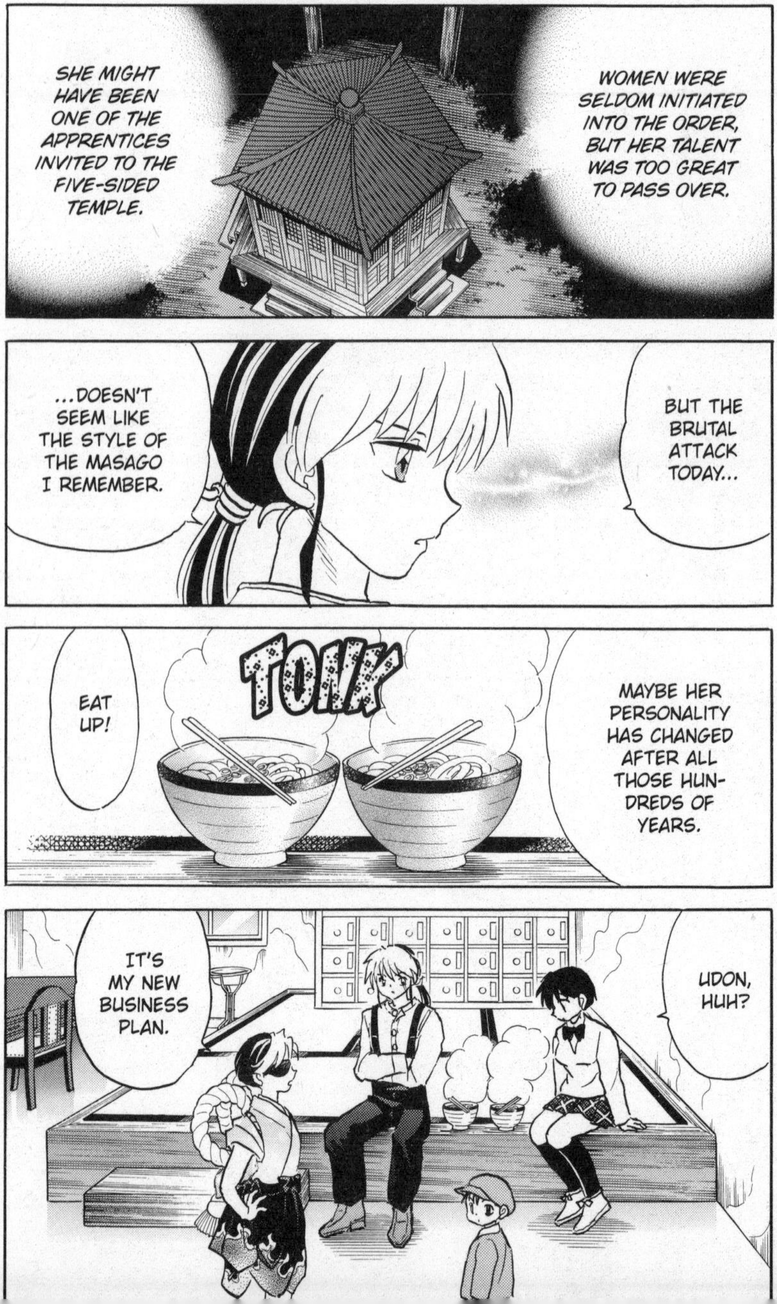
WOMEN WERE SELDOM INITIATED INTO THE ORDER, BUT HER TALENT WAS TOO GREAT TO PASS OVER.
SHE MIGHT HAVE BEEN ONE OF THE APPRENTICES INVITED TO THE FIVE-SIDED TEMPLE.
BUT THE BRUTAL ATTACK TODAY...
...DOESN'T SEEM LIKE THE STYLE OF THE MASAGO I REMEMBER.
MAYBE HER PERSONALITY HAS CHANGED AFTER ALL THOSE HUN-DREDS OF YEARS.
TONK
EAT UP!
UDON, HUH?
IT'S MY NEW BUSINESS PLAN.

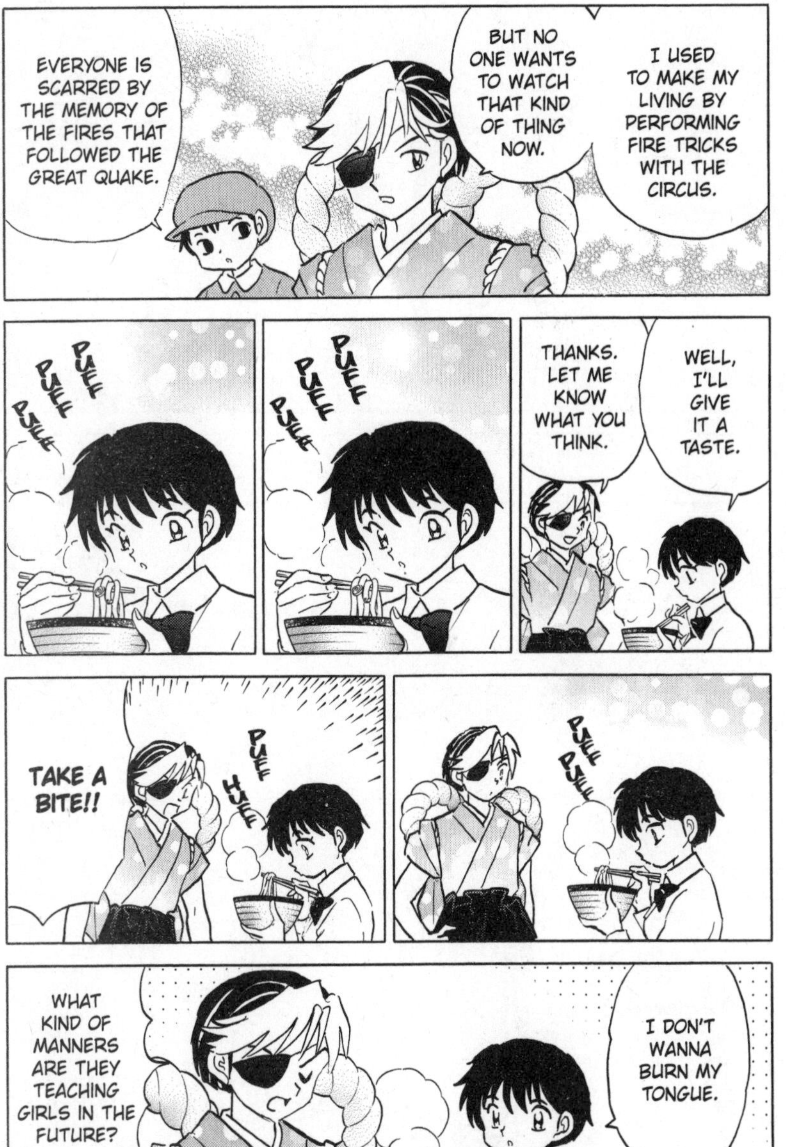
I USED TO MAKE MY LIVING BY PERFORMING FIRE TRICKS WITH THE CIRCUS.
BUT NO ONE WANTS TO WATCH THAT KIND OF THING NOW.
EVERYONE IS SCARRED BY THE MEMORY OF THE FIRES THAT FOLLOWED THE GREAT QUAKE.
WELL, I'LL GIVE IT A TASTE.
THANKS. LET ME KNOW WHAT YOU THINK.
PUFF
PUFF
PUFF
PUFF
PUFF
PUFF
PUFF
PUFF
PUFF
HUFF
TAKE A BITE!!
I DON'T WANNA BURN MY TONGUE.
WHAT KIND OF MANNERS ARE THEY TEACHING GIRLS IN THE FUTURE?

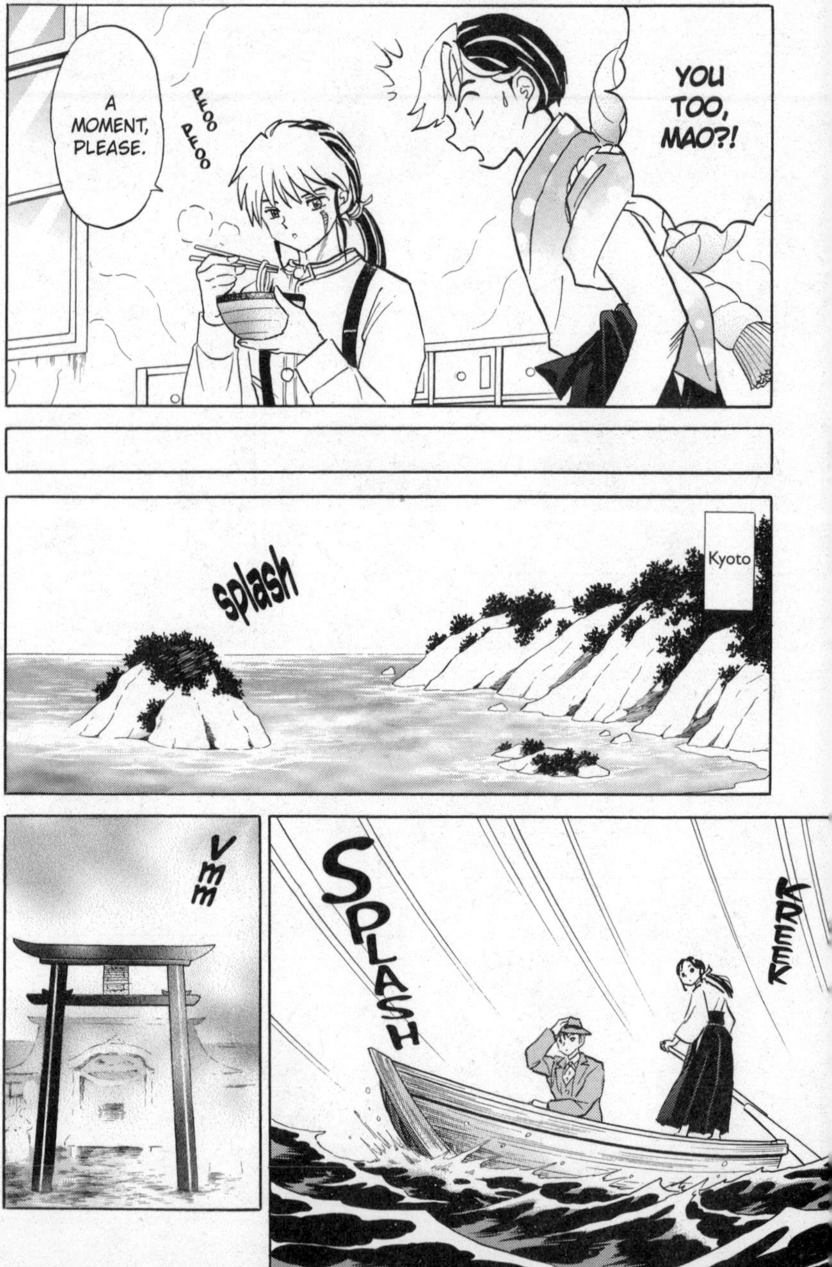
YOU TOO, MAO?!
PFOO PFOO
A MOMENT, PLEASE.
Kyoto
splash
KREEK
SPLASH
Vmm

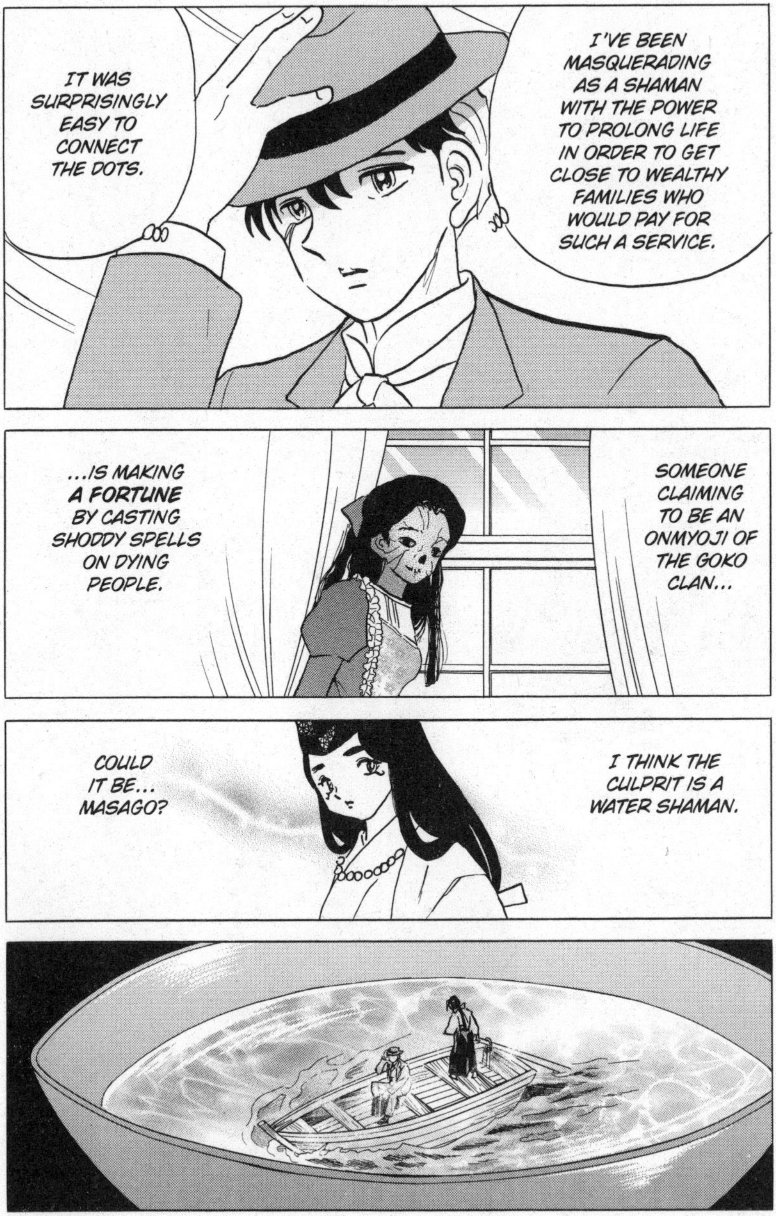
I'VE BEEN MASQUERADING AS A SHAMAN WITH THE POWER TO PROLONG LIFE IN ORDER TO GET CLOSE TO WEALTHY FAMILIES WHO WOULD PAY FOR SUCH A SERVICE.
IT WAS SURPRISINGLY EASY TO CONNECT THE DOTS.
SOMEONE CLAIMING TO BE AN ONMYOJI OF THE GOKO CLAN...
...IS MAKING **A FORTUNE** BY CASTING SHODDY SPELLS ON DYING PEOPLE.
I THINK THE CULPRIT IS A WATER SHAMAN.
COULD IT BE... MASAGO?

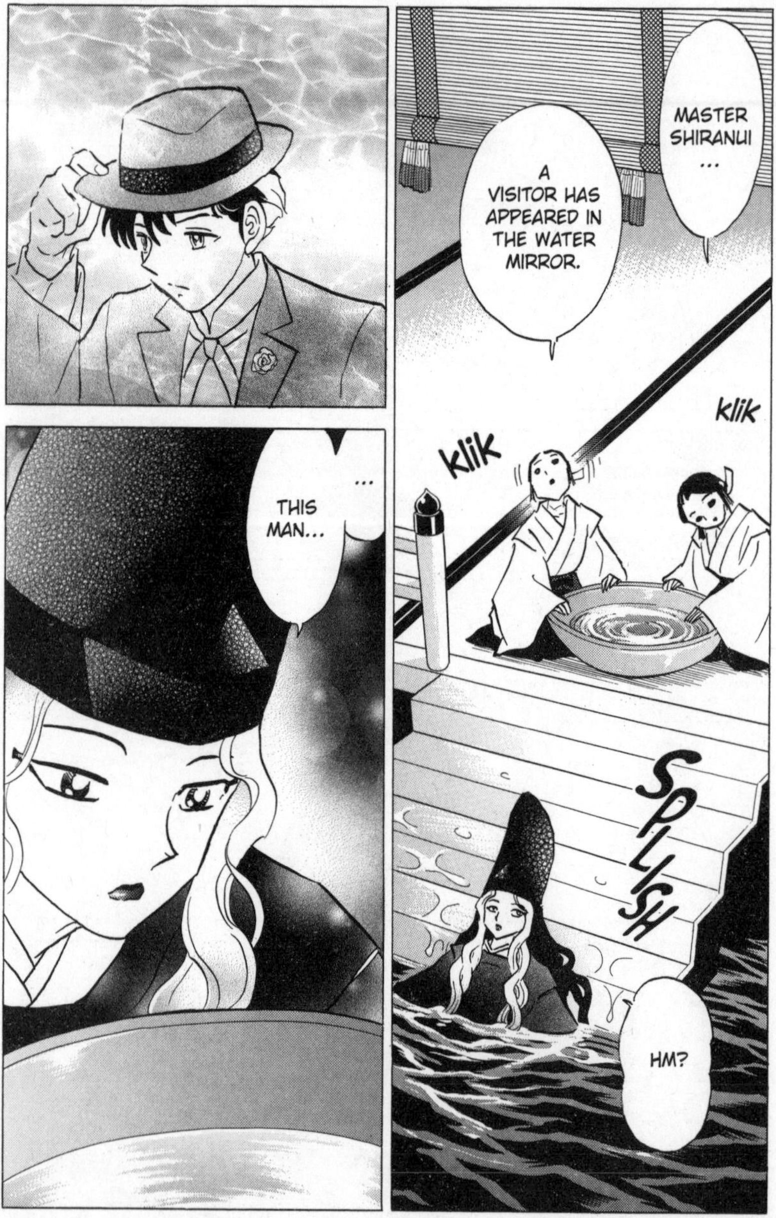
MASTER SHIRANUI ...
A VISITOR HAS APPEARED IN THE WATER MIRROR.
klik
klik
SPLISH
HM?
... THIS MAN...

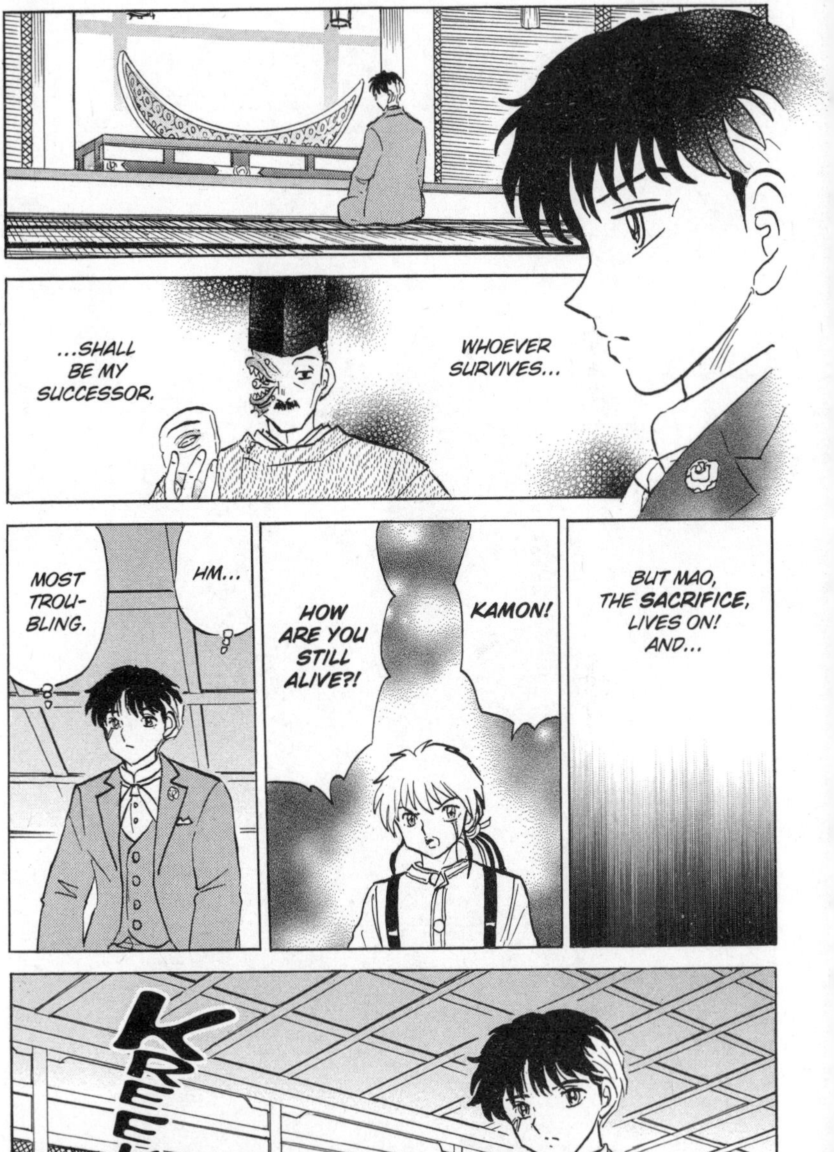
WHOEVER SURVIVES...
...SHALL BE MY SUCCESSOR.
BUT MAO, THE SACRIFICE, LIVES ON! AND...
KAMON!
HOW ARE YOU STILL ALIVE?!
HM...
MOST TROU-BLING.
KREEK

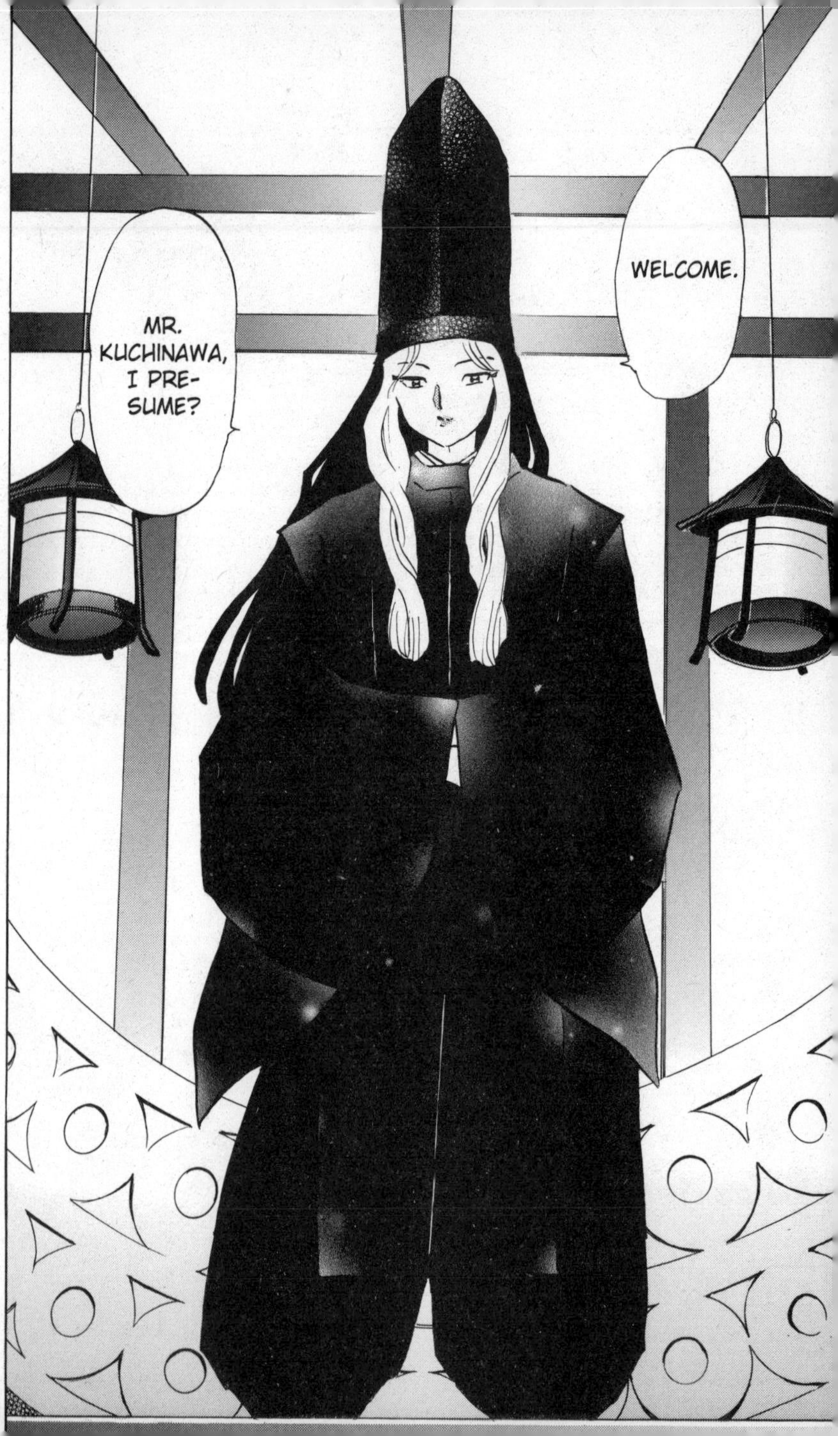
WELCOME.
MR. KUCHINAWA, I PRE-SUME?

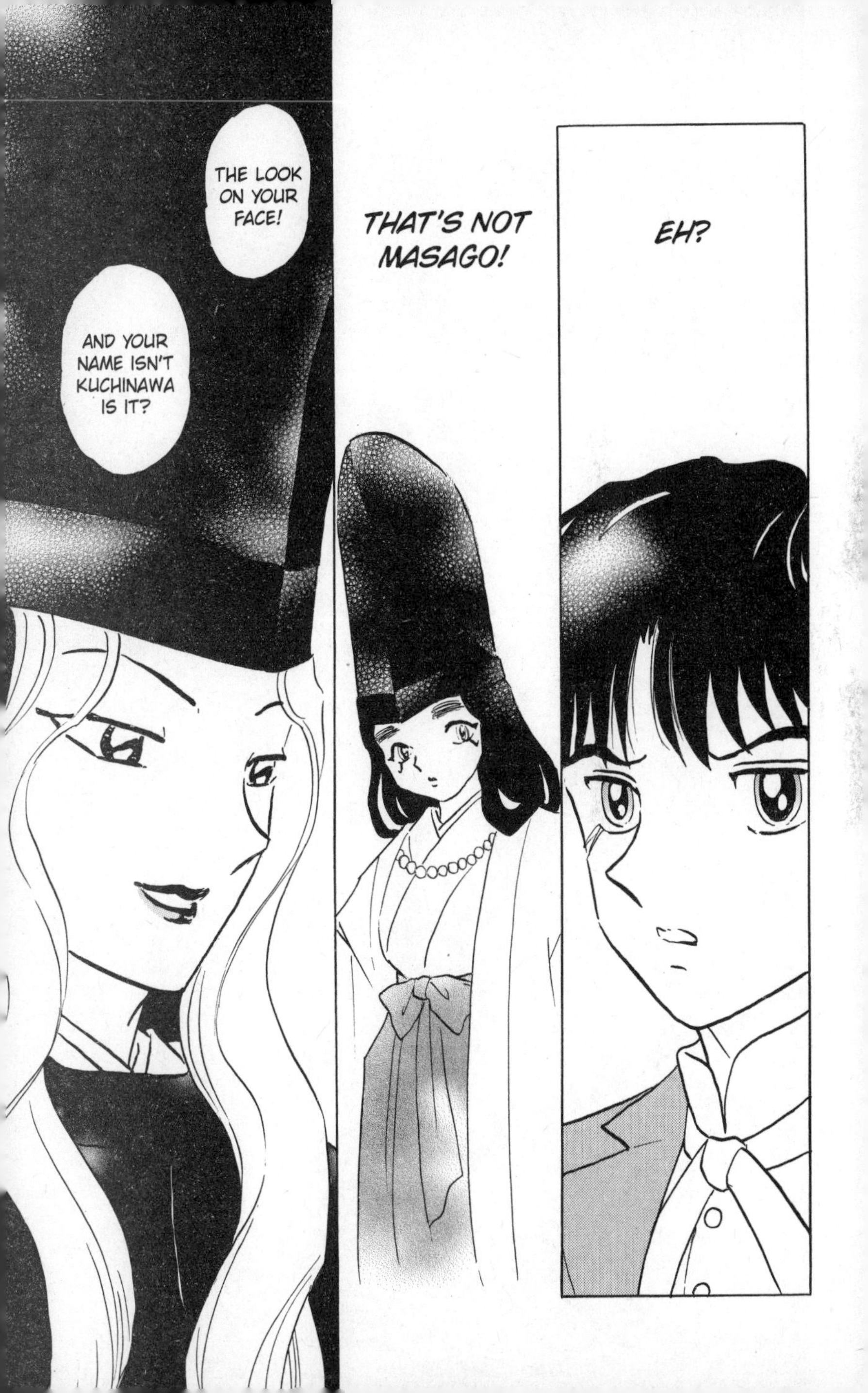
EH?
THAT'S NOT MASAGO!
THE LOOK ON YOUR FACE!
AND YOUR NAME ISN'T KUCHINAWA IS IT?

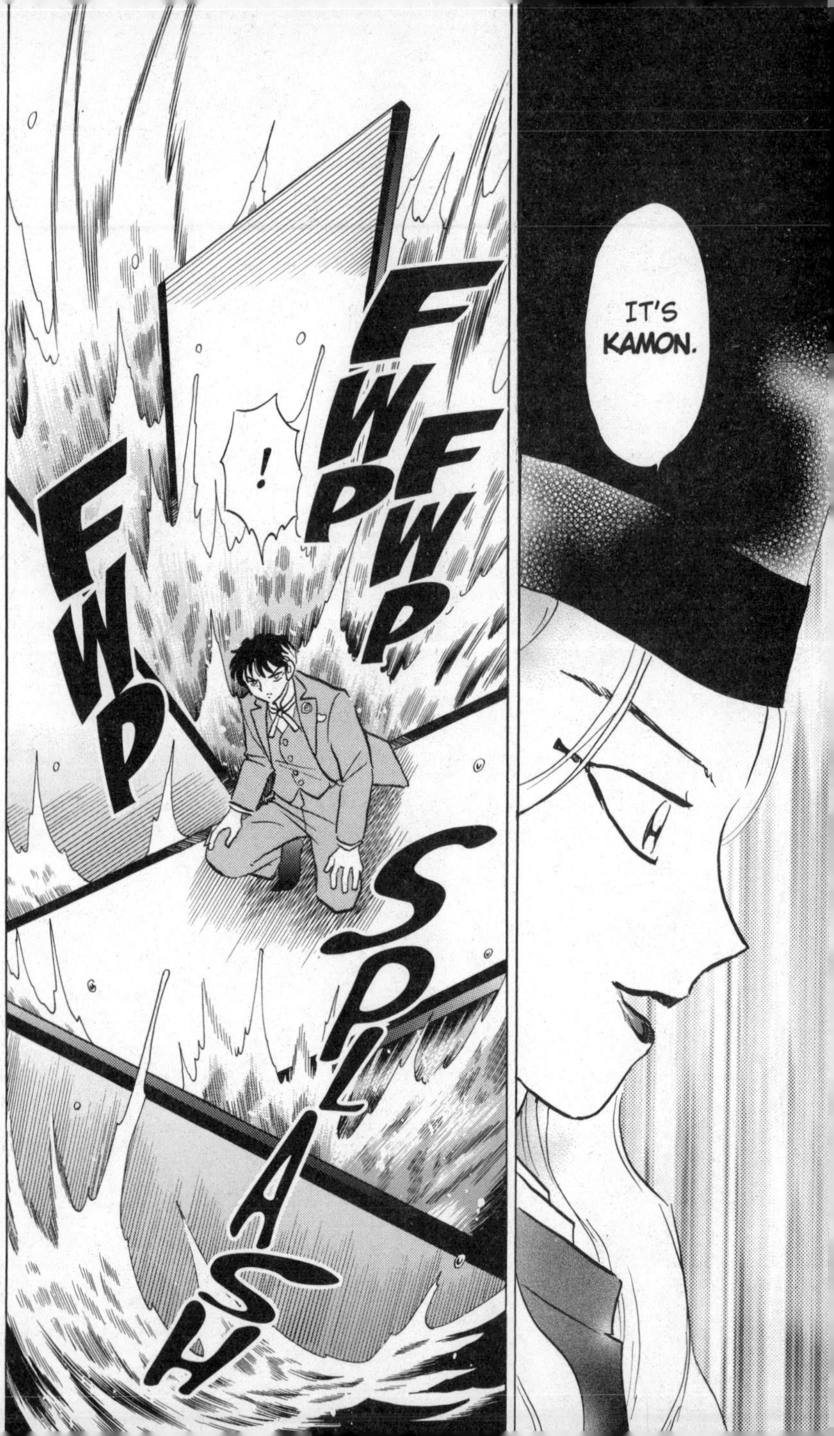
IT'S KAMON.
FWP FWP
!
FWP
SPLAASH

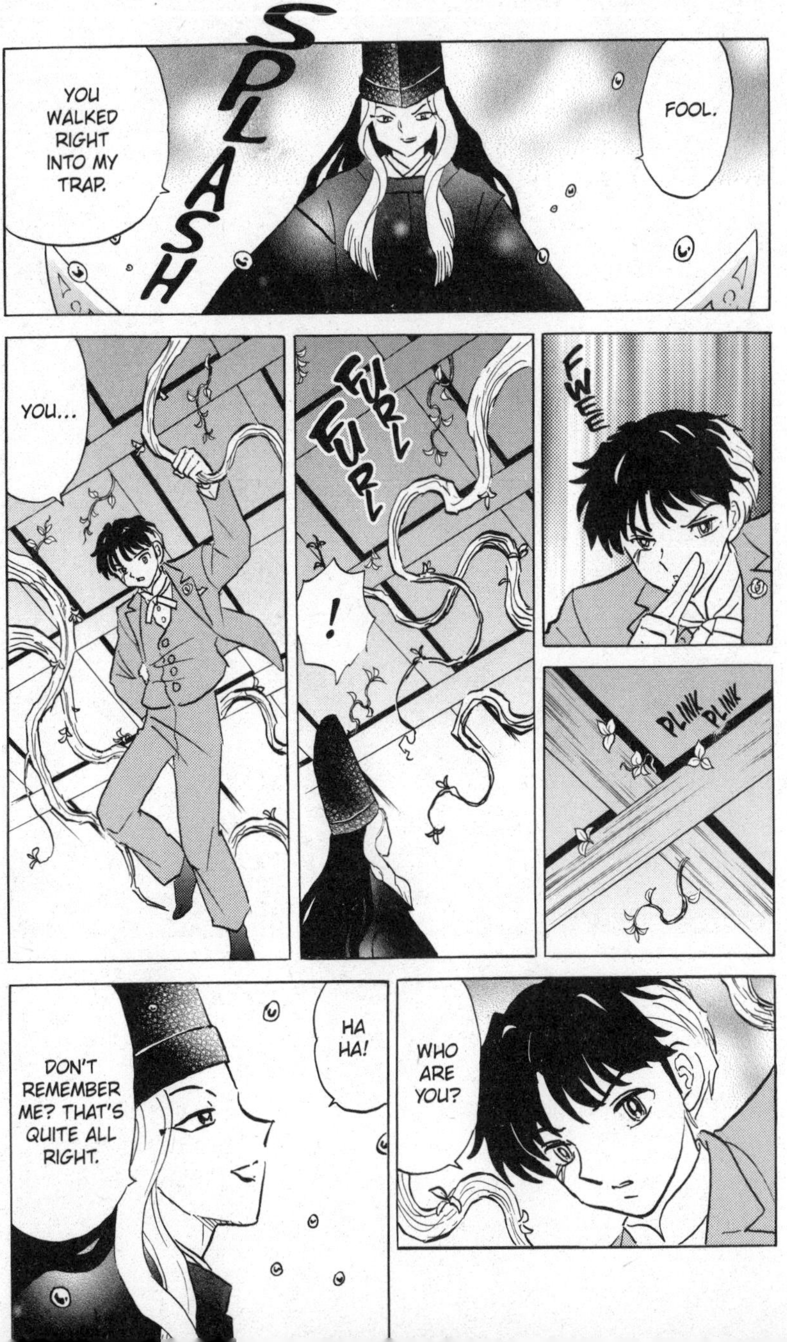
FOOL.
SPLASH
YOU WALKED RIGHT INTO MY TRAP.
FWEE
PLINK PLINK
FURI FURI
!
YOU...
WHO ARE YOU?
HA HA!
DON'T REMEMBER ME? THAT'S QUITE ALL RIGHT.

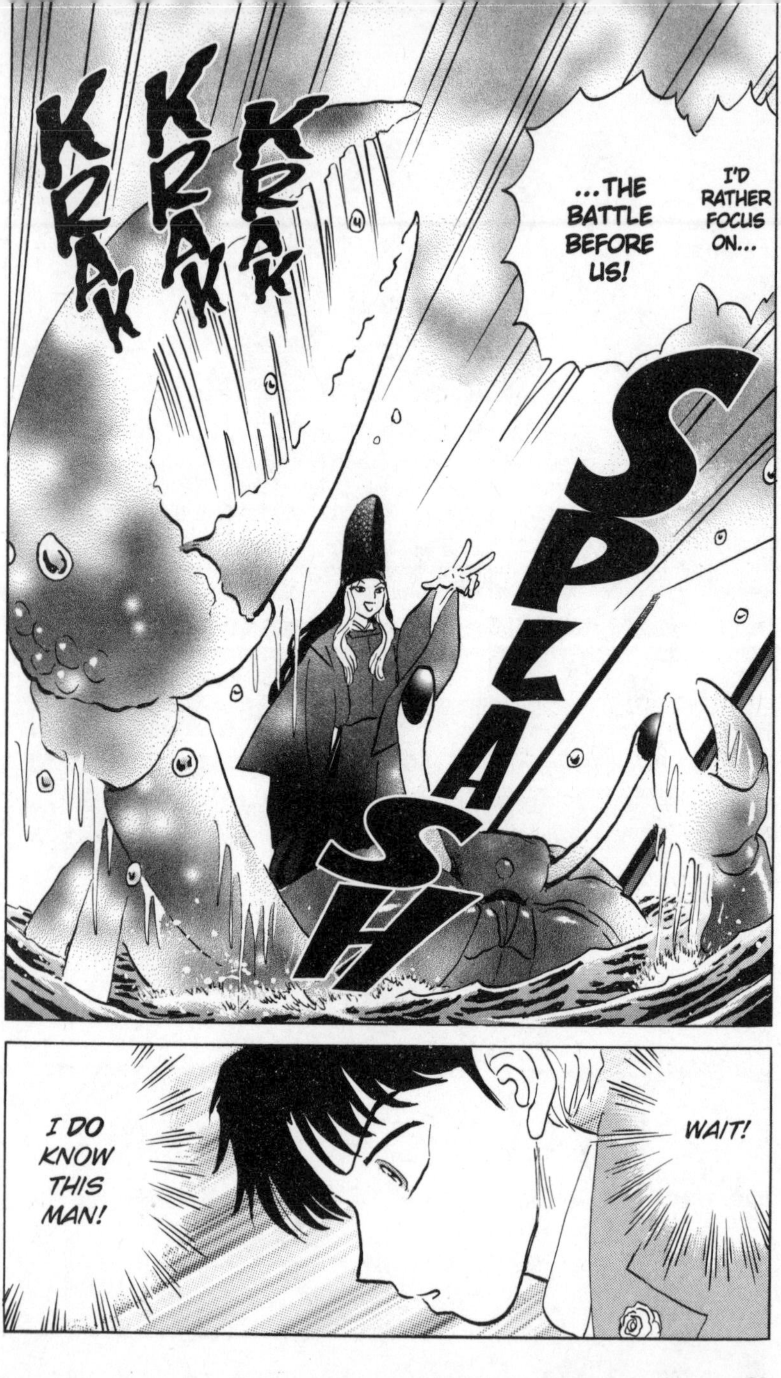
I'D RATHER FOCUS ON...
...THE BATTLE BEFORE US!
KRAK
KRAK
KRAK
SPLASH
WAIT!
I DO KNOW THIS MAN!

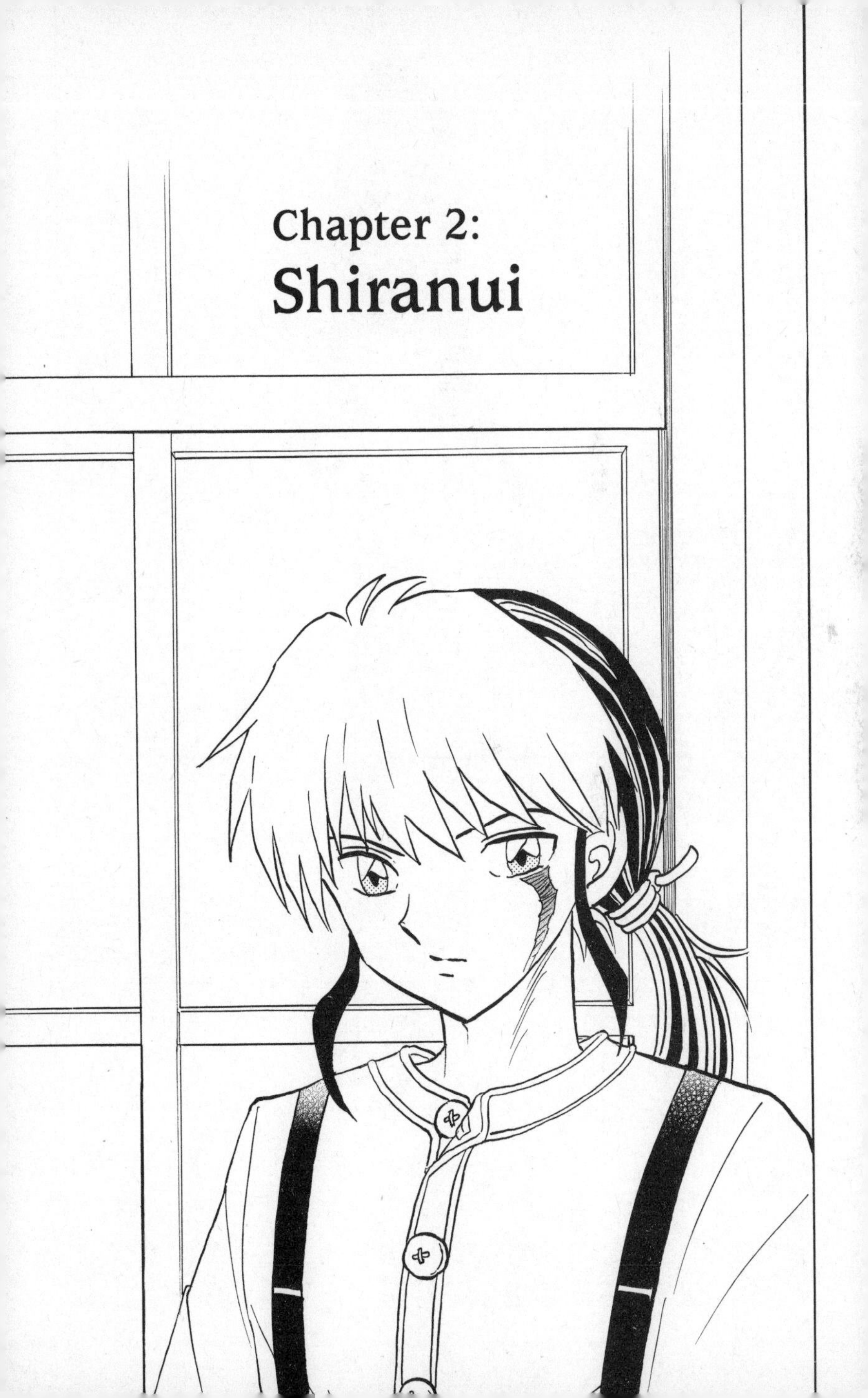
Chapter 2:
Shiranui

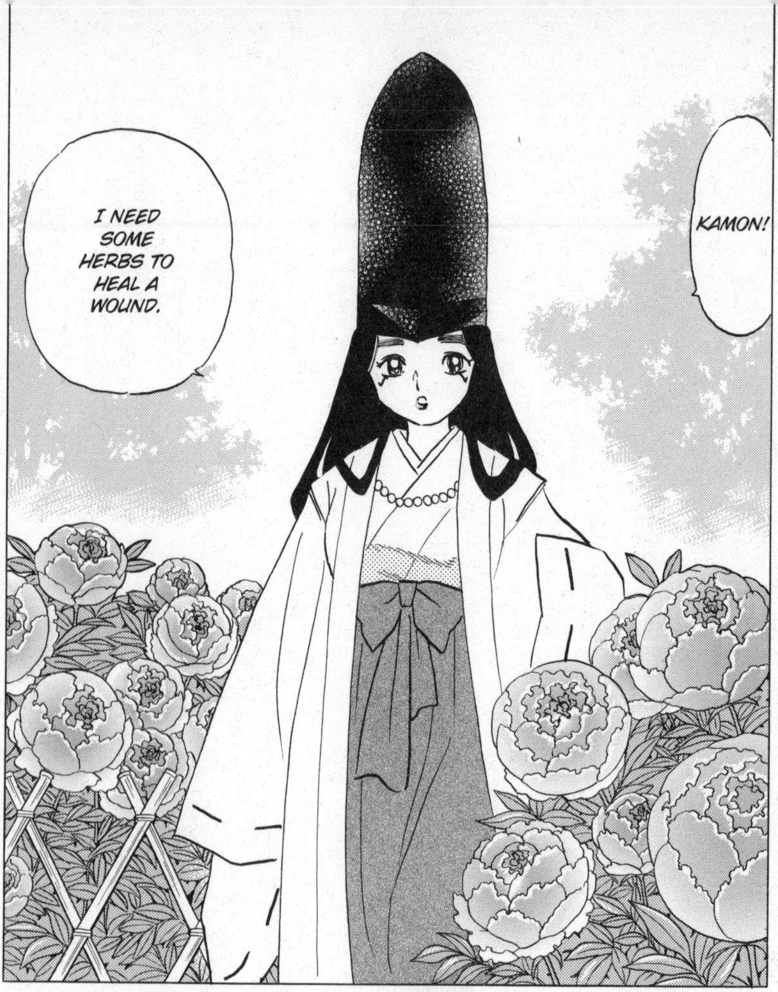
KAMON!
I NEED SOME HERBS TO HEAL A WOUND.

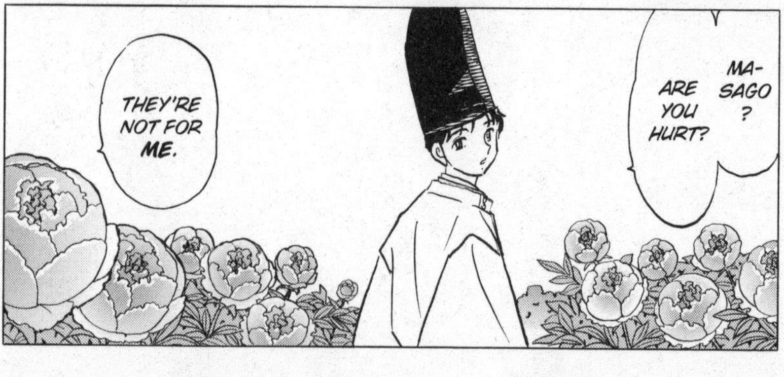
MA-SAGO?
ARE YOU HURT?
THEY'RE NOT FOR **ME.**

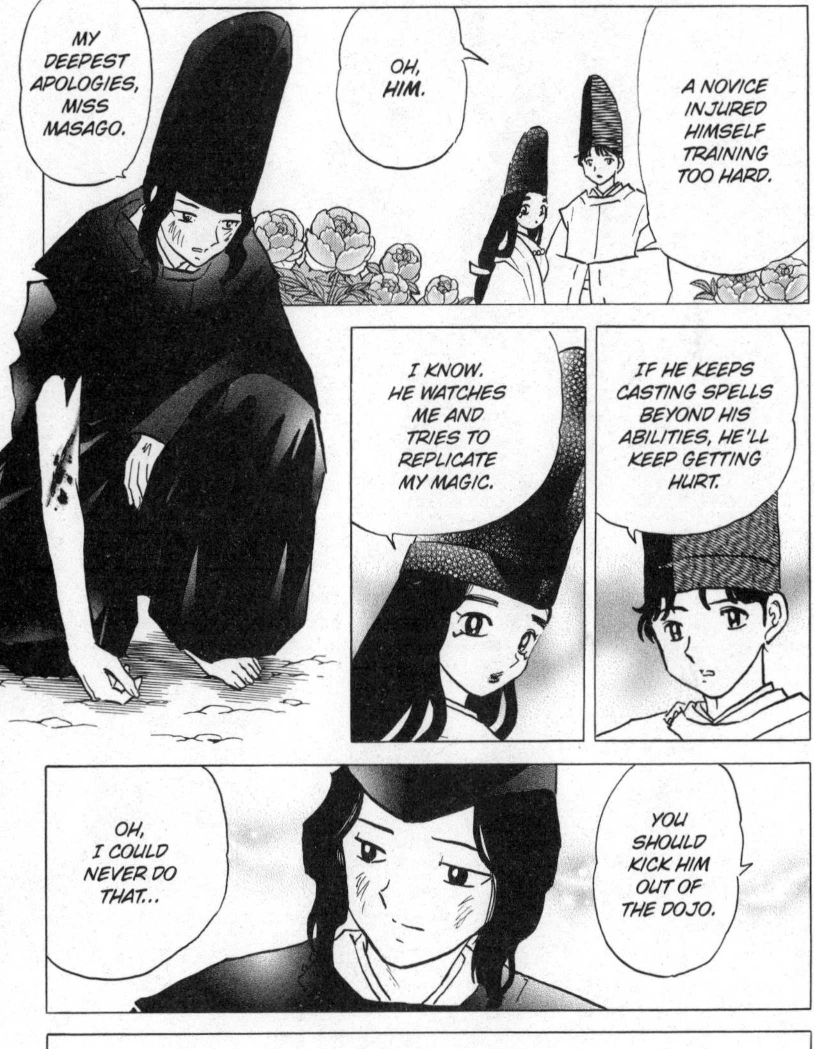
A NOVICE INJURED HIMSELF TRAINING TOO HARD.
OH, HIM.
MY DEEPEST APOLOGIES, MISS MASAGO.
IF HE KEEPS CASTING SPELLS BEYOND HIS ABILITIES, HE'LL KEEP GETTING HURT.
I KNOW. HE WATCHES ME AND TRIES TO REPLICATE MY MAGIC.
YOU SHOULD KICK HIM OUT OF THE DOJO.
OH, I COULD NEVER DO THAT...
MASAGO ALWAYS DID HAVE A SOFT SPOT FOR THAT CLUMSY NOVICE.

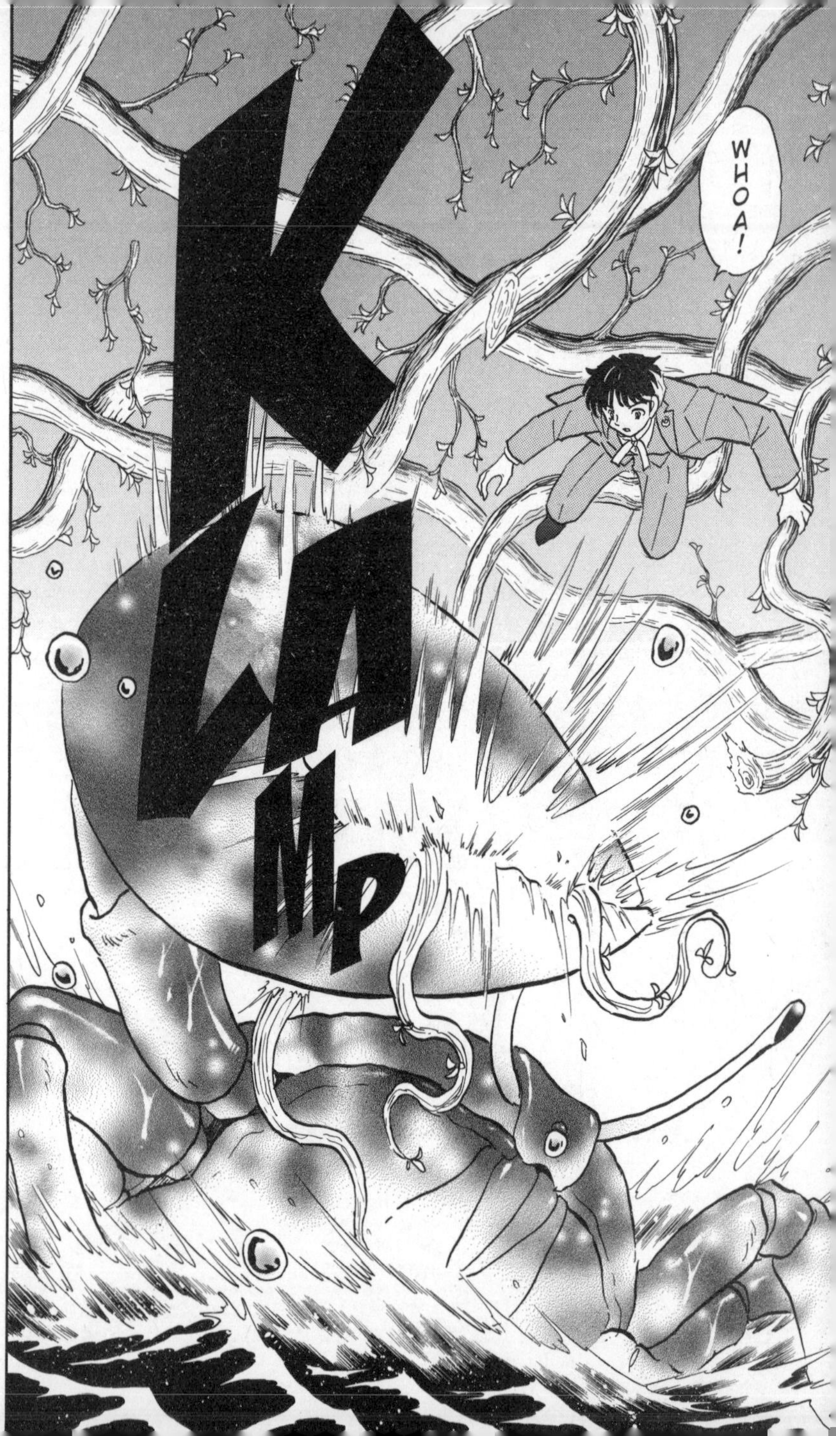
WHOA!
KLAMP

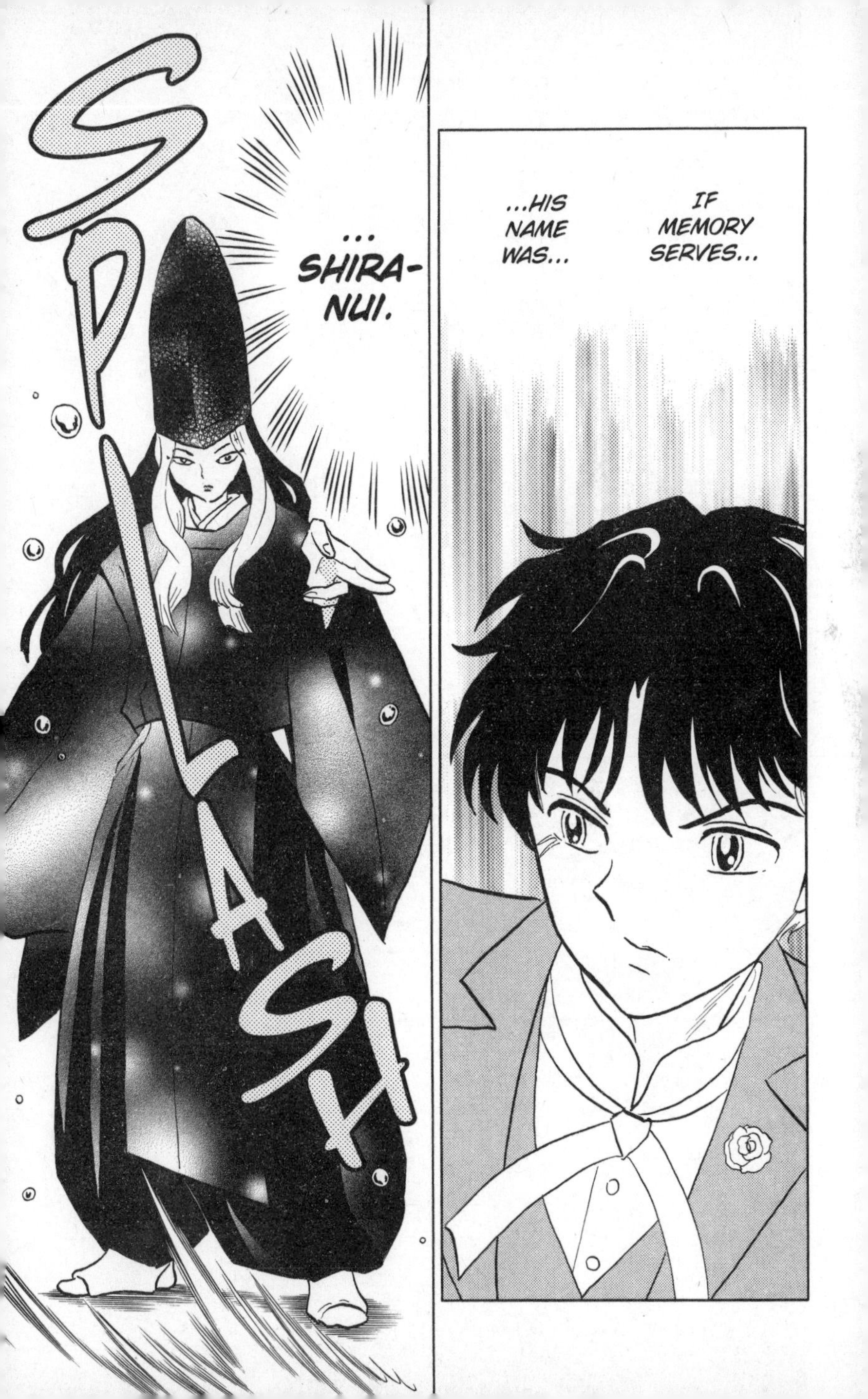
IF MEMORY SERVES...
...HIS NAME WAS...
... SHIRA-NUI.
SPLASH

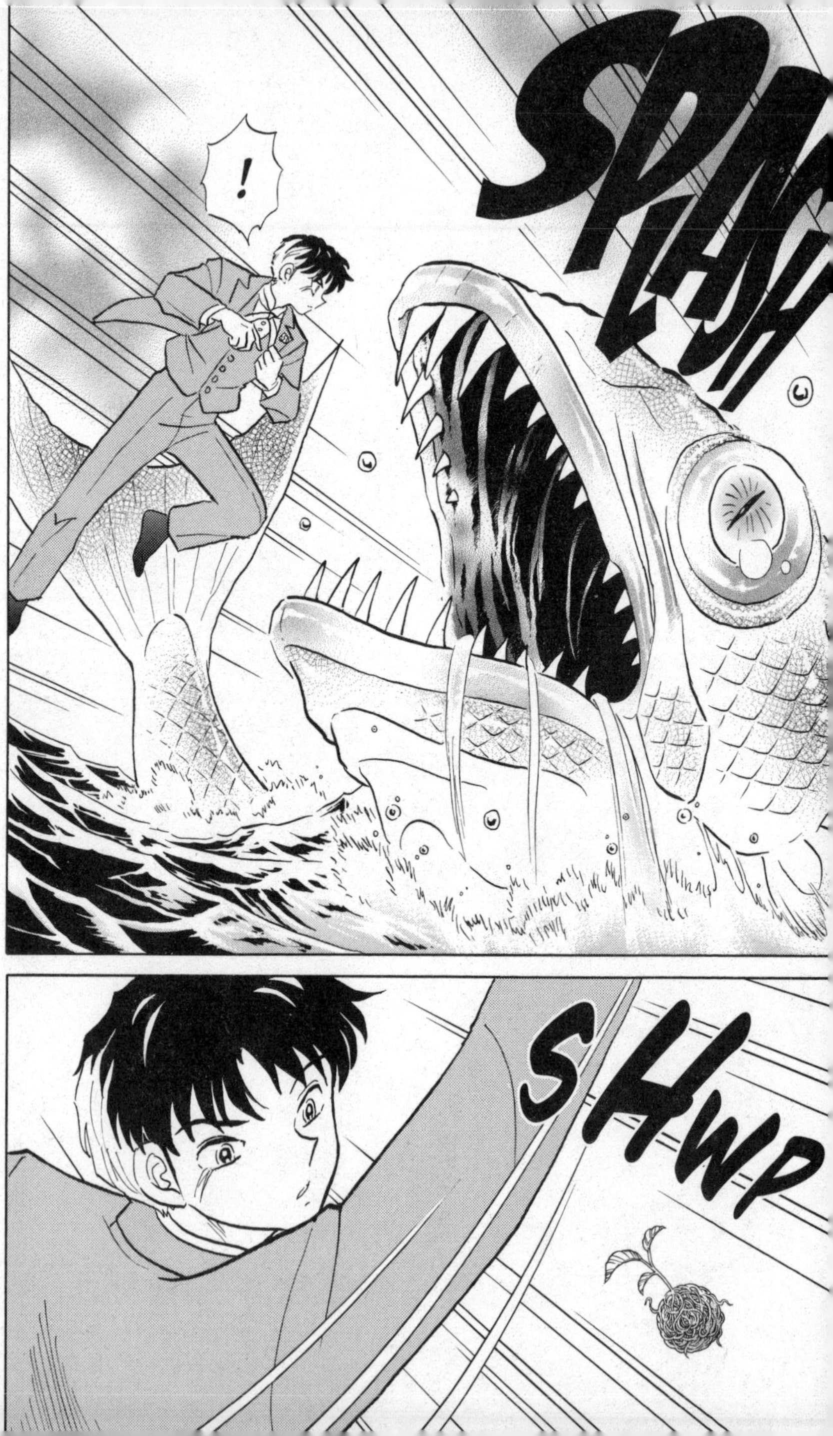
SPLASH
!
SHWP

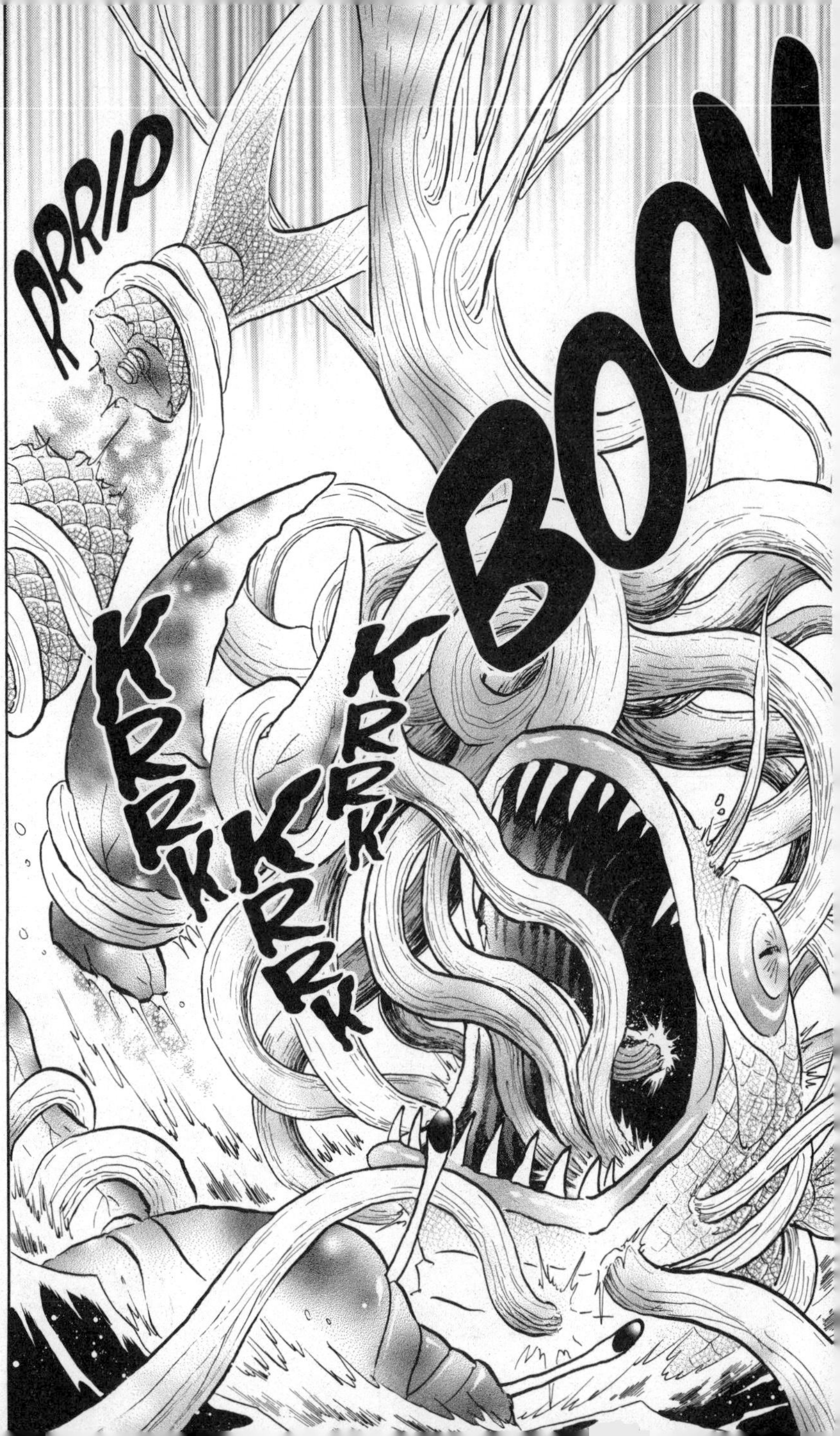
BOOM
RRRIP
KRRRK
KRRRK
KRRRK

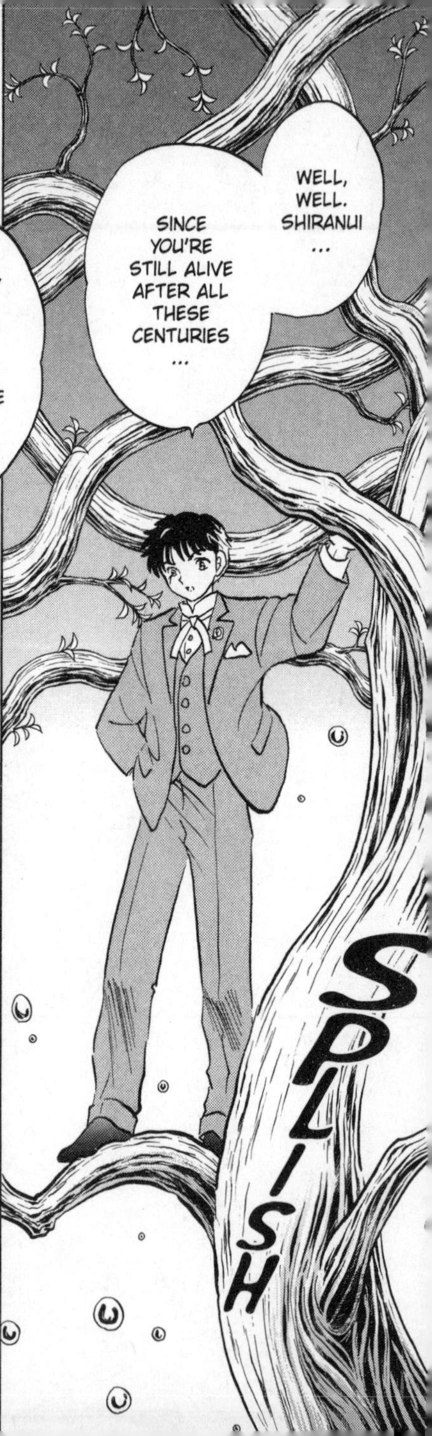
WELL, WELL. SHIRANUI...
SINCE YOU'RE STILL ALIVE AFTER ALL THESE CENTURIES...
SPLISH
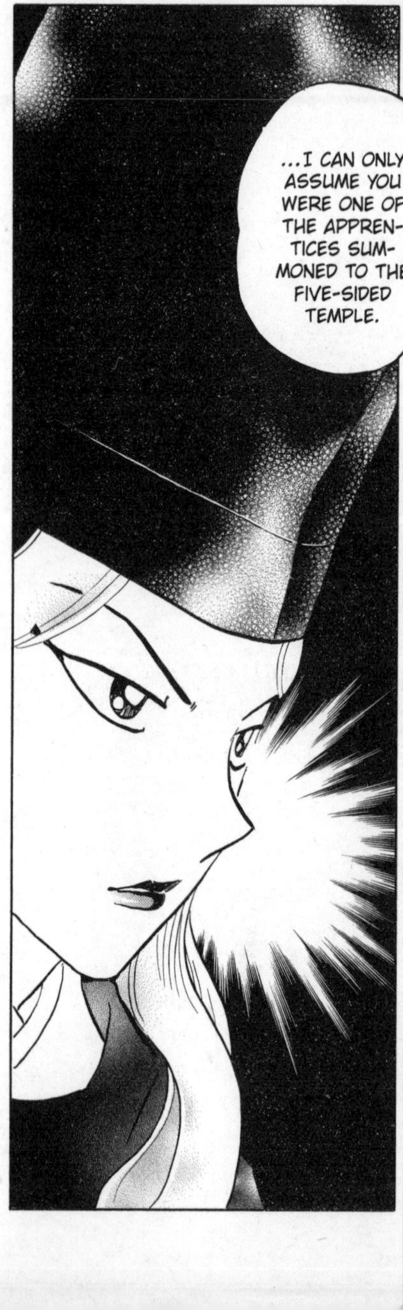
...I CAN ONLY ASSUME YOU WERE ONE OF THE APPREN-TICES SUM-MONED TO THE FIVE-SIDED TEMPLE.

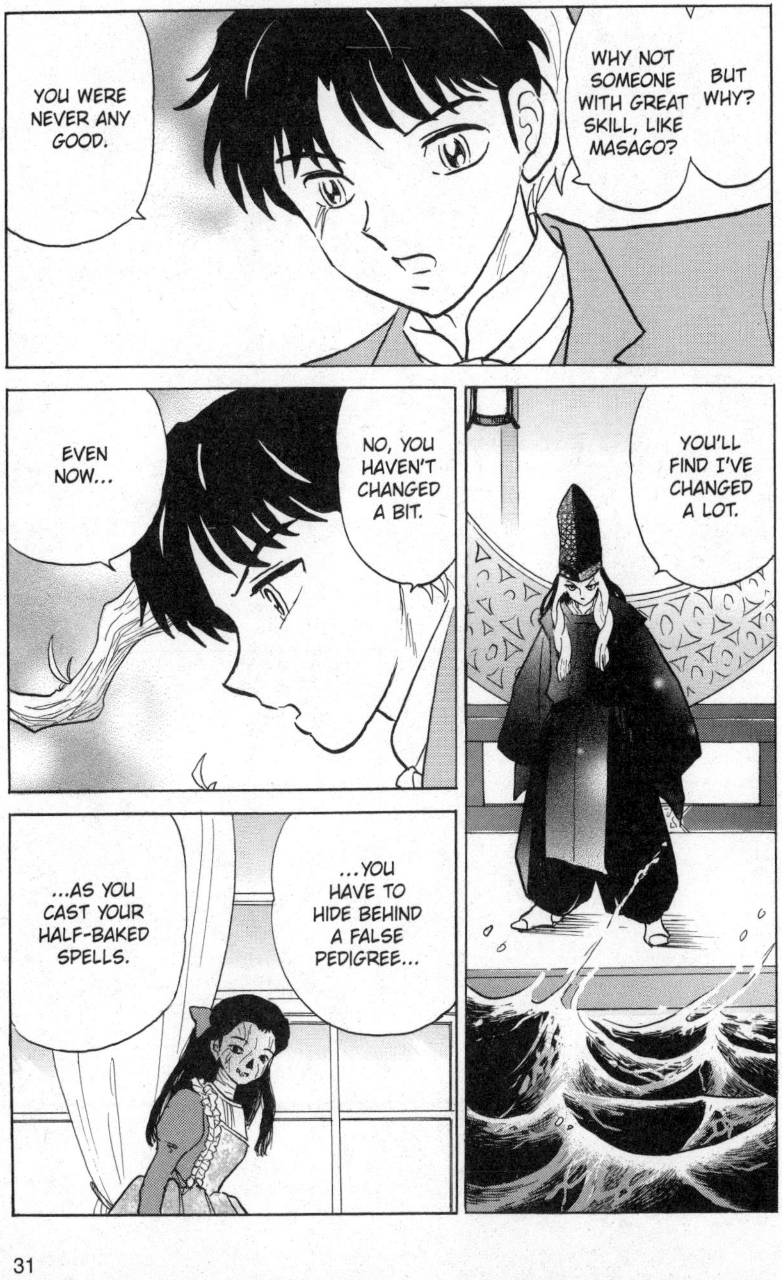
BUT WHY?
WHY NOT SOMEONE WITH GREAT SKILL, LIKE MASAGO?
YOU WERE NEVER ANY GOOD.
YOU'LL FIND I'VE CHANGED A LOT.
NO, YOU HAVEN'T CHANGED A BIT.
EVEN NOW...
...YOU HAVE TO HIDE BEHIND A FALSE PEDIGREE...
...AS YOU CAST YOUR HALF-BAKED SPELLS.

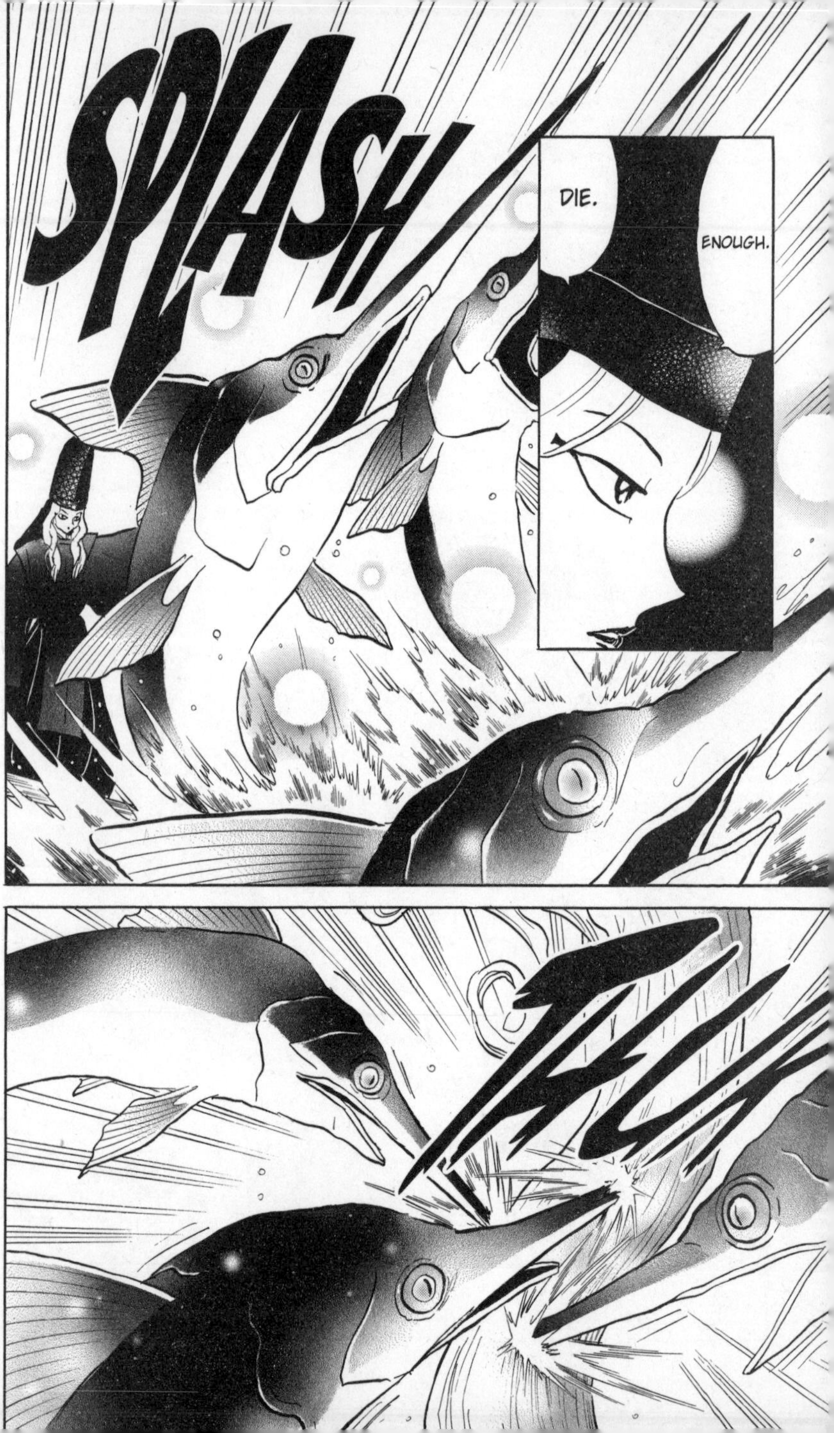
ENOUGH.
DIE.
SPLASH
THUK

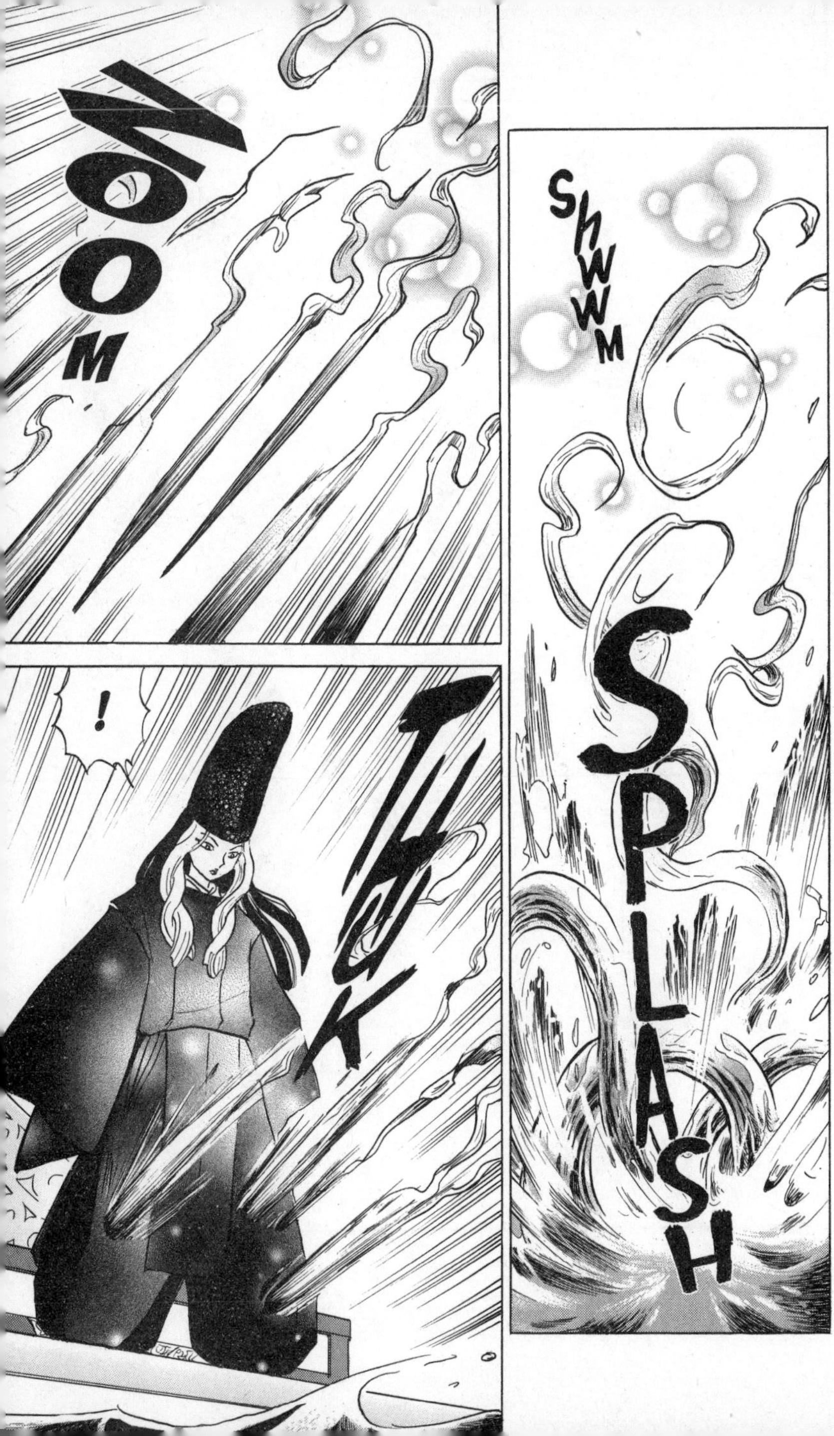
SHWWM
SPLASH
ZOOM
!
THUK

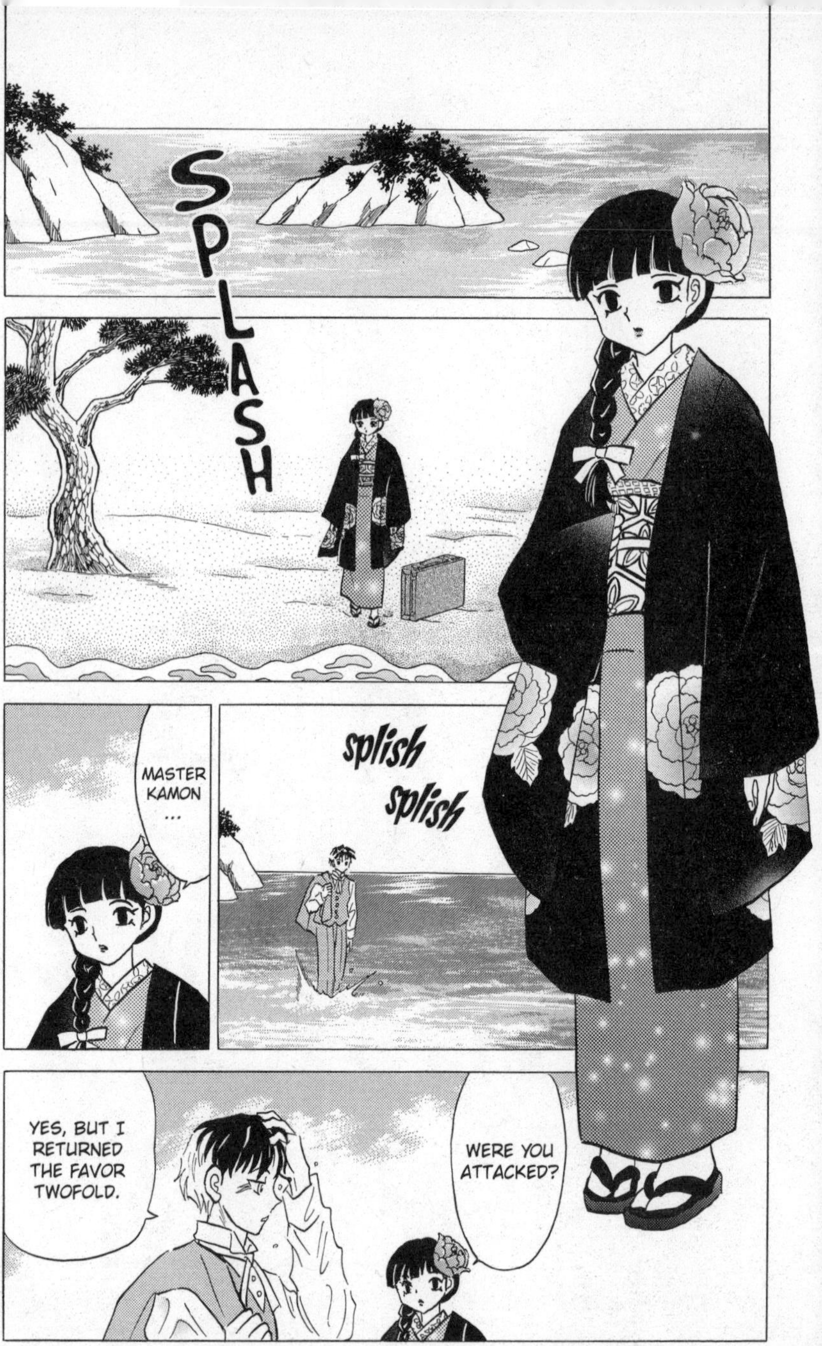
SPLASH
splish
splish
MASTER KAMON ...
WERE YOU ATTACKED?
YES, BUT I RETURNED THE FAVOR TWOFOLD.

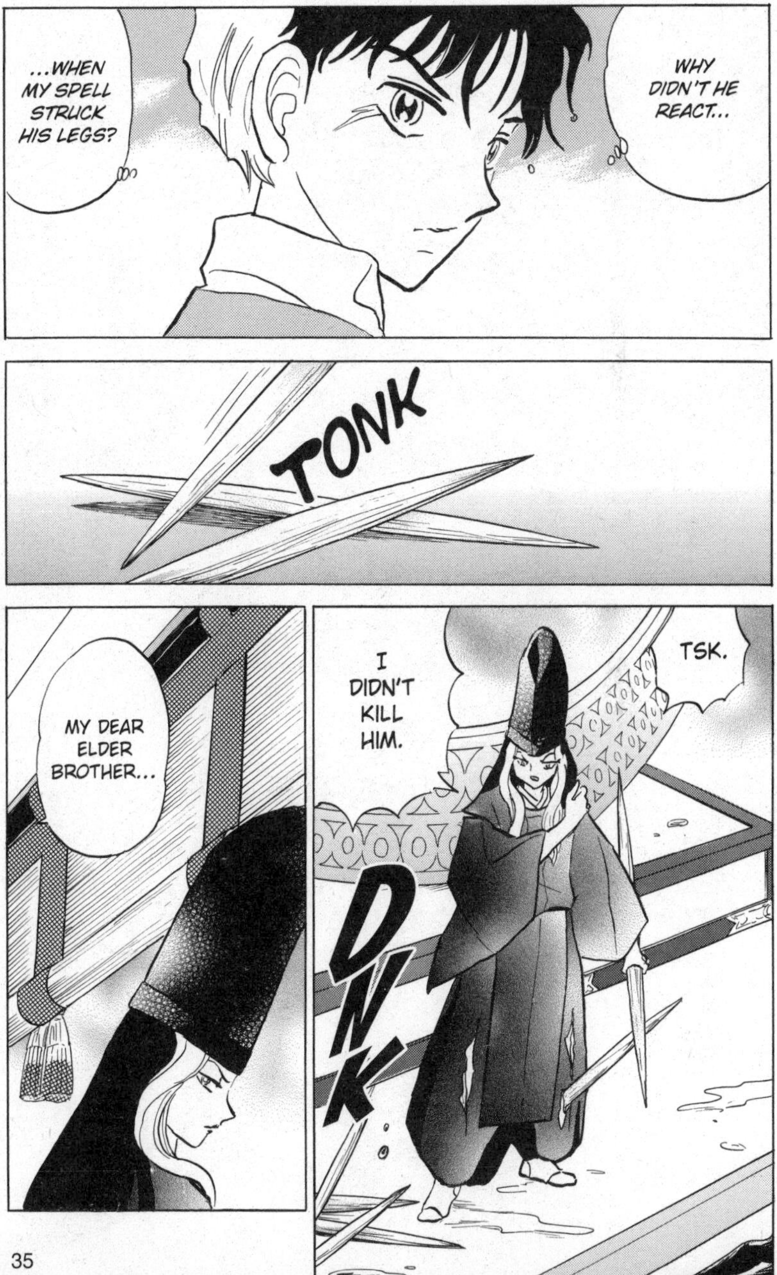
WHY DIDN'T HE REACT...
...WHEN MY SPELL STRUCK HIS LEGS?
TONK
TSK.
I DIDN'T KILL HIM.
DINK
MY DEAR ELDER BROTHER...

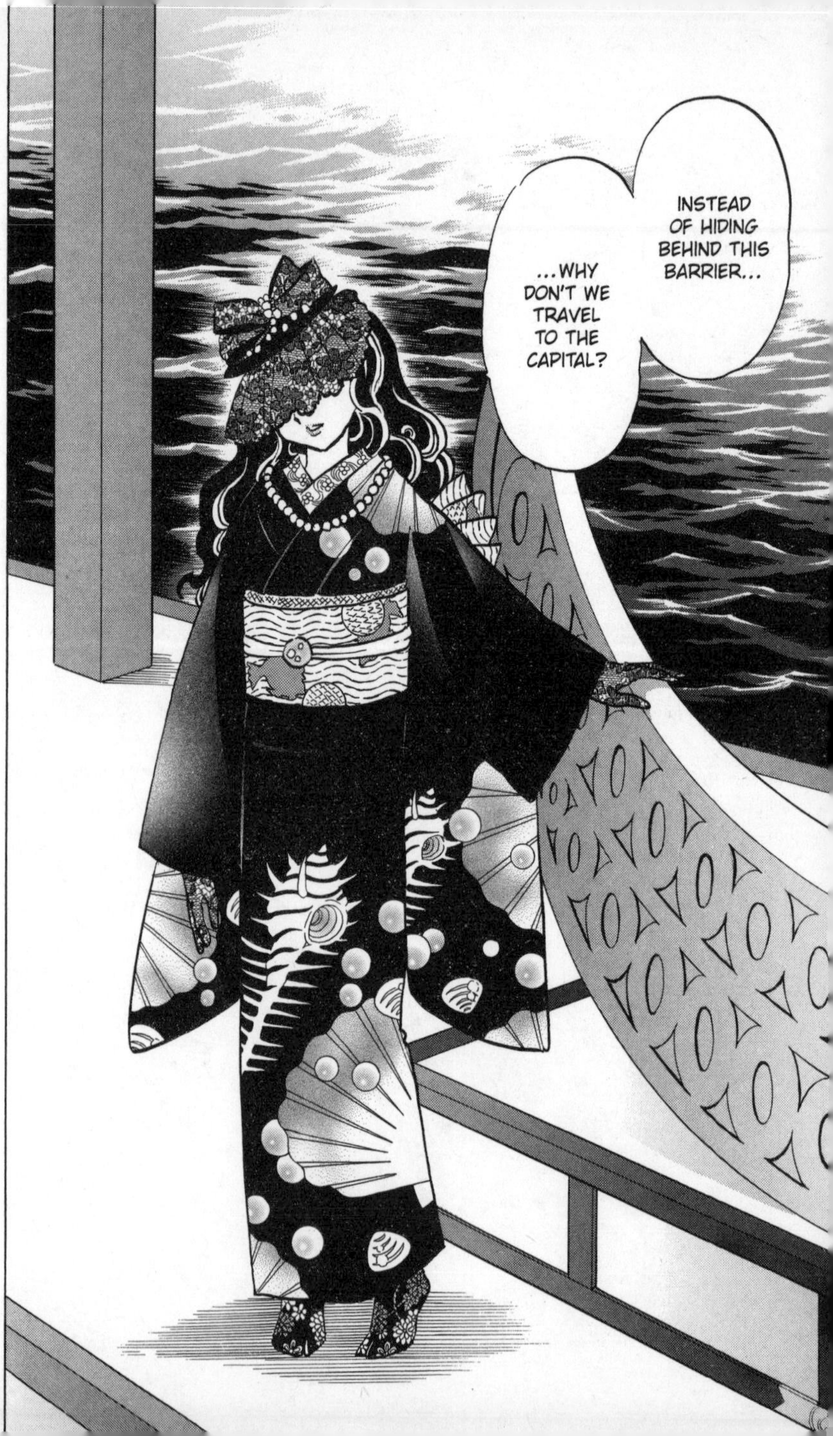
INSTEAD OF HIDING BEHIND THIS BARRIER...
...WHY DON'T WE TRAVEL TO THE CAPITAL?

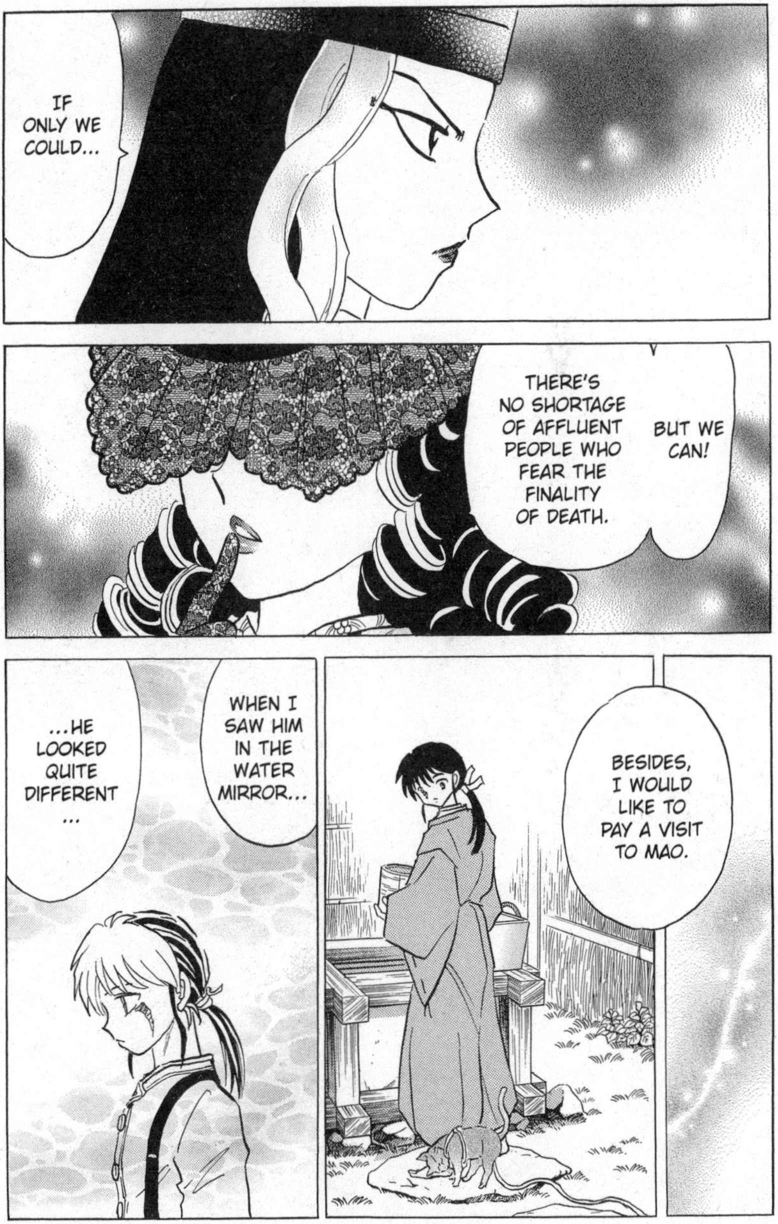

IF ONLY WE COULD...
BUT WE CAN!
THERE'S NO SHORTAGE OF AFFLUENT PEOPLE WHO FEAR THE FINALITY OF DEATH.
BESIDES, I WOULD LIKE TO PAY A VISIT TO MAO.
WHEN I SAW HIM IN THE WATER MIRROR...
...HE LOOKED QUITE DIFFERENT...

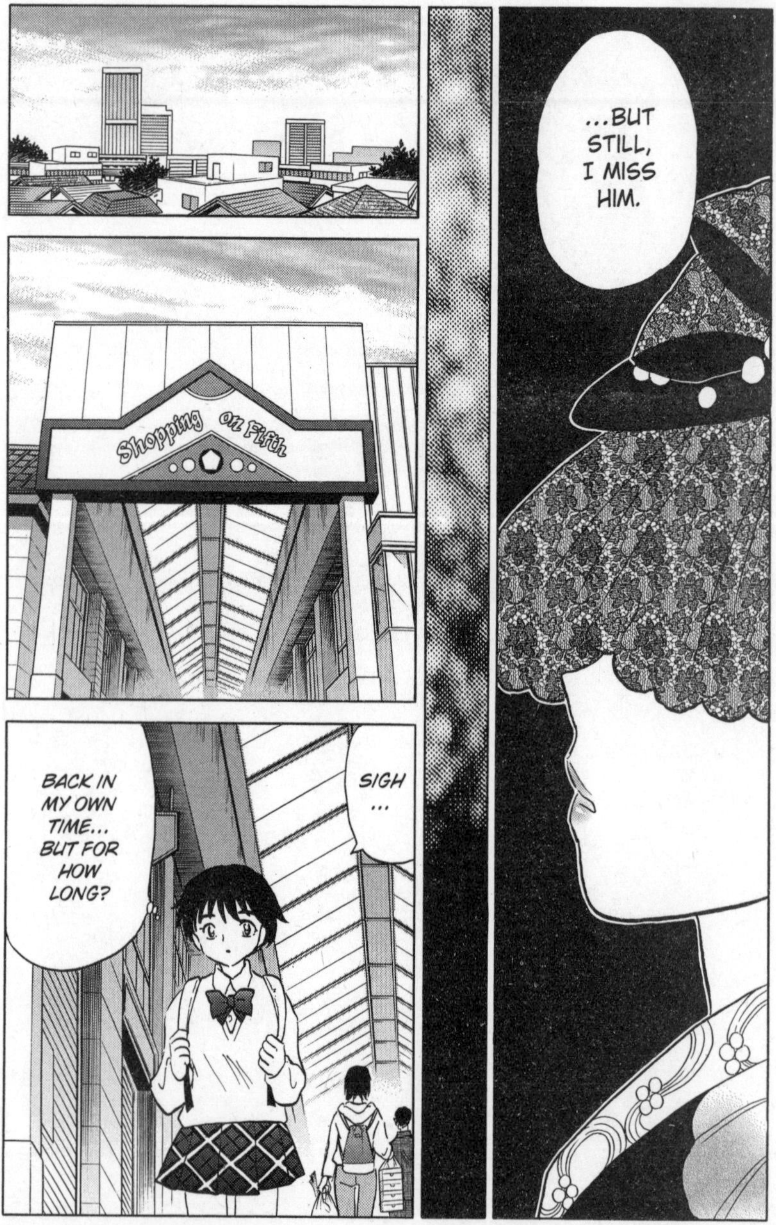
...BUT STILL, I MISS HIM.
Shopping on Fifth
SIGH ...
BACK IN MY OWN TIME... BUT FOR HOW LONG?

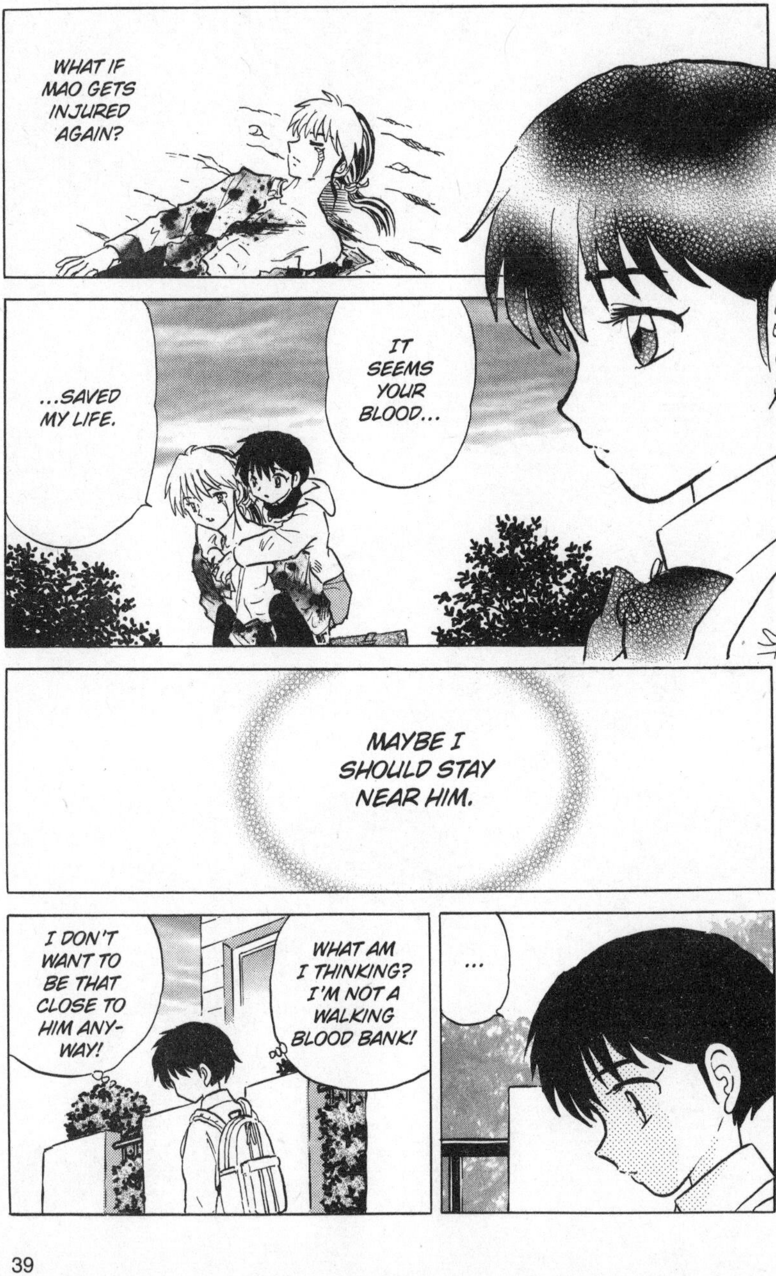
WHAT IF MAO GETS INJURED AGAIN?
IT SEEMS YOUR BLOOD...
...SAVED MY LIFE.
MAYBE I SHOULD STAY NEAR HIM.
...
WHAT AM I THINKING? I'M NOT A WALKING BLOOD BANK!
I DON'T WANT TO BE THAT CLOSE TO HIM ANY-WAY!

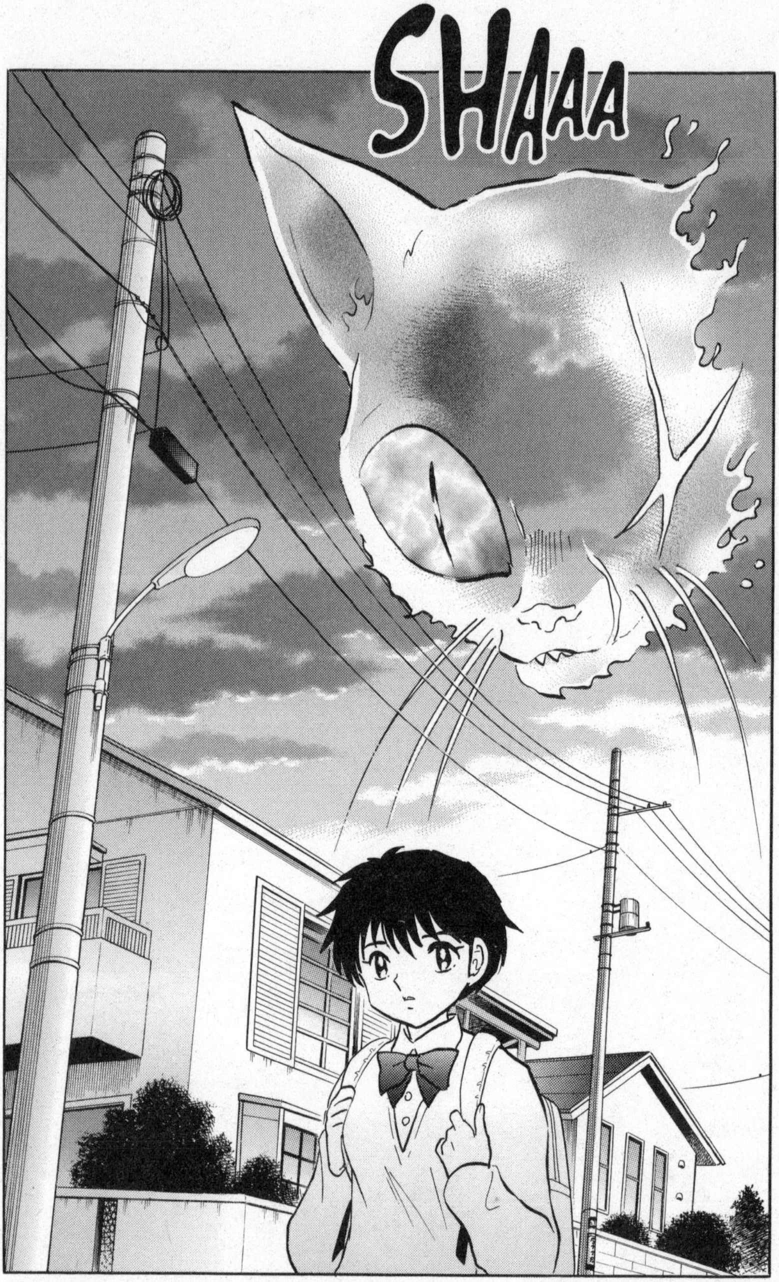
SHAAA

Chapter 3:
Warning

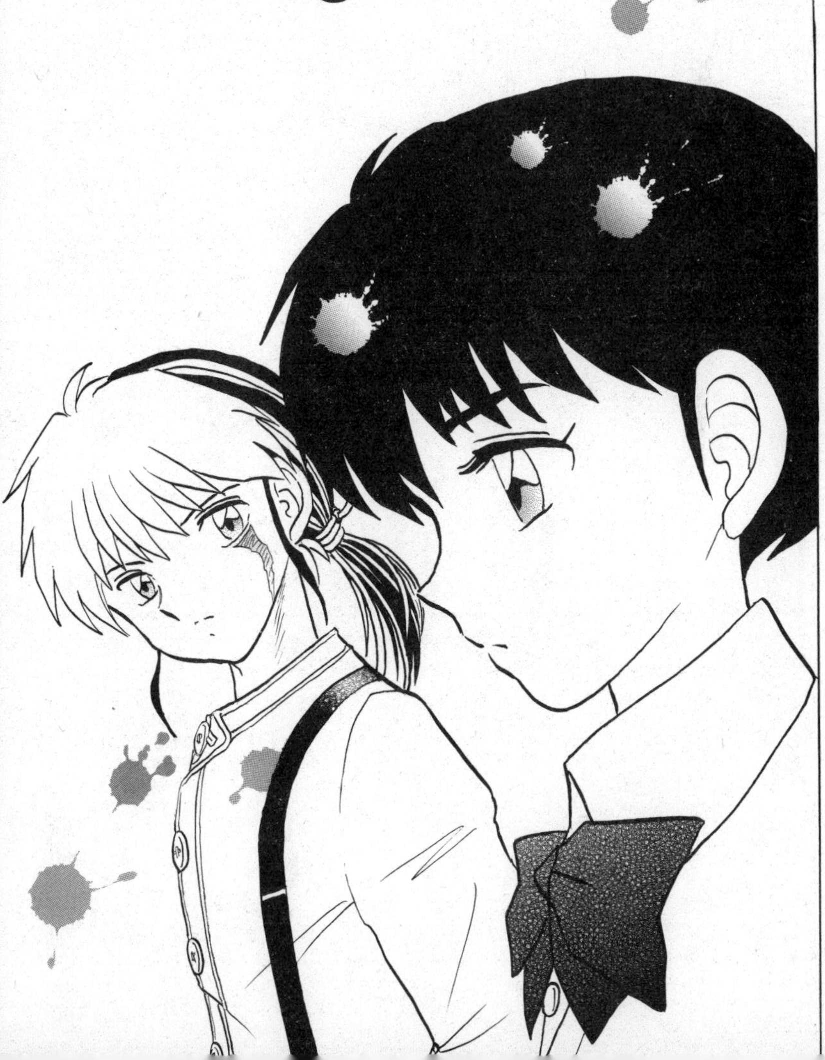

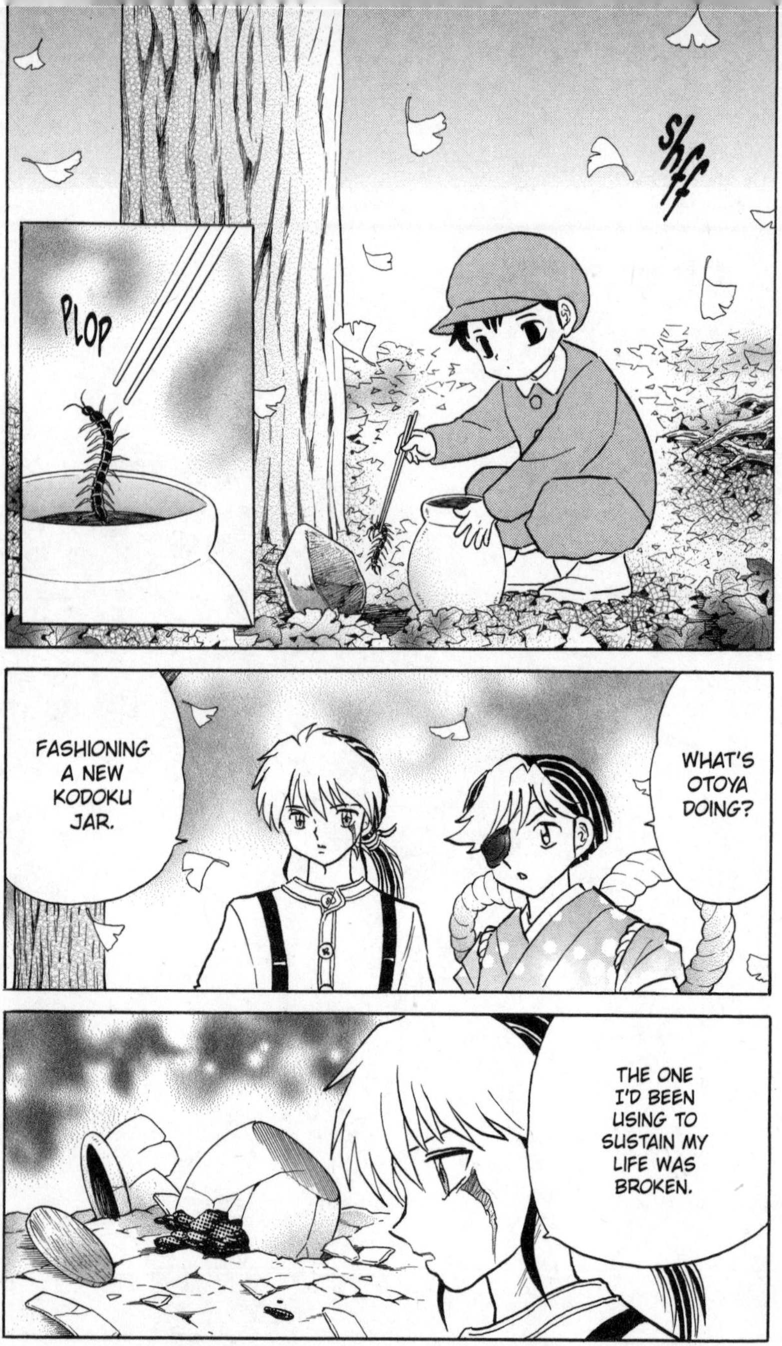
SHFF
PLOP
WHAT'S OTOYA DOING?
FASHIONING A NEW KODOKU JAR.
THE ONE I'D BEEN USING TO SUSTAIN MY LIFE WAS BROKEN.

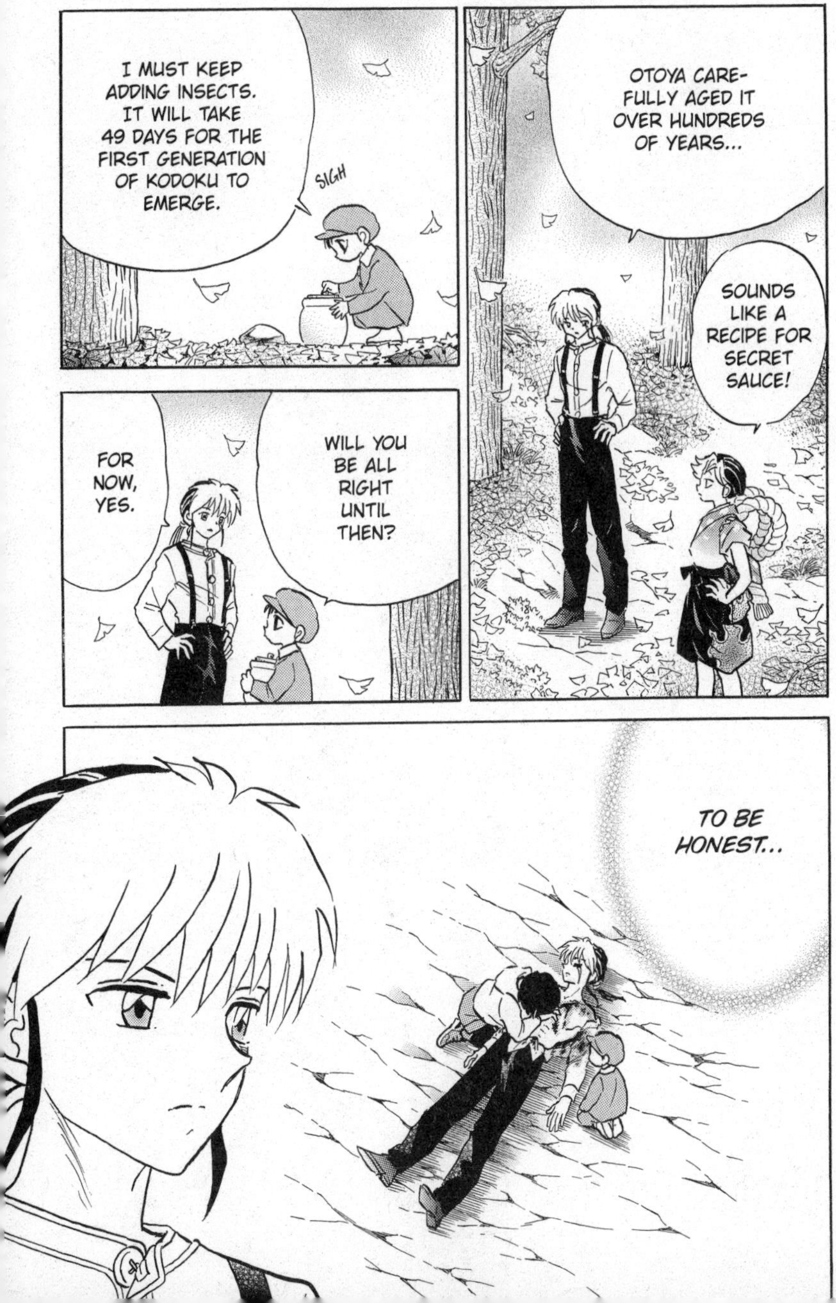
OTOYA CAREFULLY AGED IT OVER HUNDREDS OF YEARS...
SOUNDS LIKE A RECIPE FOR SECRET SAUCE!
I MUST KEEP ADDING INSECTS. IT WILL TAKE 49 DAYS FOR THE FIRST GENERATION OF KODOKU TO EMERGE.
SIGH
WILL YOU BE ALL RIGHT UNTIL THEN?
FOR NOW, YES.
TO BE HONEST...

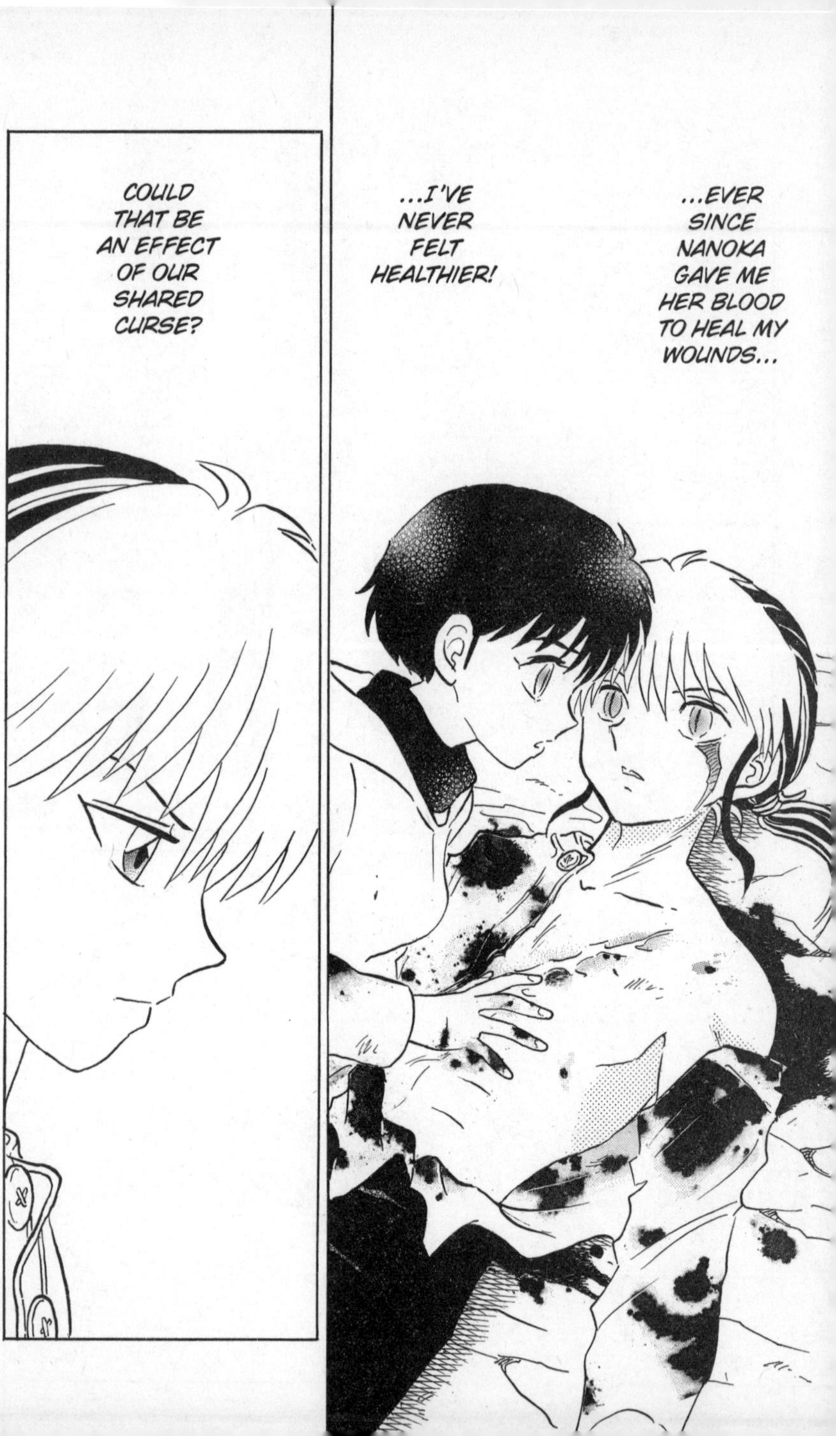
...EVER SINCE NANOKA GAVE ME HER BLOOD TO HEAL MY WOUNDS...
...I'VE NEVER FELT HEALTHIER!
COULD THAT BE AN EFFECT OF OUR SHARED CURSE?

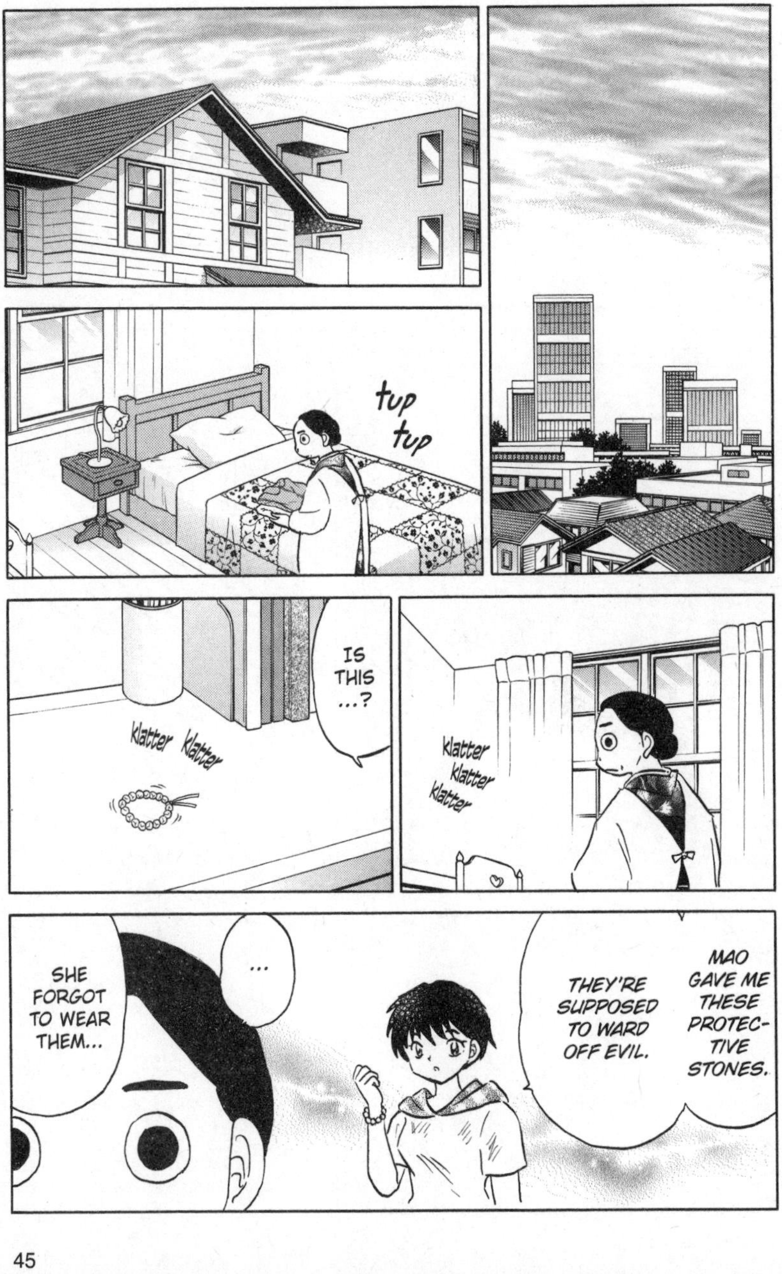
tup tup
klatter klatter klatter
klatter klatter
IS THIS ...?
MAO GAVE ME THESE PROTEC-TIVE STONES.
THEY'RE SUPPOSED TO WARD OFF EVIL.
...
SHE FORGOT TO WEAR THEM...

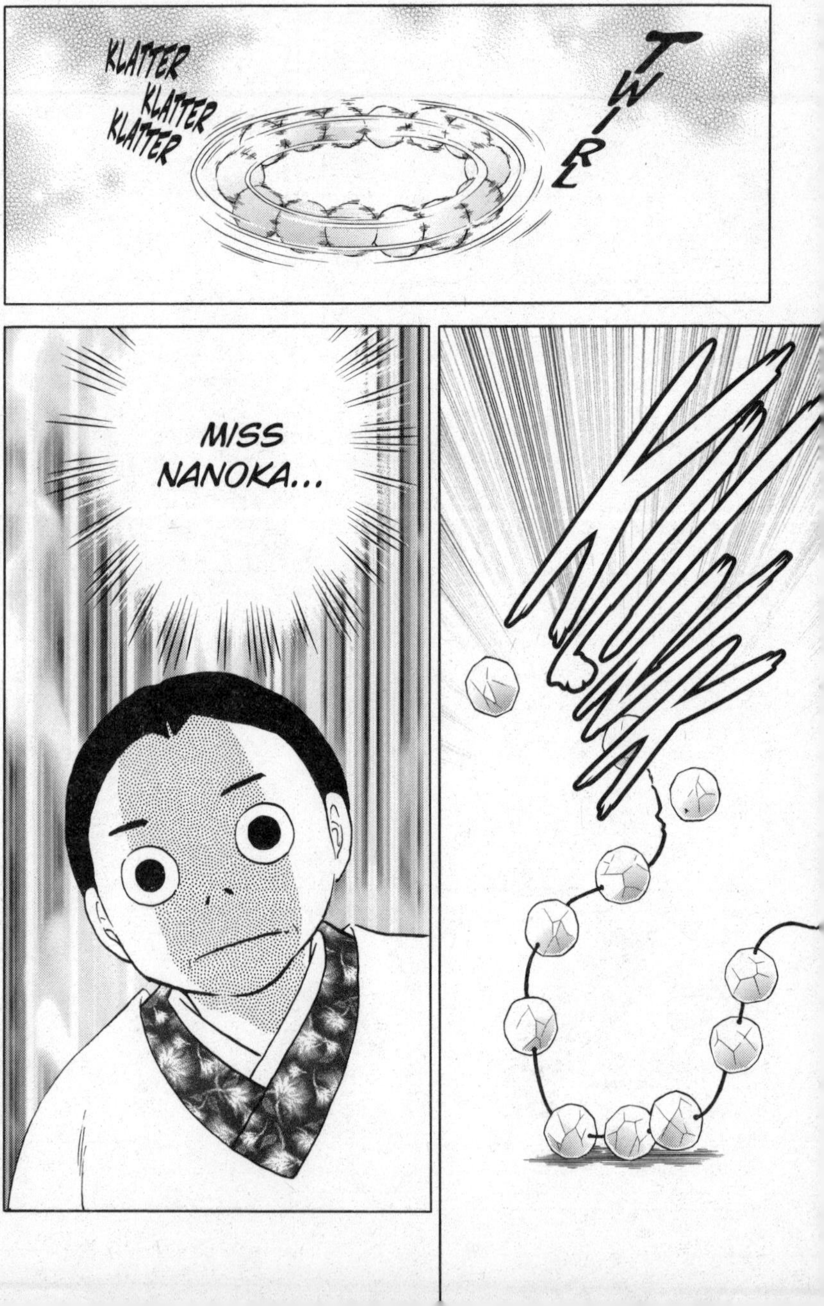
TWIRL
KLATTER KLATTER KLATTER
MISS NANOKA...

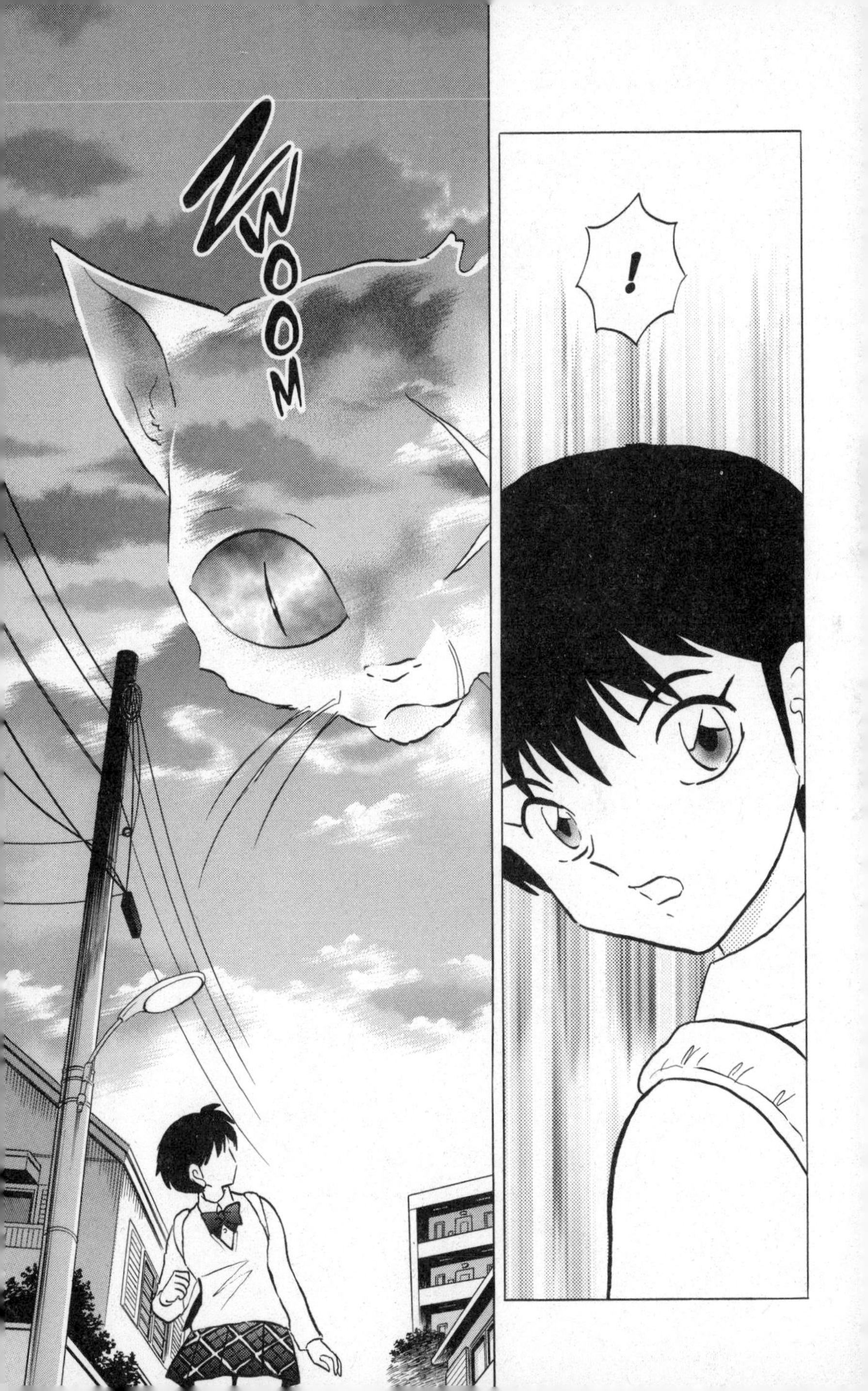
!
WOOM

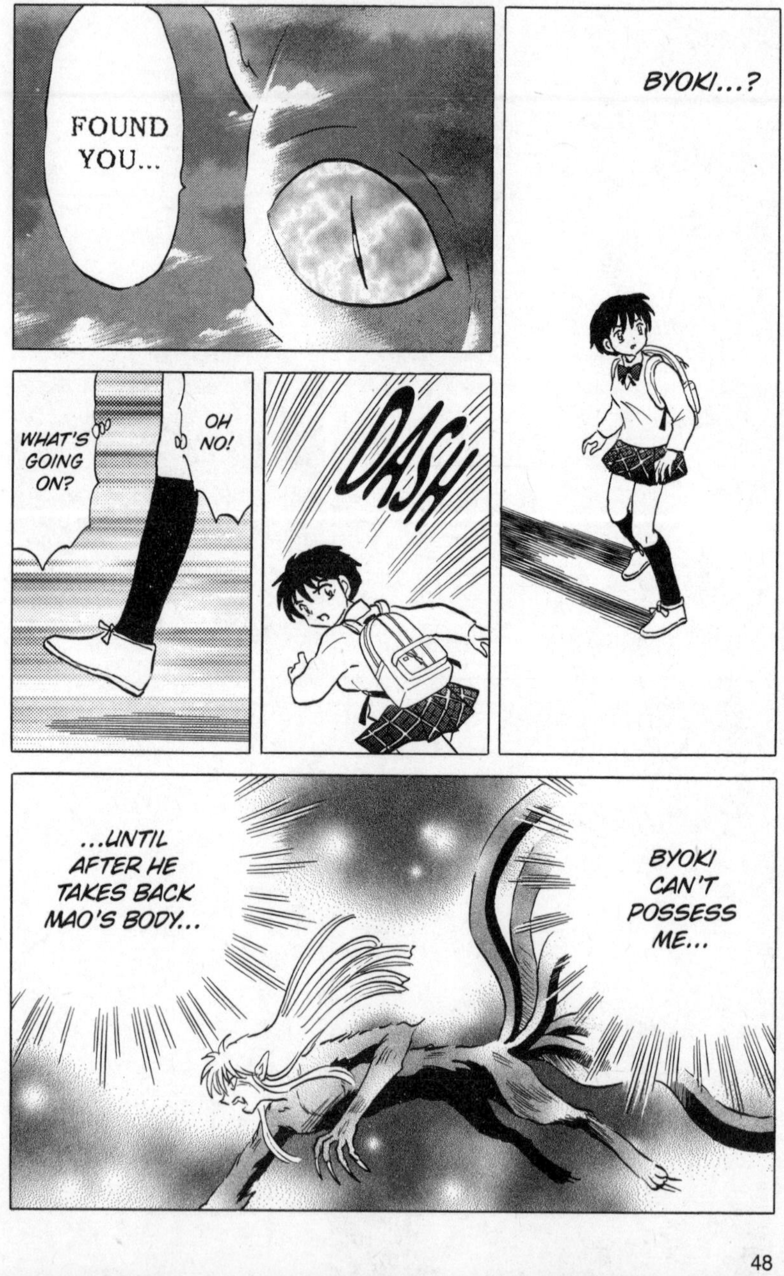
BYOKI...?
FOUND YOU...
DASH
OH NO!
WHAT'S GOING ON?
BYOKI CAN'T POSSESS ME...
...UNTIL AFTER HE TAKES BACK MAO'S BODY...

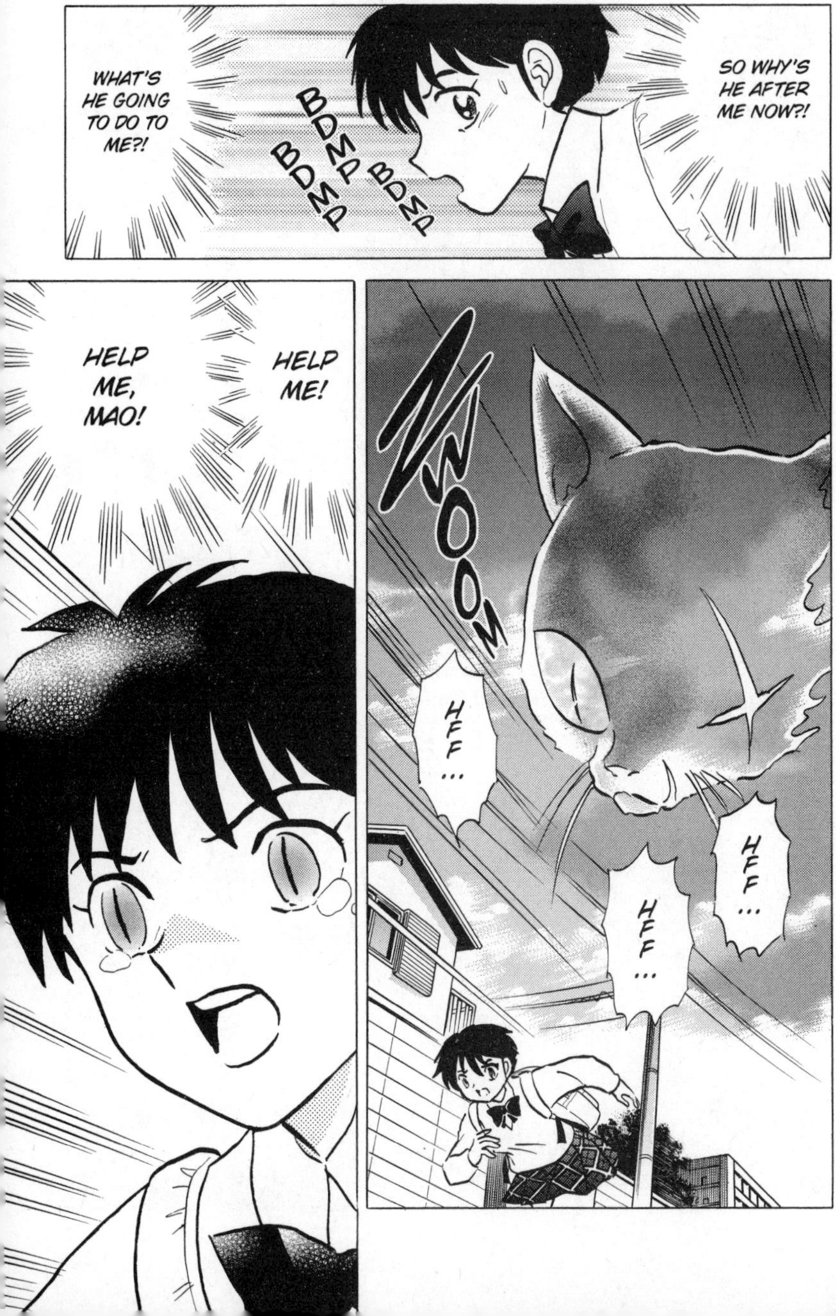
SO WHY'S HE AFTER ME NOW?!
BDMP
BDMP
BDMP
WHAT'S HE GOING TO DO TO ME?!
WOOOM
HFF...
HFF...
HFF...
HELP ME!
HELP ME, MAO!

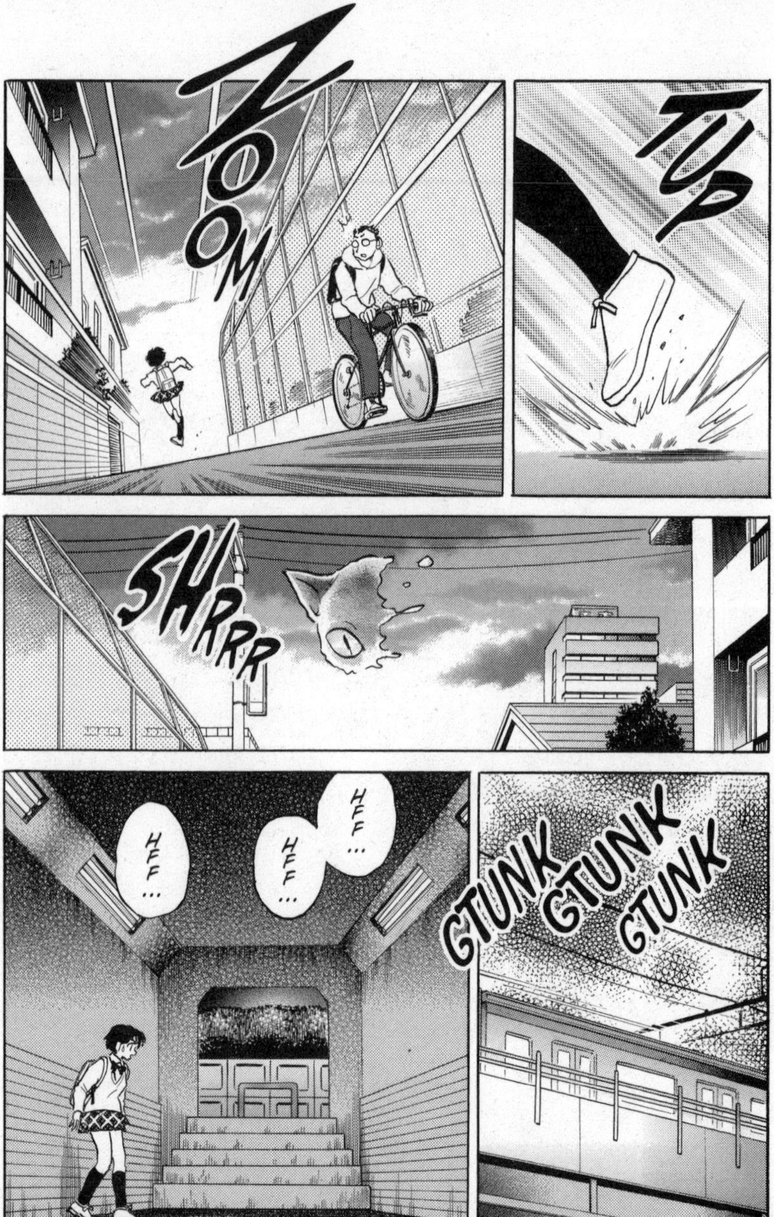
TUP
ZOOM
SHRRRR
GTUNK GTUNK GTUNK
HFF...
HFF...
HFF...

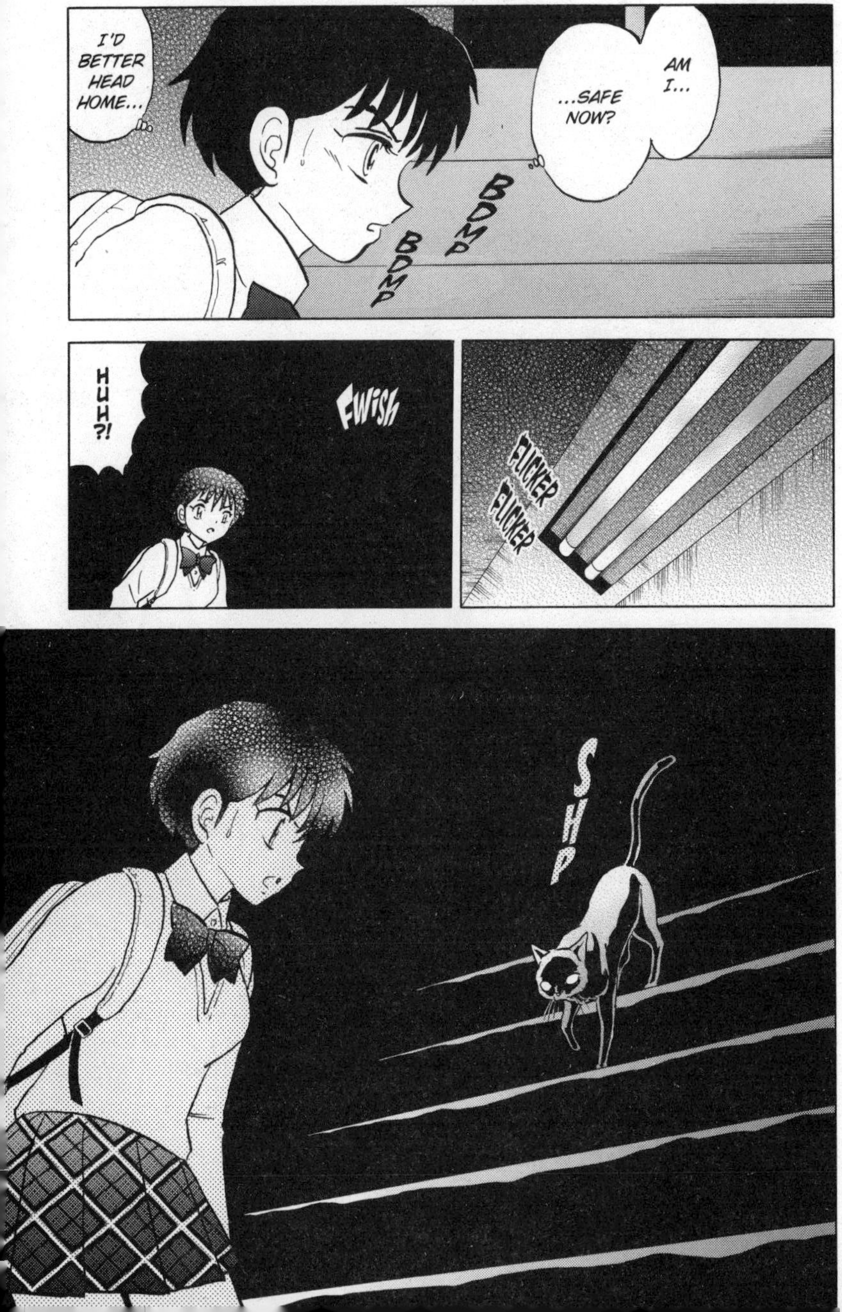
AM I...
...SAFE NOW?
BDOMP
BDOMP
I'D BETTER HEAD HOME...
FLICKER
FLICKER
FWISH
HUH?!
SHP

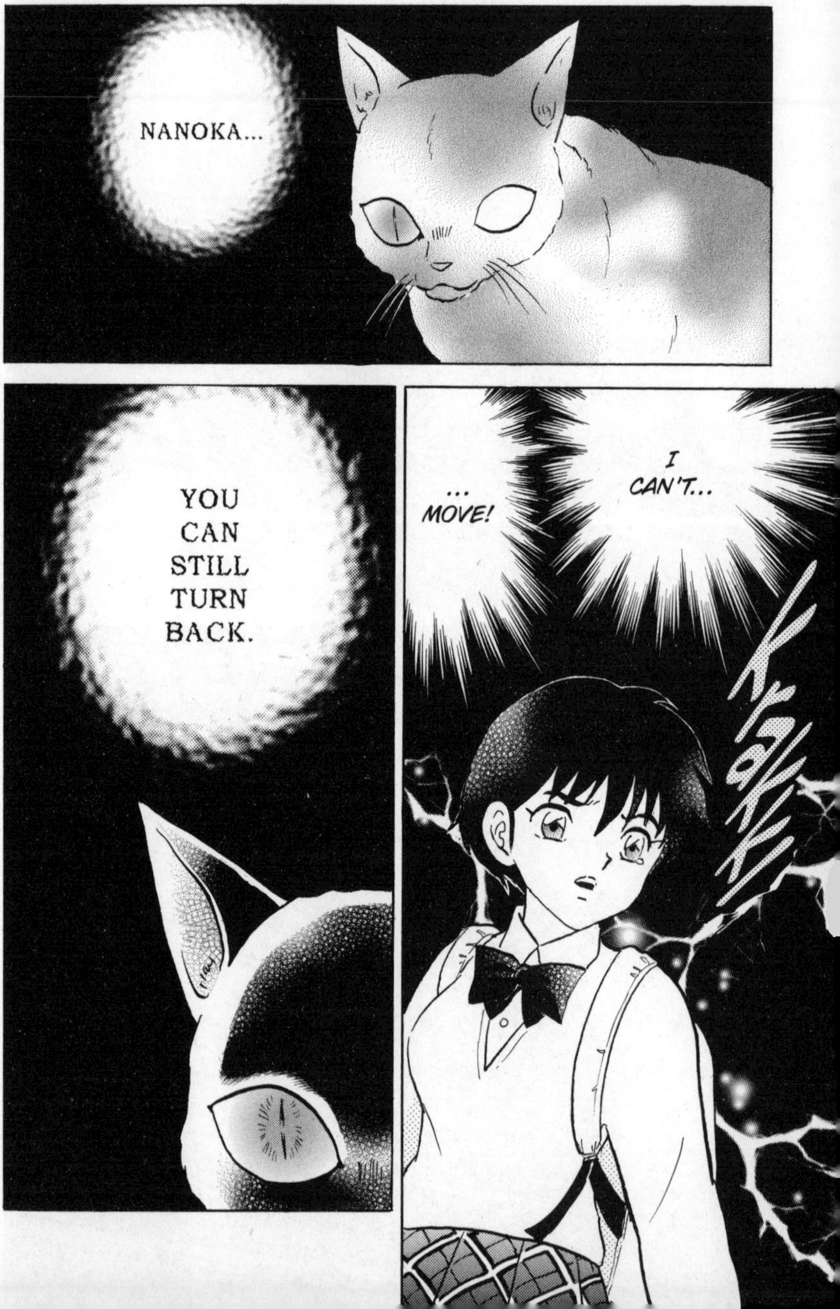
NANOKA...
I CAN'T...
...MOVE!
KRAKKK
YOU CAN STILL TURN BACK.

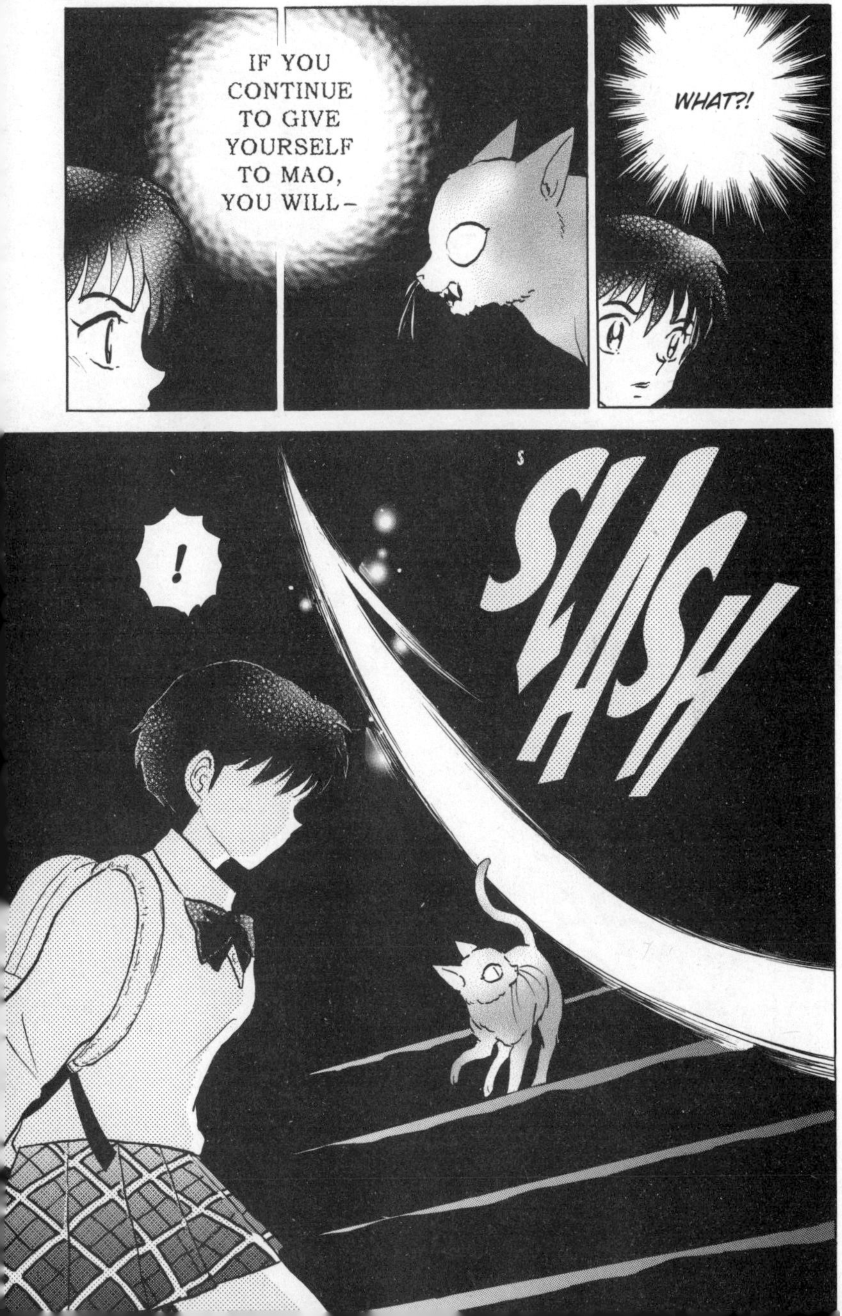
WHAT?!
IF YOU CONTINUE TO GIVE YOURSELF TO MAO, YOU WILL–
SLASH
!

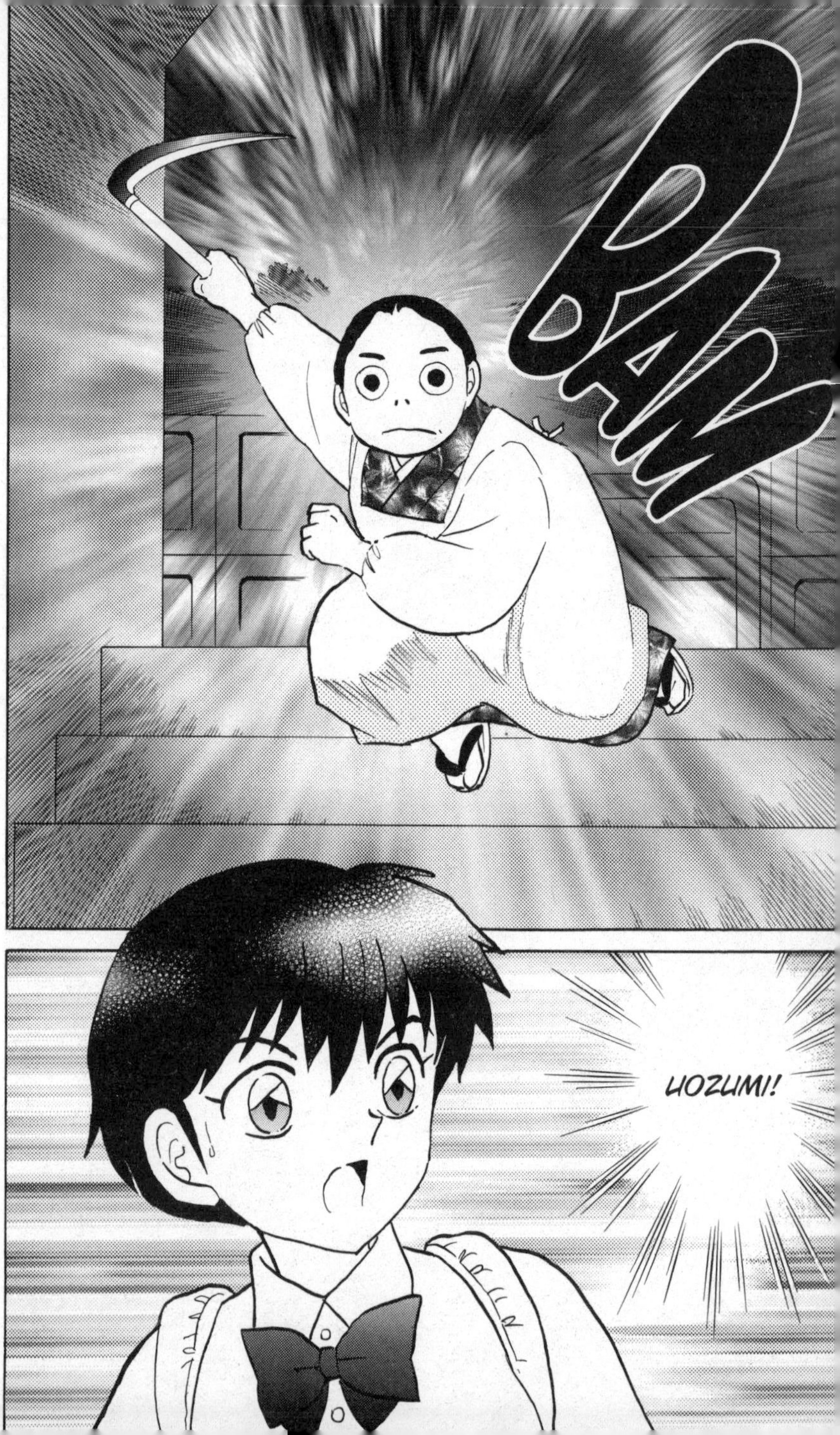
BAM
UOZUMI!

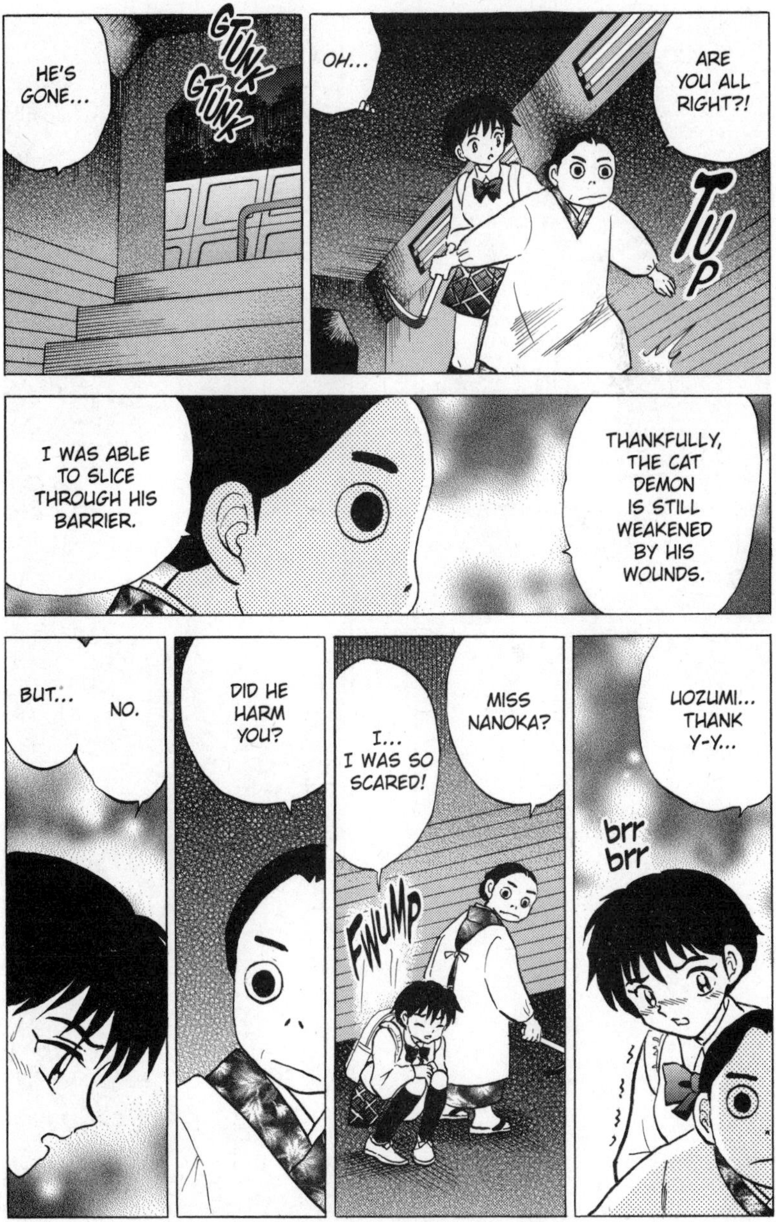
ARE YOU ALL RIGHT?!
TUP
OH...
GTUNK GTUNK
HE'S GONE...
THANKFULLY, THE CAT DEMON IS STILL WEAKENED BY HIS WOUNDS.
I WAS ABLE TO SLICE THROUGH HIS BARRIER.
UOZUMI... THANK Y-Y...
brr brr
MISS NANOKA?
I... I WAS SO SCARED!
FWUMP
DID HE HARM YOU?
NO.
BUT...

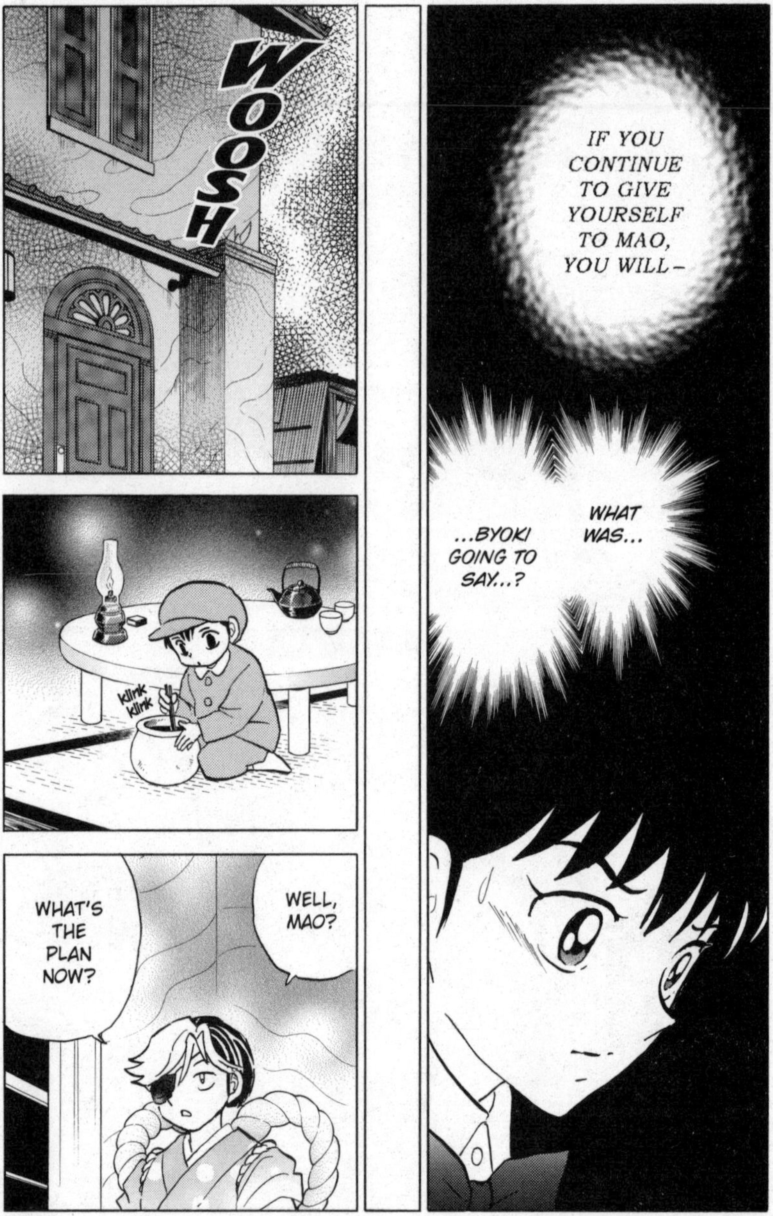
IF YOU CONTINUE TO GIVE YOURSELF TO MAO, YOU WILL–
WHAT WAS...
...BYOKI GOING TO SAY...?
WOOSH
klink klink
WELL, MAO?
WHAT'S THE PLAN NOW?

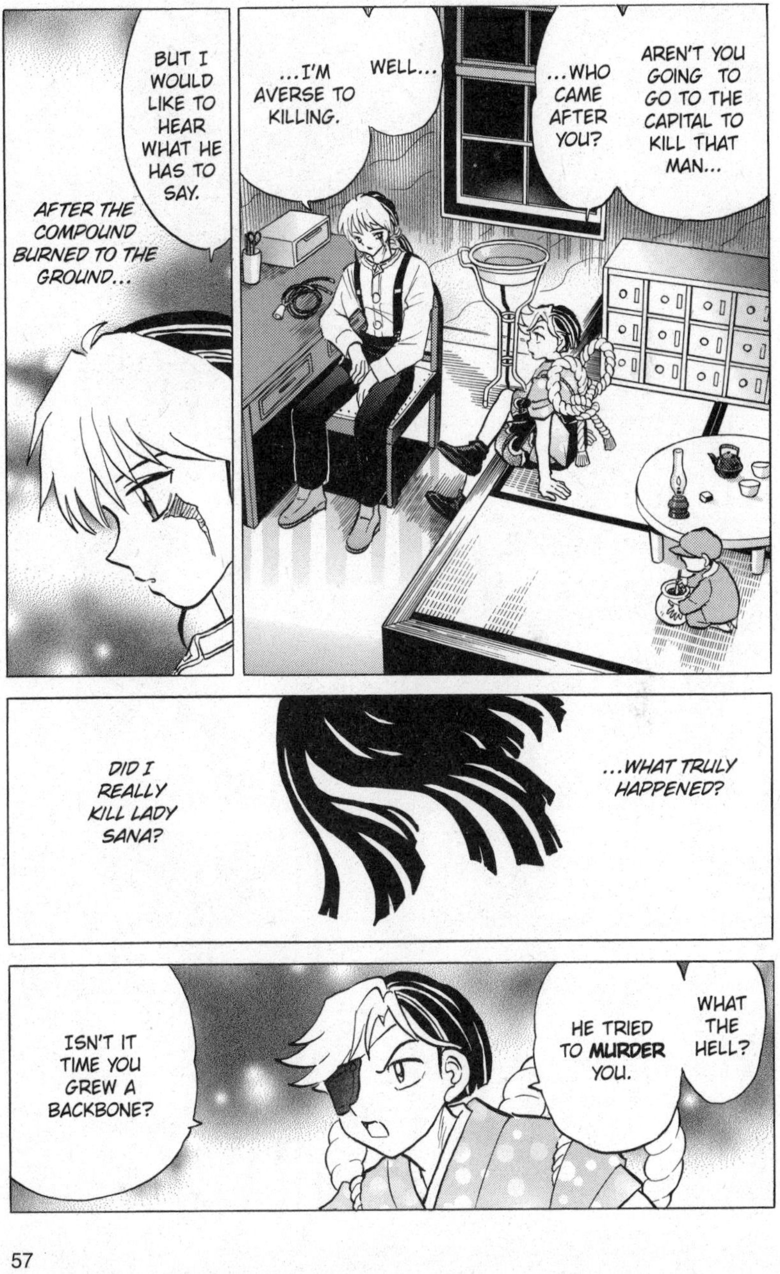
AREN'T YOU GOING TO GO TO THE CAPITAL TO KILL THAT MAN...
...WHO CAME AFTER YOU?
WELL...
...I'M AVERSE TO KILLING.
BUT I WOULD LIKE TO HEAR WHAT HE HAS TO SAY.
AFTER THE COMPOUND BURNED TO THE GROUND...
...WHAT TRULY HAPPENED?
DID I REALLY KILL LADY SANA?
WHAT THE HELL?
HE TRIED TO **MURDER** YOU.
ISN'T IT TIME YOU GREW A BACKBONE?

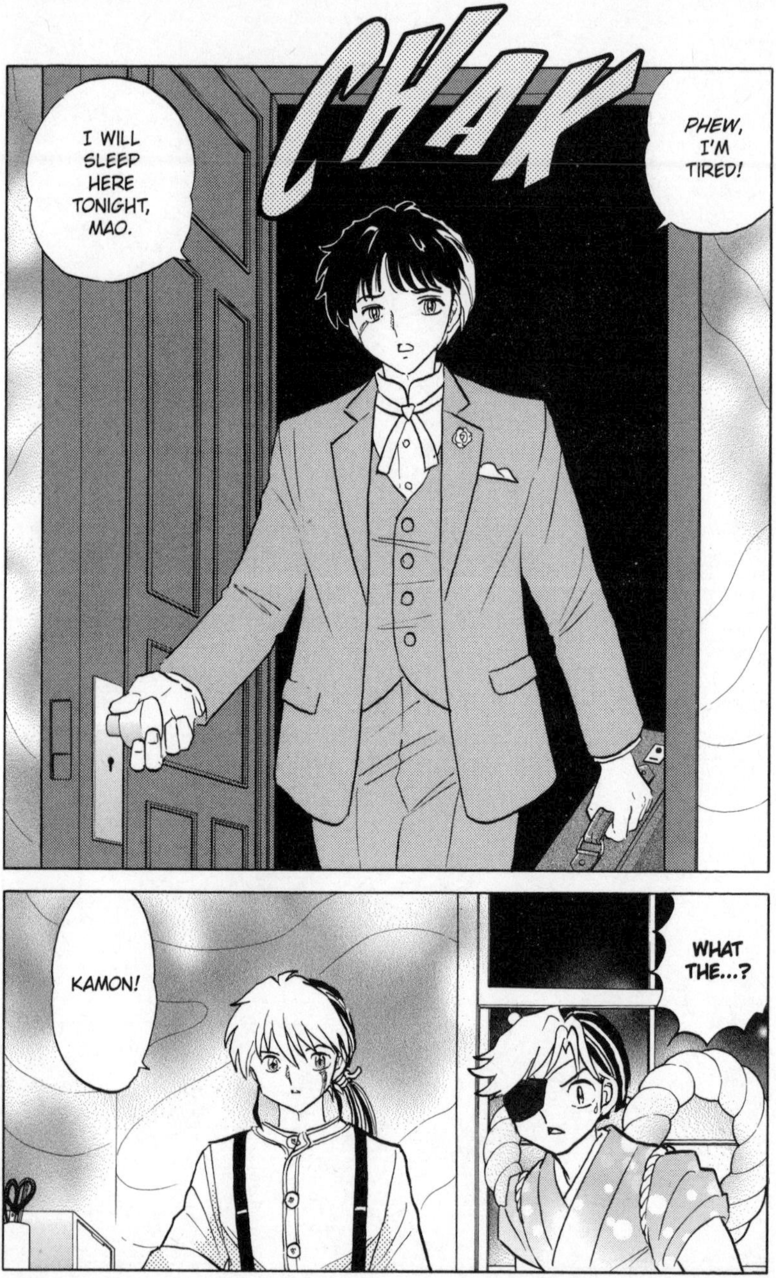
CHAK
PHEW, I'M TIRED!
I WILL SLEEP HERE TONIGHT, MAO.
WHAT THE...?
KAMON!

Chapter 4:
Three-Way Conversation

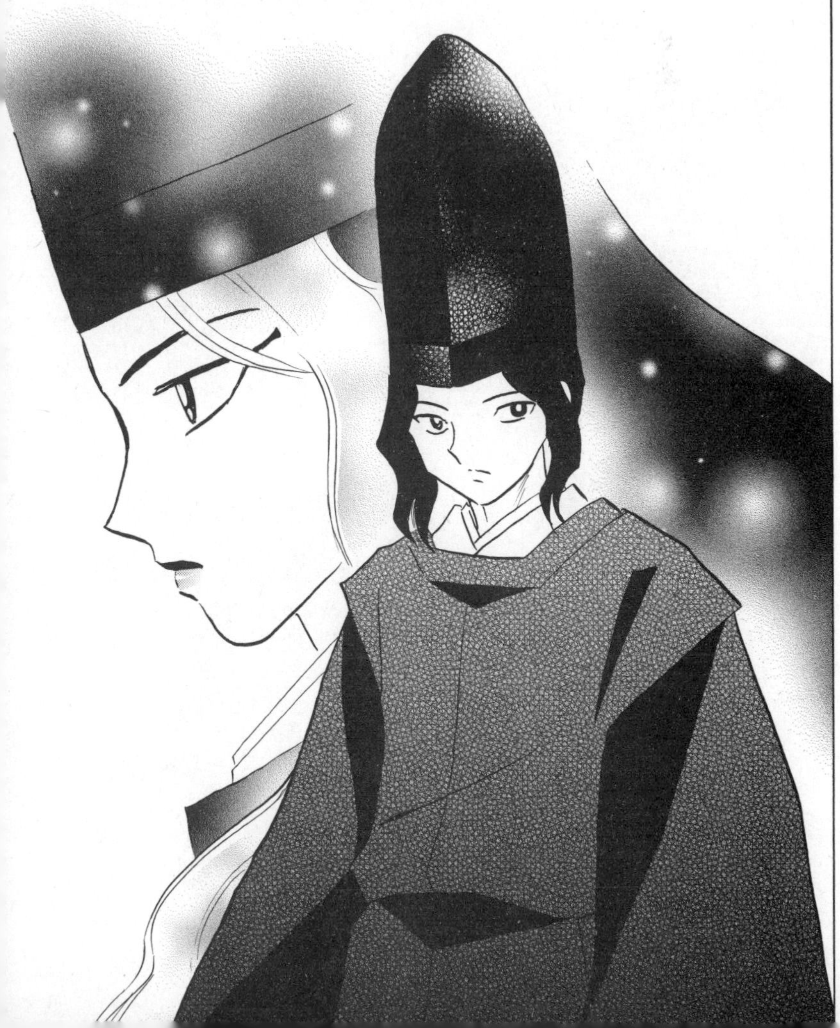

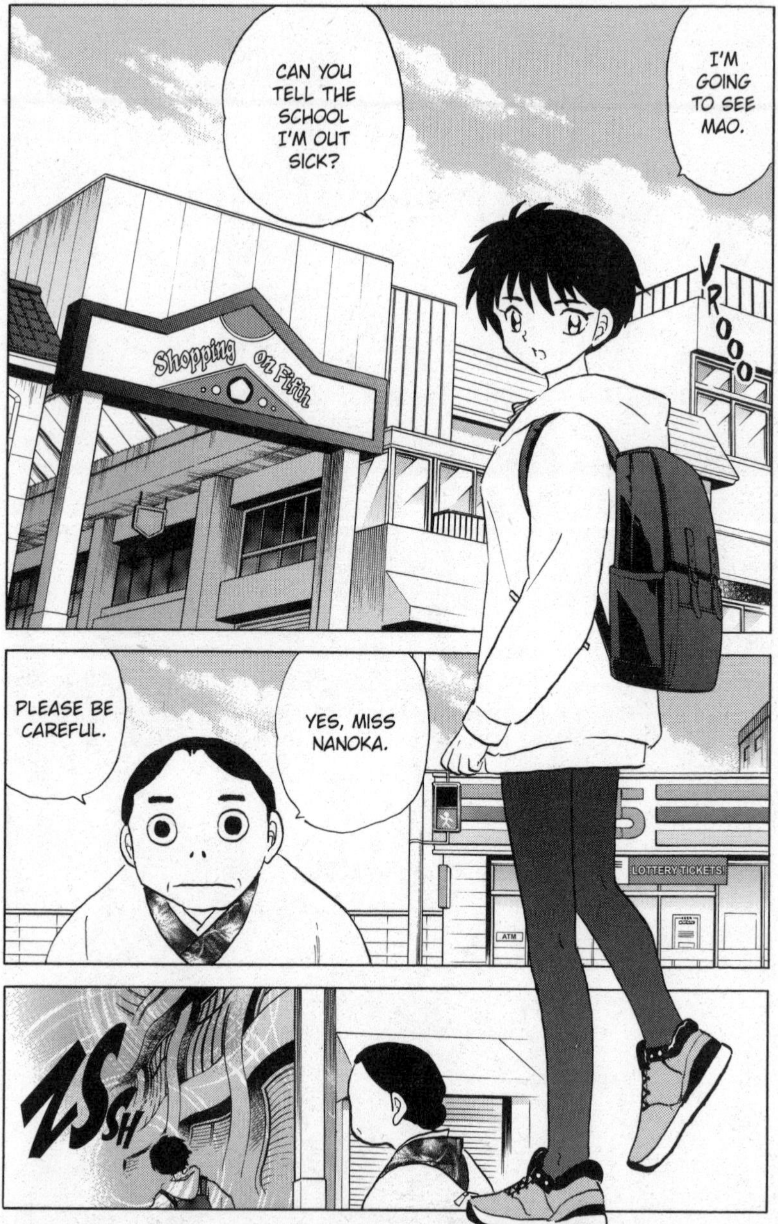
I'M GOING TO SEE MAO.
CAN YOU TELL THE SCHOOL I'M OUT SICK?
VROOOO
Shopping on Fifth
YES, MISS NANOKA.
PLEASE BE CAREFUL.
LOTTERY TICKETS
ATM
ZSSH

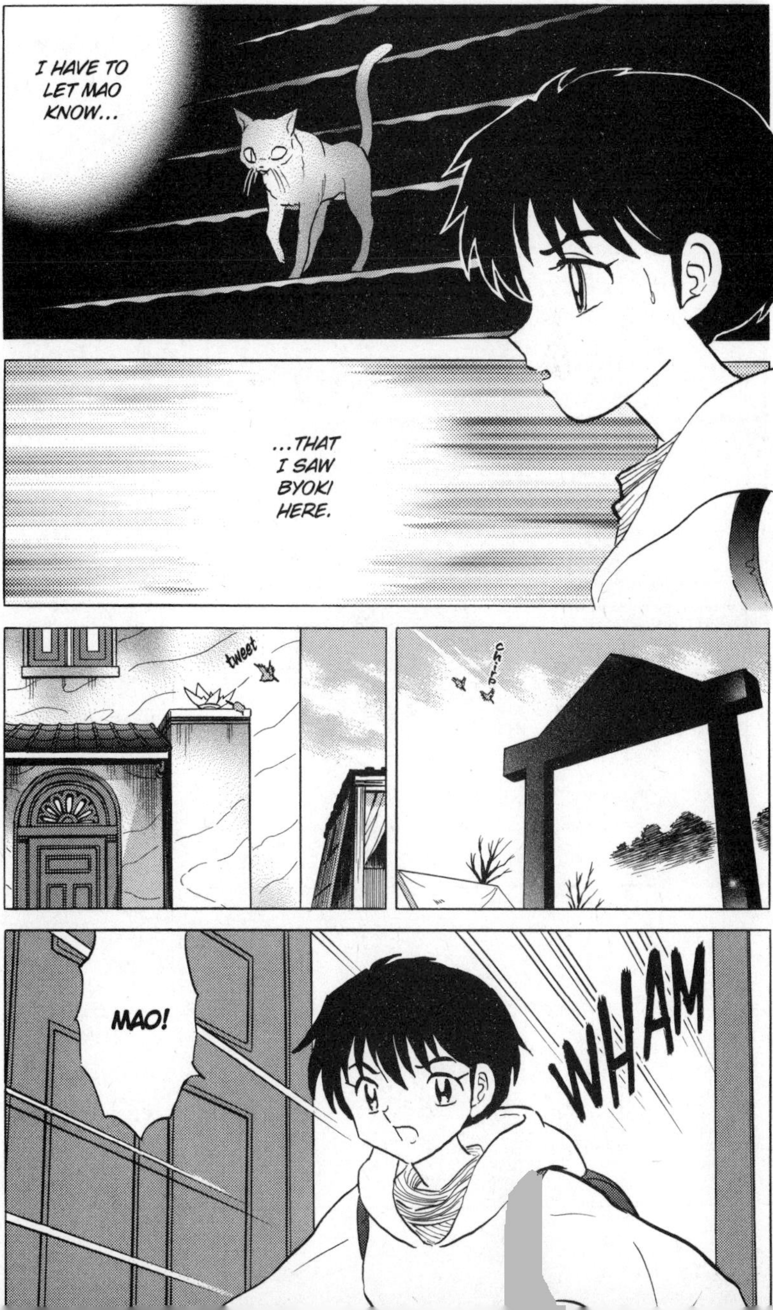
I HAVE TO LET MAO KNOW...
...THAT I SAW BYOKI HERE.
chirp
tweet
MAO!
WHAM

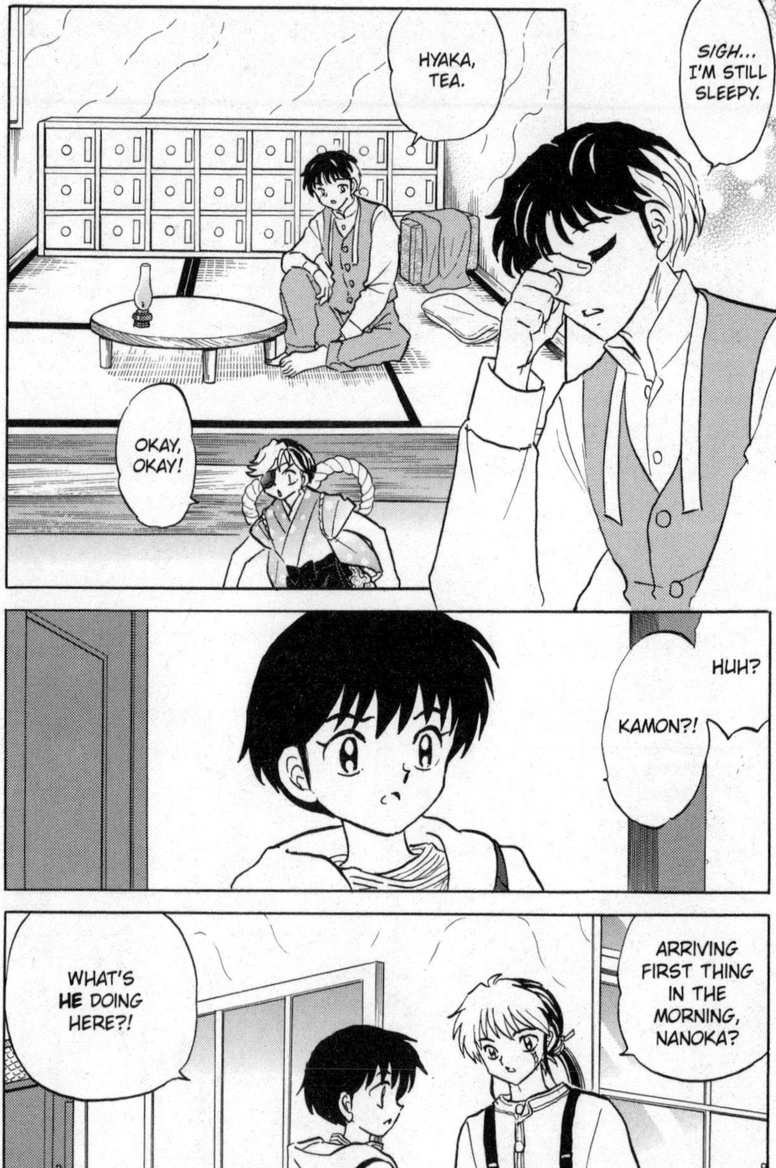
SIGH... I'M STILL SLEEPY.
HYAKA, TEA.
OKAY, OKAY!
HUH?
KAMON?!
ARRIVING FIRST THING IN THE MORNING, NANOKA?
WHAT'S **HE** DOING HERE?!

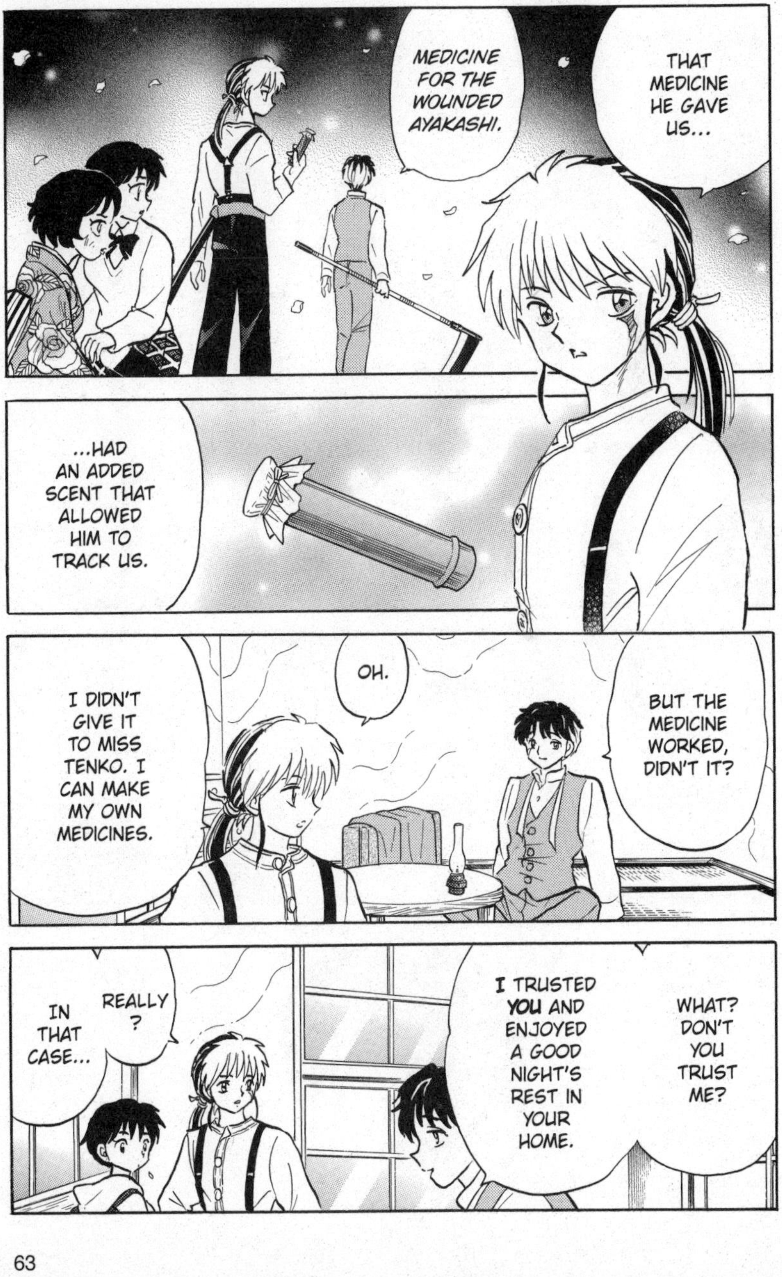
THAT MEDICINE HE GAVE US...
MEDICINE FOR THE WOUNDED AYAKASHI.
...HAD AN ADDED SCENT THAT ALLOWED HIM TO TRACK US.
BUT THE MEDICINE WORKED, DIDN'T IT?
OH.
I DIDN'T GIVE IT TO MISS TENKO. I CAN MAKE MY OWN MEDICINES.
WHAT? DON'T YOU TRUST ME?
I TRUSTED **YOU** AND ENJOYED A GOOD NIGHT'S REST IN YOUR HOME.
REALLY?
IN THAT CASE...

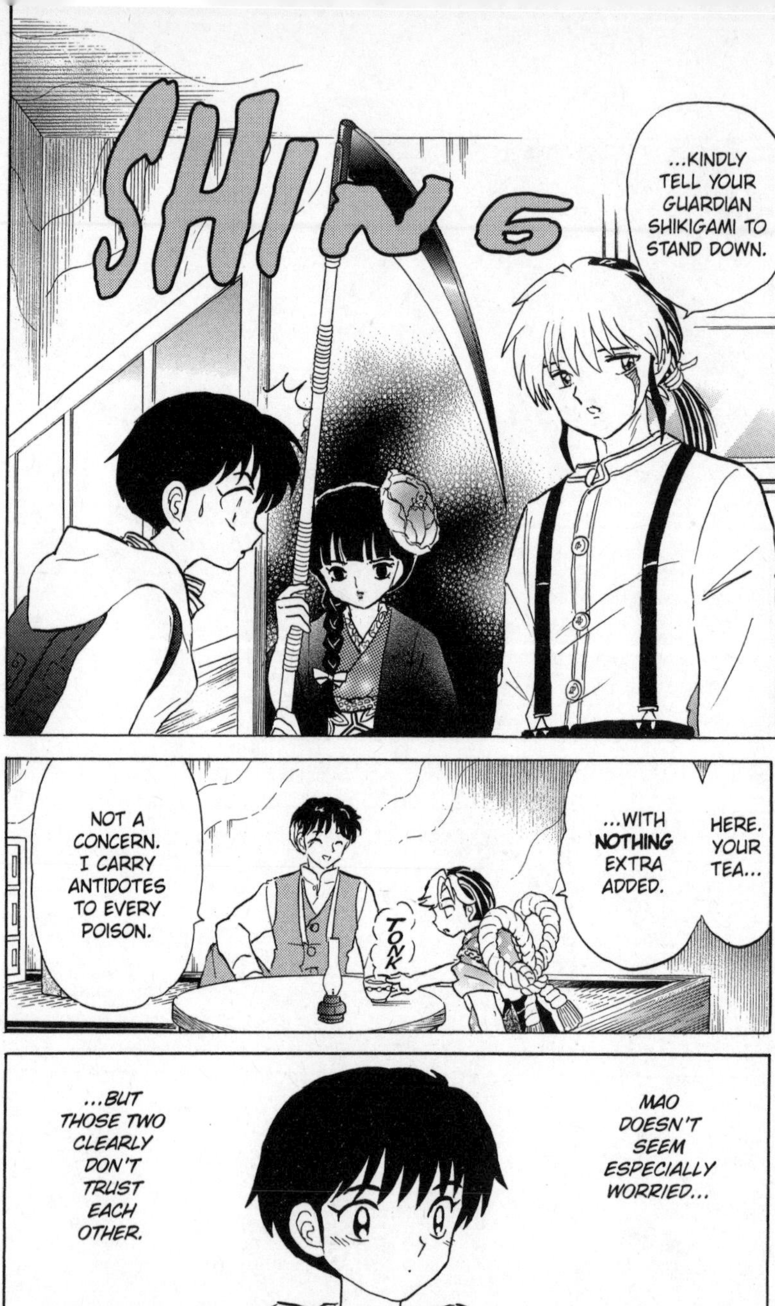
...KINDLY TELL YOUR GUARDIAN SHIKIGAMI TO STAND DOWN.
SHING
HERE. YOUR TEA...
...WITH NOTHING EXTRA ADDED.
TONK
NOT A CONCERN. I CARRY ANTIDOTES TO EVERY POISON.
MAO DOESN'T SEEM ESPECIALLY WORRIED...
...BUT THOSE TWO CLEARLY DON'T TRUST EACH OTHER.

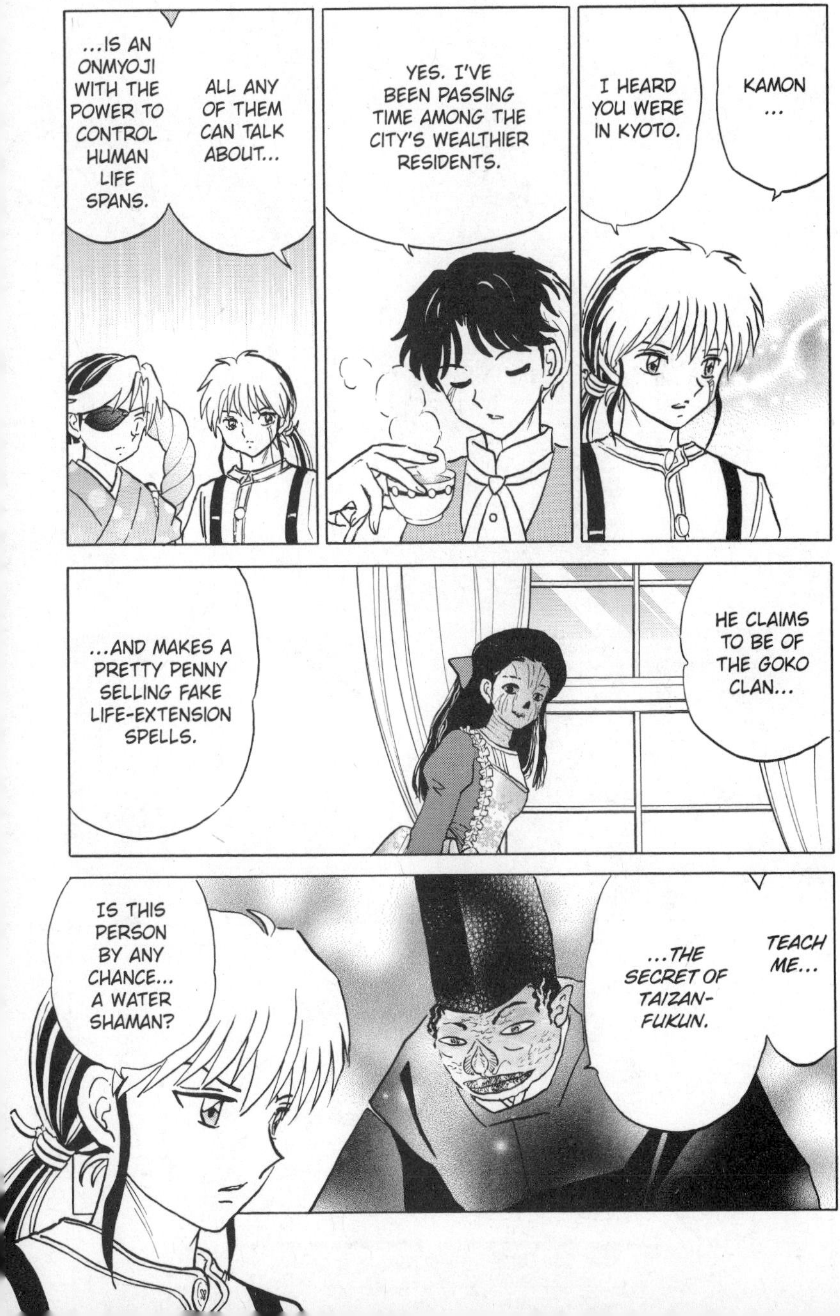
KAMON ...
I HEARD YOU WERE IN KYOTO.
YES. I'VE BEEN PASSING TIME AMONG THE CITY'S WEALTHIER RESIDENTS.
ALL ANY OF THEM CAN TALK ABOUT...
...IS AN ONMYOJI WITH THE POWER TO CONTROL HUMAN LIFE SPANS.
HE CLAIMS TO BE OF THE GOKO CLAN...
...AND MAKES A PRETTY PENNY SELLING FAKE LIFE-EXTENSION SPELLS.
TEACH ME...
...THE SECRET OF TAIZAN-FUKUN.
IS THIS PERSON BY ANY CHANCE... A WATER SHAMAN?

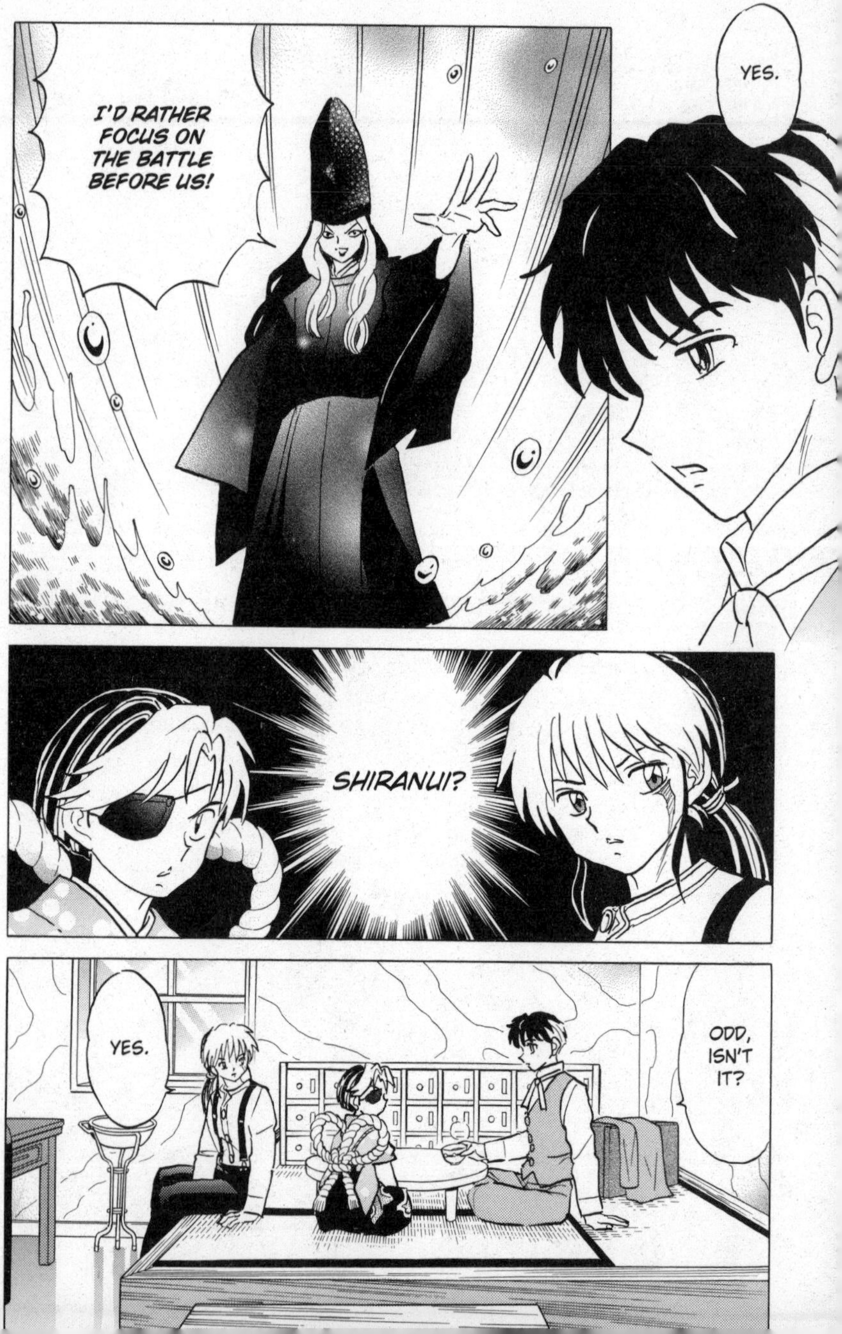
YES.
I'D RATHER FOCUS ON THE BATTLE BEFORE US!
SHIRANUI?
ODD, ISN'T IT?
YES.

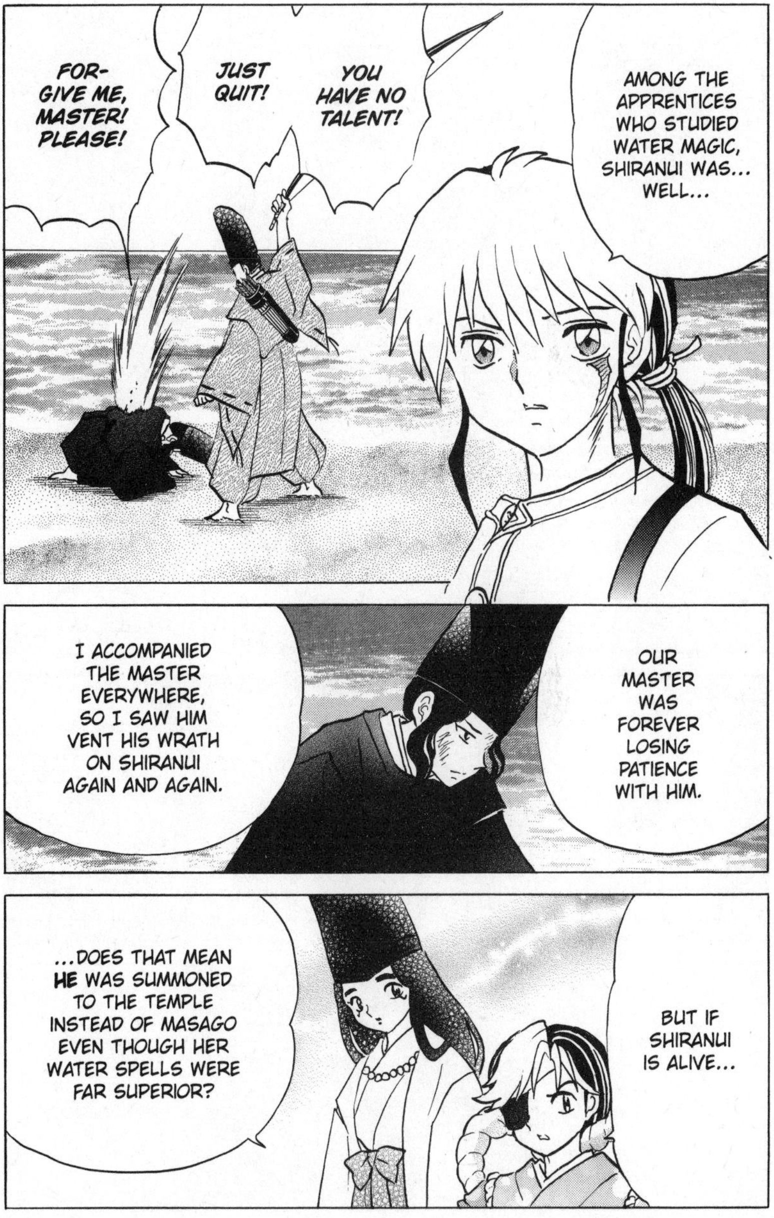
AMONG THE APPRENTICES WHO STUDIED WATER MAGIC, SHIRANUI WAS... WELL...
YOU HAVE NO TALENT!
JUST QUIT!
FOR-GIVE ME, MASTER! PLEASE!
OUR MASTER WAS FOREVER LOSING PATIENCE WITH HIM.
I ACCOMPANIED THE MASTER EVERYWHERE, SO I SAW HIM VENT HIS WRATH ON SHIRANUI AGAIN AND AGAIN.
BUT IF SHIRANUI IS ALIVE...
...DOES THAT MEAN **HE** WAS SUMMONED TO THE TEMPLE INSTEAD OF MASAGO EVEN THOUGH HER WATER SPELLS WERE FAR SUPERIOR?

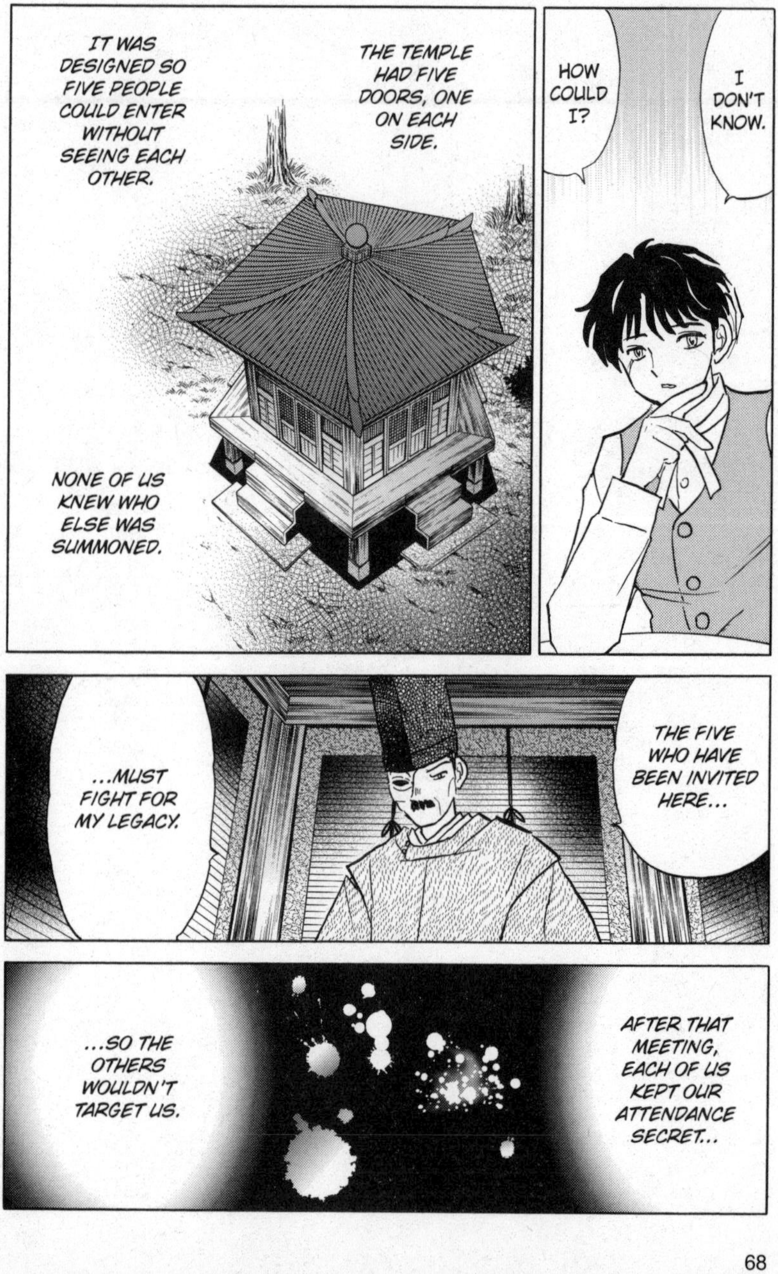
I DON'T KNOW.
HOW COULD I?
THE TEMPLE HAD FIVE DOORS, ONE ON EACH SIDE.
IT WAS DESIGNED SO FIVE PEOPLE COULD ENTER WITHOUT SEEING EACH OTHER.
NONE OF US KNEW WHO ELSE WAS SUMMONED.
THE FIVE WHO HAVE BEEN INVITED HERE...
...MUST FIGHT FOR MY LEGACY.
AFTER THAT MEETING, EACH OF US KEPT OUR ATTENDANCE SECRET...
...SO THE OTHERS WOULDN'T TARGET US.

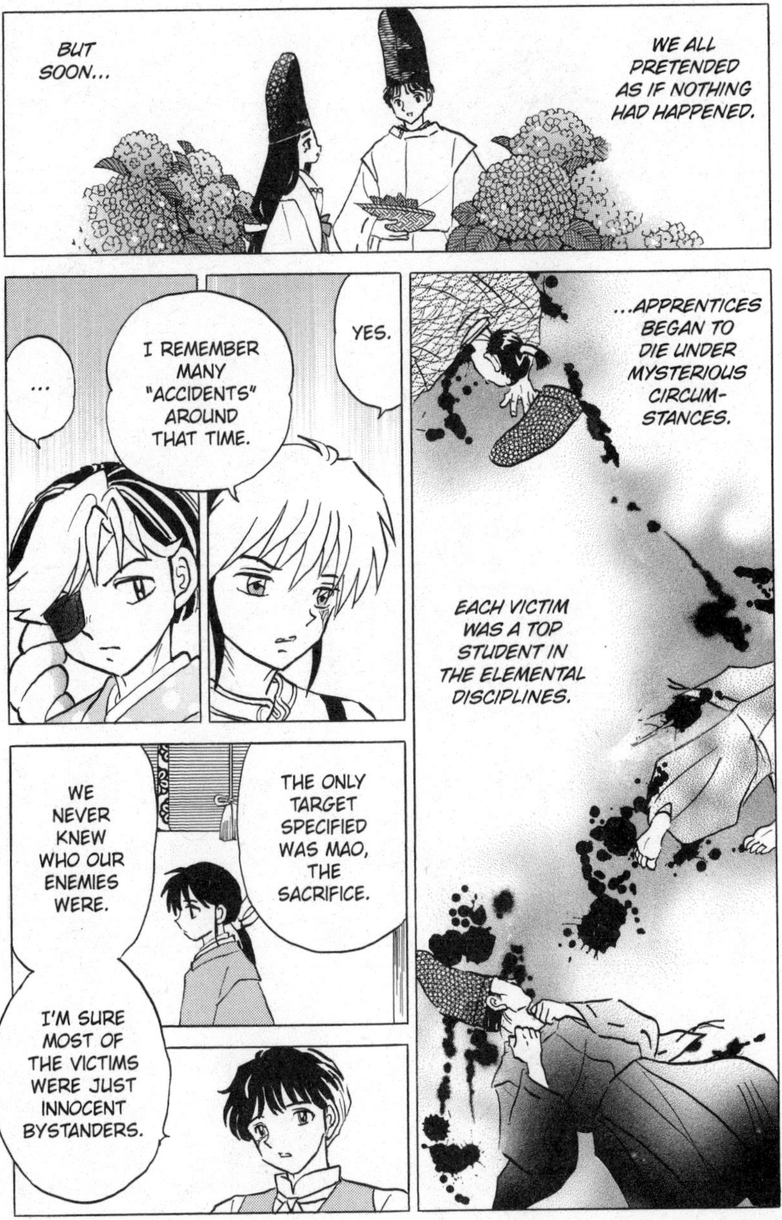
WE ALL PRETENDED AS IF NOTHING HAD HAPPENED.
BUT SOON...
...APPRENTICES BEGAN TO DIE UNDER MYSTERIOUS CIRCUM-STANCES.
EACH VICTIM WAS A TOP STUDENT IN THE ELEMENTAL DISCIPLINES.
I REMEMBER MANY "ACCIDENTS" AROUND THAT TIME.
YES.
...
THE ONLY TARGET SPECIFIED WAS MAO, THE SACRIFICE.
WE NEVER KNEW WHO OUR ENEMIES WERE.
I'M SURE MOST OF THE VICTIMS WERE JUST INNOCENT BYSTANDERS.

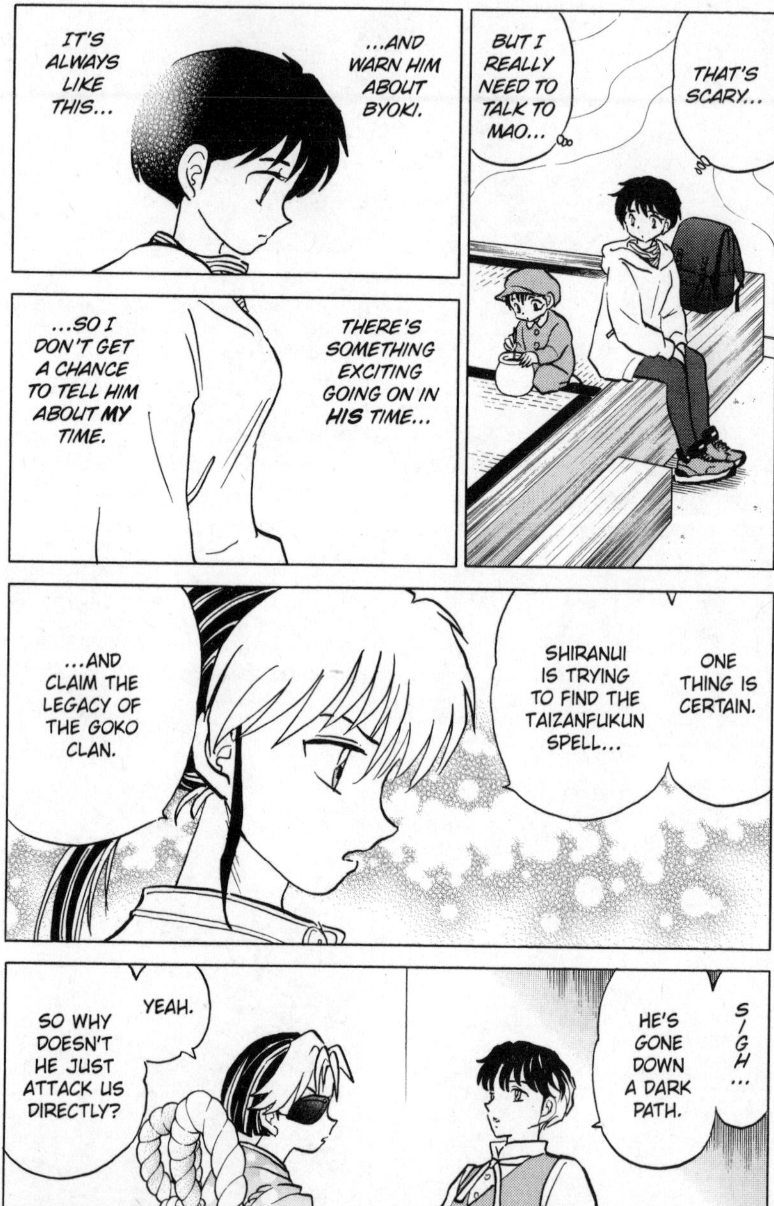
THAT'S SCARY...
BUT I REALLY NEED TO TALK TO MAO...
...AND WARN HIM ABOUT BYOKI.
IT'S ALWAYS LIKE THIS...
THERE'S SOMETHING EXCITING GOING ON IN HIS TIME...
...SO I DON'T GET A CHANCE TO TELL HIM ABOUT MY TIME.
ONE THING IS CERTAIN.
SHIRANUI IS TRYING TO FIND THE TAIZANFUKUN SPELL...
...AND CLAIM THE LEGACY OF THE GOKO CLAN.
SIGH...
HE'S GONE DOWN A DARK PATH.
YEAH.
SO WHY DOESN'T HE JUST ATTACK US DIRECTLY?

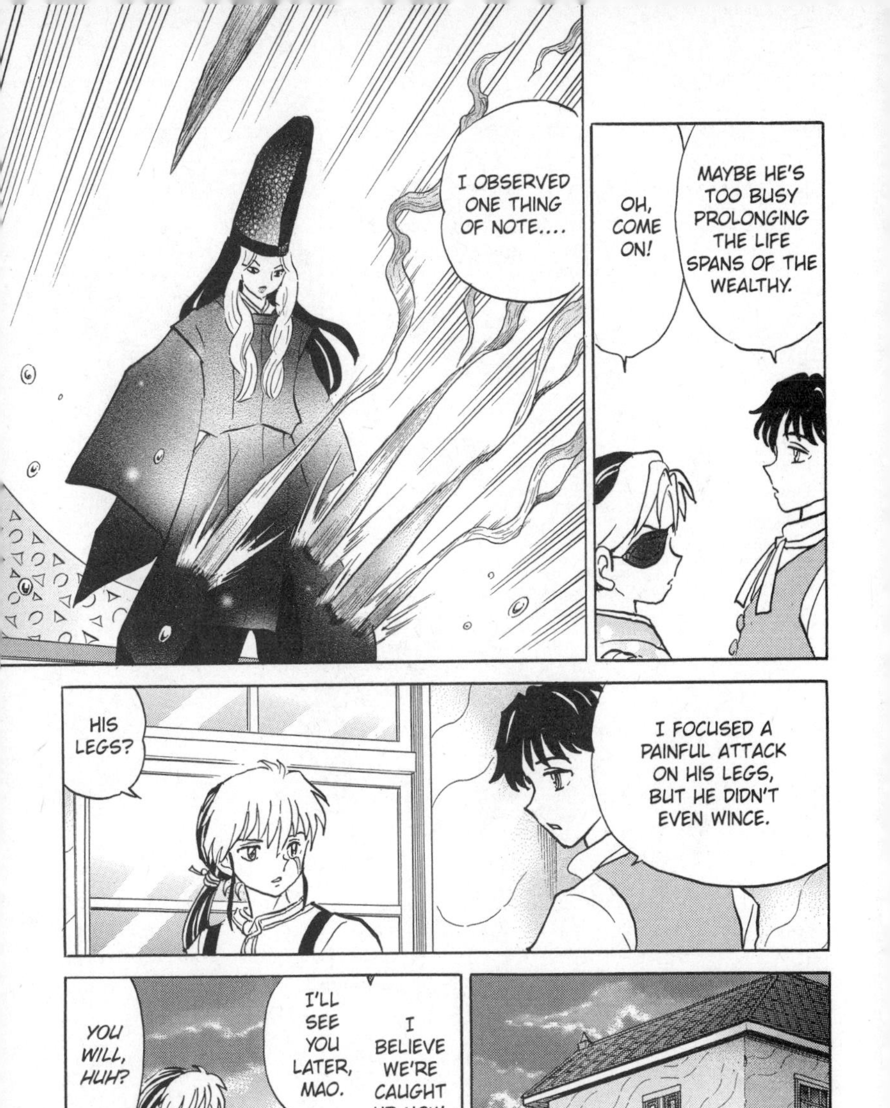
MAYBE HE'S TOO BUSY PROLONGING THE LIFE SPANS OF THE WEALTHY.
OH, COME ON!
I OBSERVED ONE THING OF NOTE....
I FOCUSED A PAINFUL ATTACK ON HIS LEGS, BUT HE DIDN'T EVEN WINCE.
HIS LEGS?
I BELIEVE WE'RE CAUGHT UP NOW.
I'LL SEE YOU LATER, MAO.
YOU WILL, HUH?

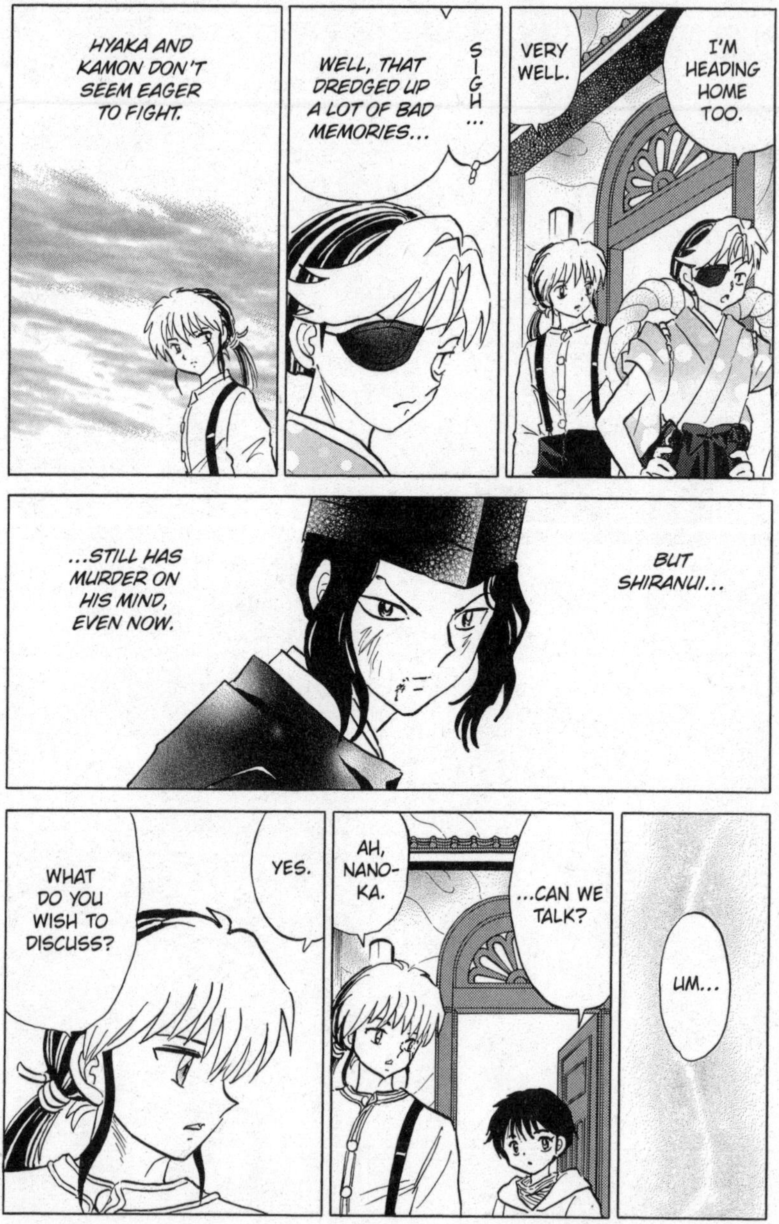
I'M HEADING HOME TOO.
VERY WELL.
SIGH...
WELL, THAT DREDGED UP A LOT OF BAD MEMORIES...
HYAKA AND KAMON DON'T SEEM EAGER TO FIGHT.
BUT SHIRANUI...
...STILL HAS MURDER ON HIS MIND, EVEN NOW.
UM...
...CAN WE TALK?
AH, NANOKA.
YES.
WHAT DO YOU WISH TO DISCUSS?

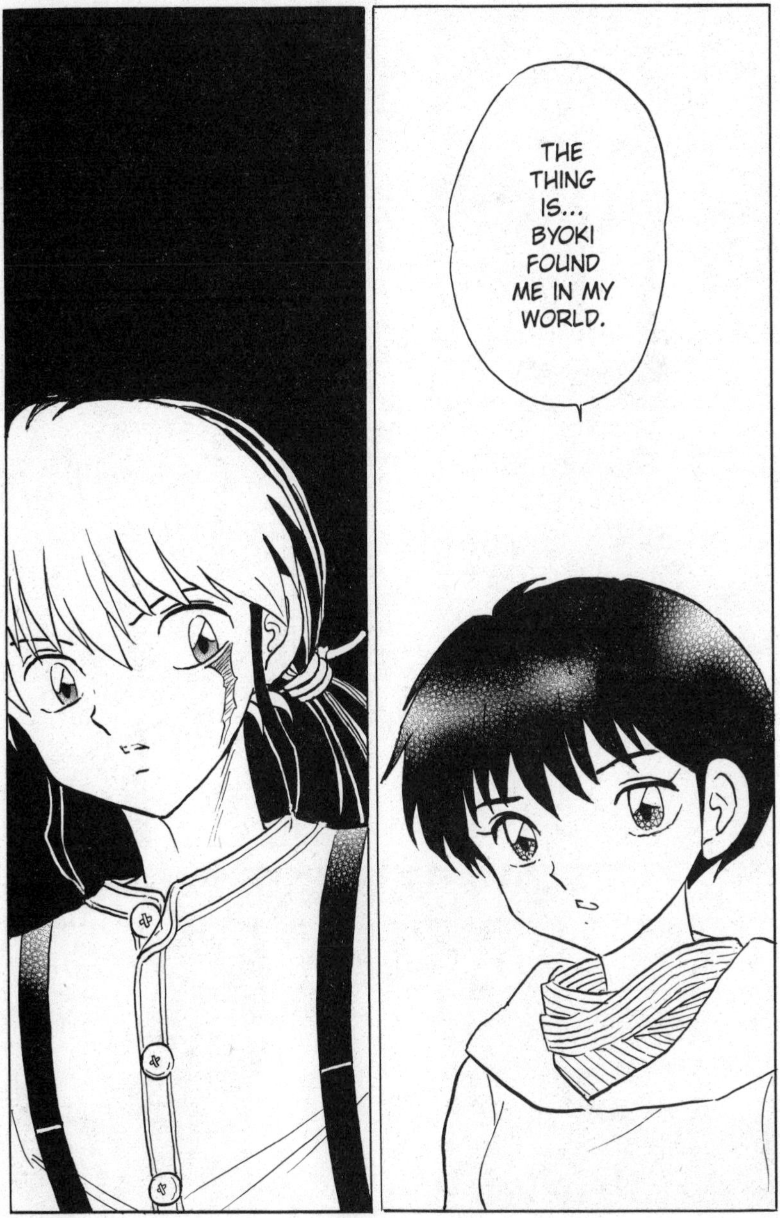
THE THING IS... BYOKI FOUND ME IN MY WORLD.

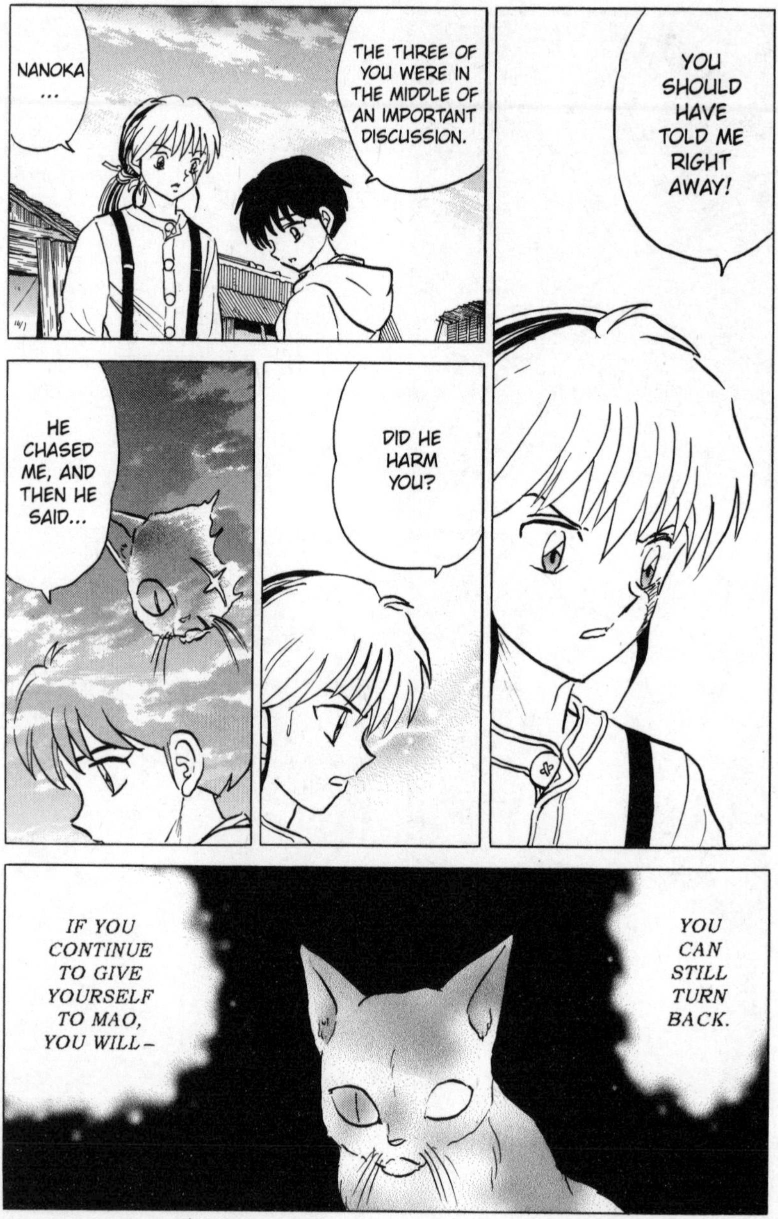
YOU SHOULD HAVE TOLD ME RIGHT AWAY!
THE THREE OF YOU WERE IN THE MIDDLE OF AN IMPORTANT DISCUSSION.
NANOKA ...
DID HE HARM YOU?
HE CHASED ME, AND THEN HE SAID...
YOU CAN STILL TURN BACK.
IF YOU CONTINUE TO GIVE YOURSELF TO MAO, YOU WILL–

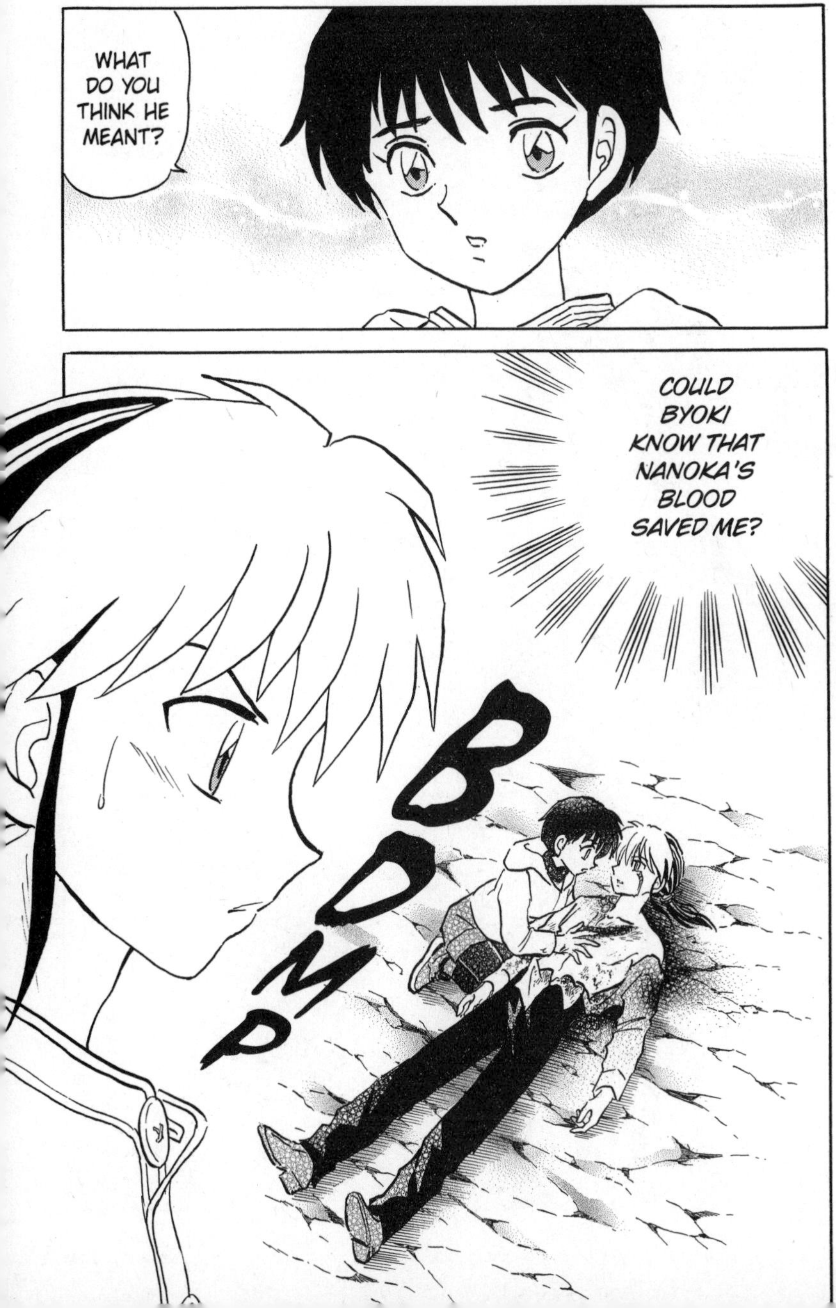
WHAT DO YOU THINK HE MEANT?
COULD BYOKI KNOW THAT NANOKA'S BLOOD SAVED ME?
BDMP

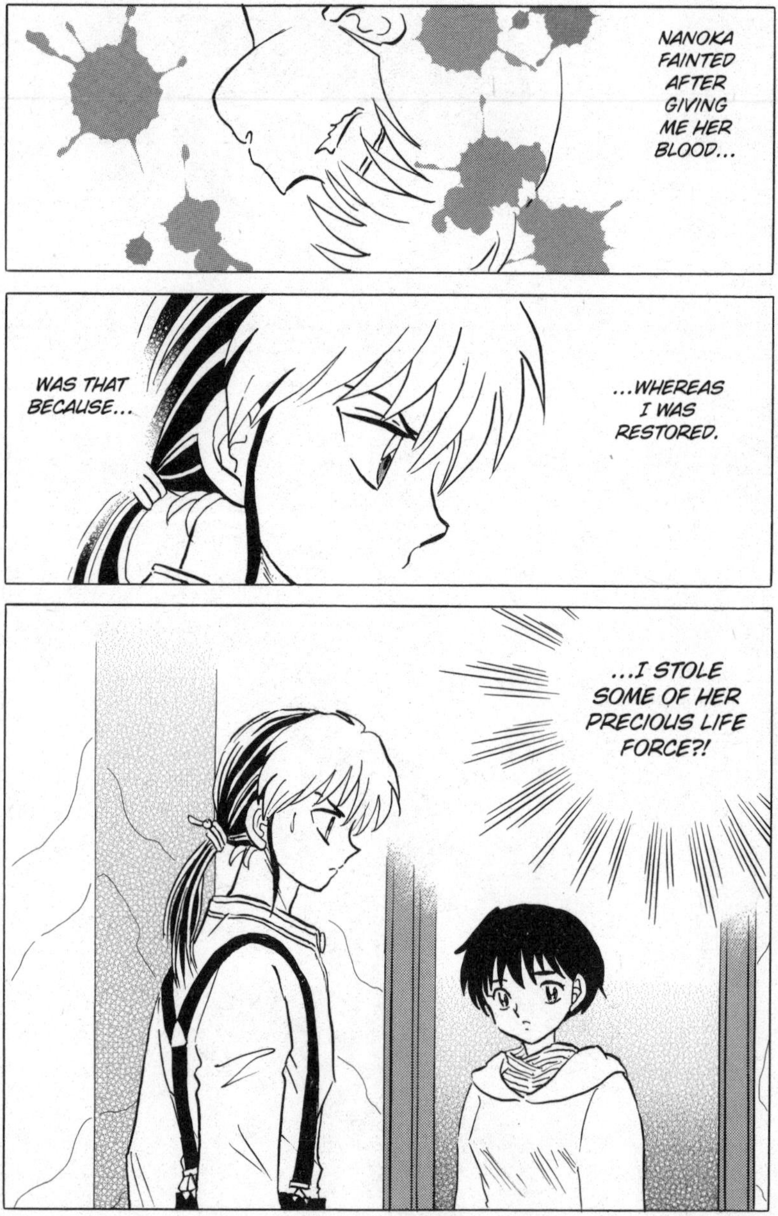
NANOKA FAINTED AFTER GIVING ME HER BLOOD...
...WHEREAS I WAS RESTORED.
WAS THAT BECAUSE...
...I STOLE SOME OF HER PRECIOUS LIFE FORCE?!

Chapter 5: The Donor

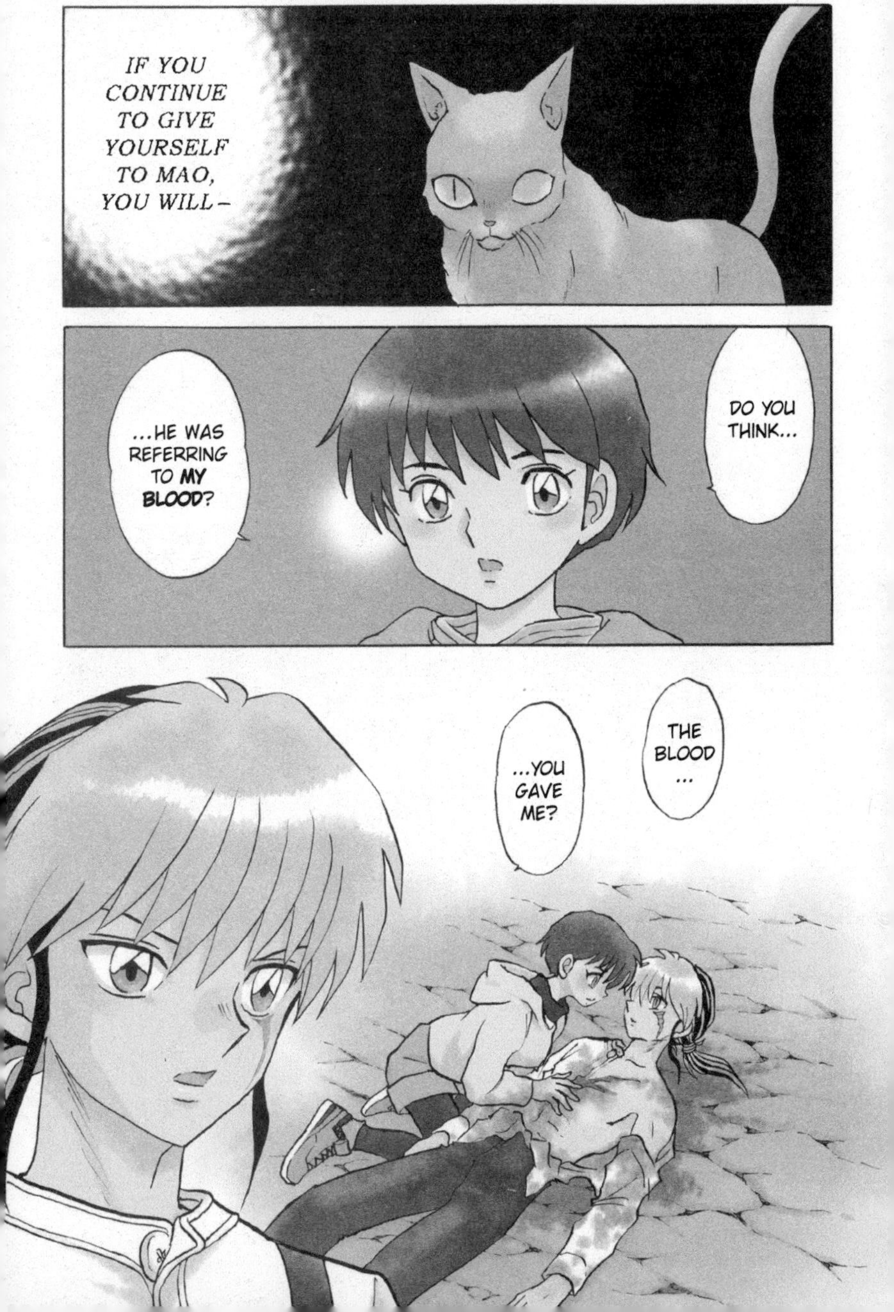
IF YOU CONTINUE TO GIVE YOURSELF TO MAO, YOU WILL–
DO YOU THINK...
...HE WAS REFERRING TO **MY BLOOD**?
THE BLOOD...
...YOU GAVE ME?

Chapter 5:
The Donor

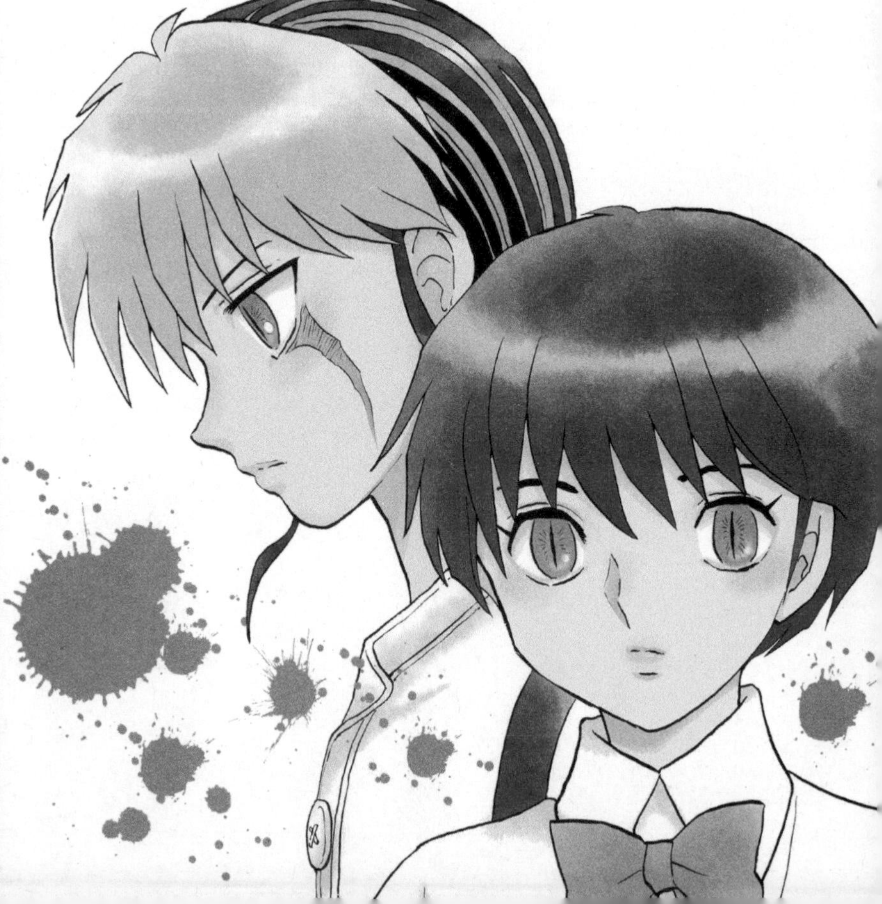

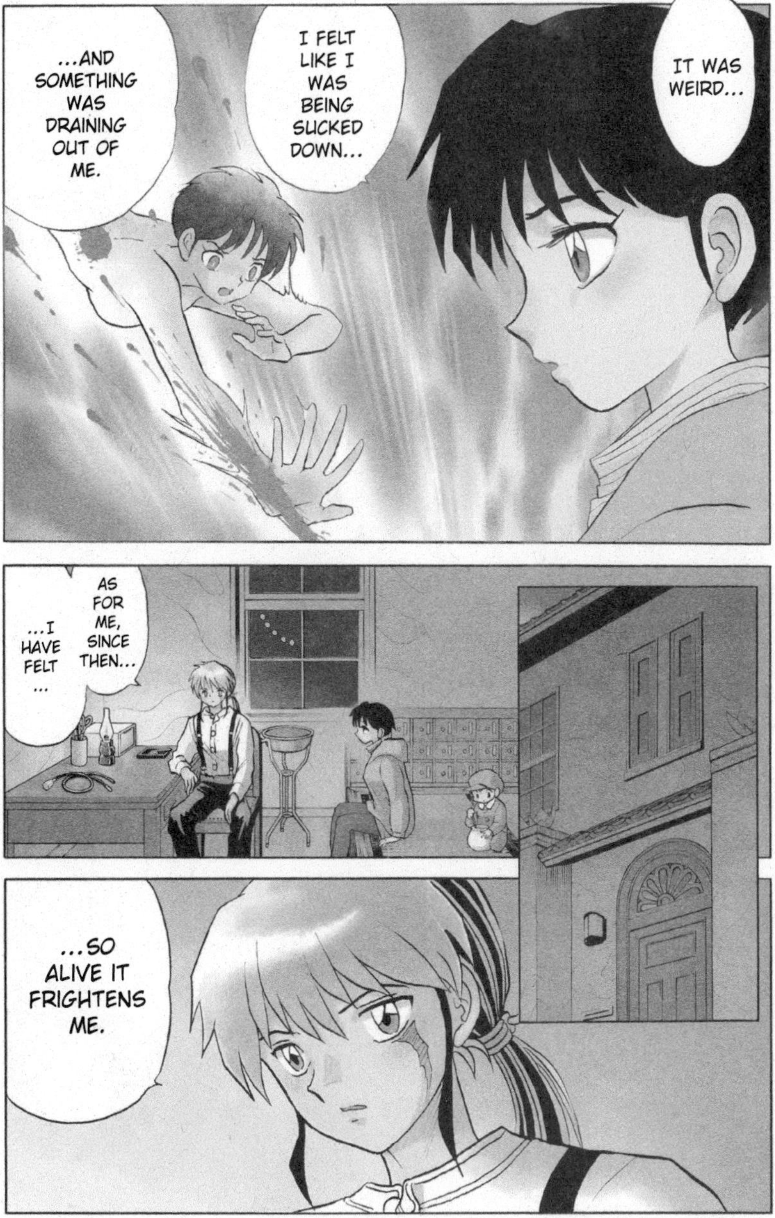
IT WAS WEIRD...
I FELT LIKE I WAS BEING SUCKED DOWN...
...AND SOMETHING WAS DRAINING OUT OF ME.
AS FOR ME, SINCE THEN...
...I HAVE FELT ...
...SO ALIVE IT FRIGHTENS ME.

MAO

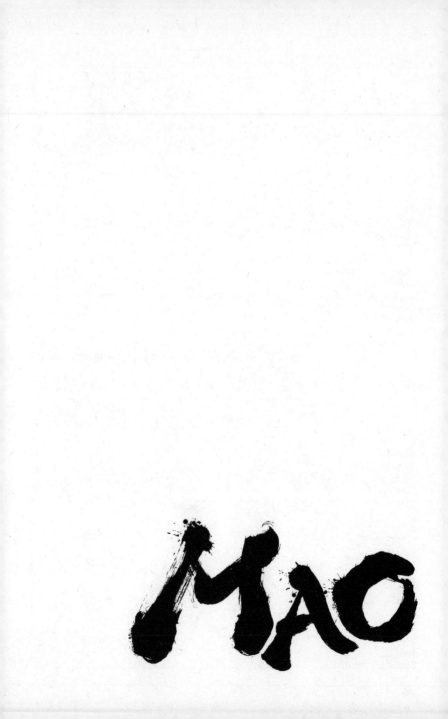

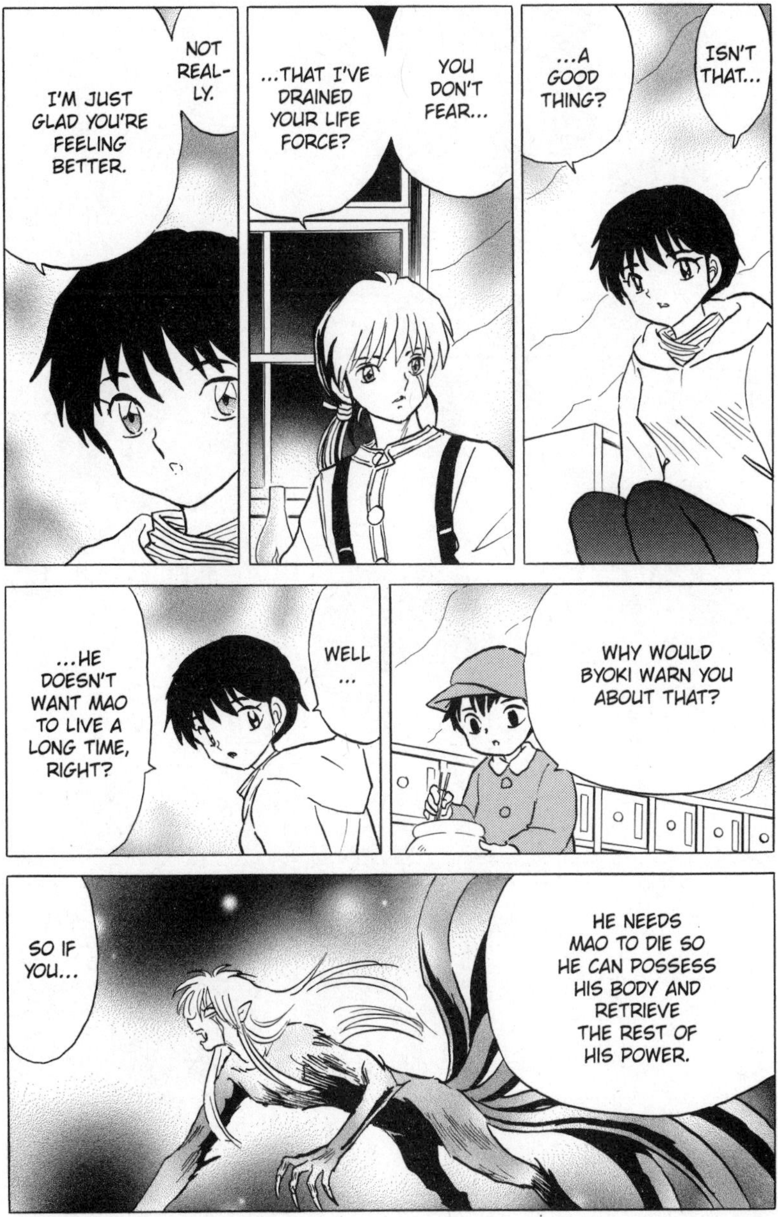
ISN'T THAT...
...A GOOD THING?
YOU DON'T FEAR...
...THAT I'VE DRAINED YOUR LIFE FORCE?
NOT REAL-LY.
I'M JUST GLAD YOU'RE FEELING BETTER.
WHY WOULD BYOKI WARN YOU ABOUT THAT?
WELL ...
...HE DOESN'T WANT MAO TO LIVE A LONG TIME, RIGHT?
HE NEEDS MAO TO DIE SO HE CAN POSSESS HIS BODY AND RETRIEVE THE REST OF HIS POWER.
SO IF YOU...

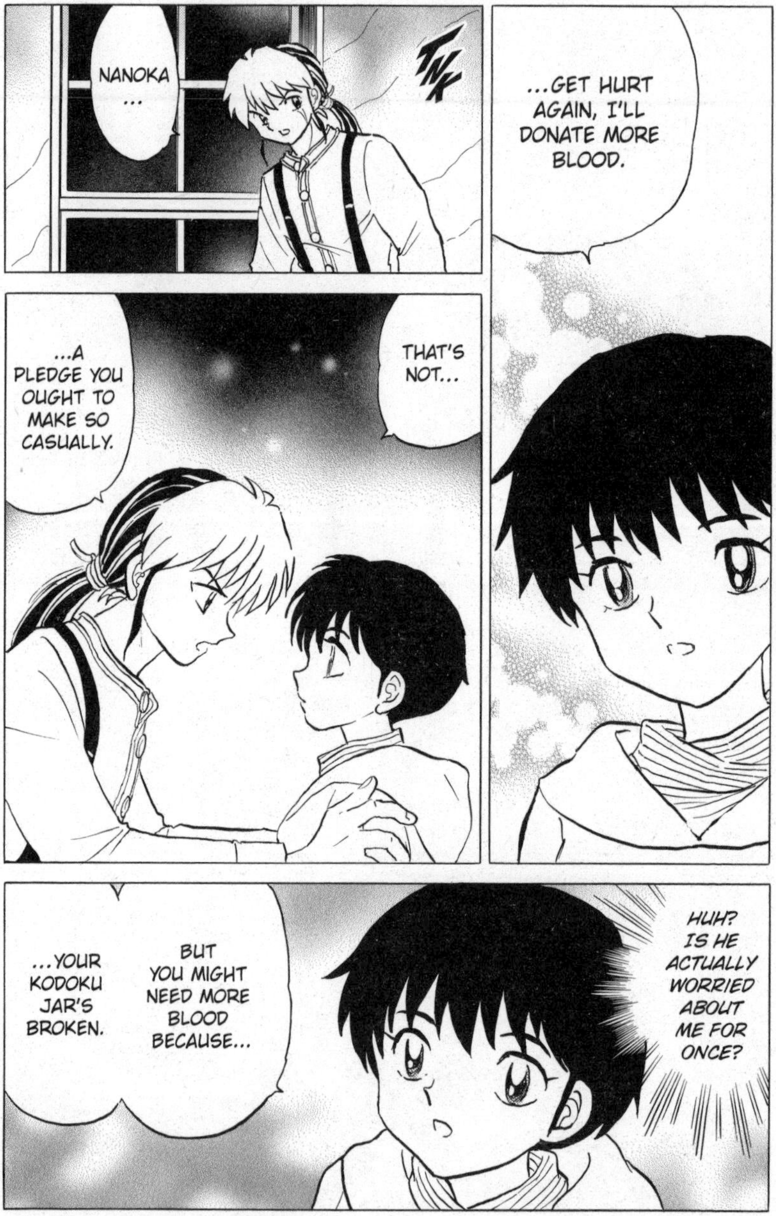
...GET HURT AGAIN, I'LL DONATE MORE BLOOD.
TNK
NANOKA ...
THAT'S NOT...
...A PLEDGE YOU OUGHT TO MAKE SO CASUALLY.
HUH? IS HE ACTUALLY WORRIED ABOUT ME FOR ONCE?
BUT YOU MIGHT NEED MORE BLOOD BECAUSE...
...YOUR KODOKU JAR'S BROKEN.

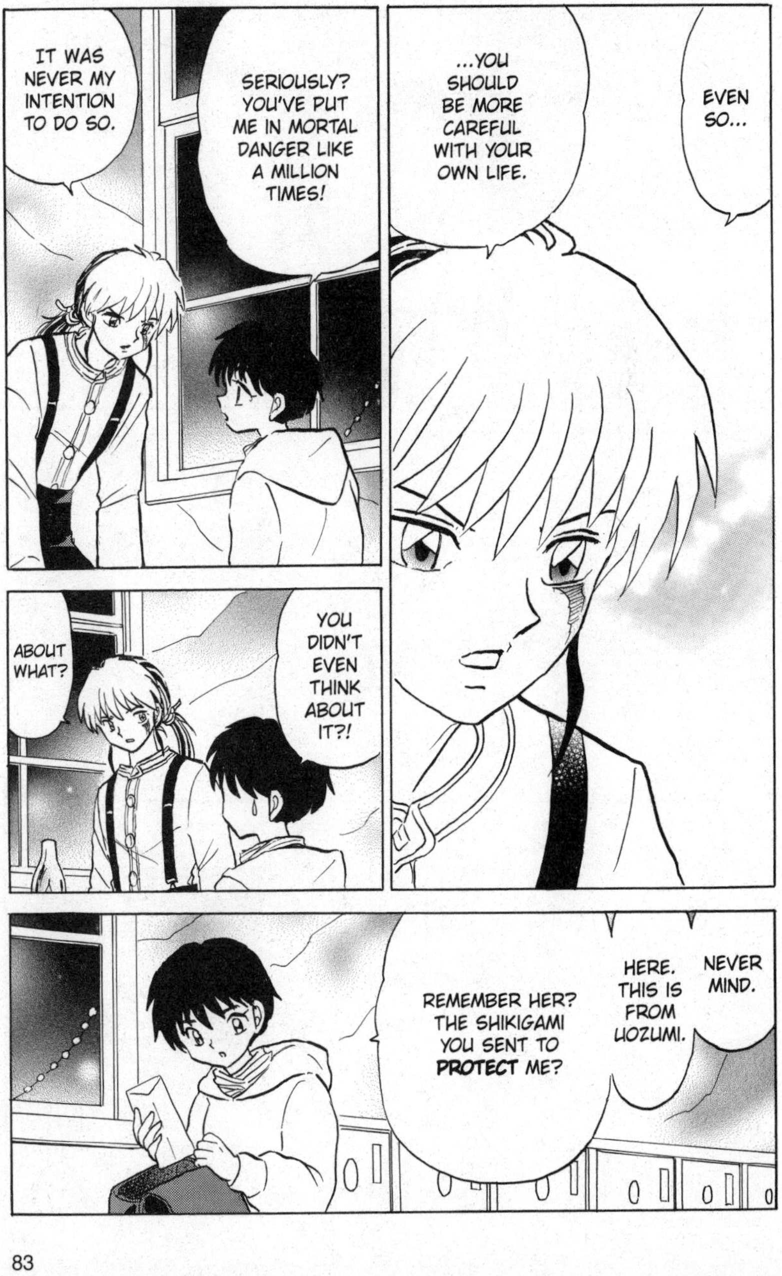
EVEN SO...
...YOU SHOULD BE MORE CAREFUL WITH YOUR OWN LIFE.
SERIOUSLY? YOU'VE PUT ME IN MORTAL DANGER LIKE A MILLION TIMES!
IT WAS NEVER MY INTENTION TO DO SO.
YOU DIDN'T EVEN THINK ABOUT IT?!
ABOUT WHAT?
NEVER MIND.
HERE. THIS IS FROM UOZUMI.
REMEMBER HER? THE SHIKIGAMI YOU SENT TO **PROTECT** ME?

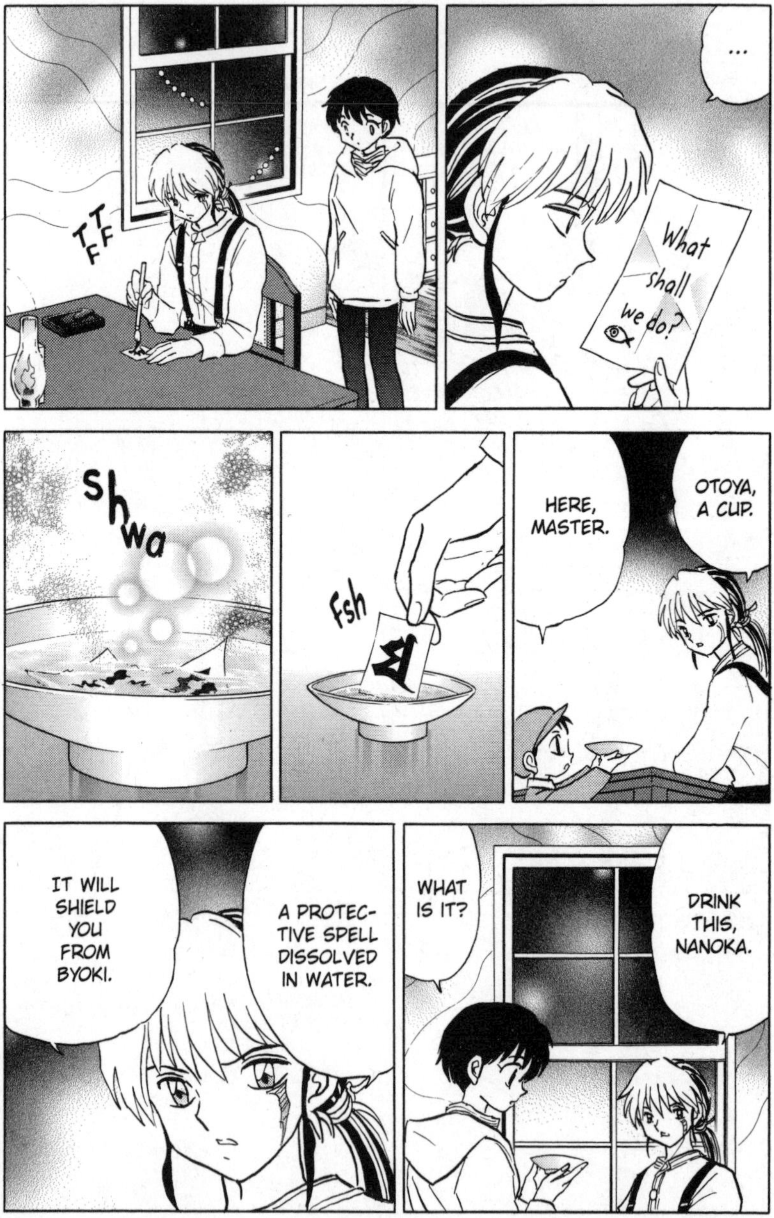
...
What shall we do?
TTFF
OTOYA, A CUP.
HERE, MASTER.
Fsh
shwa
DRINK THIS, NANOKA.
WHAT IS IT?
A PROTEC-TIVE SPELL DISSOLVED IN WATER.
IT WILL SHIELD YOU FROM BYOKI.

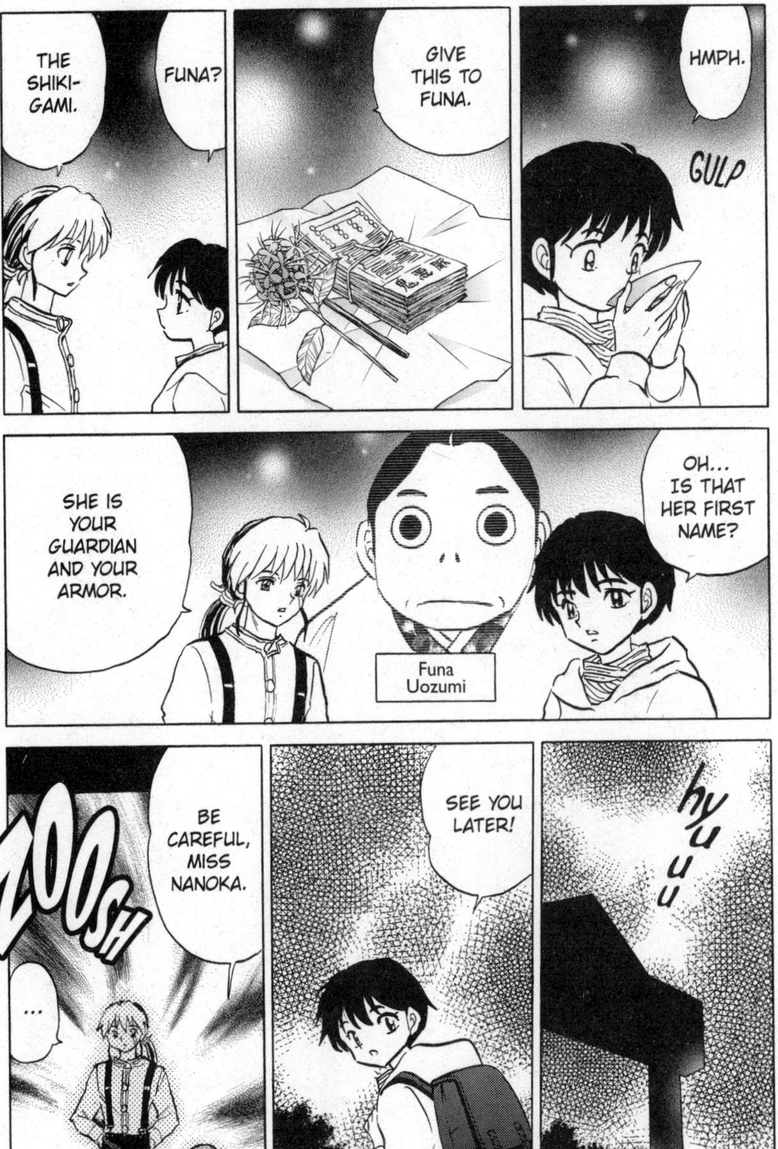
HMPH.
GULP
GIVE THIS TO FUNA.
FUNA?
THE SHIKI-GAMI.
OH... IS THAT HER FIRST NAME?
Funa Uozumi
SHE IS YOUR GUARDIAN AND YOUR ARMOR.
hyuuuu
SEE YOU LATER!
BE CAREFUL, MISS NANOKA.
ZOOSH
...

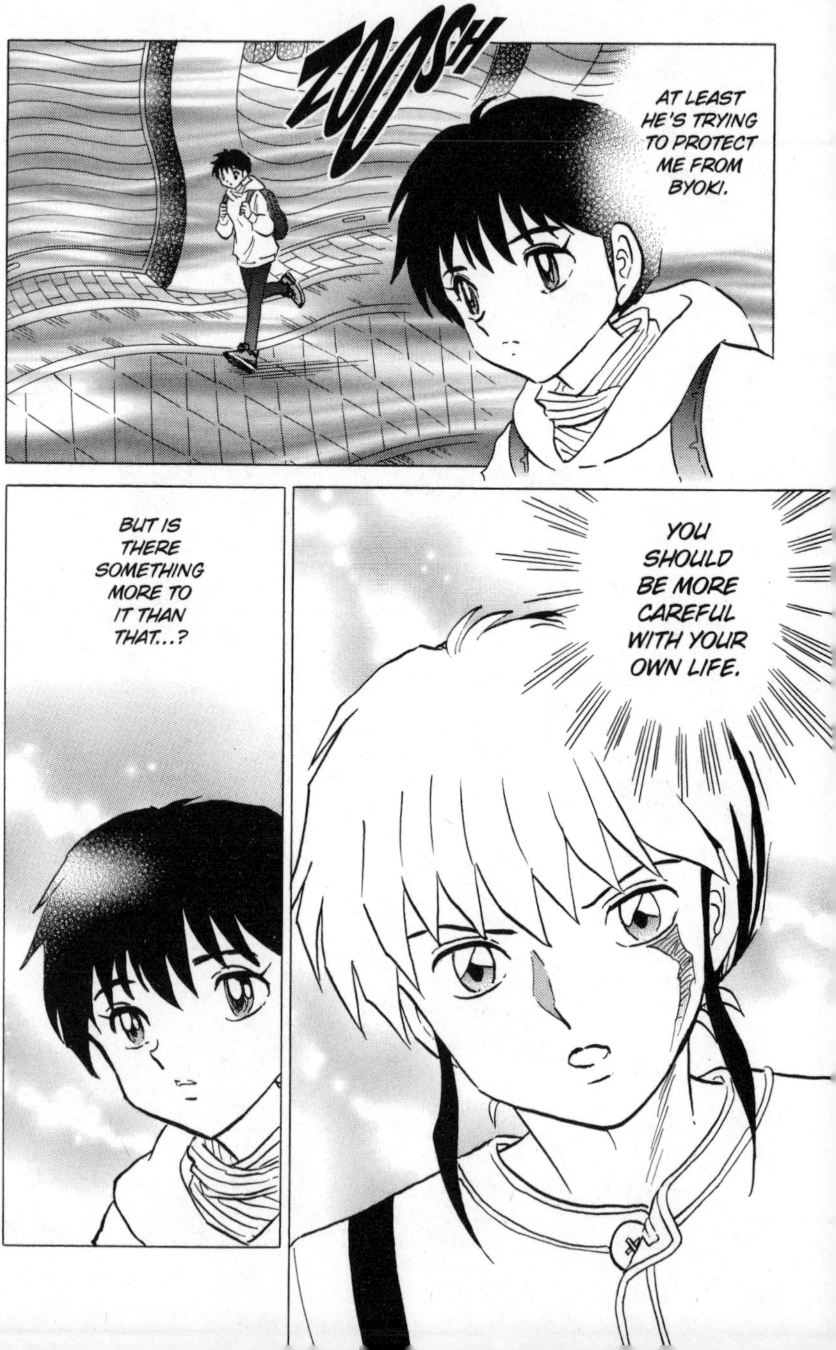
ZOOSH
AT LEAST HE'S TRYING TO PROTECT ME FROM BYOKI.
YOU SHOULD BE MORE CAREFUL WITH YOUR OWN LIFE.
BUT IS THERE SOMETHING MORE TO IT THAN THAT...?

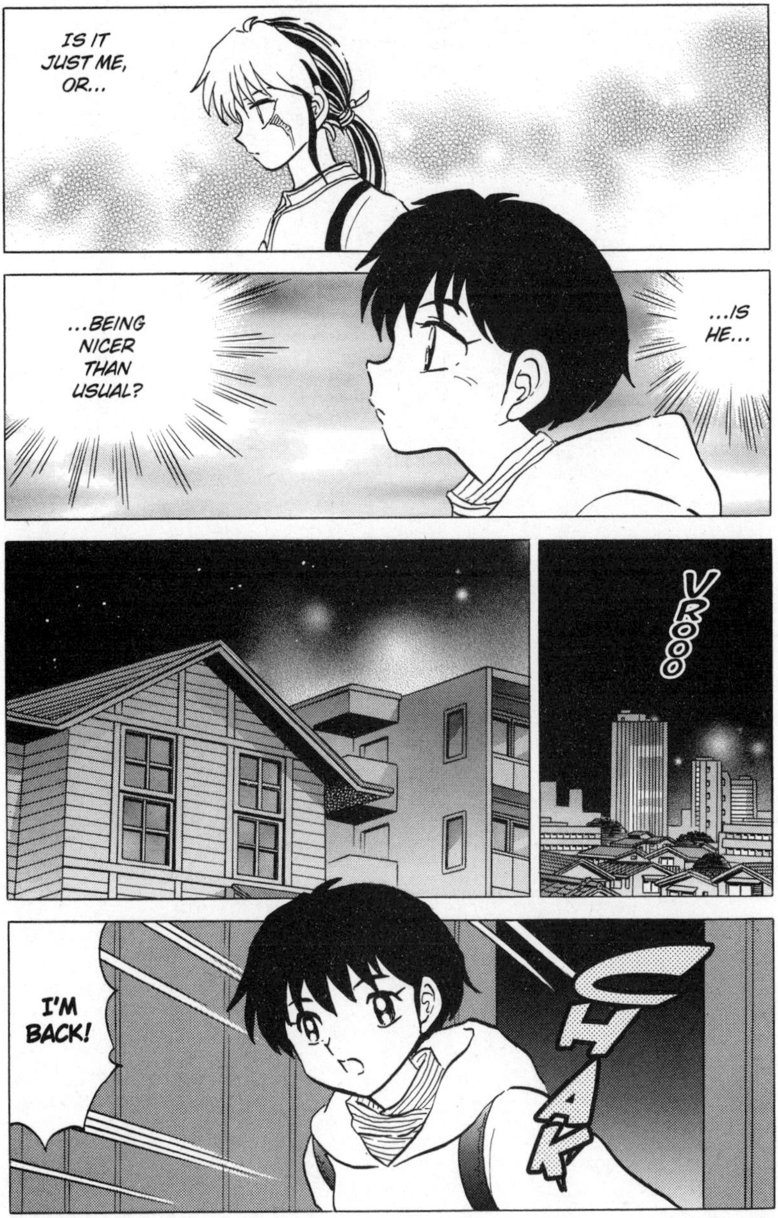
IS IT JUST ME, OR...
...IS HE...
...BEING NICER THAN USUAL?
VROOOO
CHAK
I'M BACK!

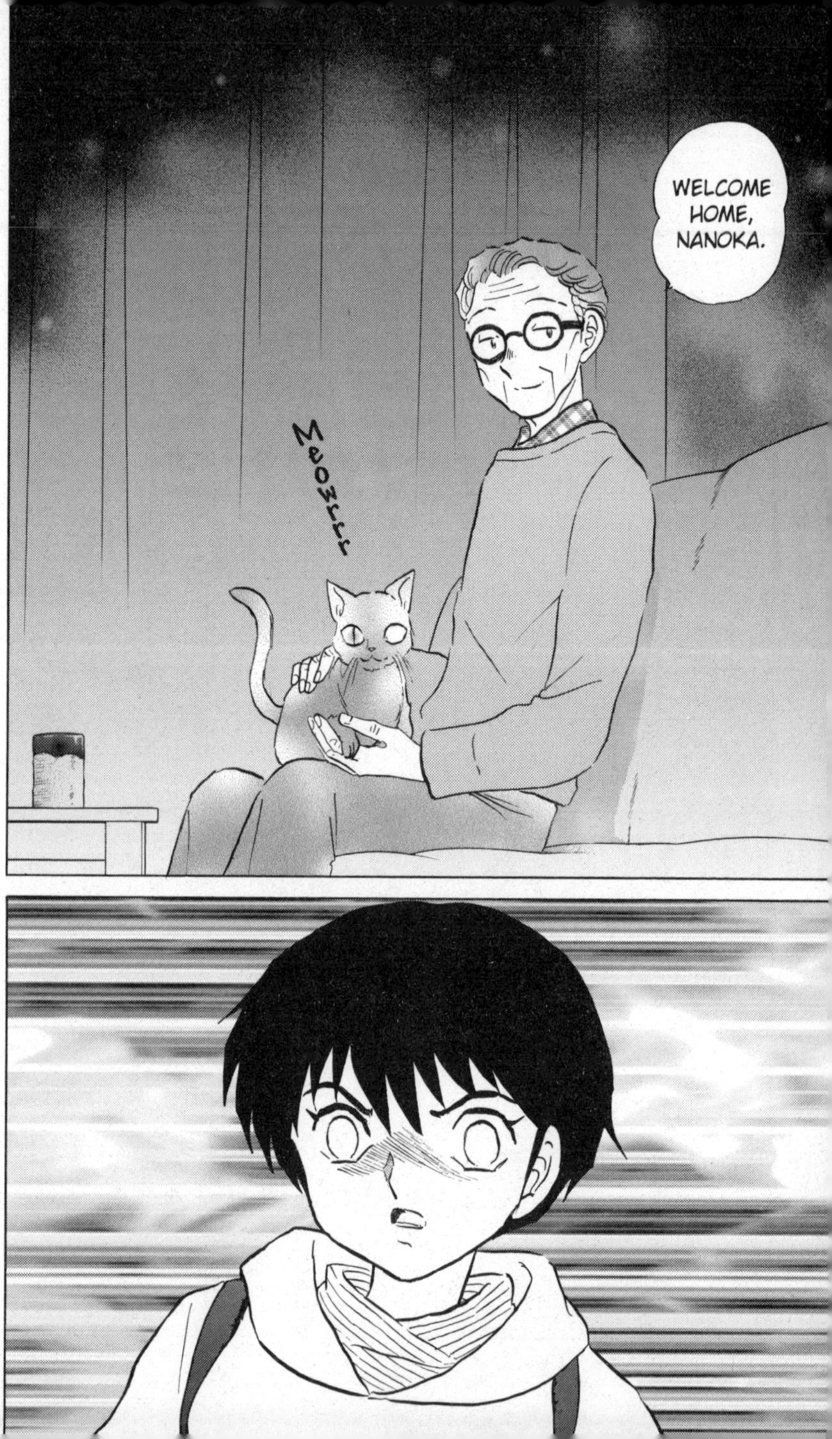
WELCOME HOME, NANOKA.
Meowrrr

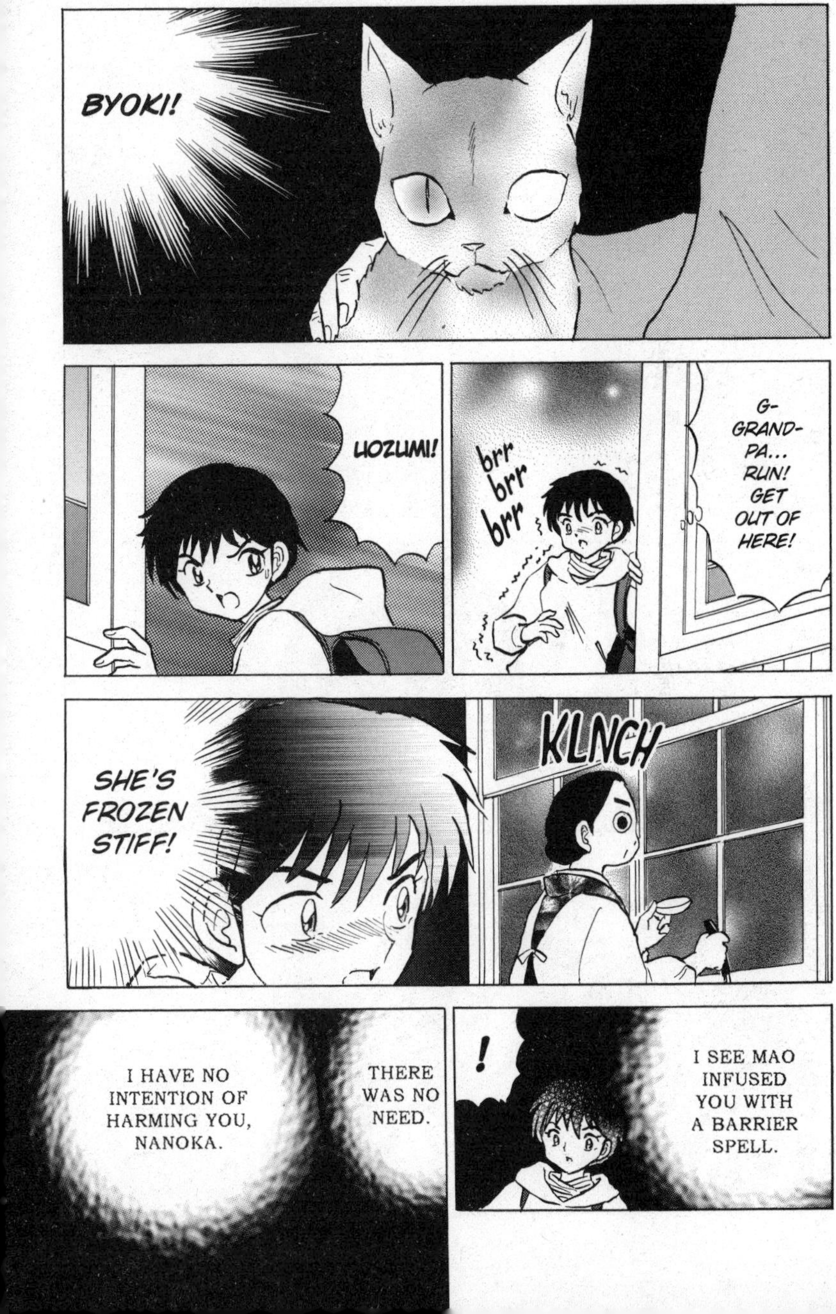
BYOKI!
G-GRANDPA... RUN! GET OUT OF HERE!
brr brr brr
UOZUMI!
KLNCH
SHE'S FROZEN STIFF!
I SEE MAO INFUSED YOU WITH A BARRIER SPELL.
!
THERE WAS NO NEED.
I HAVE NO INTENTION OF HARMING YOU, NANOKA.

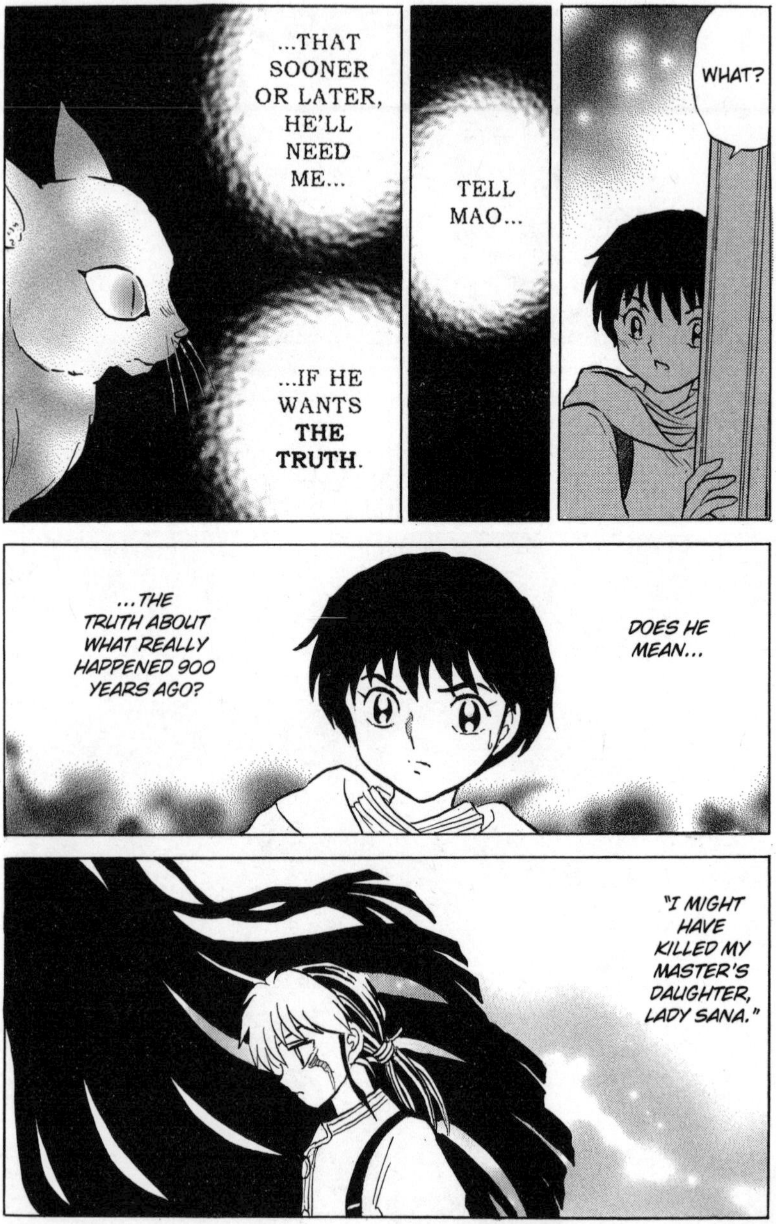
WHAT?
TELL MAO...
...THAT SOONER OR LATER, HE'LL NEED ME...
...IF HE WANTS THE TRUTH.
DOES HE MEAN...
...THE TRUTH ABOUT WHAT REALLY HAPPENED 900 YEARS AGO?
"I MIGHT HAVE KILLED MY MASTER'S DAUGHTER, LADY SANA."

NANO-KA...
...IF YOU WISH TO SUMMON ME, JUST CALL MY NAME.
PSH
HE'S GONE.
WHAT'S WRONG, NANOKA?
GRANDPA! ARE YOU OKAY?!
EH?
THAT CAT...
OH...
DRAT.
I DIDN'T THINK HE'D BE SO BRAZEN AS TO COME INTO THE HOUSE!
GRR
UOZUMI...
UOZUMI HATES CATS.

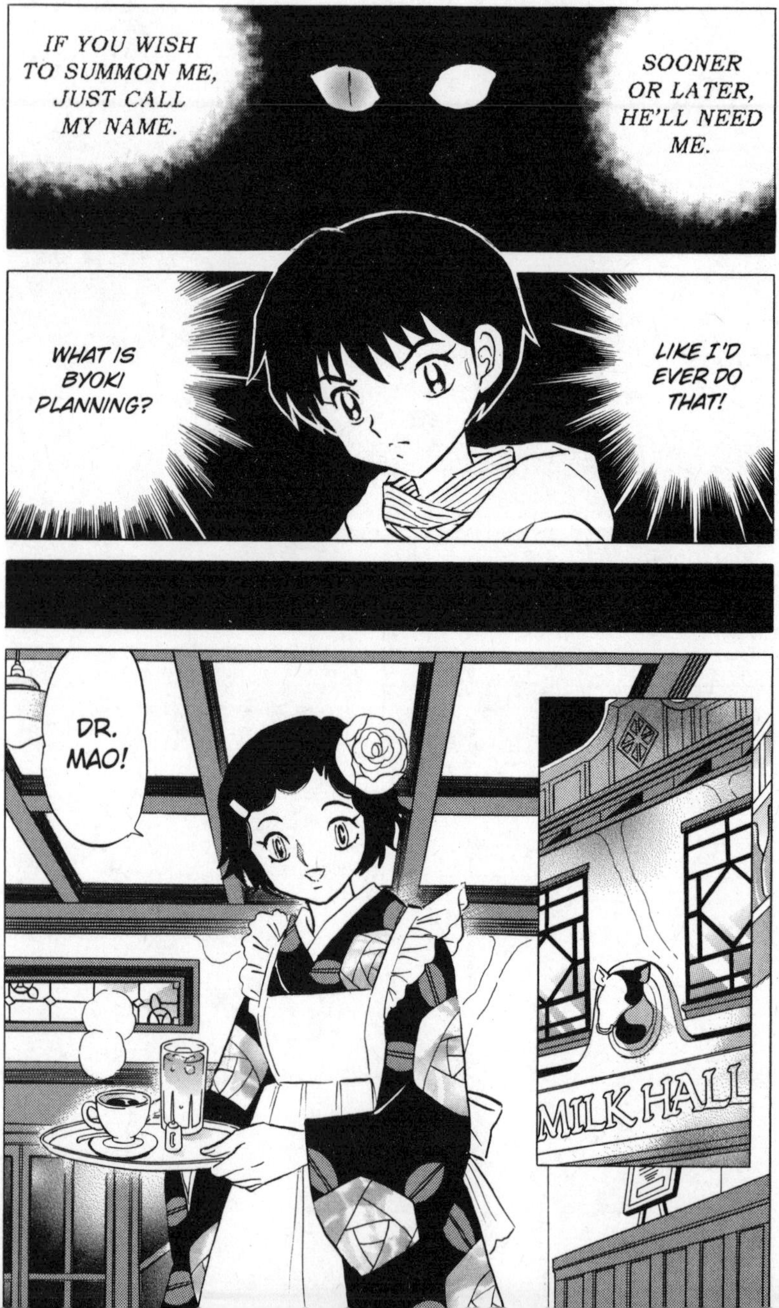
SOONER OR LATER, HE'LL NEED ME.
IF YOU WISH TO SUMMON ME, JUST CALL MY NAME.
LIKE I'D EVER DO THAT!
WHAT IS BYOKI PLANNING?
MILK HALL
DR. MAO!

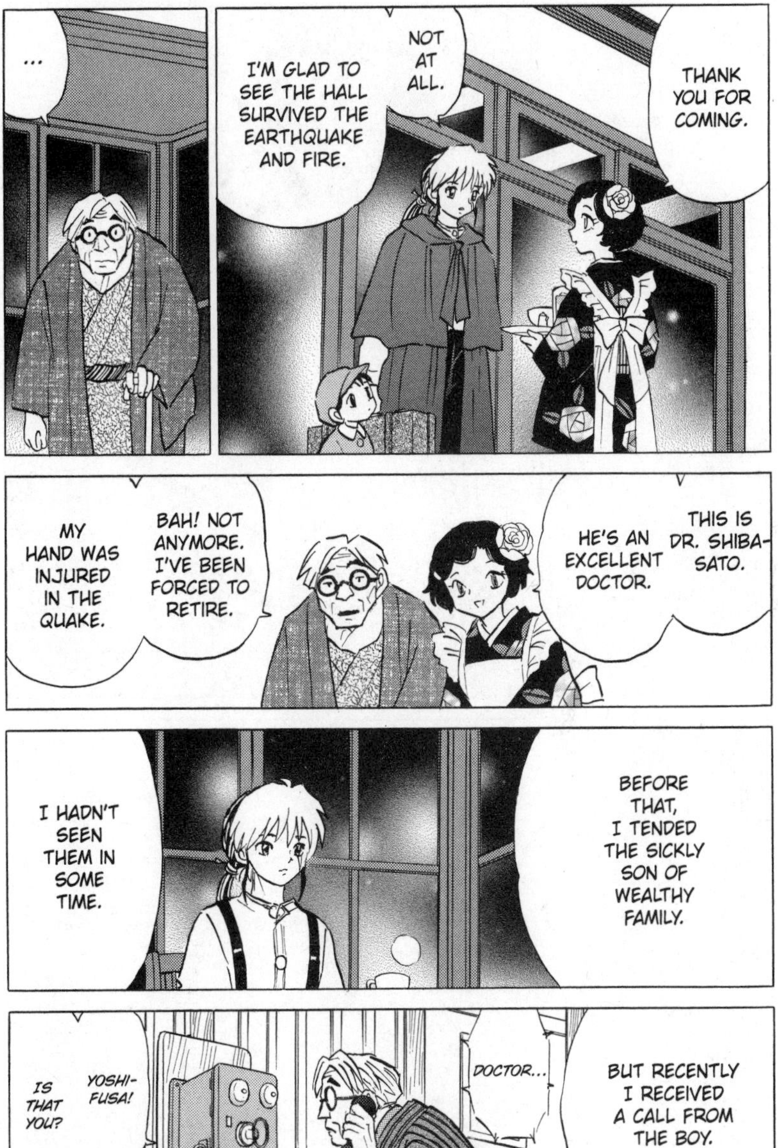
THANK YOU FOR COMING.
NOT AT ALL.
I'M GLAD TO SEE THE HALL SURVIVED THE EARTHQUAKE AND FIRE.
...
THIS IS DR. SHIBA-SATO.
HE'S AN EXCELLENT DOCTOR.
BAH! NOT ANYMORE. I'VE BEEN FORCED TO RETIRE.
MY HAND WAS INJURED IN THE QUAKE.
BEFORE THAT, I TENDED THE SICKLY SON OF WEALTHY FAMILY.
I HADN'T SEEN THEM IN SOME TIME.
BUT RECENTLY I RECEIVED A CALL FROM THE BOY.
DOCTOR...
YOSHI-FUSA!
IS THAT YOU?

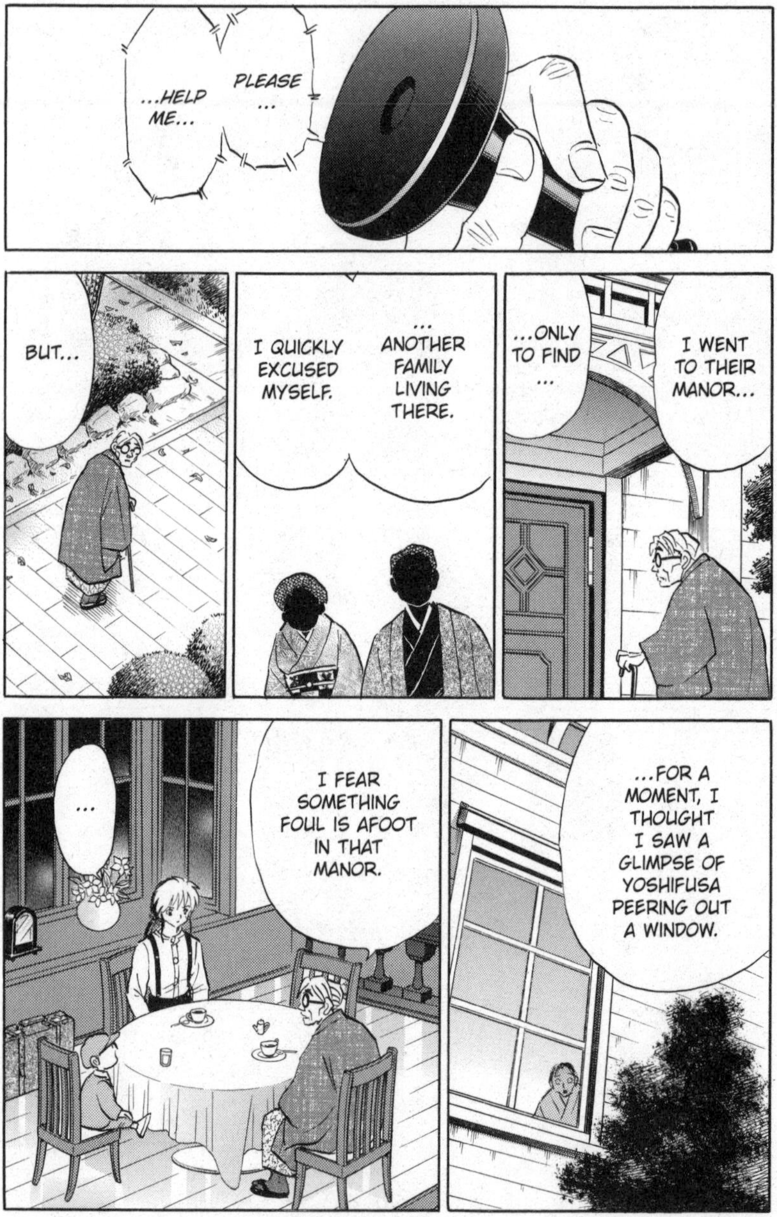
PLEASE...
...HELP ME...
I WENT TO THEIR MANOR...
...ONLY TO FIND...
...ANOTHER FAMILY LIVING THERE.
I QUICKLY EXCUSED MYSELF.
BUT...
...FOR A MOMENT, I THOUGHT I SAW A GLIMPSE OF YOSHIFUSA PEERING OUT A WINDOW.
I FEAR SOMETHING FOUL IS AFOOT IN THAT MANOR.
...

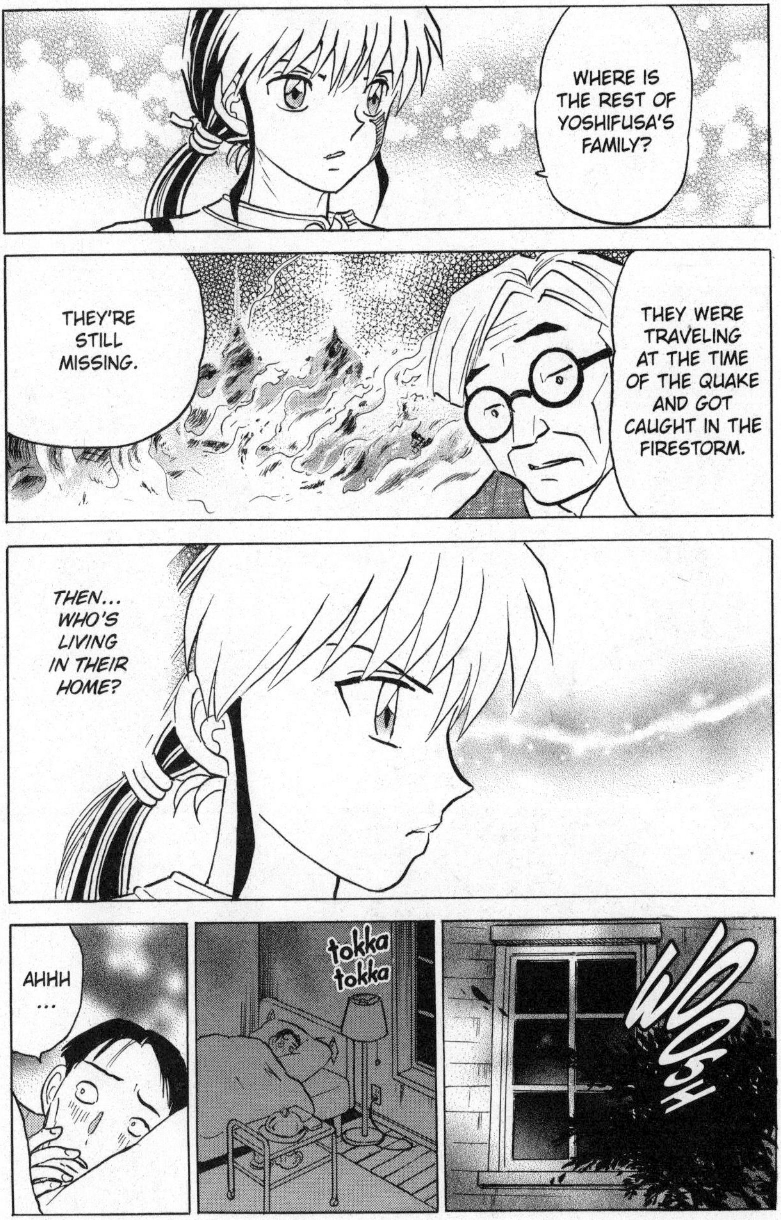
WHERE IS THE REST OF YOSHIFUSA'S FAMILY?
THEY WERE TRAVELING AT THE TIME OF THE QUAKE AND GOT CAUGHT IN THE FIRESTORM.
THEY'RE STILL MISSING.
THEN... WHO'S LIVING IN THEIR HOME?
WHOOSH
tokka tokka
AHHH ...

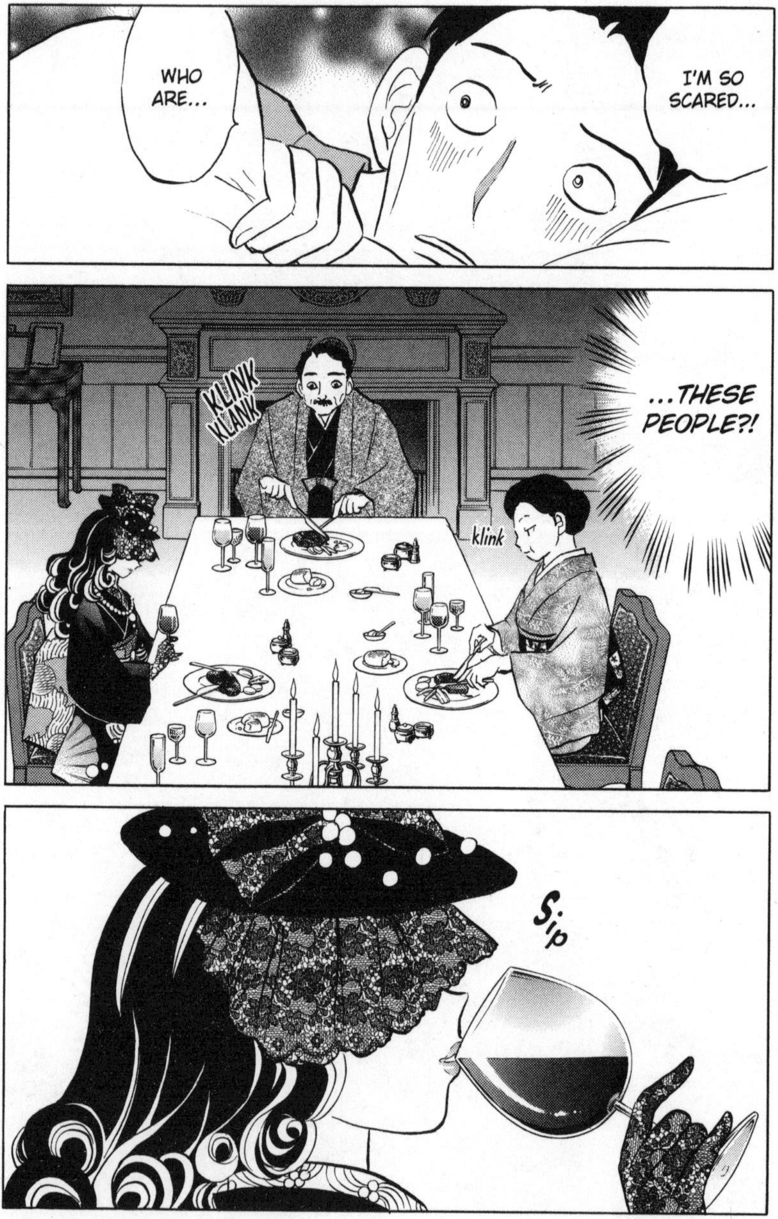
I'M SO SCARED...
WHO ARE...
...THESE PEOPLE?!
klink
KLINK KLANK
Sip

Chapter 6:
Missed Connection

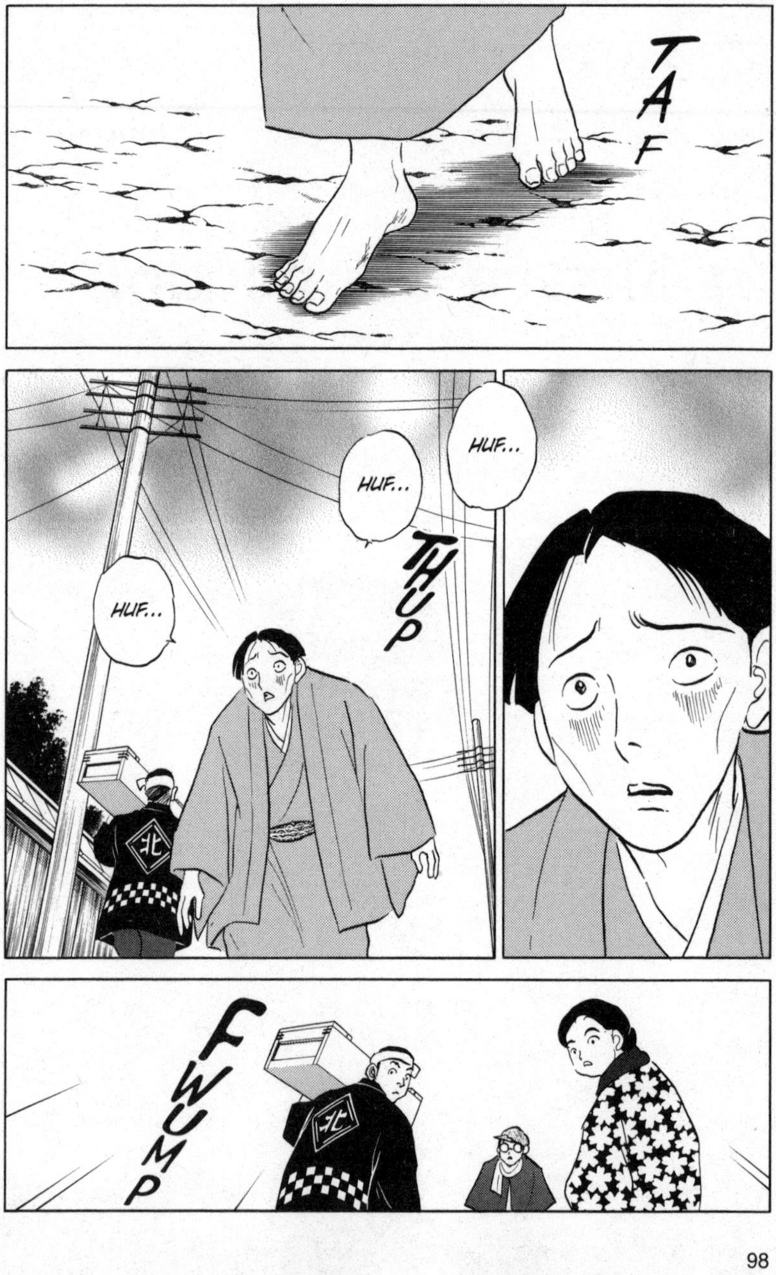
TAF
HUF...
HUF...
THUP
HUF...
FWUMP

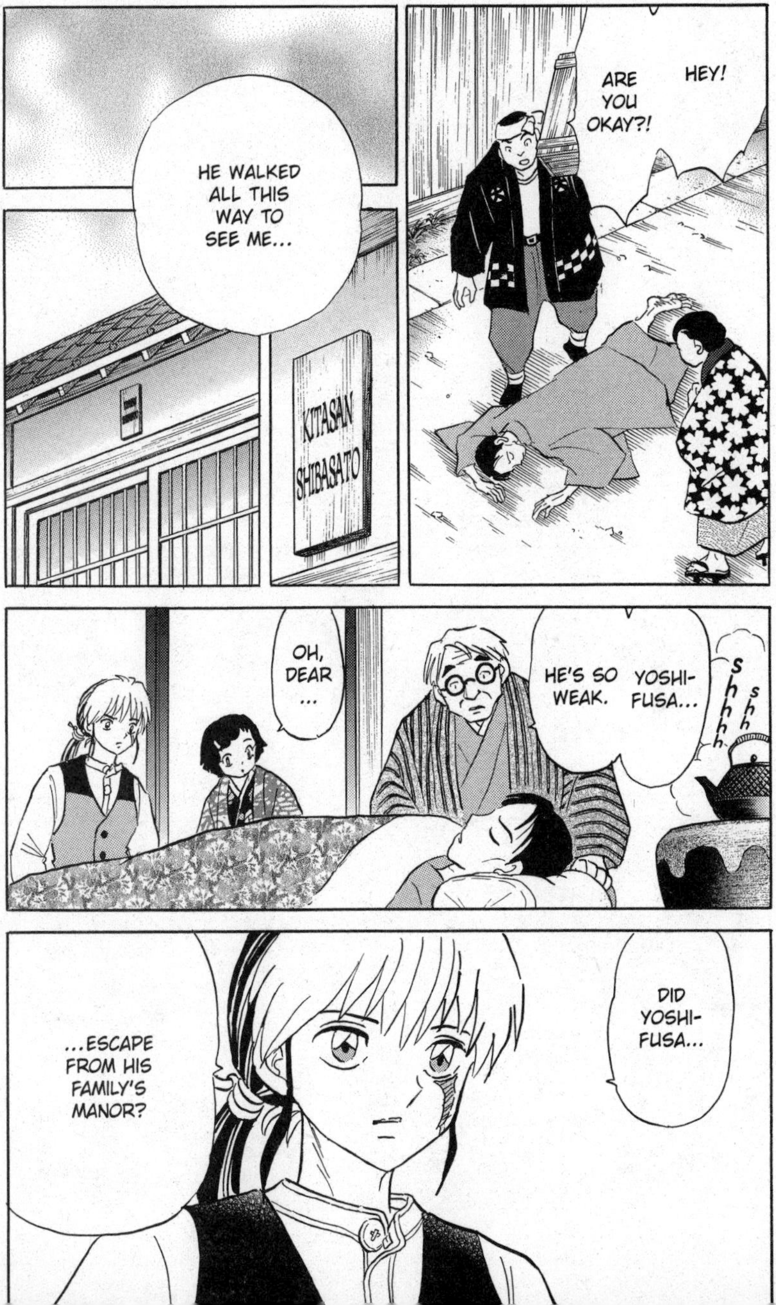
HEY!
ARE YOU OKAY?!
HE WALKED ALL THIS WAY TO SEE ME...
KITASAN SHIBASATO
YOSHI-FUSA...
HE'S SO WEAK.
shhhh
shh
OH, DEAR ...
DID YOSHI-FUSA...
...ESCAPE FROM HIS FAMILY'S MANOR?

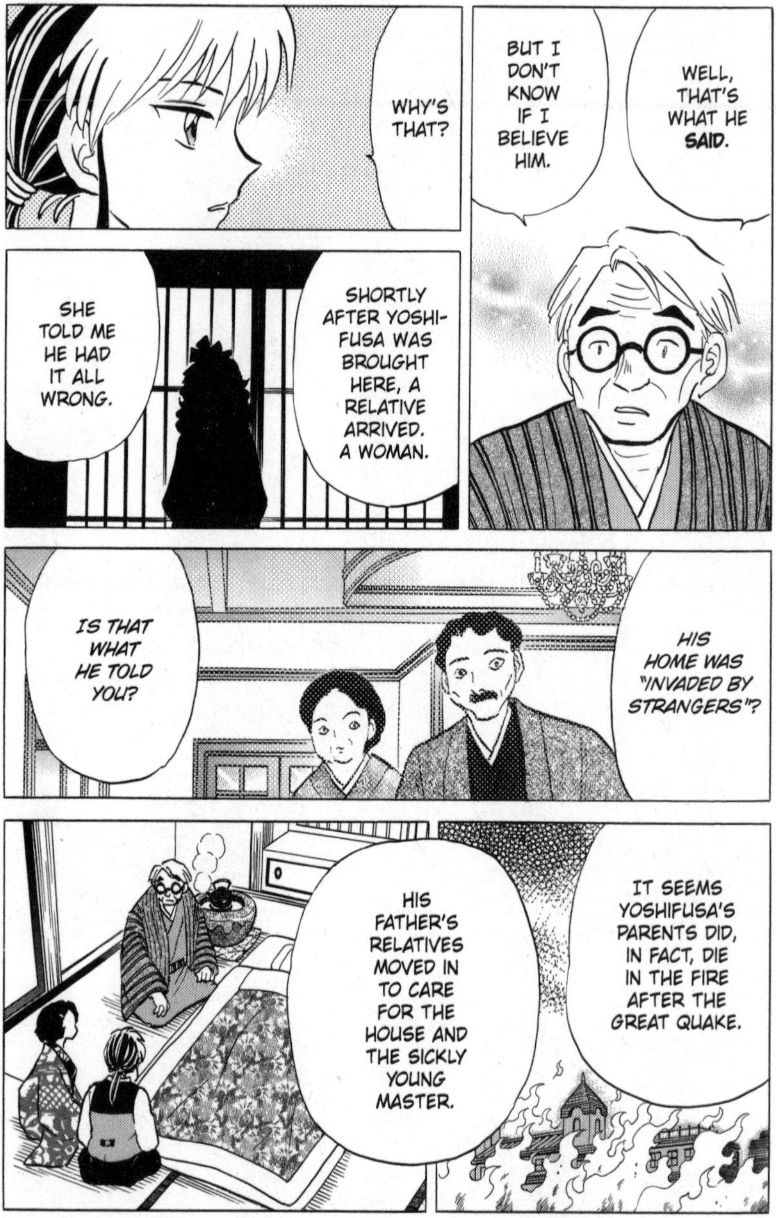

WELL, THAT'S WHAT HE SAID.
BUT I DON'T KNOW IF I BELIEVE HIM.
WHY'S THAT?
SHORTLY AFTER YOSHIFUSA WAS BROUGHT HERE, A RELATIVE ARRIVED. A WOMAN.
SHE TOLD ME HE HAD IT ALL WRONG.
HIS HOME WAS "INVADED BY STRANGERS"?
IS THAT WHAT HE TOLD YOU?
IT SEEMS YOSHIFUSA'S PARENTS DID, IN FACT, DIE IN THE FIRE AFTER THE GREAT QUAKE.
HIS FATHER'S RELATIVES MOVED IN TO CARE FOR THE HOUSE AND THE SICKLY YOUNG MASTER.

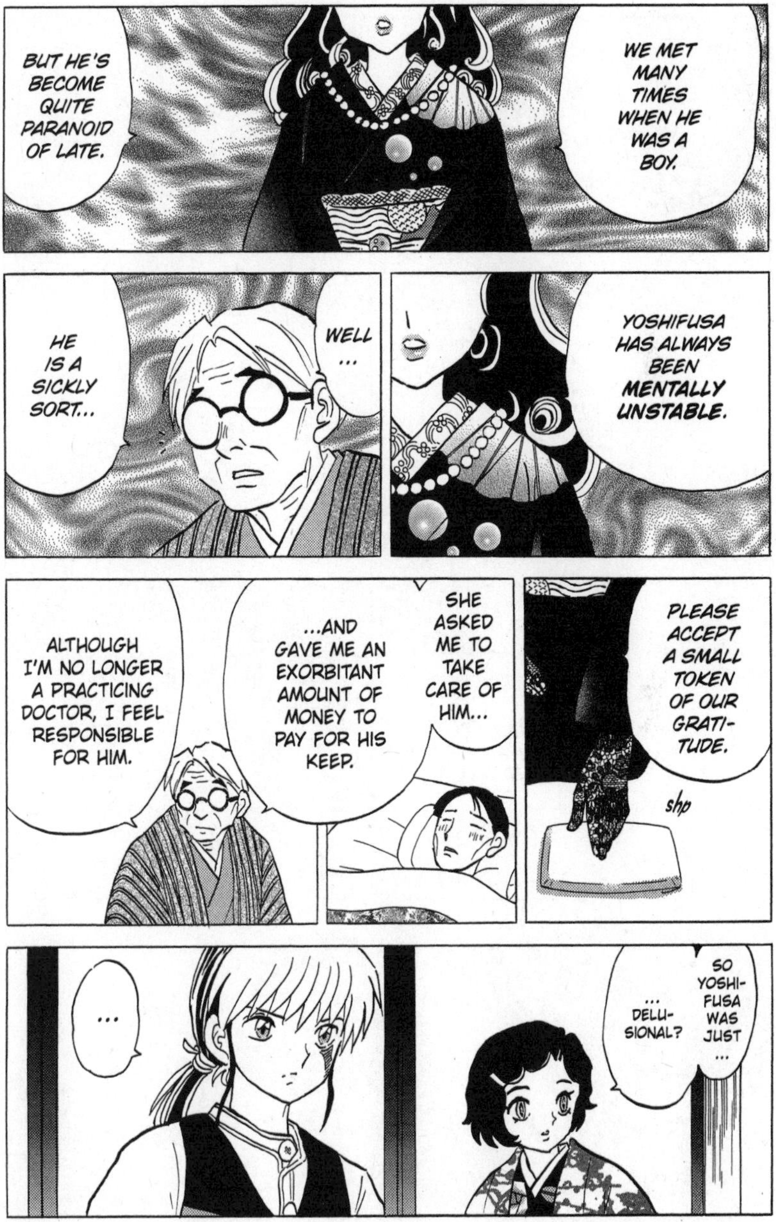
WE MET MANY TIMES WHEN HE WAS A BOY.
BUT HE'S BECOME QUITE PARANOID OF LATE.
YOSHIFUSA HAS ALWAYS BEEN MENTALLY UNSTABLE.
WELL ...
HE IS A SICKLY SORT...
PLEASE ACCEPT A SMALL TOKEN OF OUR GRATI-TUDE.
shp
SHE ASKED ME TO TAKE CARE OF HIM...
...AND GAVE ME AN EXORBITANT AMOUNT OF MONEY TO PAY FOR HIS KEEP.
ALTHOUGH I'M NO LONGER A PRACTICING DOCTOR, I FEEL RESPONSIBLE FOR HIM.
SO YOSHI-FUSA WAS JUST ...
... DELU-SIONAL?
...

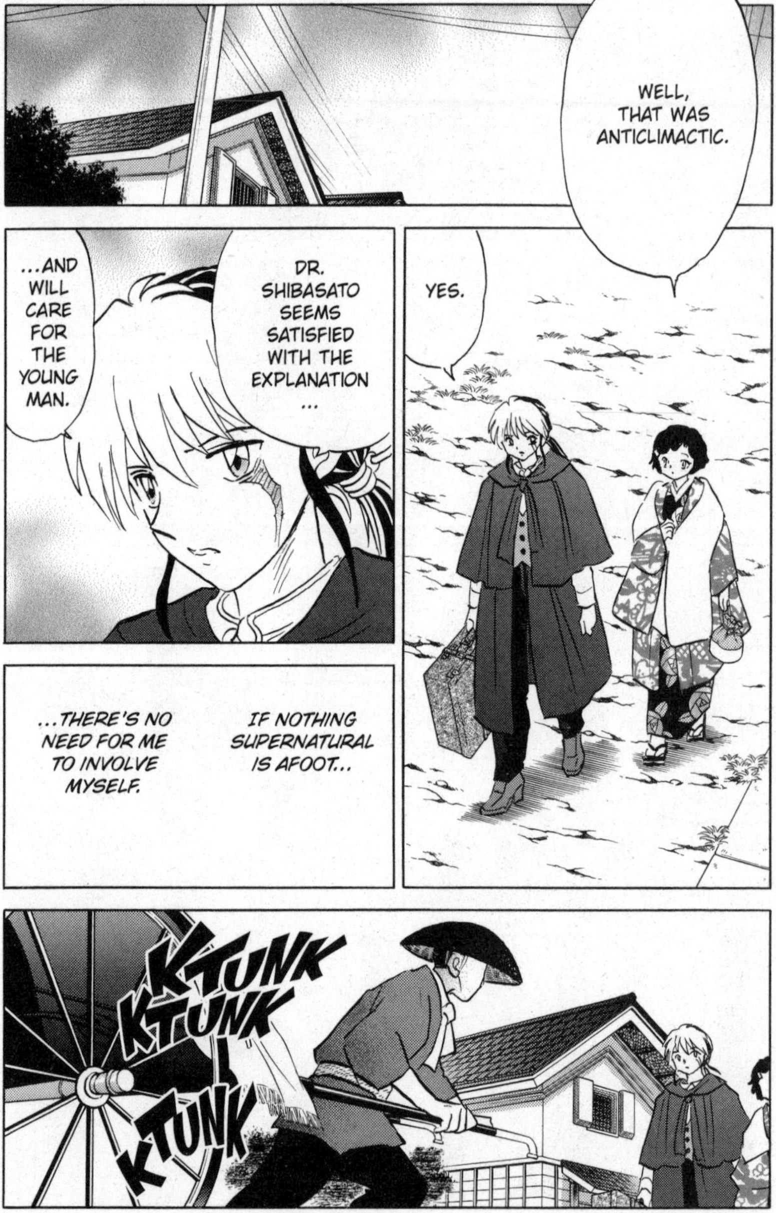
WELL, THAT WAS ANTICLIMACTIC.
YES.
DR. SHIBASATO SEEMS SATISFIED WITH THE EXPLANATION...
...AND WILL CARE FOR THE YOUNG MAN.
IF NOTHING SUPERNATURAL IS AFOOT...
...THERE'S NO NEED FOR ME TO INVOLVE MYSELF.
KTUNK KTUNK KTUNK KTUNK

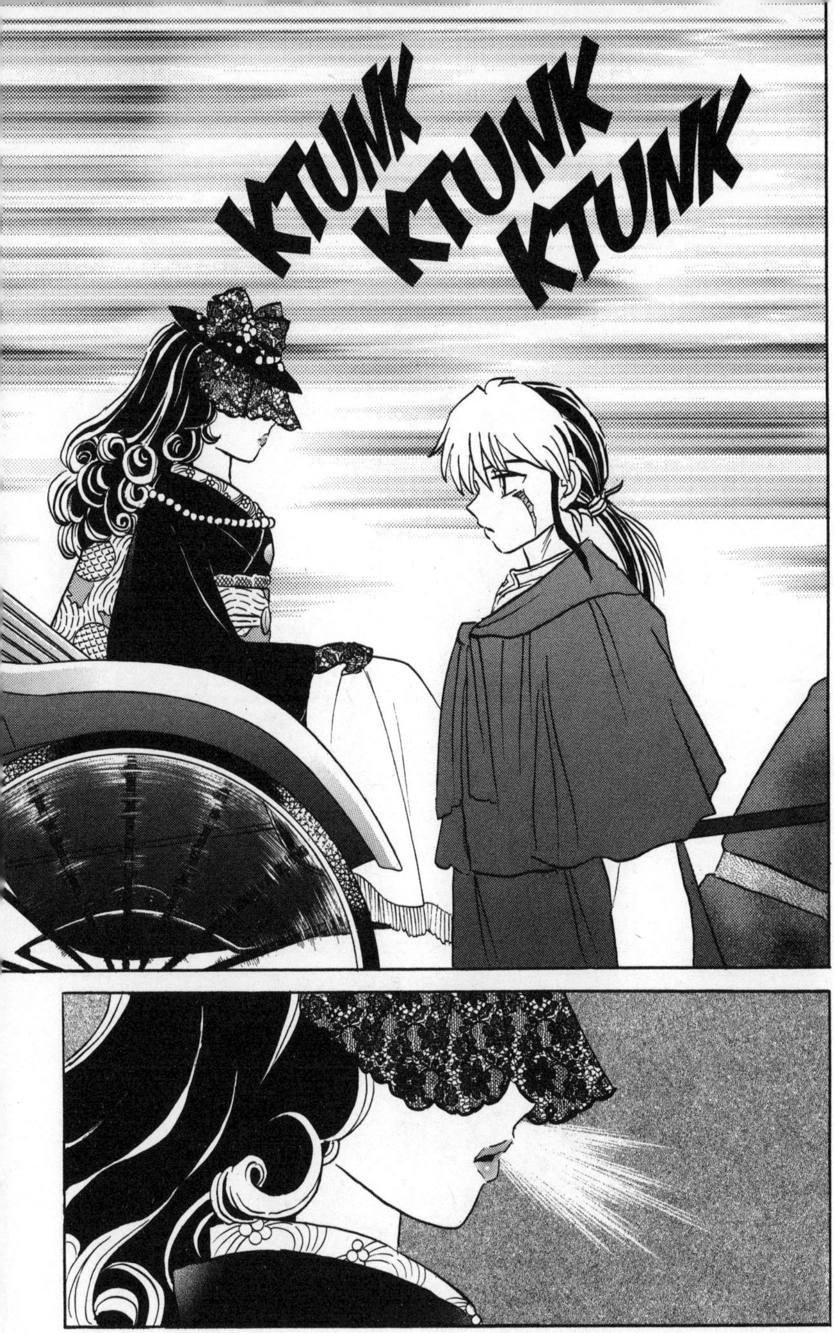
KTUNK
KTUNK
KTUNK

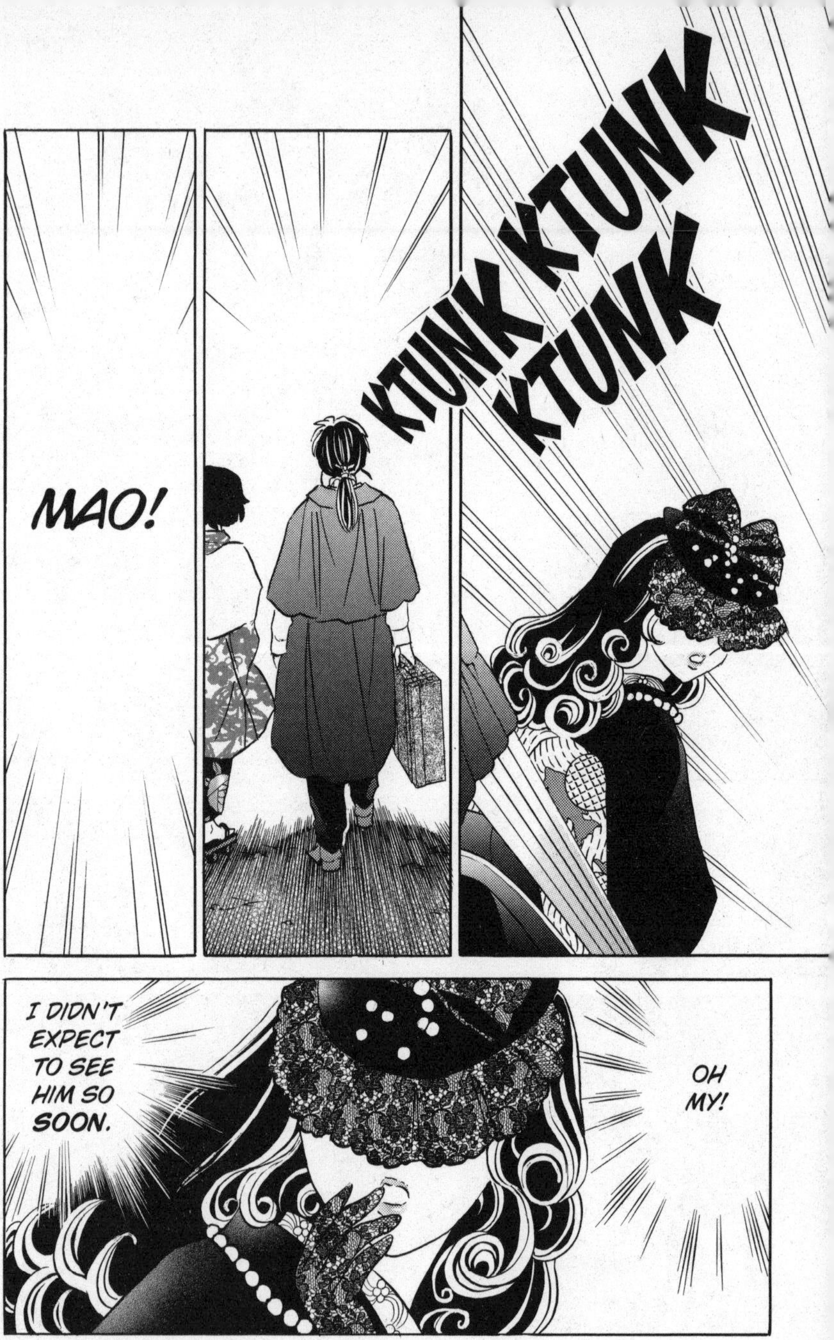
KTUNK KTUNK
KTUNK
MAO!
OH MY!
I DIDN'T EXPECT TO SEE HIM SO SOON.

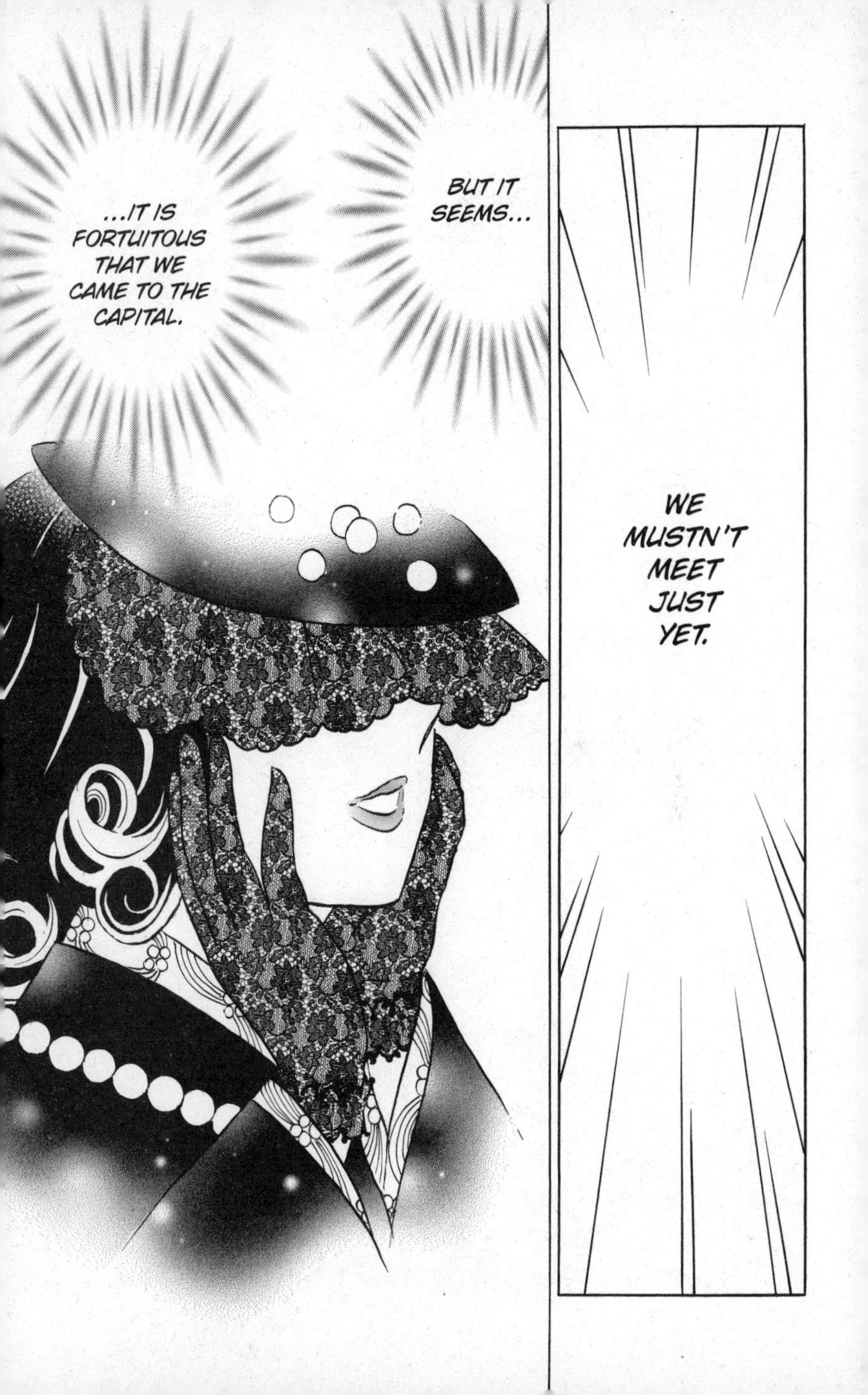
...IT IS FORTUITOUS THAT WE CAME TO THE CAPITAL.
BUT IT SEEMS...
WE MUSTN'T MEET JUST YET.

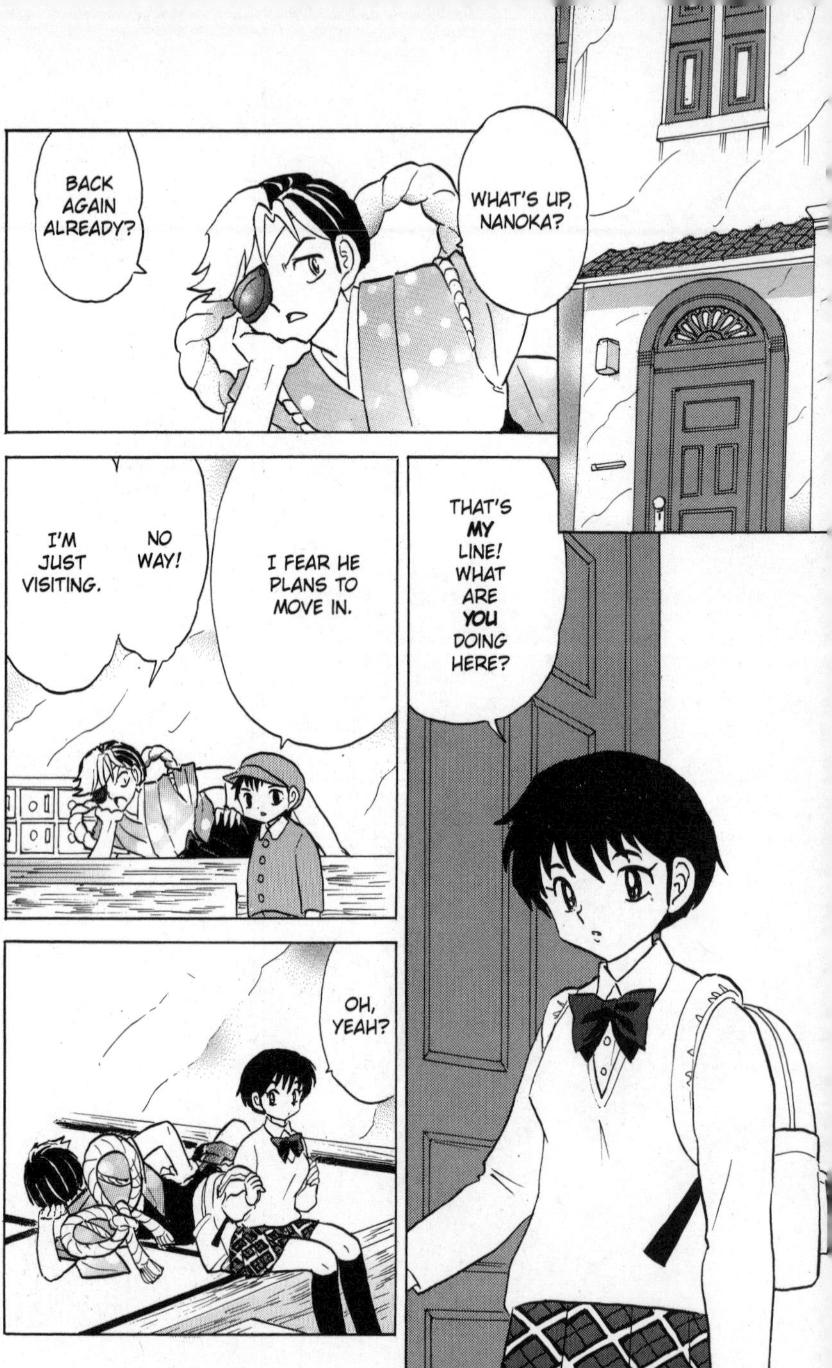
WHAT'S UP, NANOKA?
BACK AGAIN ALREADY?
THAT'S MY LINE! WHAT ARE YOU DOING HERE?
I FEAR HE PLANS TO MOVE IN.
NO WAY!
I'M JUST VISITING.
OH, YEAH?

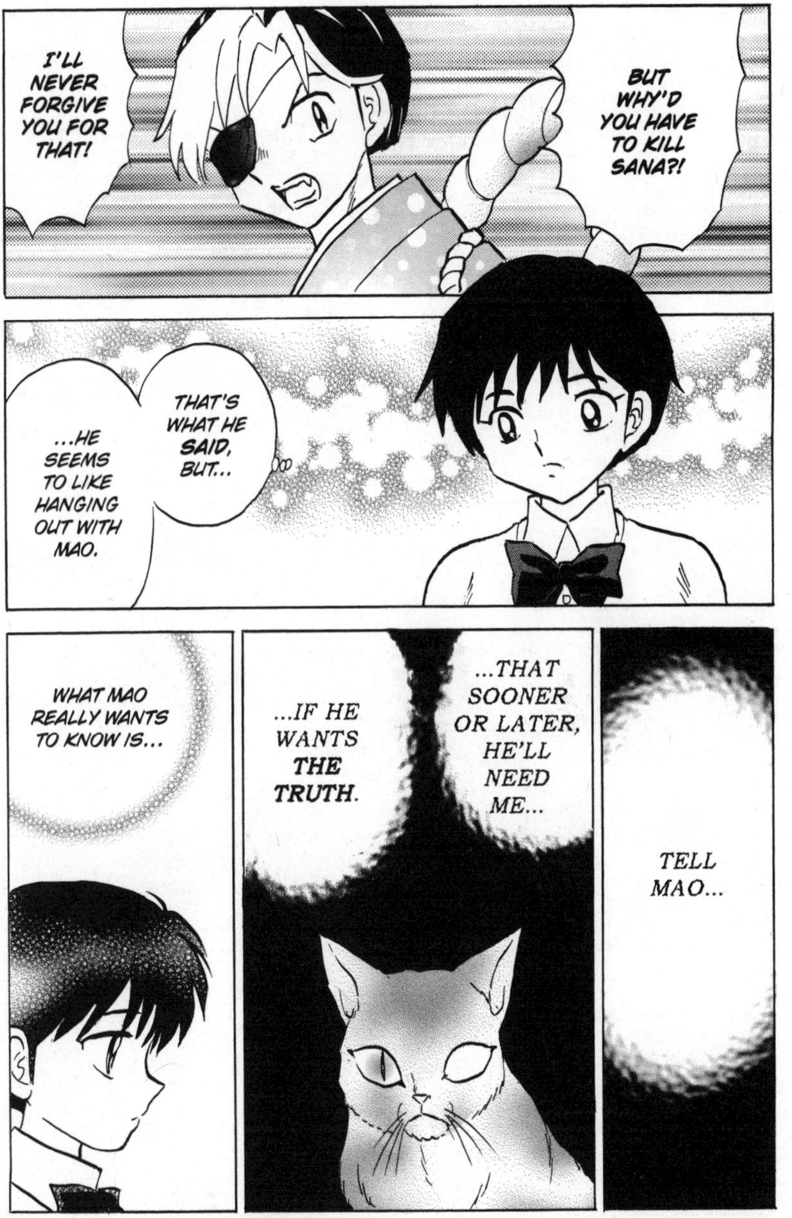
BUT WHY'D YOU HAVE TO KILL SANA?!
I'LL NEVER FORGIVE YOU FOR THAT!
THAT'S WHAT HE SAID, BUT...
...HE SEEMS TO LIKE HANGING OUT WITH MAO.
TELL MAO...
...THAT SOONER OR LATER, HE'LL NEED ME...
...IF HE WANTS **THE TRUTH**.
WHAT MAO REALLY WANTS TO KNOW IS...

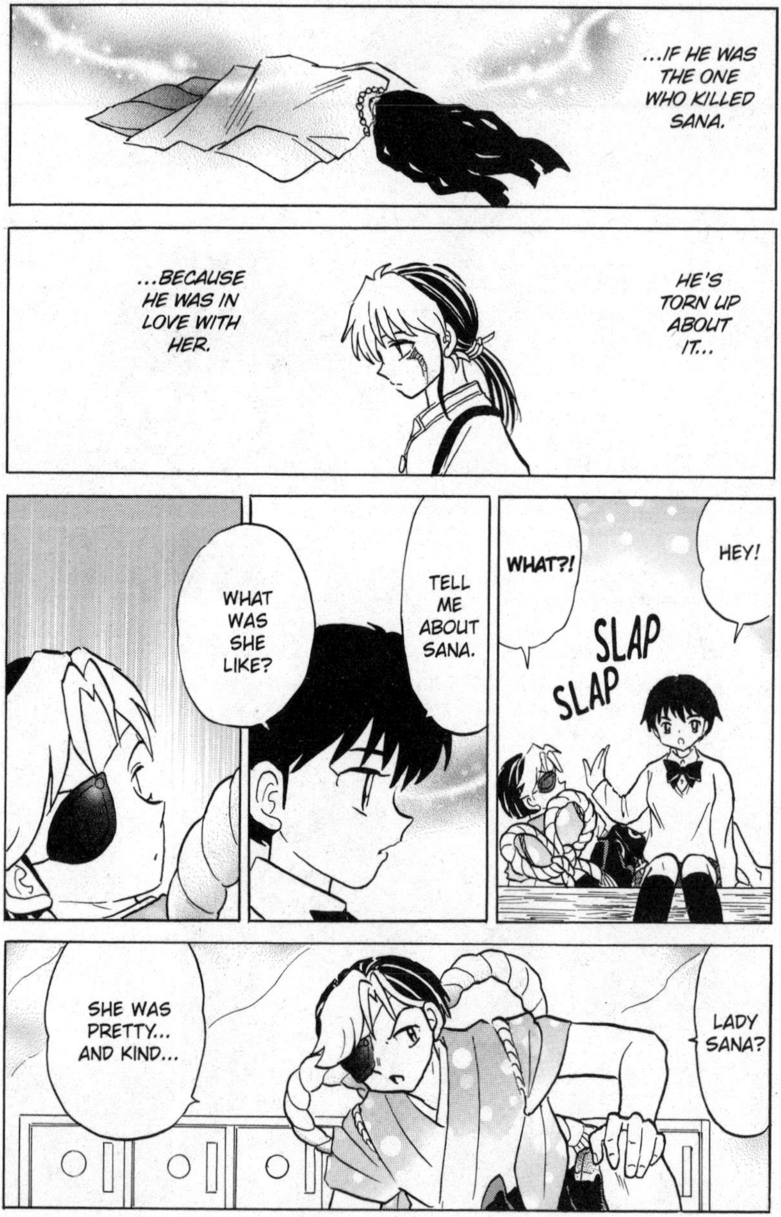
...IF HE WAS THE ONE WHO KILLED SANA.
HE'S TORN UP ABOUT IT...
...BECAUSE HE WAS IN LOVE WITH HER.
HEY!
WHAT?!
SLAP
SLAP
TELL ME ABOUT SANA.
WHAT WAS SHE LIKE?
LADY SANA?
SHE WAS PRETTY... AND KIND...

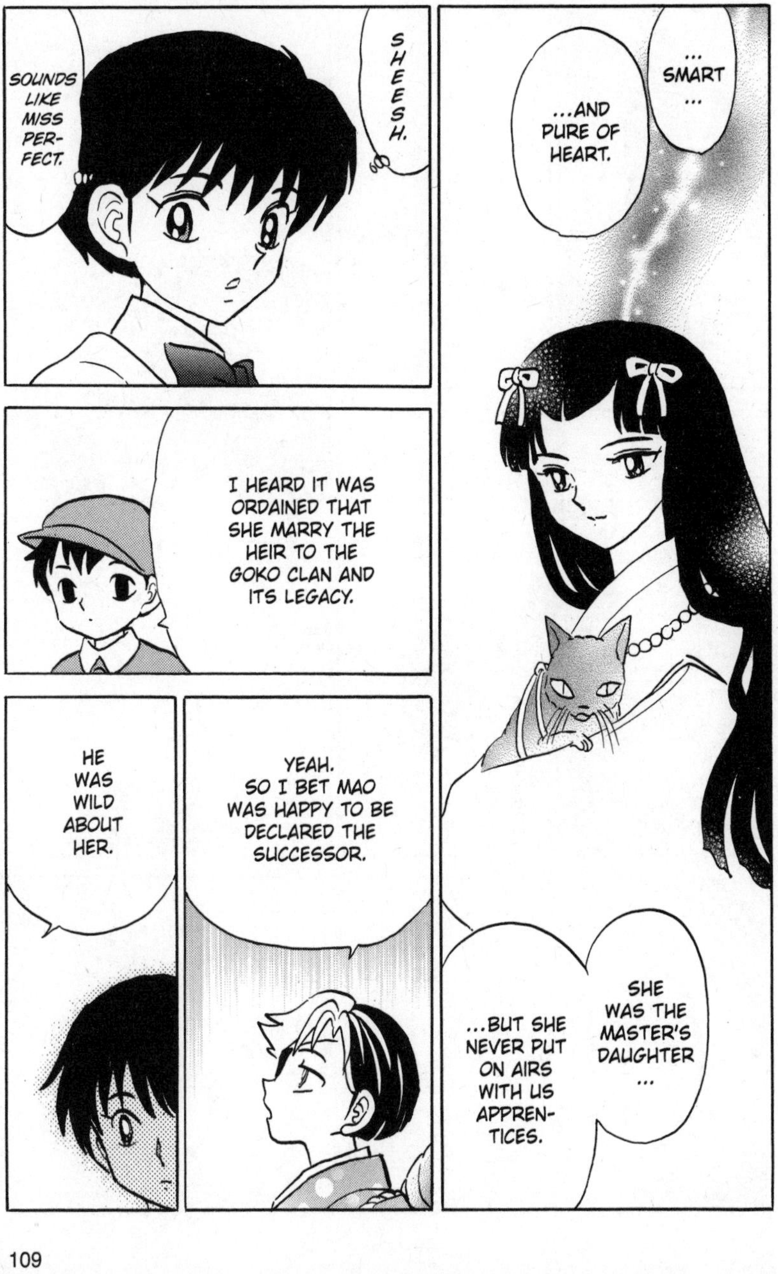
...SMART...
...AND PURE OF HEART.
SHE WAS THE MASTER'S DAUGHTER...
...BUT SHE NEVER PUT ON AIRS WITH US APPRENTICES.
SHEESH.
SOUNDS LIKE MISS PERFECT.
I HEARD IT WAS ORDAINED THAT SHE MARRY THE HEIR TO THE GOKO CLAN AND ITS LEGACY.
YEAH. SO I BET MAO WAS HAPPY TO BE DECLARED THE SUCCESSOR.
HE WAS WILD ABOUT HER.

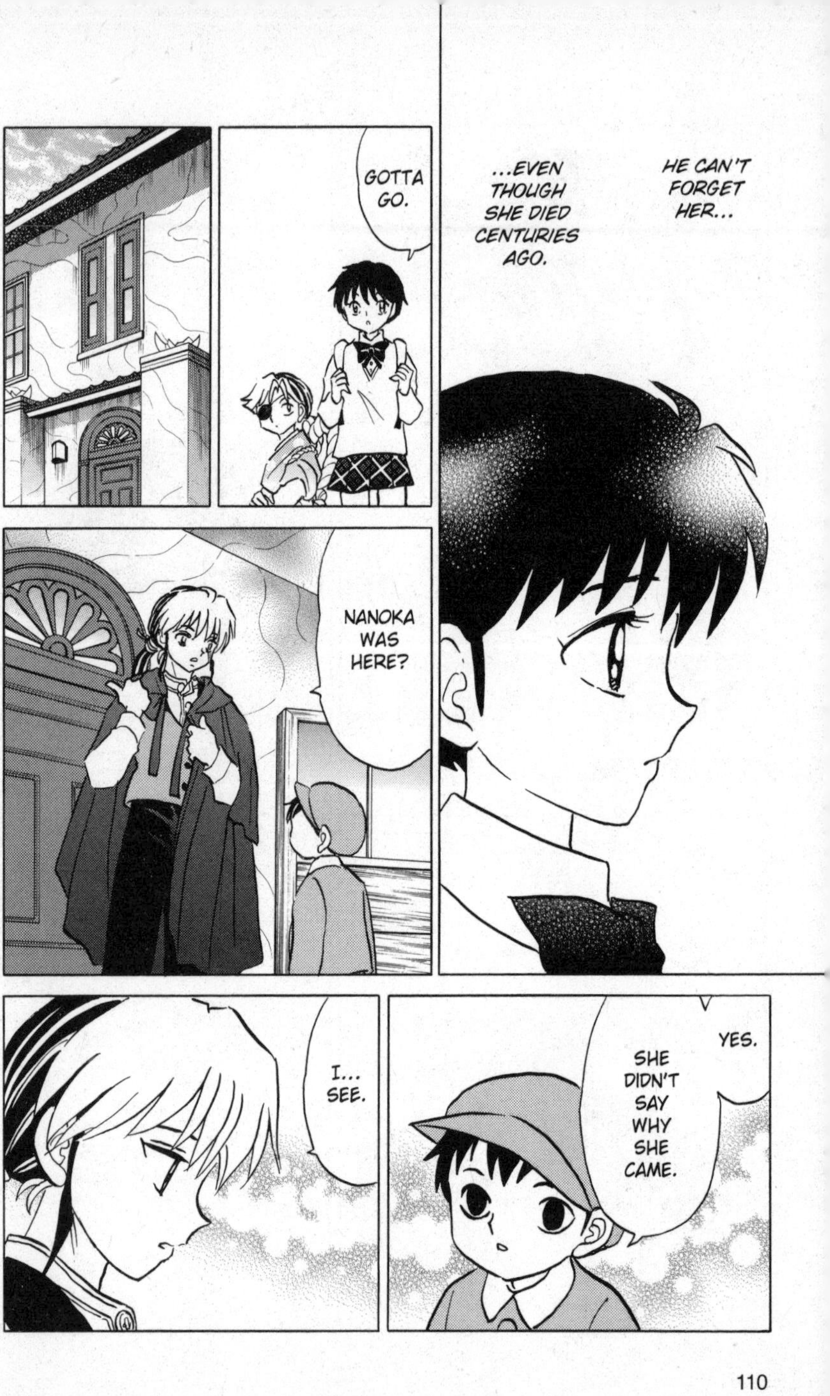
HE CAN'T FORGET HER...
...EVEN THOUGH SHE DIED CENTURIES AGO.
GOTTA GO.
NANOKA WAS HERE?
YES.
SHE DIDN'T SAY WHY SHE CAME.
I... SEE.

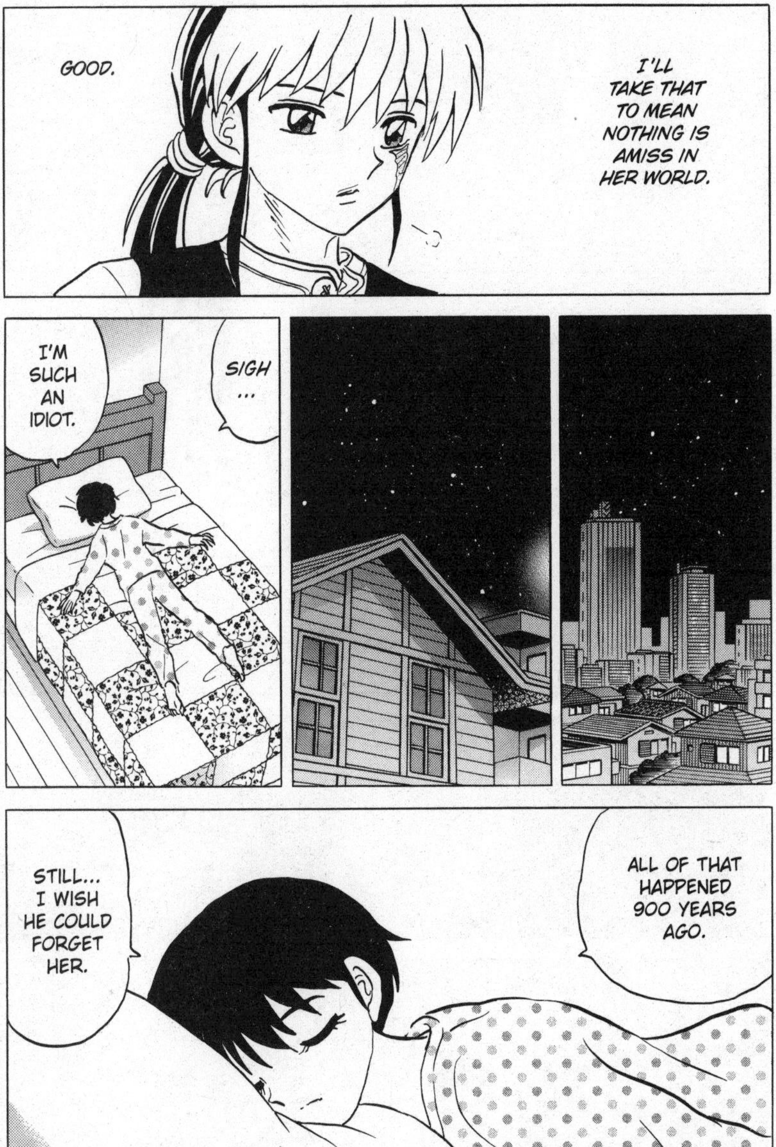
I'LL TAKE THAT TO MEAN NOTHING IS AMISS IN HER WORLD.
GOOD.
SIGH...
I'M SUCH AN IDIOT.
ALL OF THAT HAPPENED 900 YEARS AGO.
STILL... I WISH HE COULD FORGET HER.

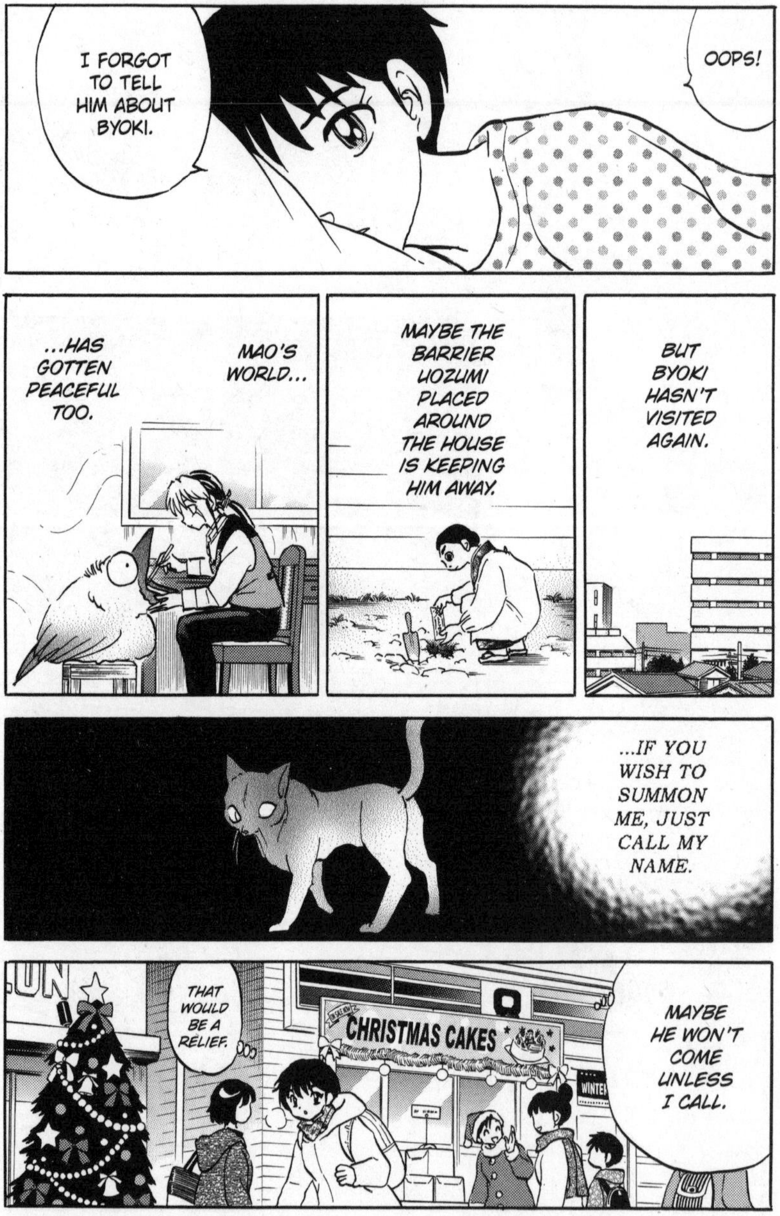
OOPS!
I FORGOT TO TELL HIM ABOUT BYOKI.
BUT BYOKI HASN'T VISITED AGAIN.
MAYBE THE BARRIER UOZUMI PLACED AROUND THE HOUSE IS KEEPING HIM AWAY.
MAO'S WORLD...
...HAS GOTTEN PEACEFUL TOO.
...IF YOU WISH TO SUMMON ME, JUST CALL MY NAME.
MAYBE HE WON'T COME UNLESS I CALL.
CHRISTMAS CAKES
THAT WOULD BE A RELIEF.

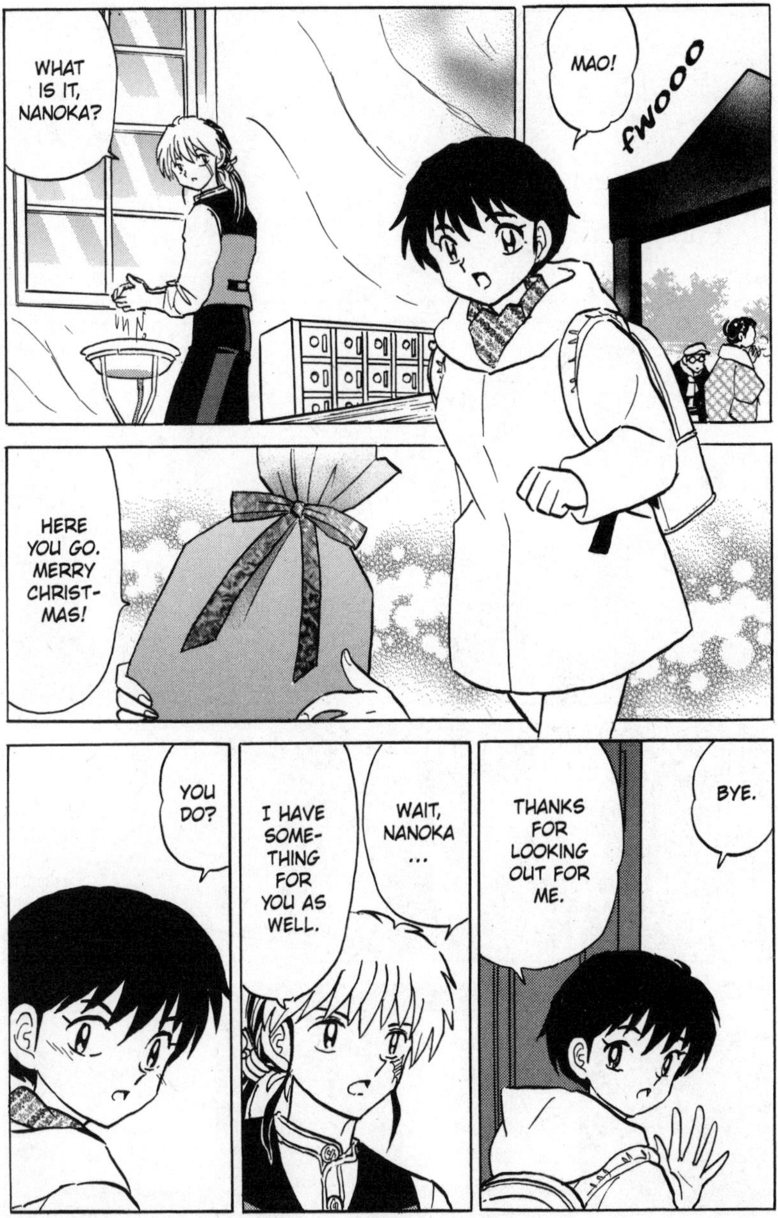
MAO!
fwooo
WHAT IS IT, NANOKA?
HERE YOU GO. MERRY CHRIST-MAS!
BYE.
THANKS FOR LOOKING OUT FOR ME.
WAIT, NANOKA ...
I HAVE SOME-THING FOR YOU AS WELL.
YOU DO?

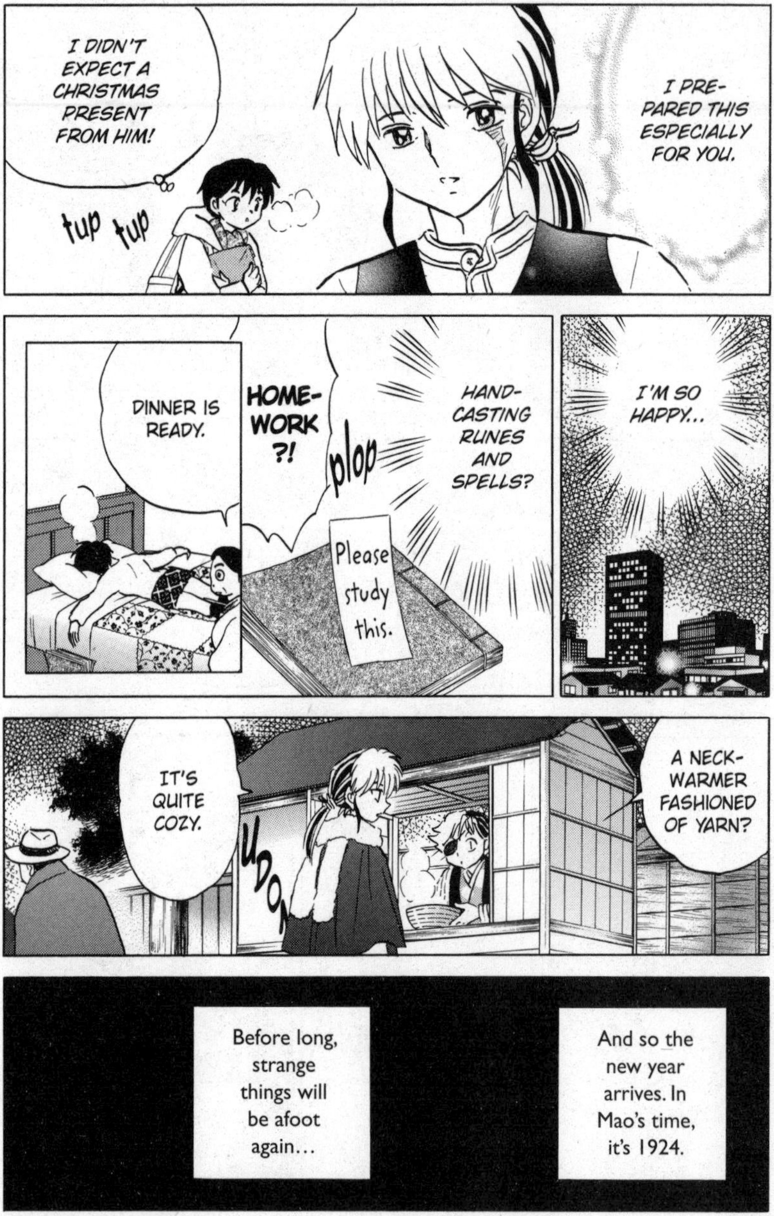

I PRE-PARED THIS ESPECIALLY FOR YOU.
I DIDN'T EXPECT A CHRISTMAS PRESENT FROM HIM!
tup tup
I'M SO HAPPY...
HAND-CASTING RUNES AND SPELLS?
plop
Please study this.
HOME-WORK ?!
DINNER IS READY.
A NECK-WARMER FASHIONED OF YARN?
UDON
IT'S QUITE COZY.
And so the new year arrives. In Mao's time, it's 1924.
Before long, strange things will be afoot again…

Chapter 7:
The Iron Mask

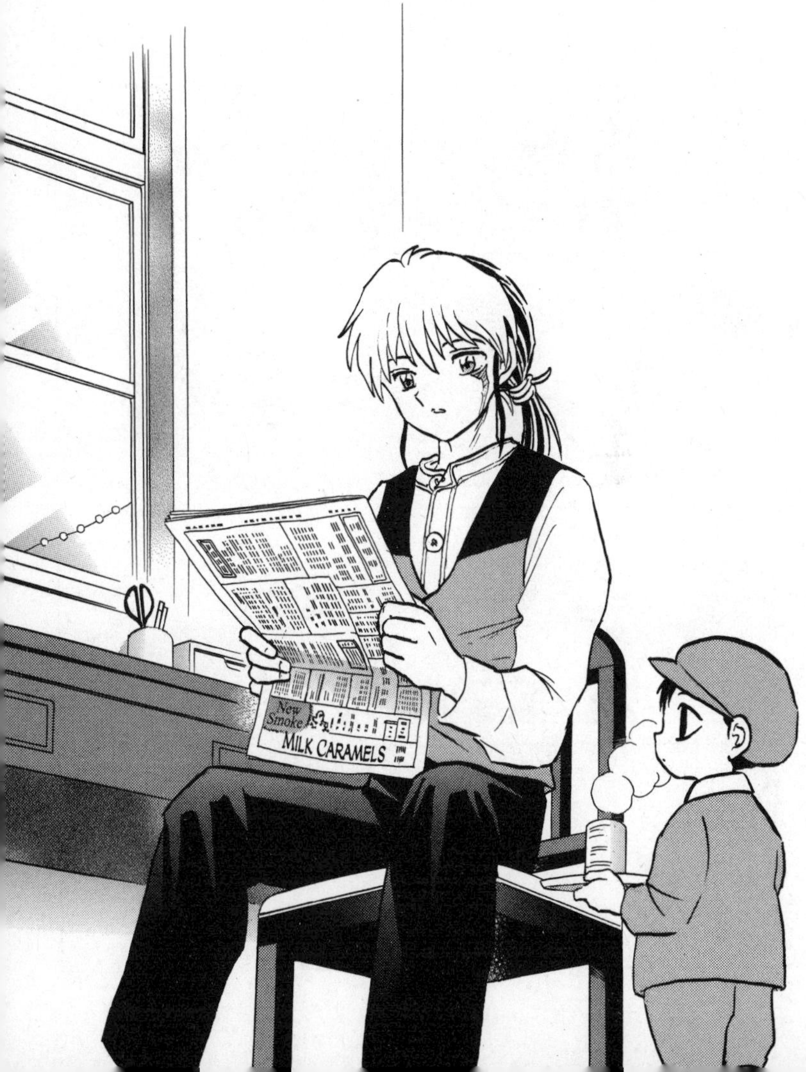
New Smoke
MILK CARAMELS

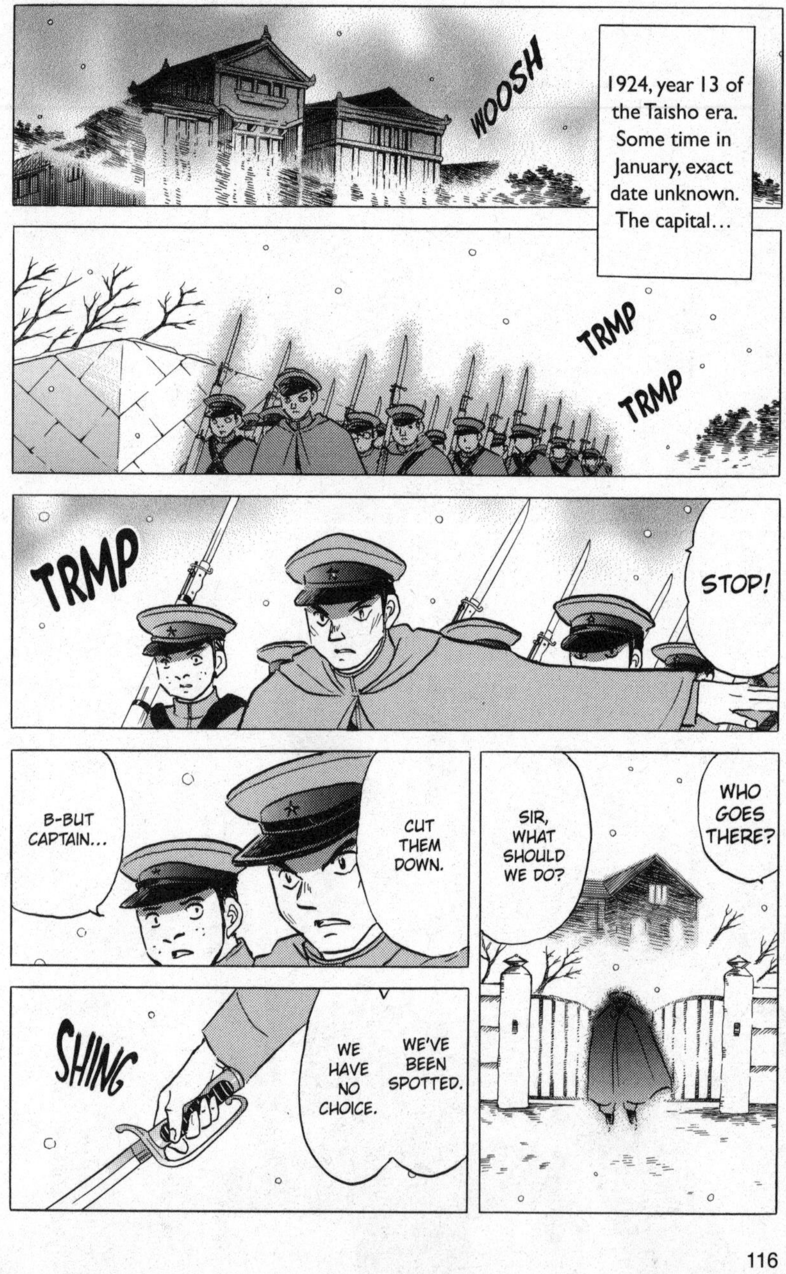
1924, year 13 of the Taisho era. Some time in January, exact date unknown. The capital…
WOOSH
TRMP
TRMP
STOP!
TRMP
WHO GOES THERE?
SIR, WHAT SHOULD WE DO?
CUT THEM DOWN.
B-BUT CAPTAIN…
WE'VE BEEN SPOTTED.
WE HAVE NO CHOICE.
SHING

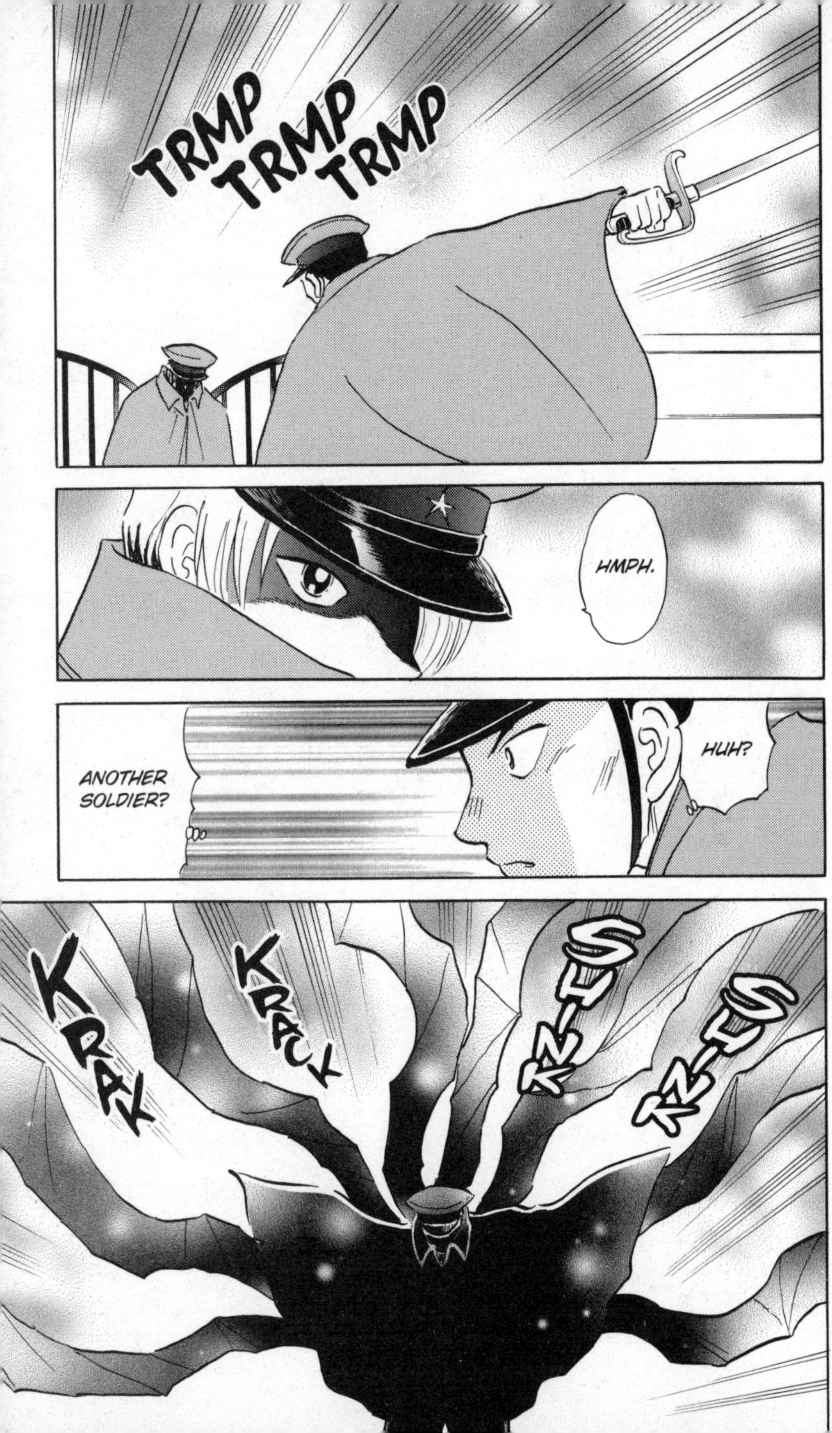
TRMP TRMP TRMP
HMPH.
HUH?
ANOTHER SOLDIER?
SHINK
SHINK
KRACK
KRAK

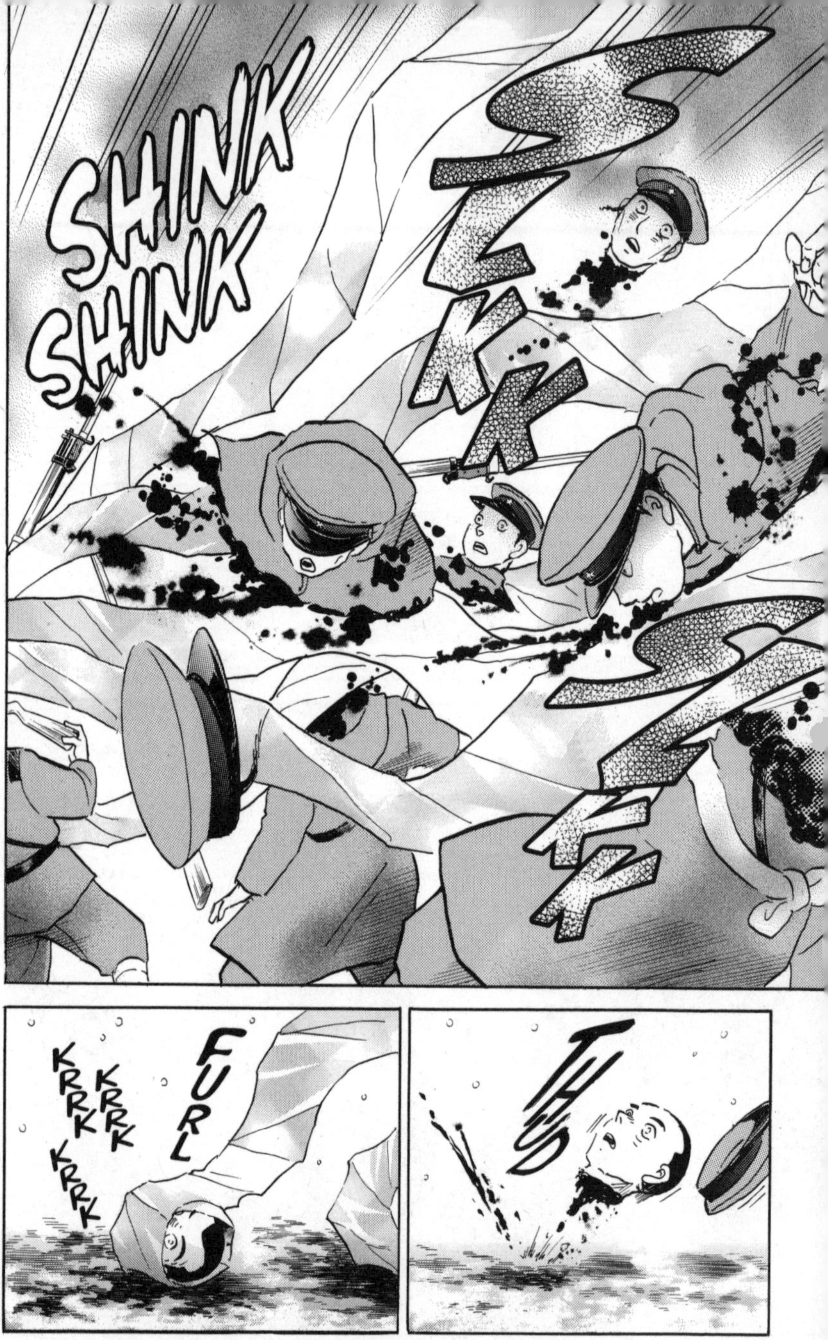
SHINK
SHINK
THUD
FURL
KRRK KRRK
KRRK

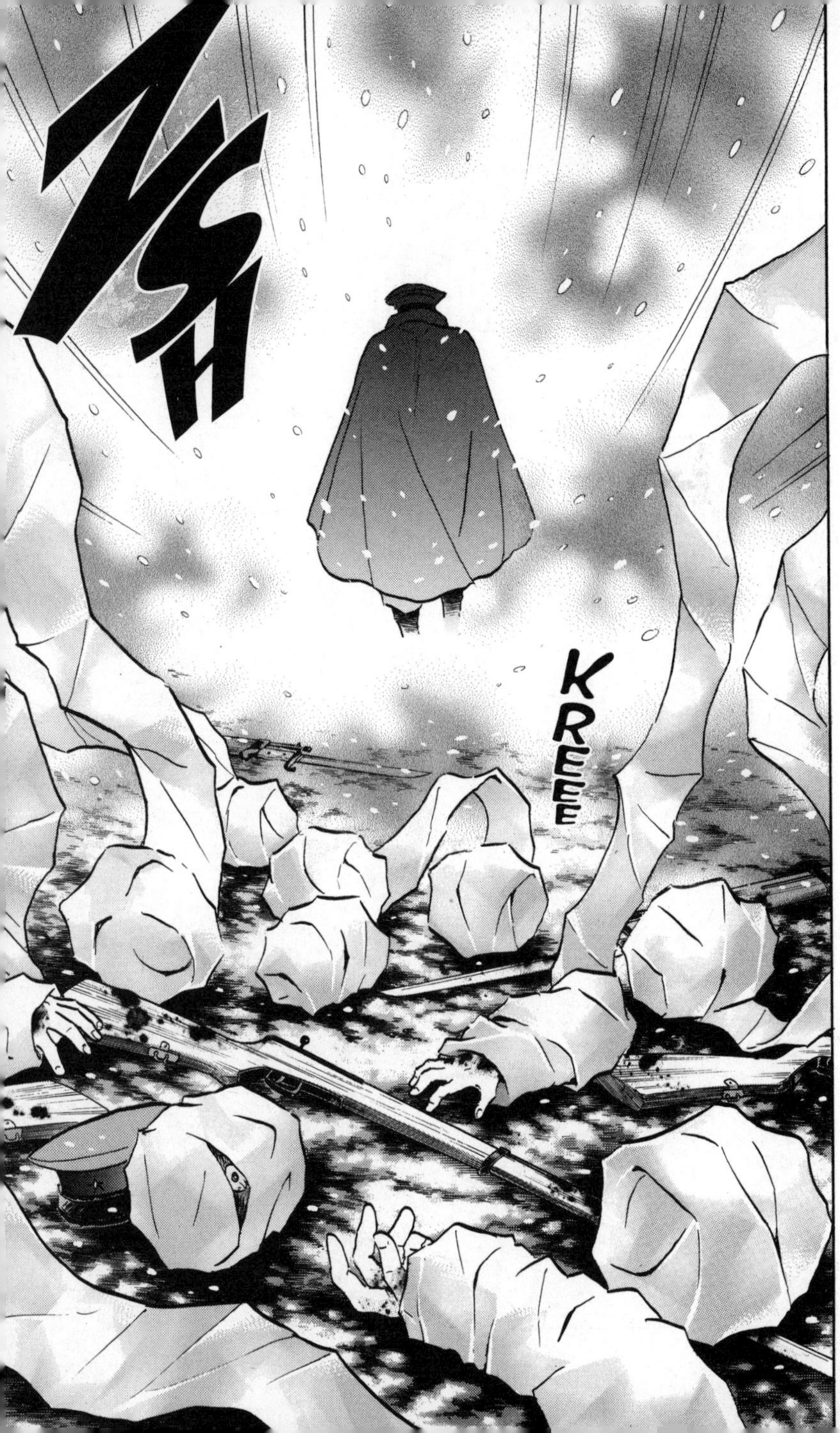
VSH
KREEE

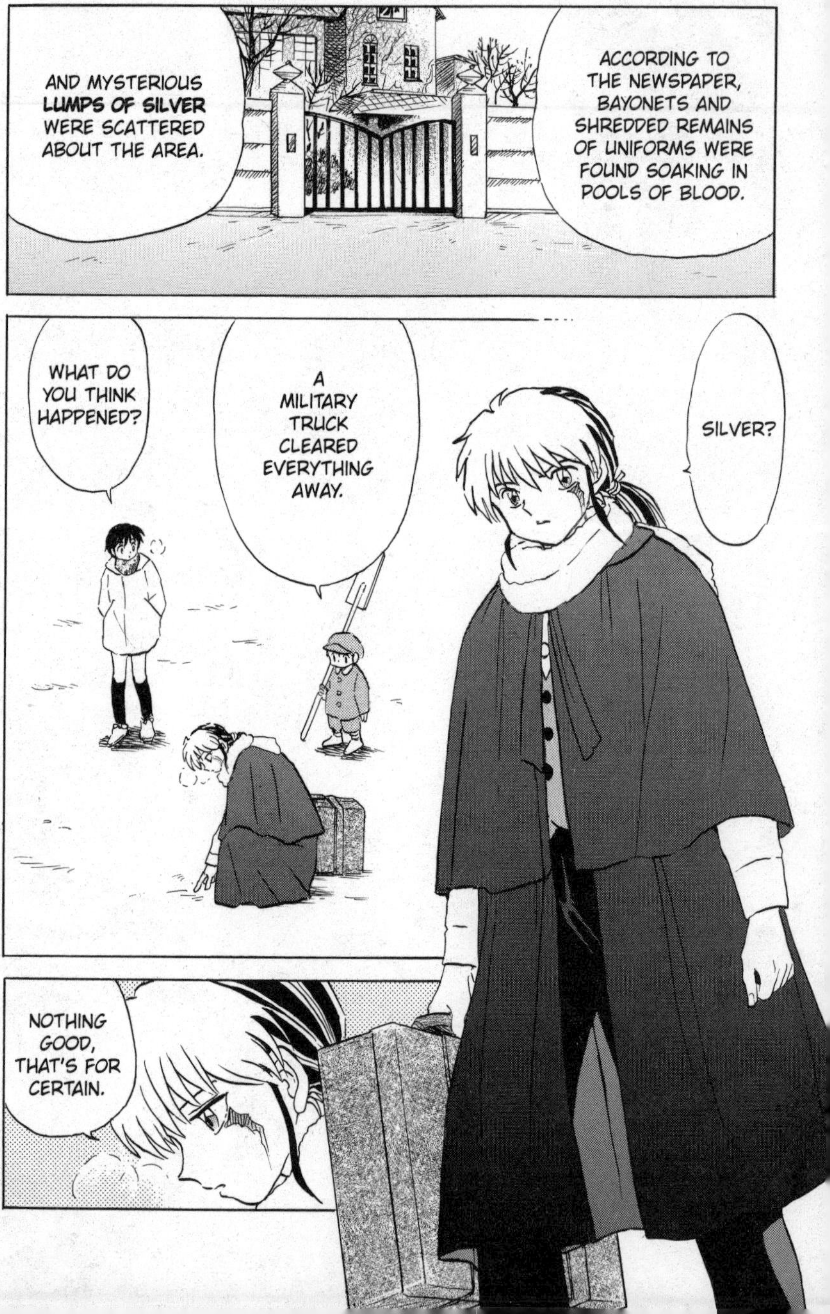
ACCORDING TO THE NEWSPAPER, BAYONETS AND SHREDDED REMAINS OF UNIFORMS WERE FOUND SOAKING IN POOLS OF BLOOD.
AND MYSTERIOUS **LUMPS OF SILVER** WERE SCATTERED ABOUT THE AREA.
SILVER?
A MILITARY TRUCK CLEARED EVERYTHING AWAY.
WHAT DO YOU THINK HAPPENED?
NOTHING GOOD, THAT'S FOR CERTAIN.

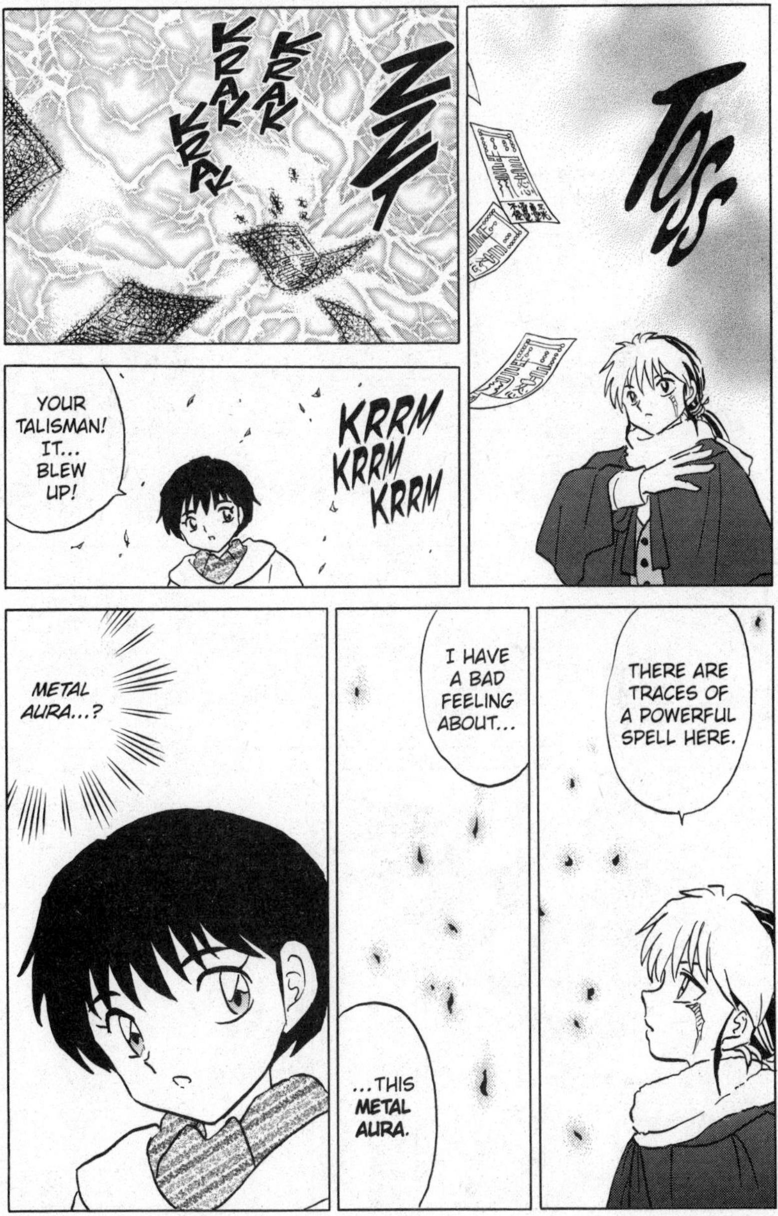
TOSS
ZZZT
KRAK KRAK KRAK
YOUR TALISMAN! IT... BLEW UP!
KRRM KRRM KRRM
THERE ARE TRACES OF A POWERFUL SPELL HERE.
I HAVE A BAD FEELING ABOUT...
...THIS **METAL AURA.**
METAL AURA...?

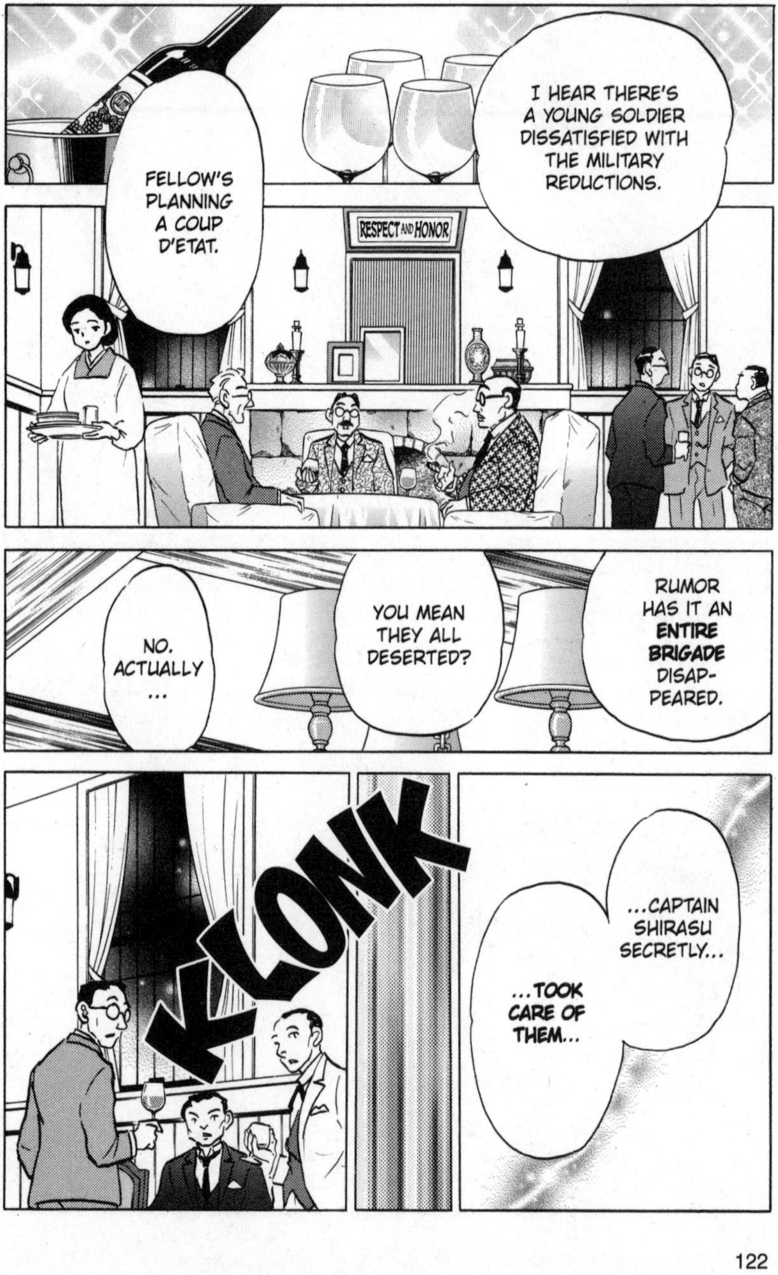
I HEAR THERE'S A YOUNG SOLDIER DISSATISFIED WITH THE MILITARY REDUCTIONS.
FELLOW'S PLANNING A COUP D'ETAT.
RESPECT AND HONOR
RUMOR HAS IT AN **ENTIRE BRIGADE** DISAP-PEARED.
YOU MEAN THEY ALL DESERTED?
NO. ACTUALLY ...
...CAPTAIN SHIRASU SECRETLY...
...TOOK CARE OF THEM...
KLONK

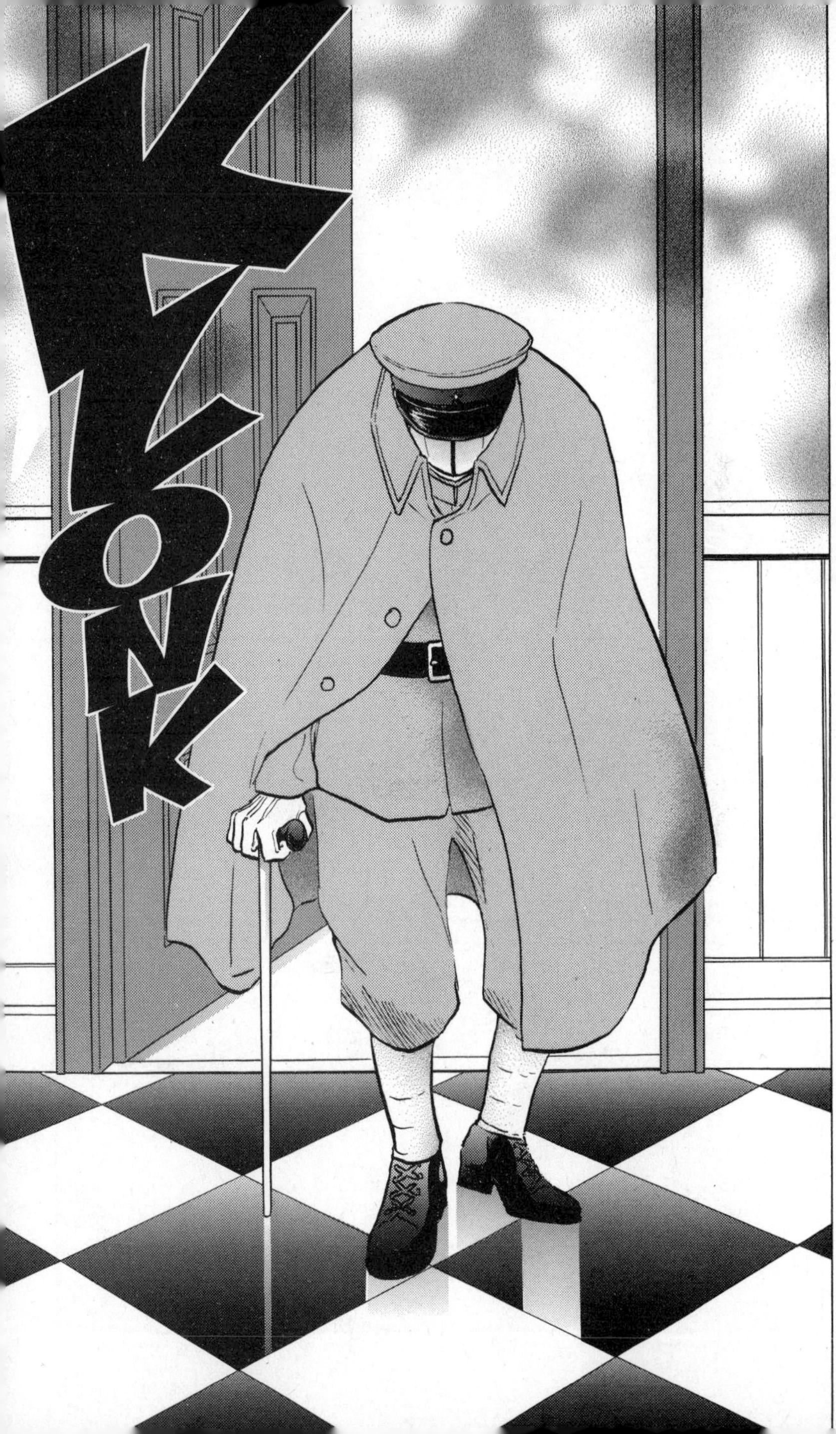
KLONK

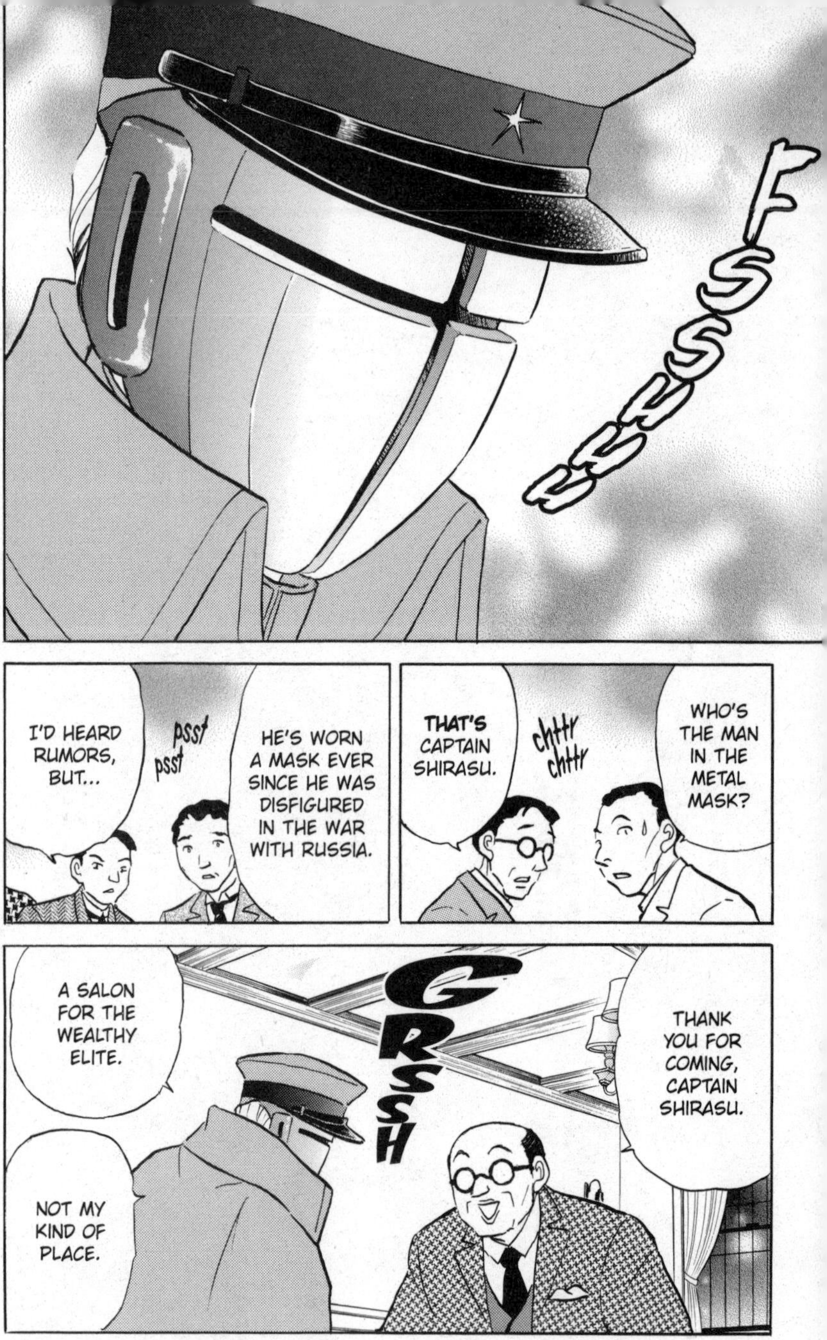
FSSHHH
WHO'S THE MAN IN THE METAL MASK?
chttr chttr
THAT'S CAPTAIN SHIRASU.
HE'S WORN A MASK EVER SINCE HE WAS DISFIGURED IN THE WAR WITH RUSSIA.
psst psst
I'D HEARD RUMORS, BUT...
THANK YOU FOR COMING, CAPTAIN SHIRASU.
GRSSH
A SALON FOR THE WEALTHY ELITE.
NOT MY KIND OF PLACE.

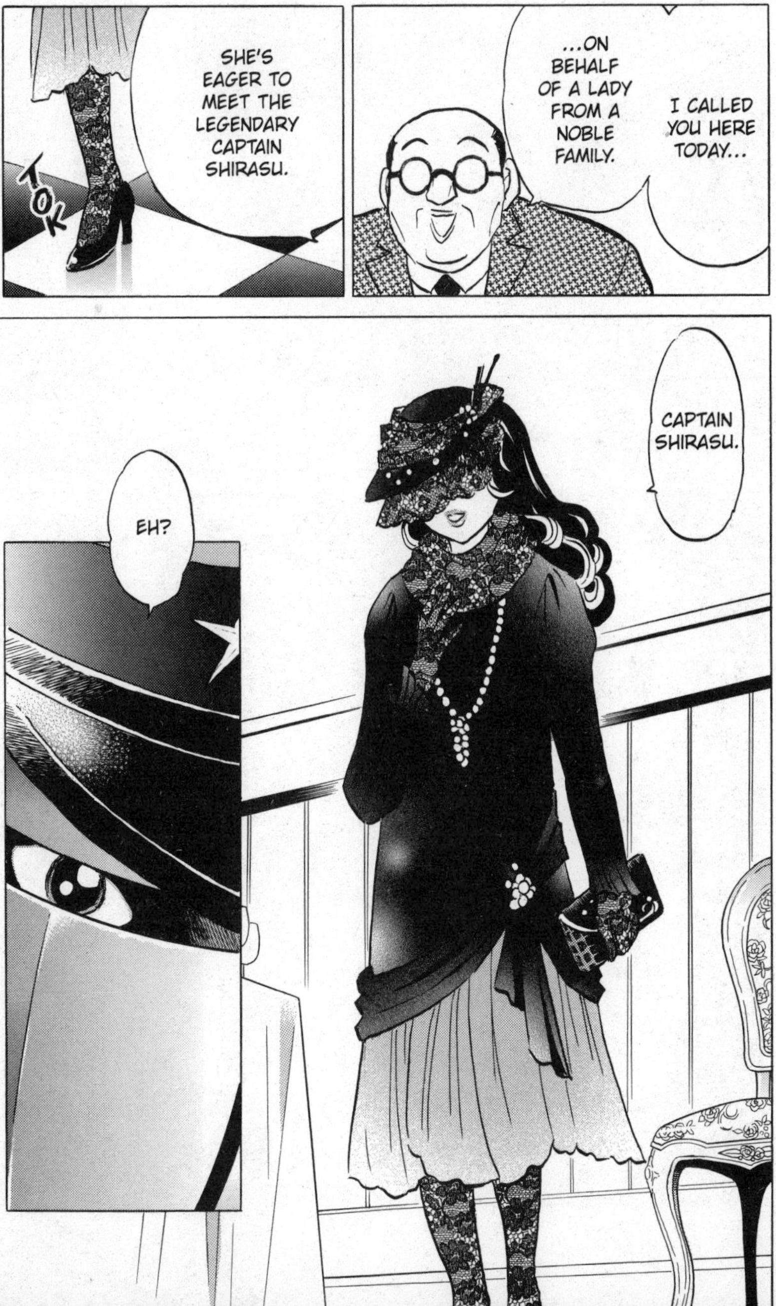
I CALLED YOU HERE TODAY...
...ON BEHALF OF A LADY FROM A NOBLE FAMILY.
SHE'S EAGER TO MEET THE LEGENDARY CAPTAIN SHIRASU.
TOK
CAPTAIN SHIRASU.
EH?

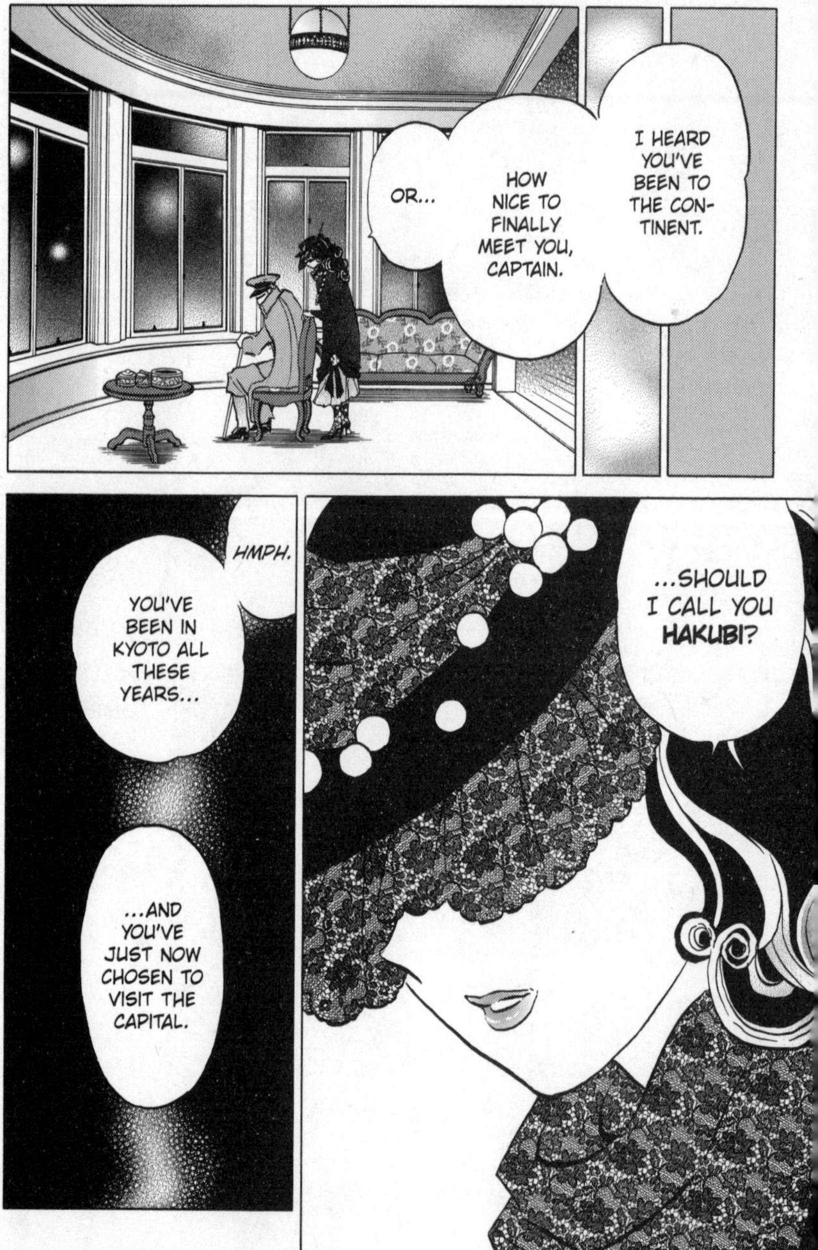
I HEARD YOU'VE BEEN TO THE CONTINENT.
HOW NICE TO FINALLY MEET YOU, CAPTAIN.
OR...
...SHOULD I CALL YOU **HAKUBI**?
HMPH.
YOU'VE BEEN IN KYOTO ALL THESE YEARS...
...AND YOU'VE JUST NOW CHOSEN TO VISIT THE CAPITAL.

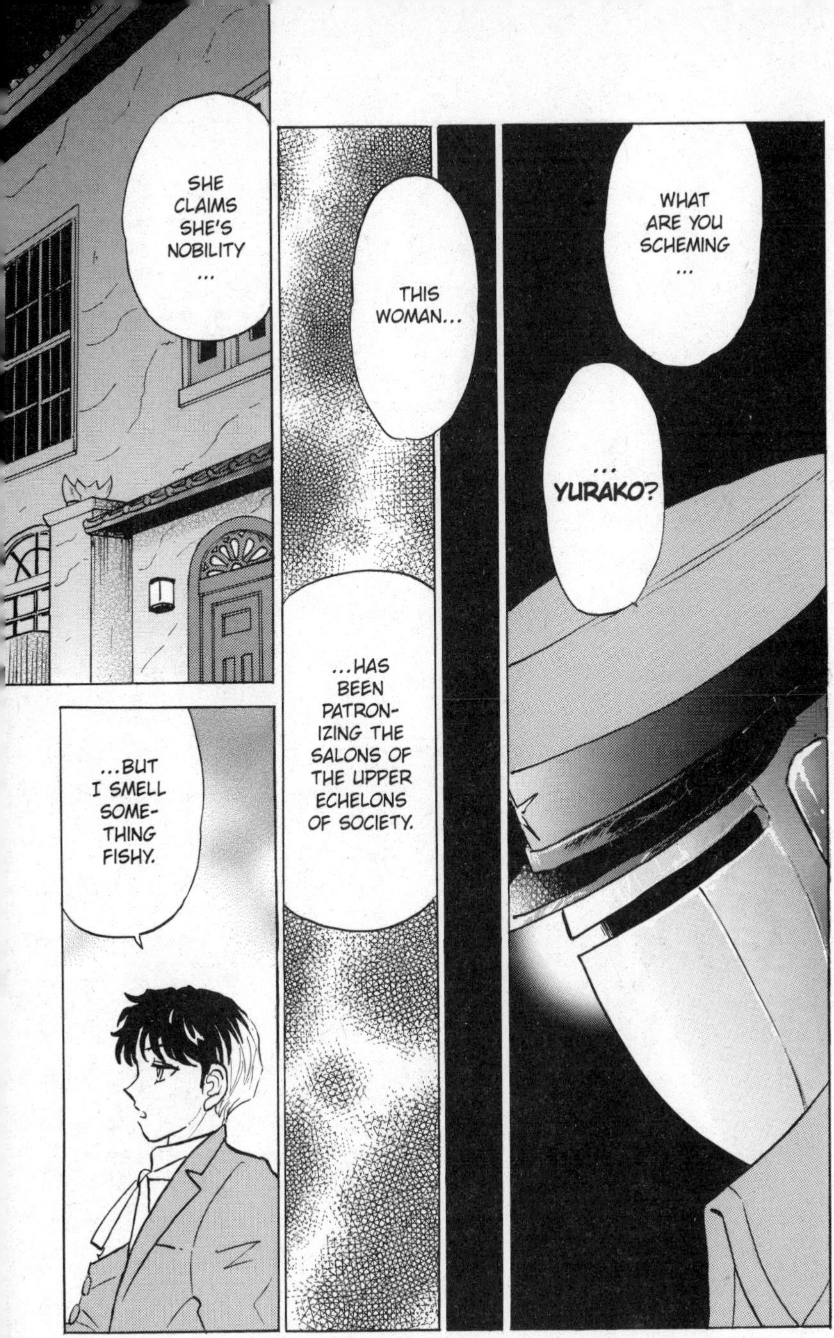
WHAT ARE YOU SCHEMING ...
... YURAKO?
THIS WOMAN...
...HAS BEEN PATRON-IZING THE SALONS OF THE UPPER ECHELONS OF SOCIETY.
SHE CLAIMS SHE'S NOBILITY ...
...BUT I SMELL SOME-THING FISHY.

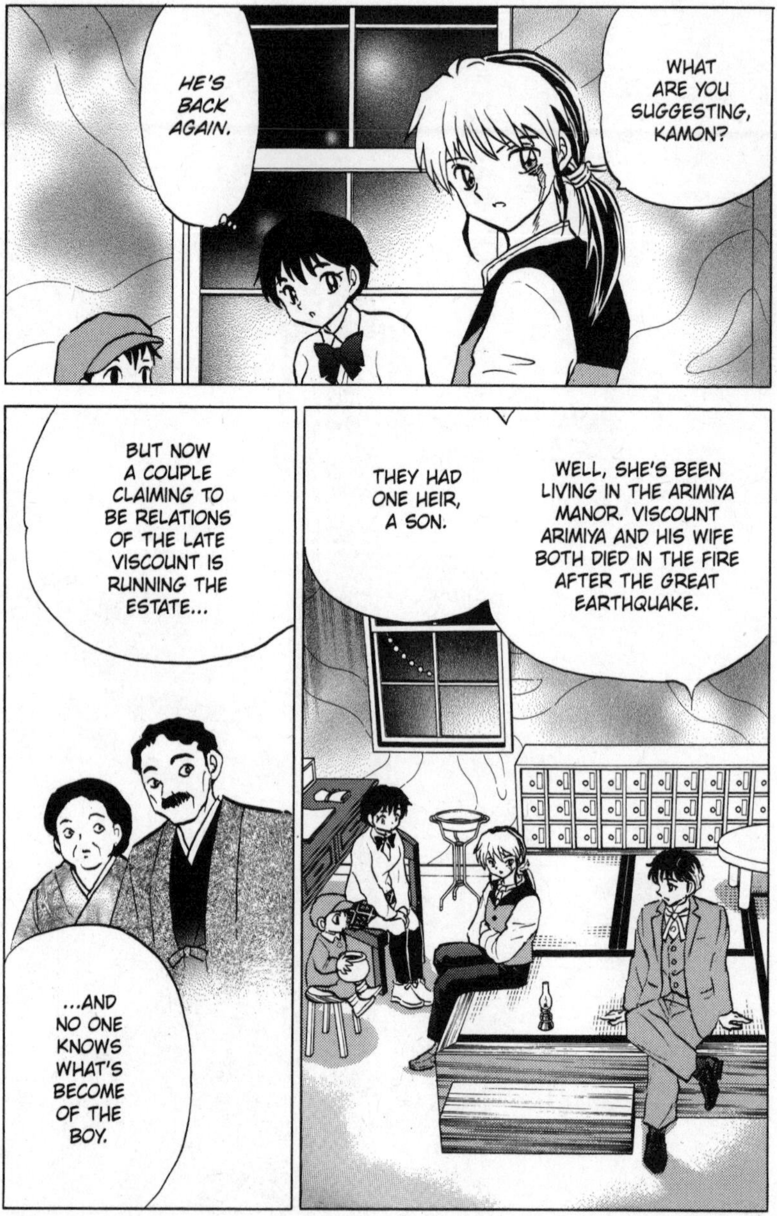
WHAT ARE YOU SUGGESTING, KAMON?
HE'S BACK AGAIN.
WELL, SHE'S BEEN LIVING IN THE ARIMIYA MANOR. VISCOUNT ARIMIYA AND HIS WIFE BOTH DIED IN THE FIRE AFTER THE GREAT EARTHQUAKE.
THEY HAD ONE HEIR, A SON.
BUT NOW A COUPLE CLAIMING TO BE RELATIONS OF THE LATE VISCOUNT IS RUNNING THE ESTATE...
...AND NO ONE KNOWS WHAT'S BECOME OF THE BOY.

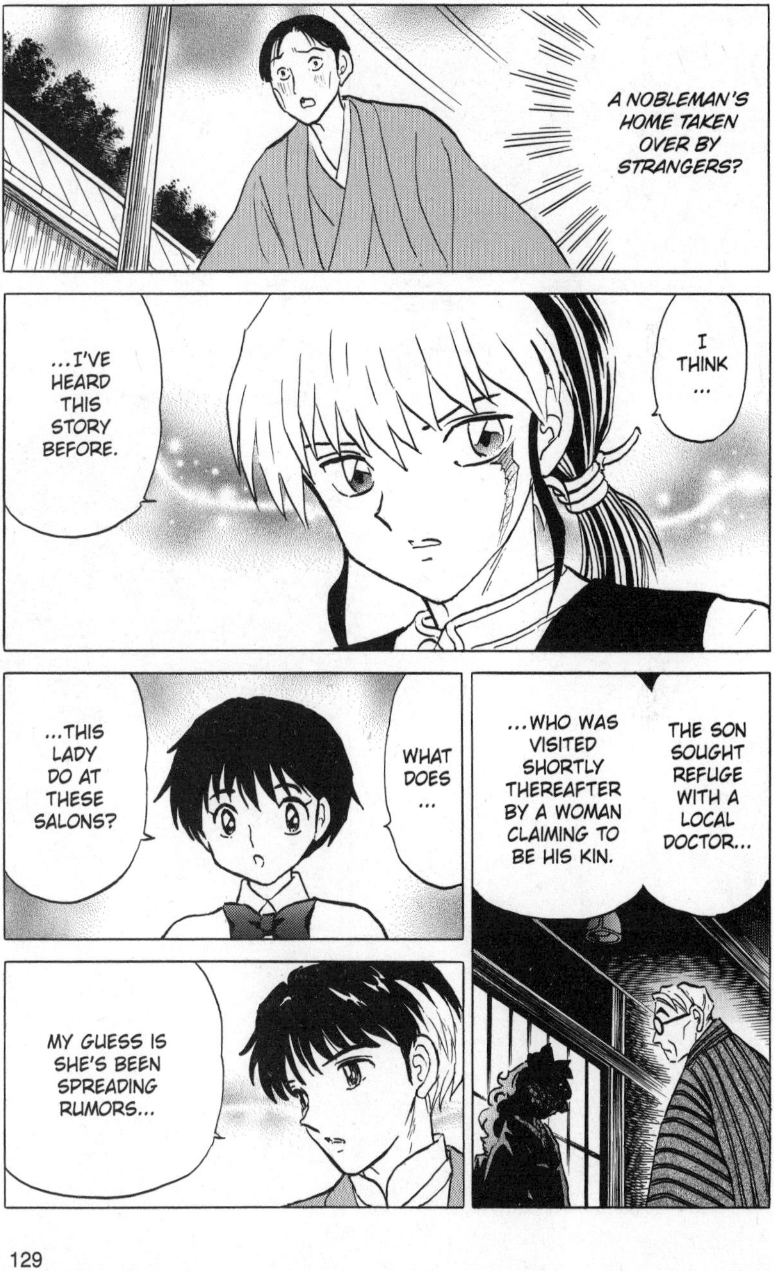
A NOBLEMAN'S HOME TAKEN OVER BY STRANGERS?
I THINK...
...I'VE HEARD THIS STORY BEFORE.
THE SON SOUGHT REFUGE WITH A LOCAL DOCTOR...
...WHO WAS VISITED SHORTLY THEREAFTER BY A WOMAN CLAIMING TO BE HIS KIN.
WHAT DOES...
...THIS LADY DO AT THESE SALONS?
MY GUESS IS SHE'S BEEN SPREADING RUMORS...

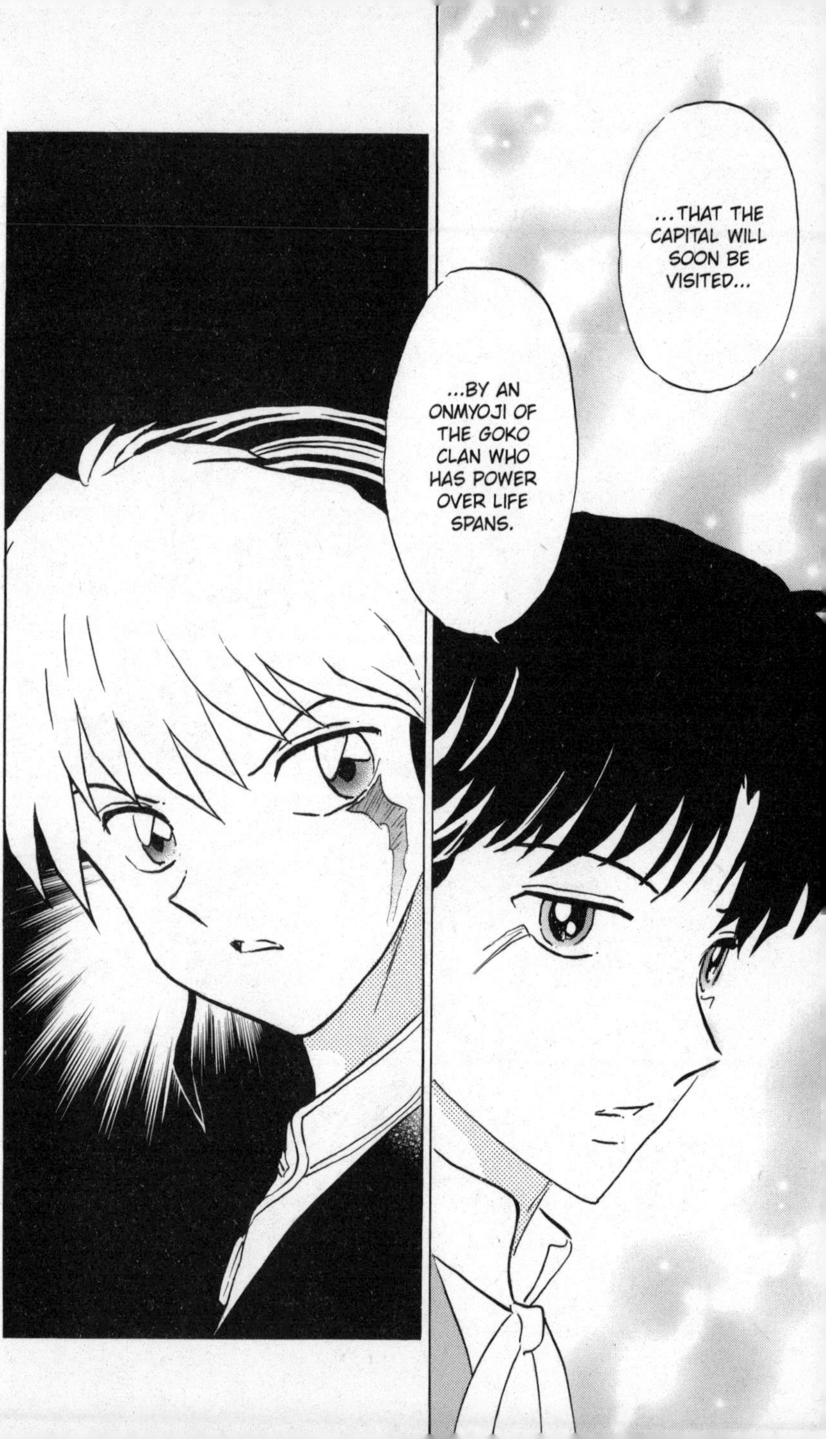
...THAT THE CAPITAL WILL SOON BE VISITED...
...BY AN ONMYOJI OF THE GOKO CLAN WHO HAS POWER OVER LIFE SPANS.

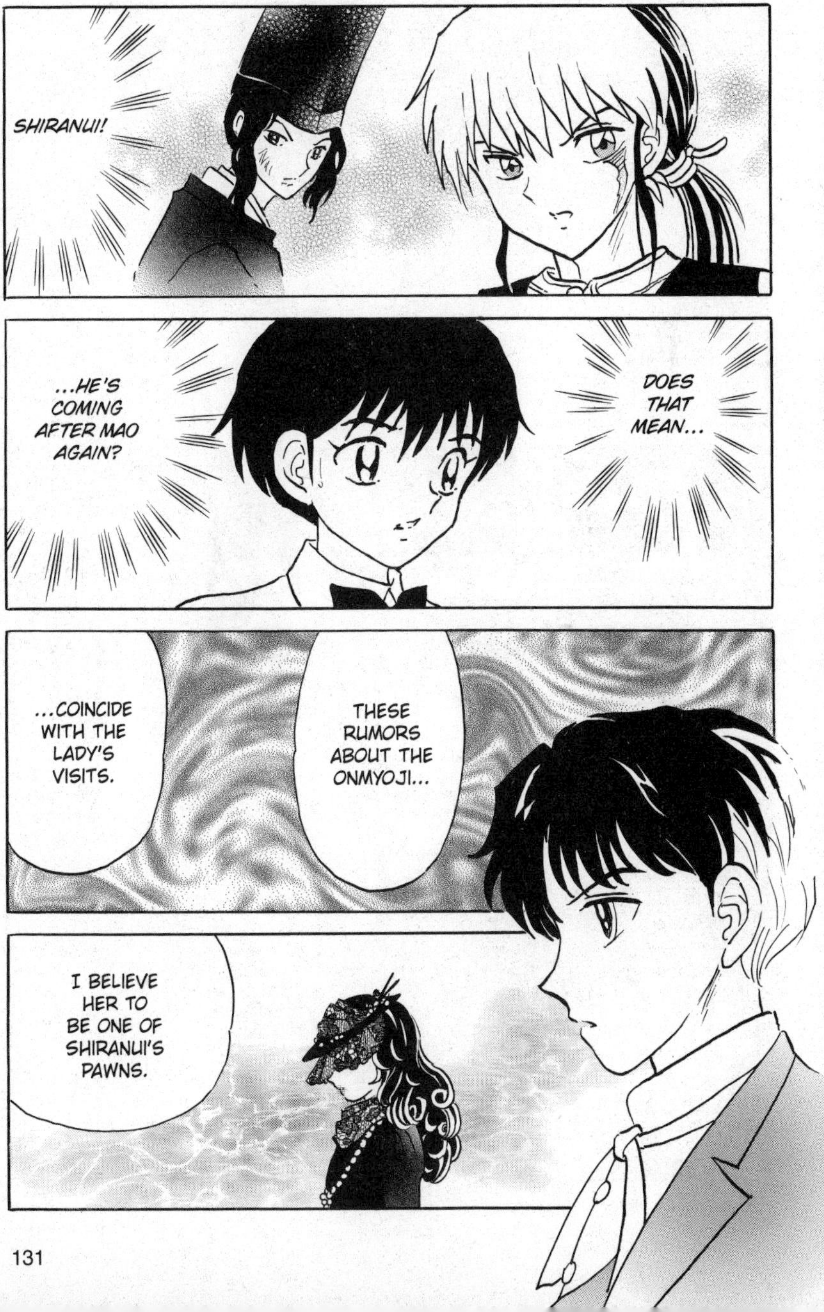
SHIRANUI!
DOES THAT MEAN...
...HE'S COMING AFTER MAO AGAIN?
THESE RUMORS ABOUT THE ONMYOJI...
...COINCIDE WITH THE LADY'S VISITS.
I BELIEVE HER TO BE ONE OF SHIRANUI'S PAWNS.

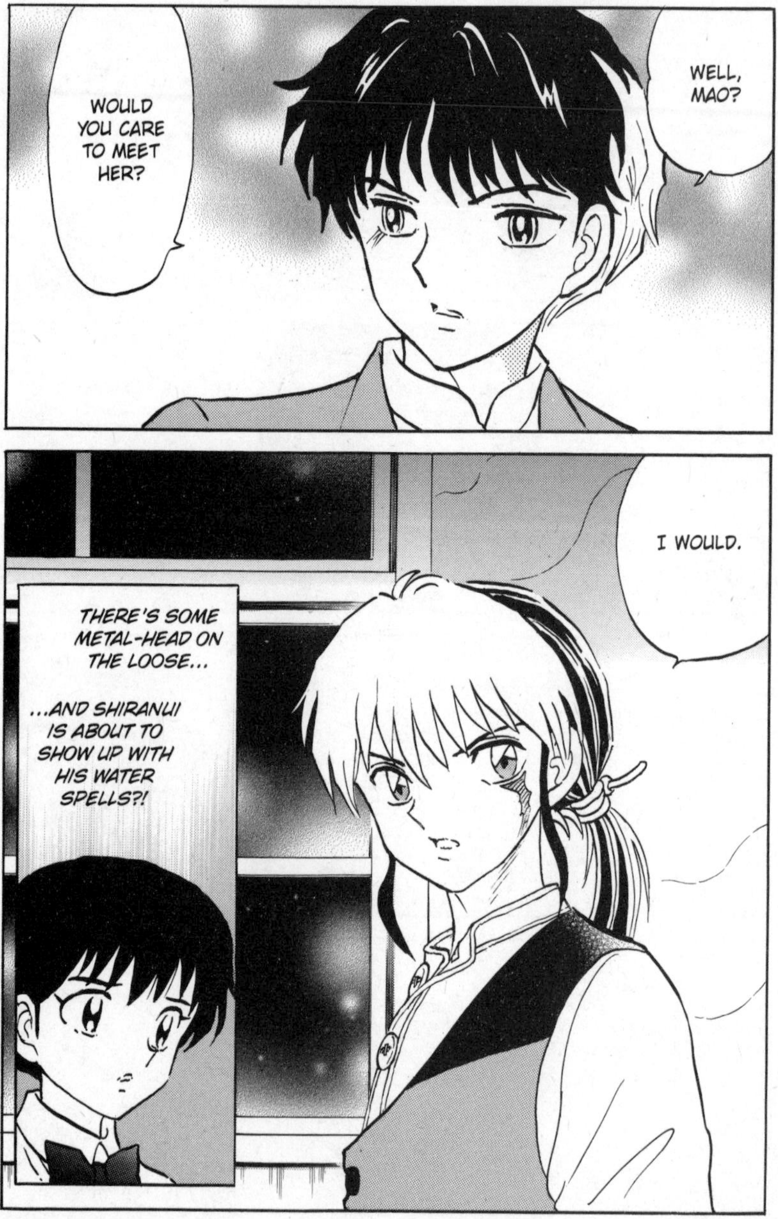
WELL, MAO?
WOULD YOU CARE TO MEET HER?
I WOULD.
THERE'S SOME METAL-HEAD ON THE LOOSE...
...AND SHIRANUI IS ABOUT TO SHOW UP WITH HIS WATER SPELLS?!

Chapter 8: Yurako

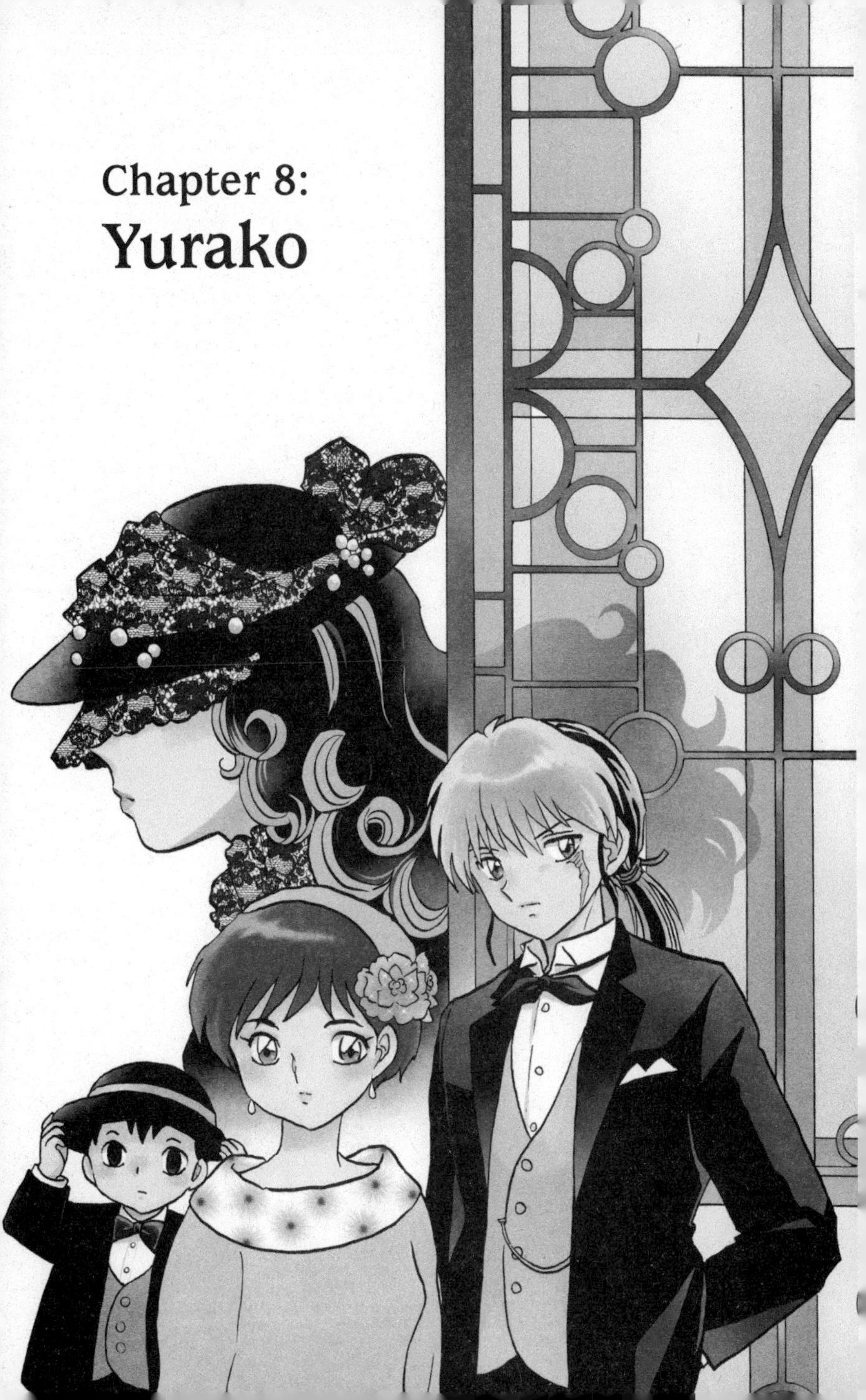

MAO

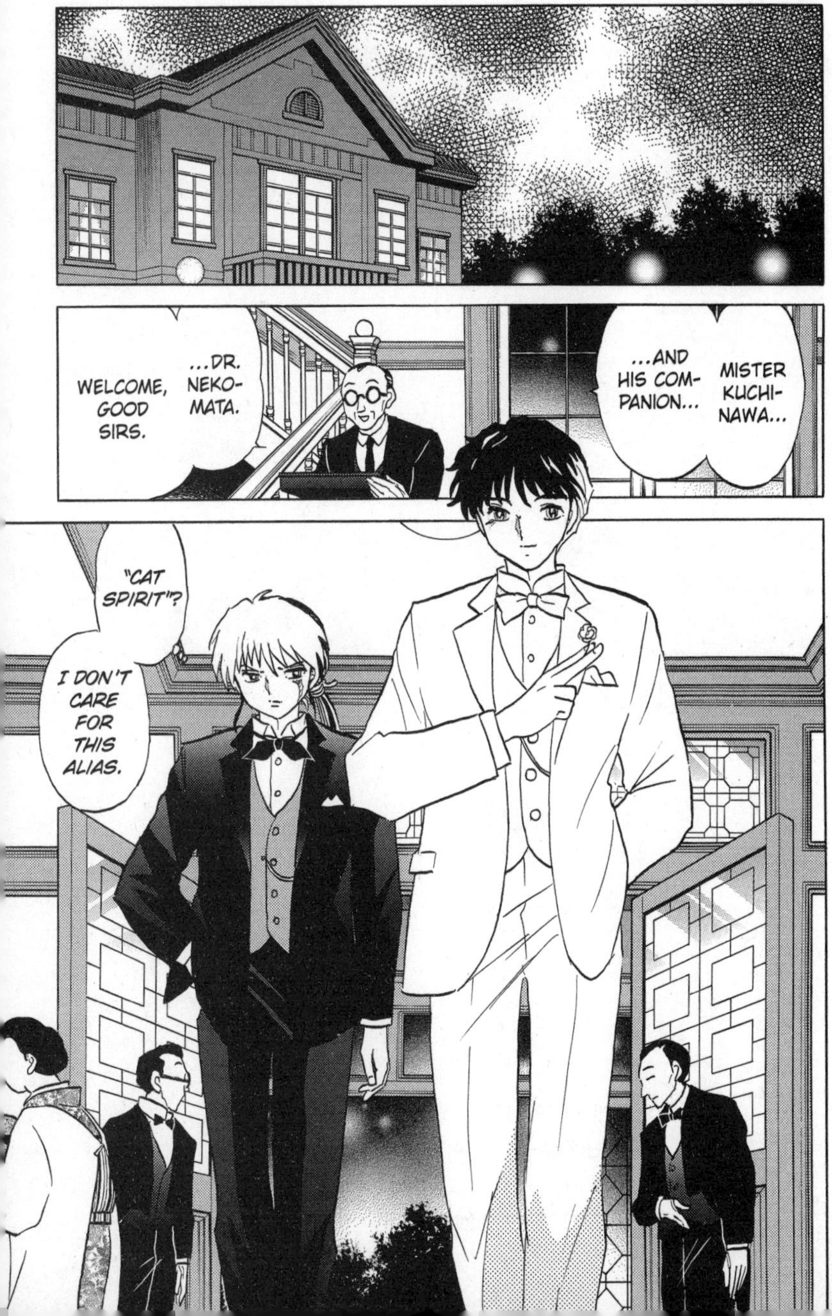
MISTER KUCHI-NAWA...
...AND HIS COM-PANION...
...DR. NEKO-MATA.
WELCOME, GOOD SIRS.
"CAT SPIRIT"?
I DON'T CARE FOR THIS ALIAS.

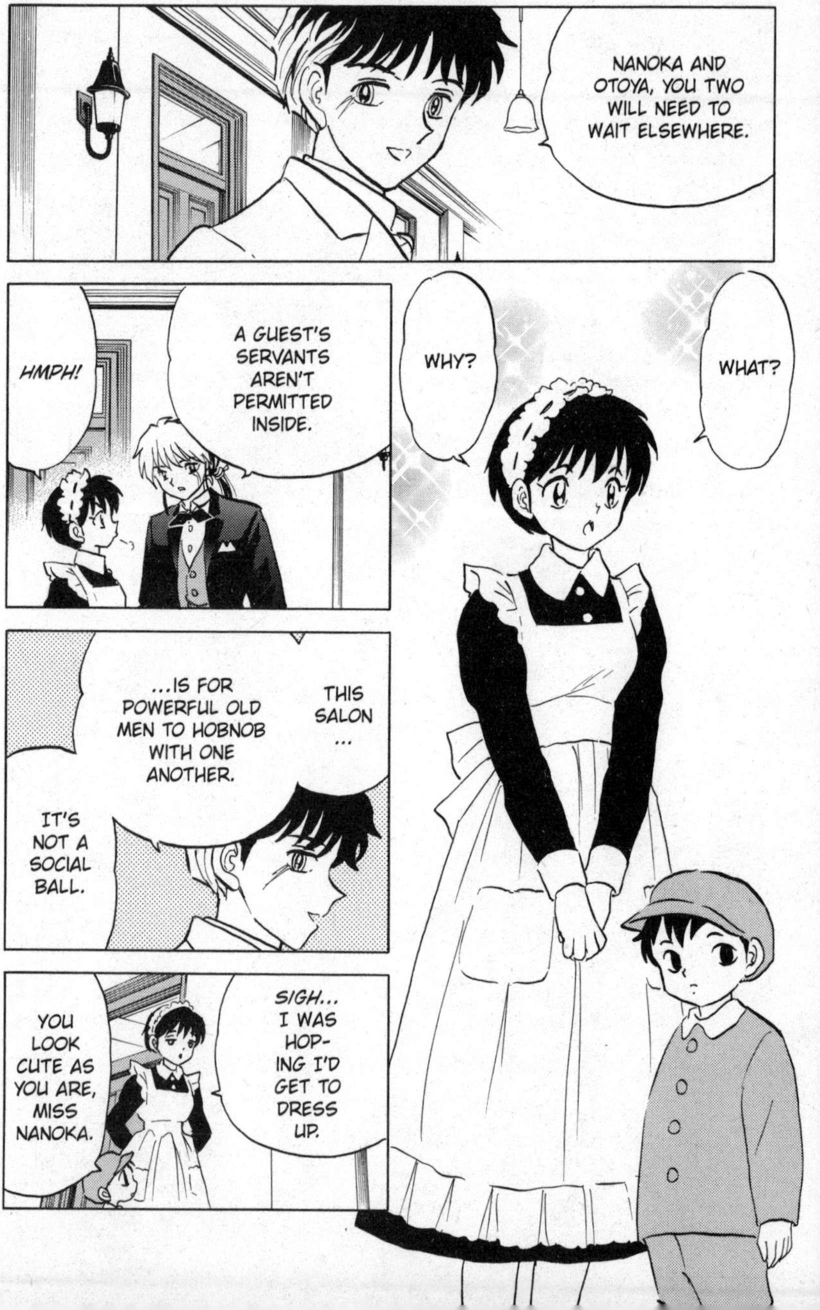
NANOKA AND OTOYA, YOU TWO WILL NEED TO WAIT ELSEWHERE.
WHAT?
WHY?
A GUEST'S SERVANTS AREN'T PERMITTED INSIDE.
HMPH!
THIS SALON...
...IS FOR POWERFUL OLD MEN TO HOBNOB WITH ONE ANOTHER.
IT'S NOT A SOCIAL BALL.
SIGH... I WAS HOPING I'D GET TO DRESS UP.
YOU LOOK CUTE AS YOU ARE, MISS NANOKA.

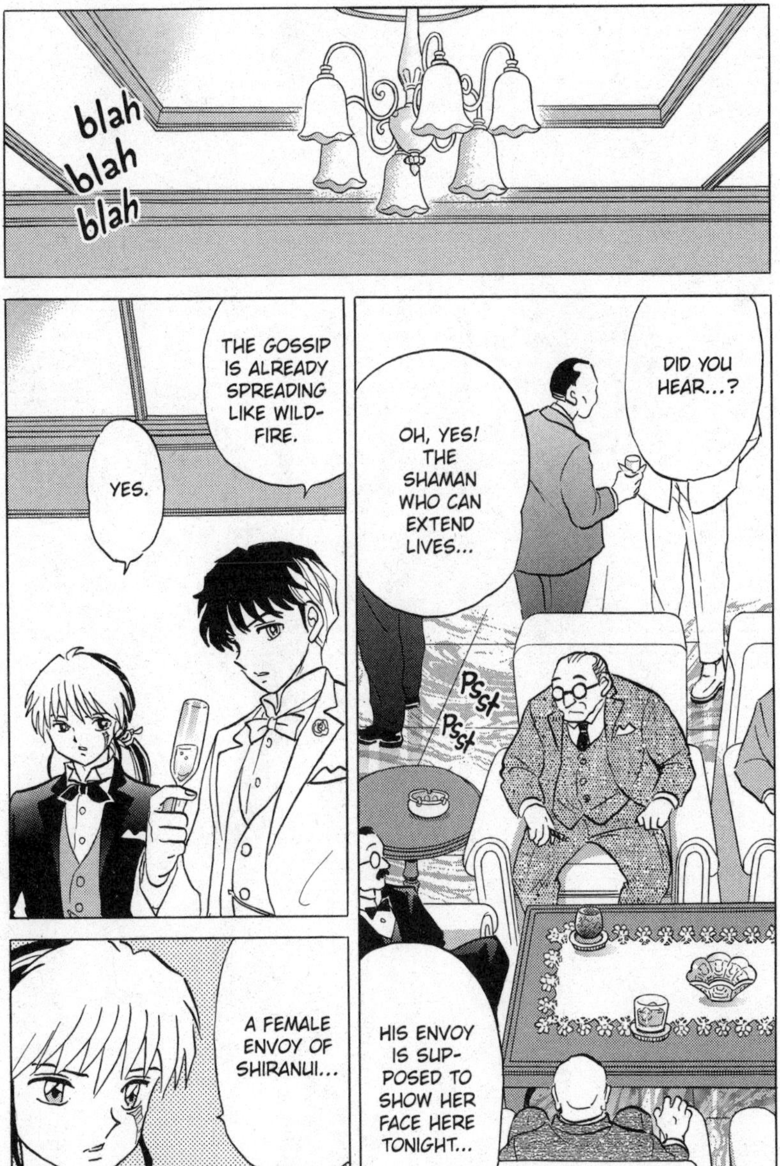
blah
blah
blah
DID YOU HEAR...?
OH, YES! THE SHAMAN WHO CAN EXTEND LIVES...
Psst
Psst
HIS ENVOY IS SUP-POSED TO SHOW HER FACE HERE TONIGHT...
THE GOSSIP IS ALREADY SPREADING LIKE WILD-FIRE.
YES.
A FEMALE ENVOY OF SHIRANUI...

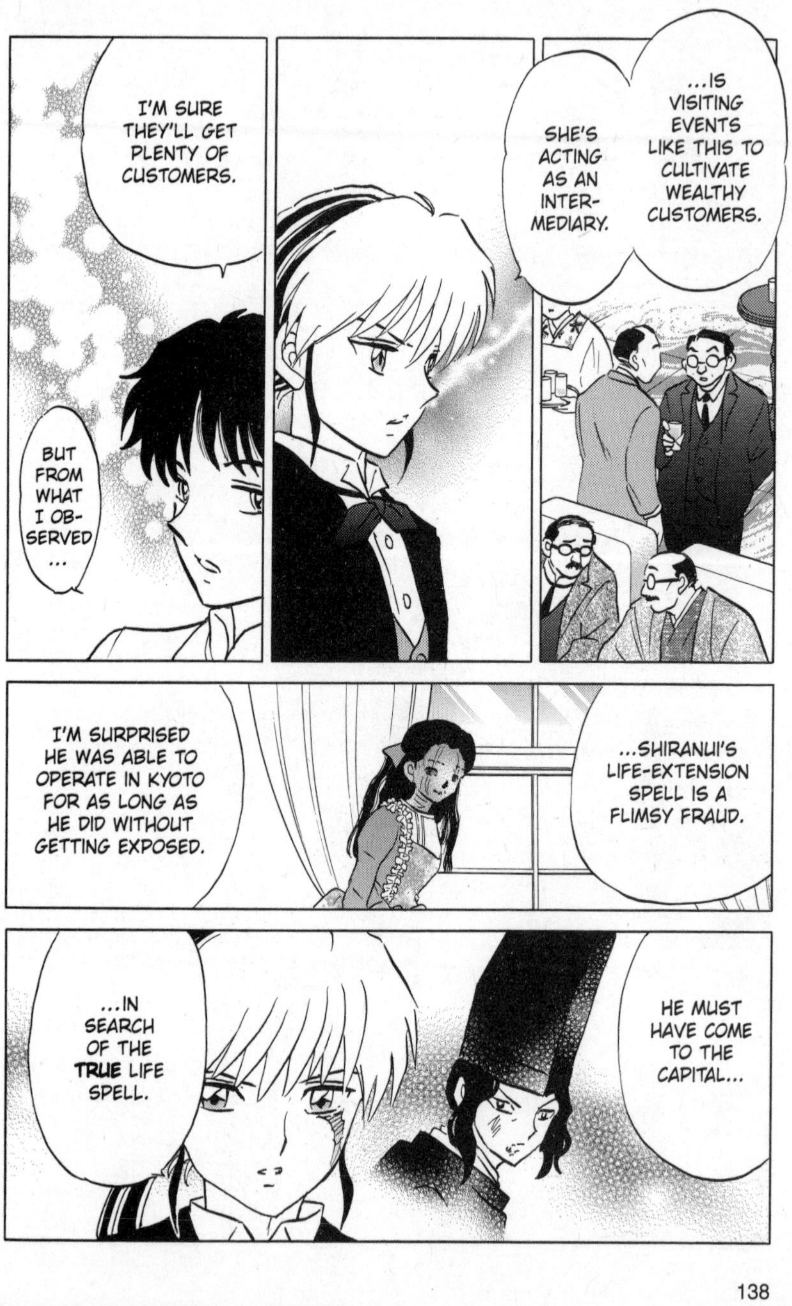
...IS VISITING EVENTS LIKE THIS TO CULTIVATE WEALTHY CUSTOMERS.
SHE'S ACTING AS AN INTER-MEDIARY.
I'M SURE THEY'LL GET PLENTY OF CUSTOMERS.
BUT FROM WHAT I OB-SERVED...
...SHIRANUI'S LIFE-EXTENSION SPELL IS A FLIMSY FRAUD.
I'M SURPRISED HE WAS ABLE TO OPERATE IN KYOTO FOR AS LONG AS HE DID WITHOUT GETTING EXPOSED.
HE MUST HAVE COME TO THE CAPITAL...
...IN SEARCH OF THE **TRUE** LIFE SPELL.

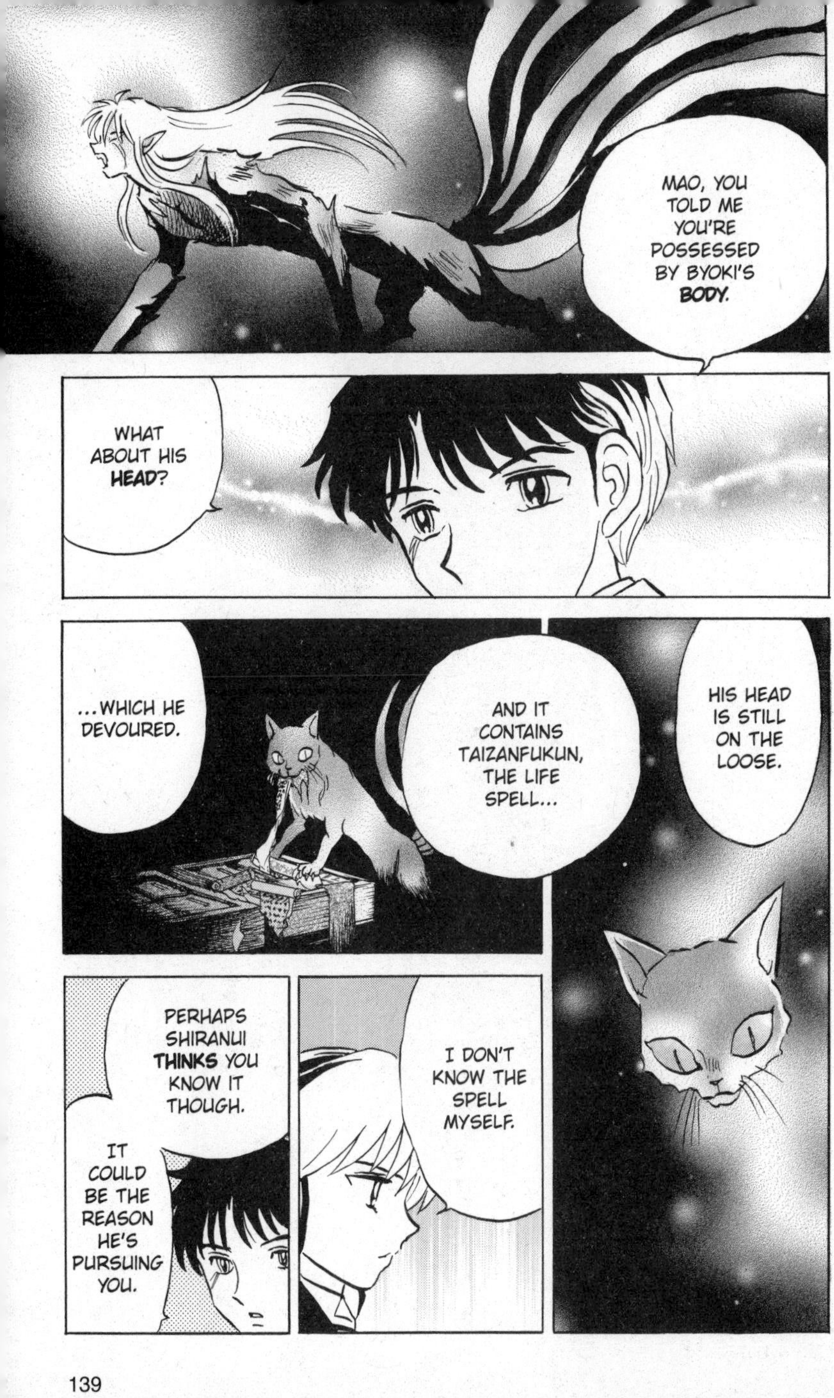
MAO, YOU TOLD ME YOU'RE POSSESSED BY BYOKI'S **BODY**.
WHAT ABOUT HIS **HEAD**?
HIS HEAD IS STILL ON THE LOOSE.
AND IT CONTAINS TAIZANFUKUN, THE LIFE SPELL...
...WHICH HE DEVOURED.
I DON'T KNOW THE SPELL MYSELF.
PERHAPS SHIRANUI **THINKS** YOU KNOW IT THOUGH.
IT COULD BE THE REASON HE'S PURSUING YOU.

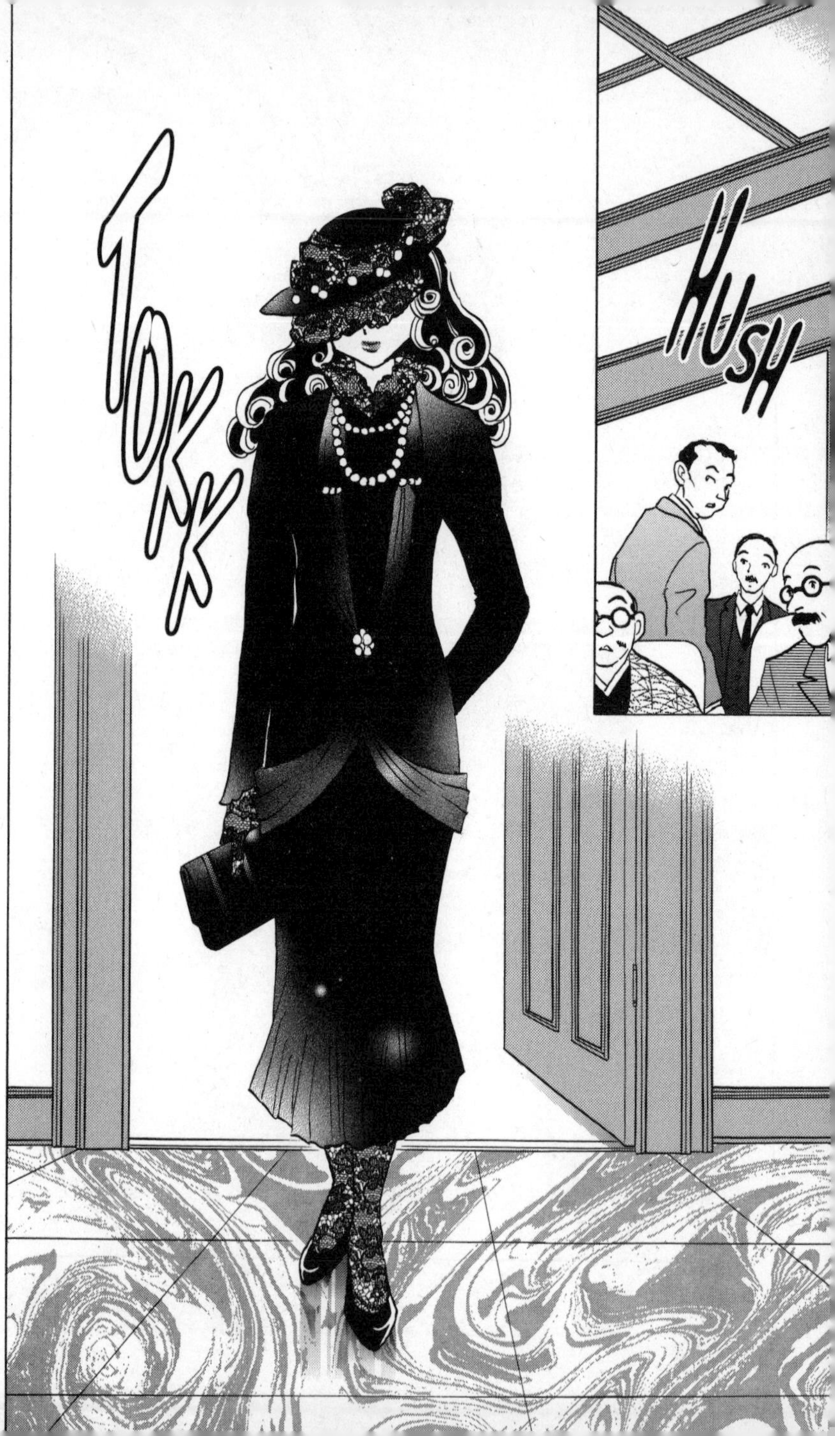
HUSH
TOKK

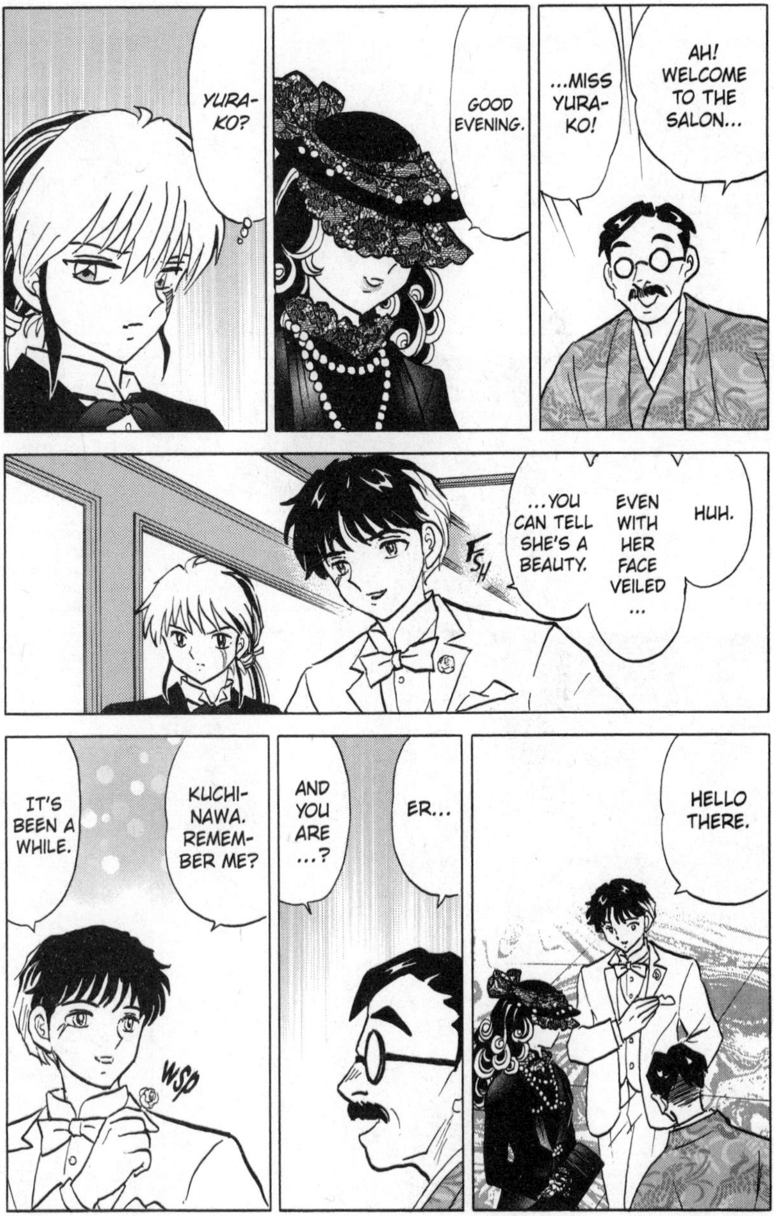
AH! WELCOME TO THE SALON...
...MISS YURA-KO!
GOOD EVENING.
YURA-KO?
HUH.
EVEN WITH HER FACE VEILED ...
...YOU CAN TELL SHE'S A BEAUTY.
FSH
HELLO THERE.
ER...
AND YOU ARE ...?
KUCHI-NAWA. REMEM-BER ME?
IT'S BEEN A WHILE.
WSP

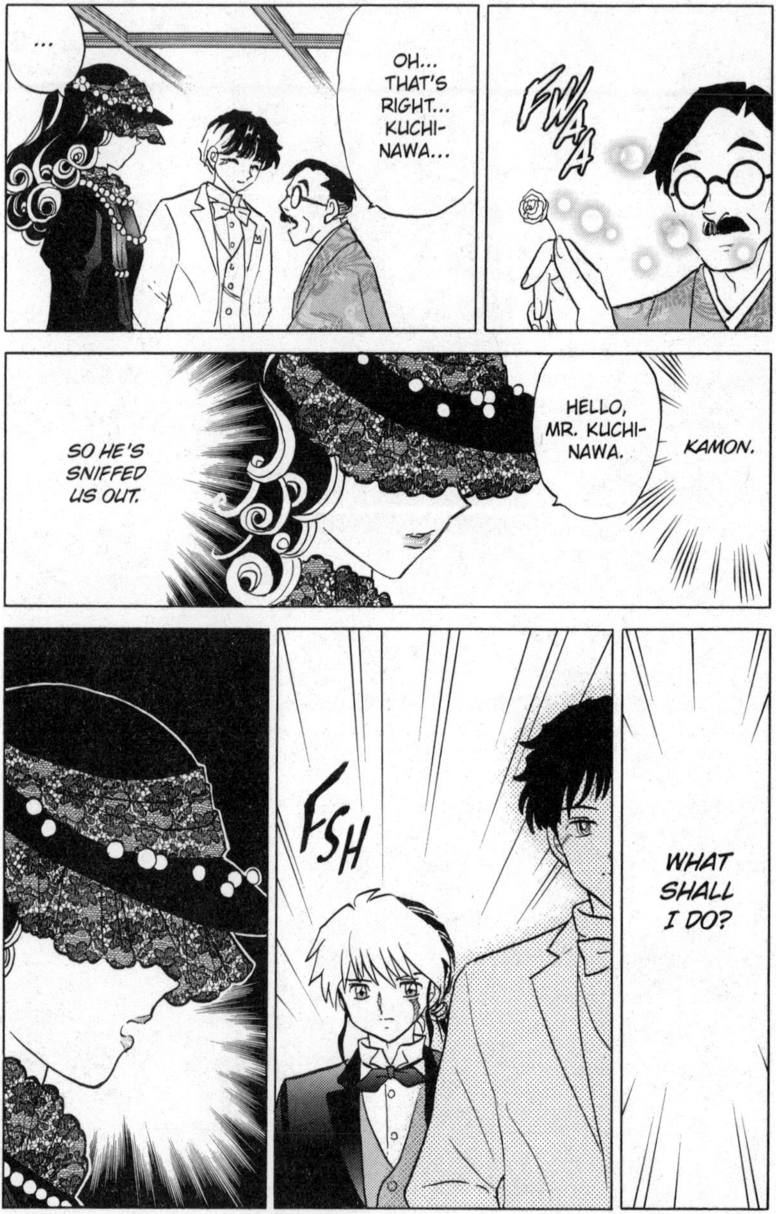
FWAA
OH... THAT'S RIGHT... KUCHI-NAWA...
...
KAMON.
HELLO, MR. KUCHI-NAWA.
SO HE'S SNIFFED US OUT.
WHAT SHALL I DO?
FSH

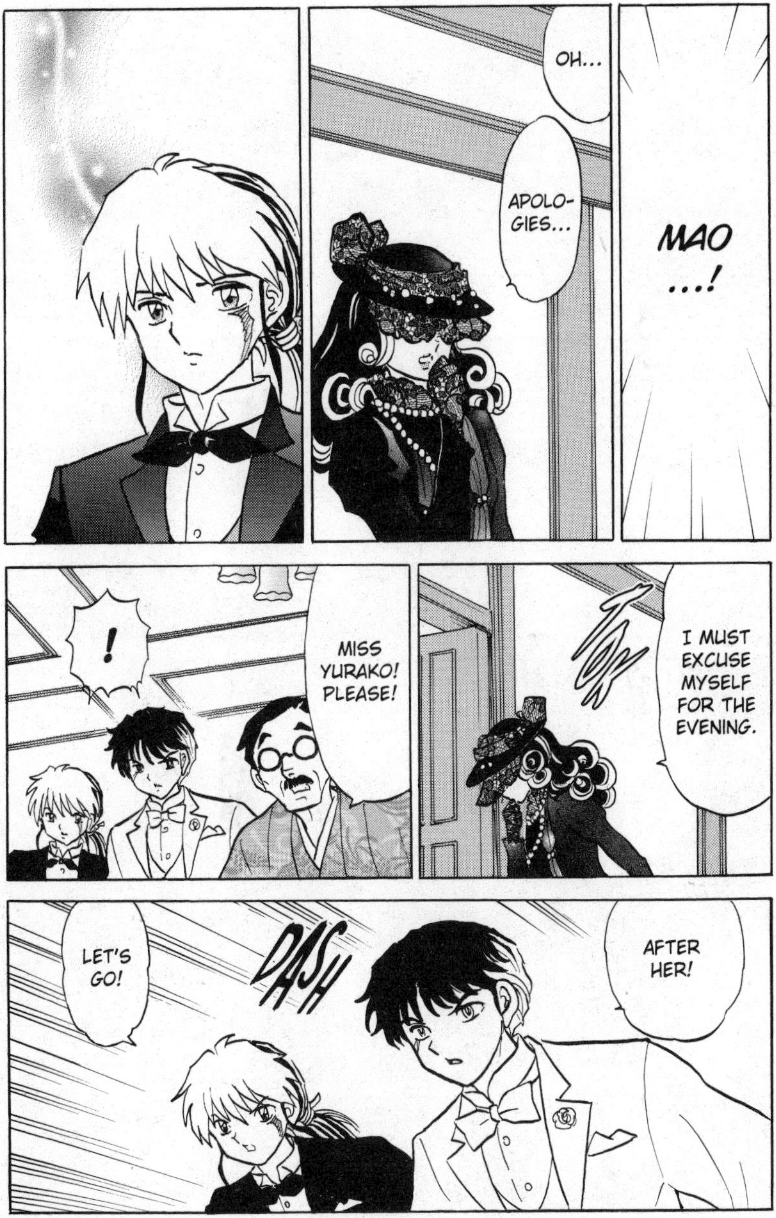
MAO ...!
OH...
APOLOGIES...
I MUST EXCUSE MYSELF FOR THE EVENING.
MISS YURAKO! PLEASE!
!
AFTER HER!
DASH
LET'S GO!

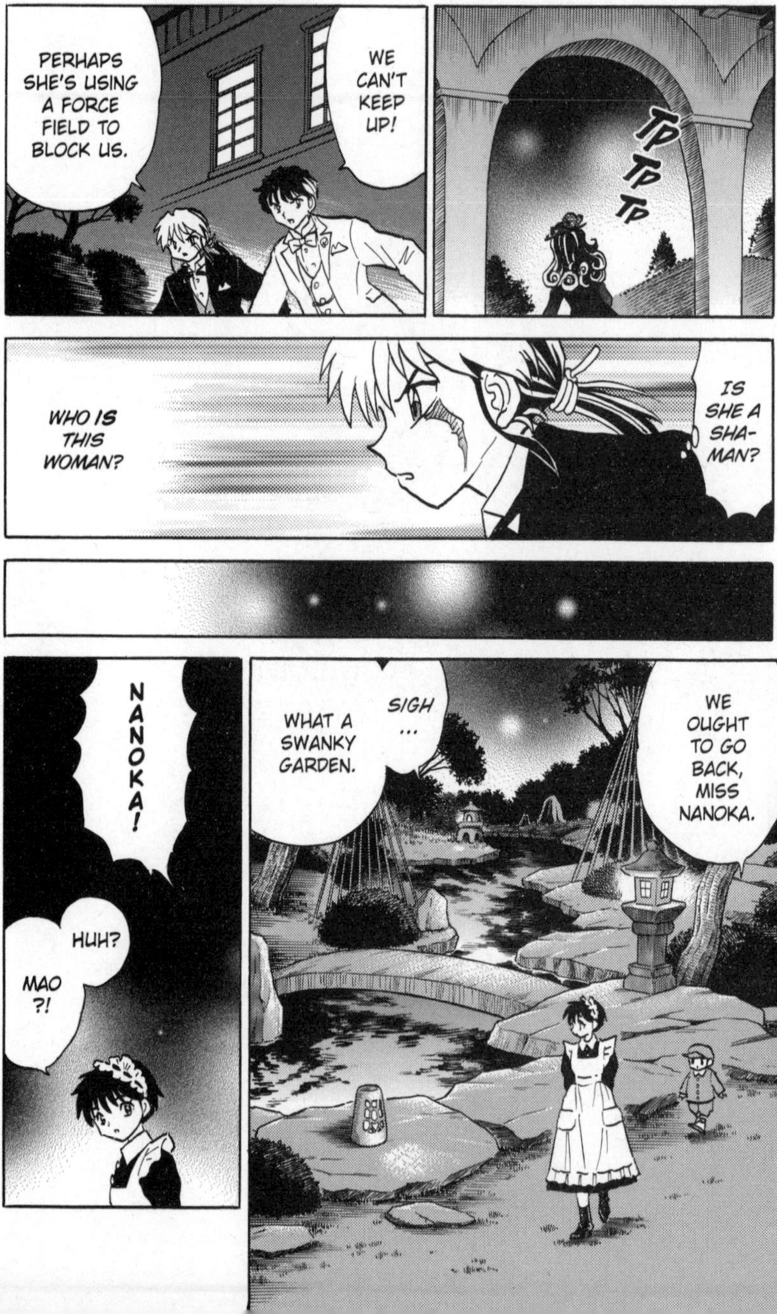
TP TP TP
WE CAN'T KEEP UP!
PERHAPS SHE'S USING A FORCE FIELD TO BLOCK US.
IS SHE A SHA-MAN?
WHO IS THIS WOMAN?
WE OUGHT TO GO BACK, MISS NANOKA.
SIGH...
WHAT A SWANKY GARDEN.
NANOKA!
HUH?
MAO?!

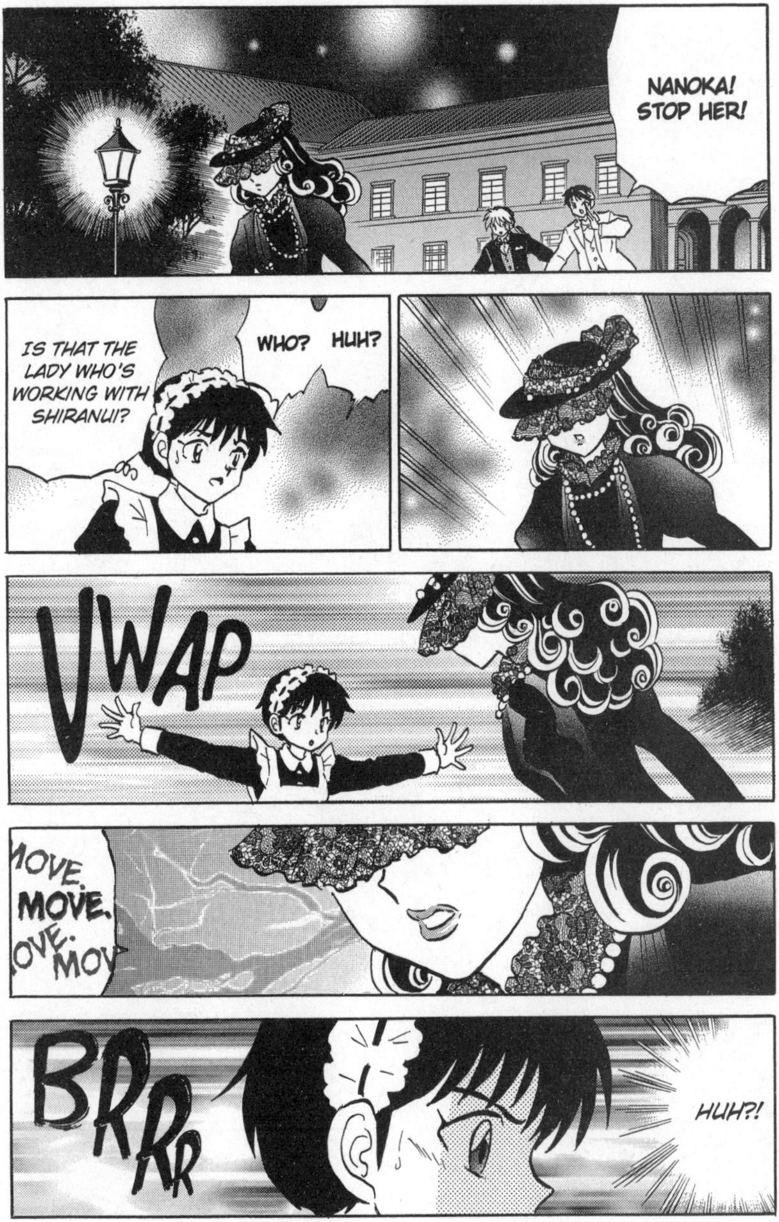
NANOKA! STOP HER!
HUH?
WHO?
IS THAT THE LADY WHO'S WORKING WITH SHIRANUI?
VWAP
MOVE. MOVE.
BRRRR
HUH?!

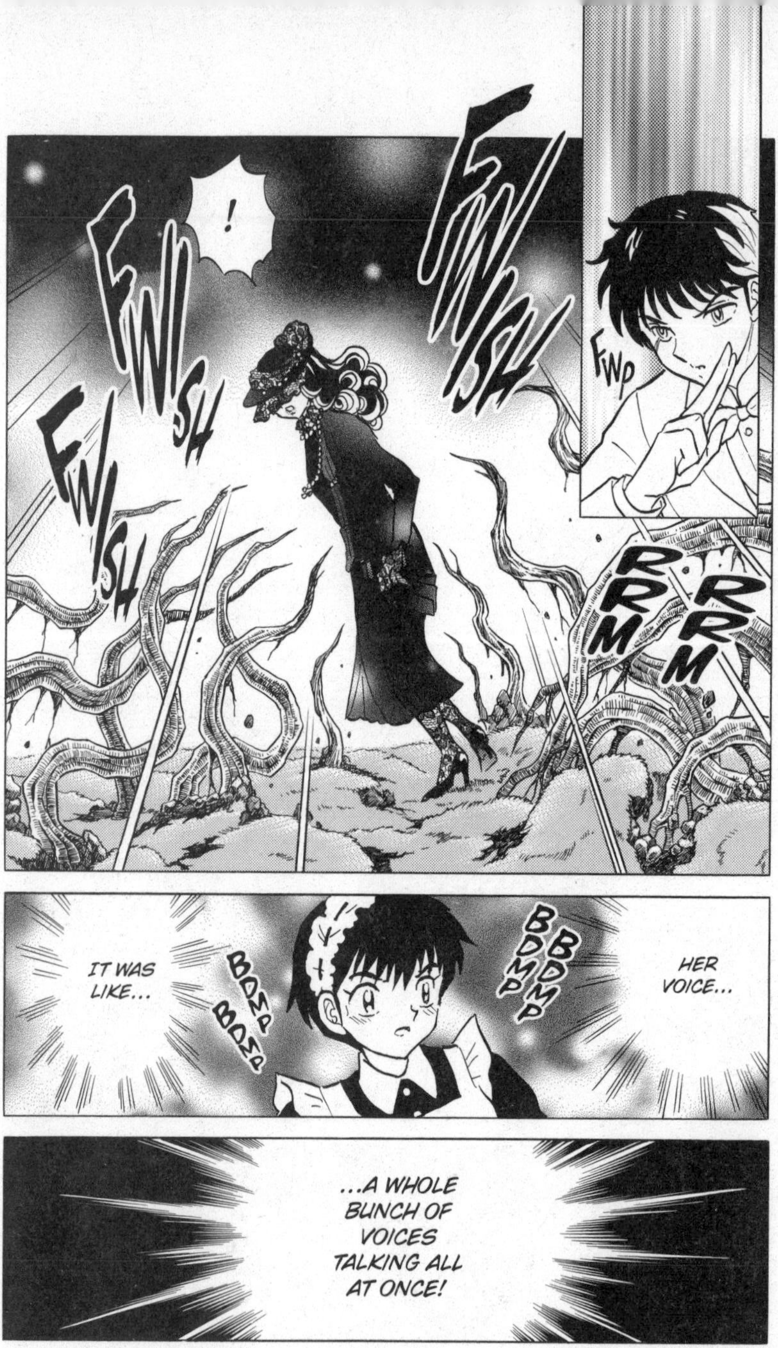
FWP
FWWISH
!
FWISH
FWISH
RRRM
RRRM
HER VOICE...
BDMP BDMP
BDMP BDMP
IT WAS LIKE...
...A WHOLE BUNCH OF VOICES TALKING ALL AT ONCE!

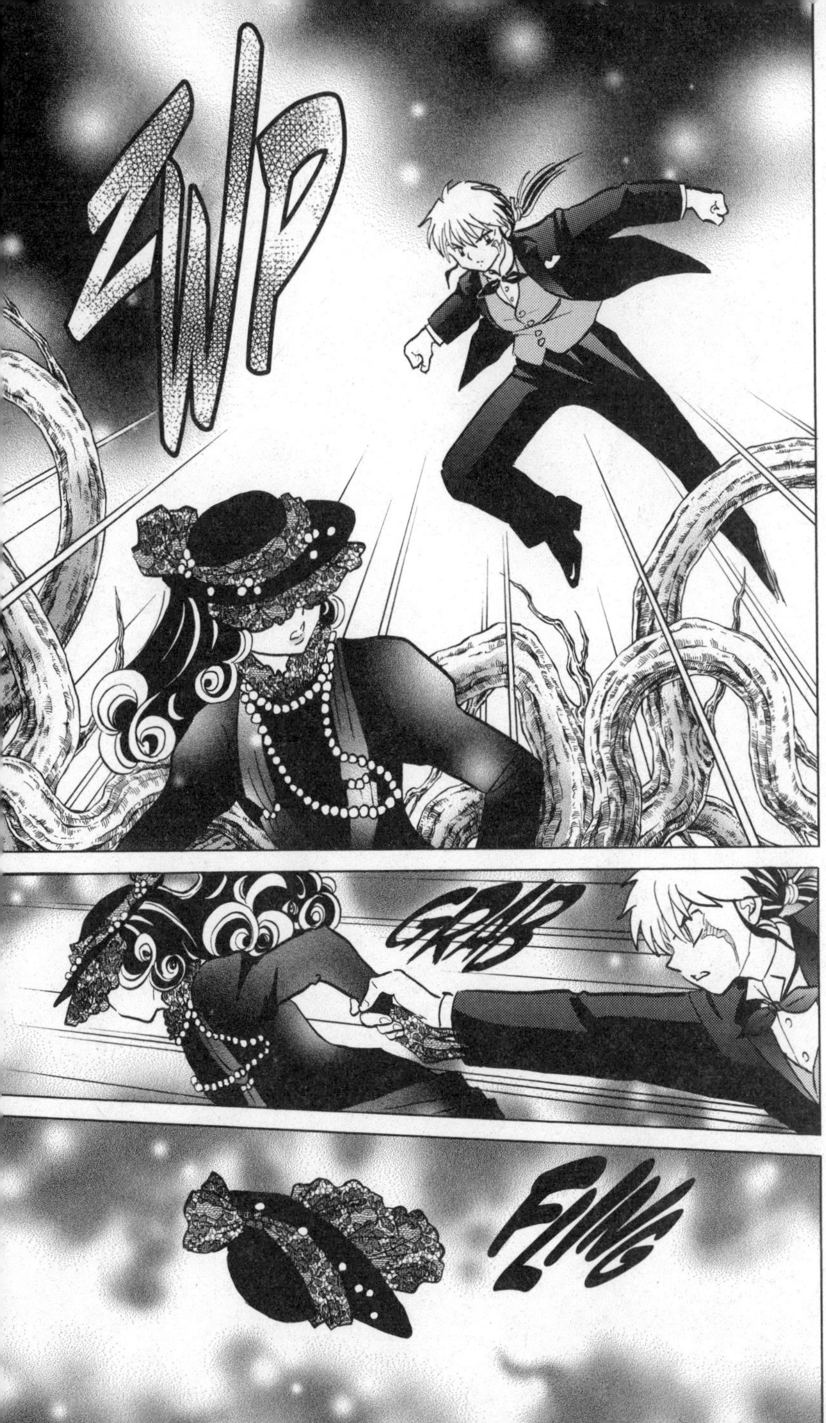
ZWIP
GRAB
FLING

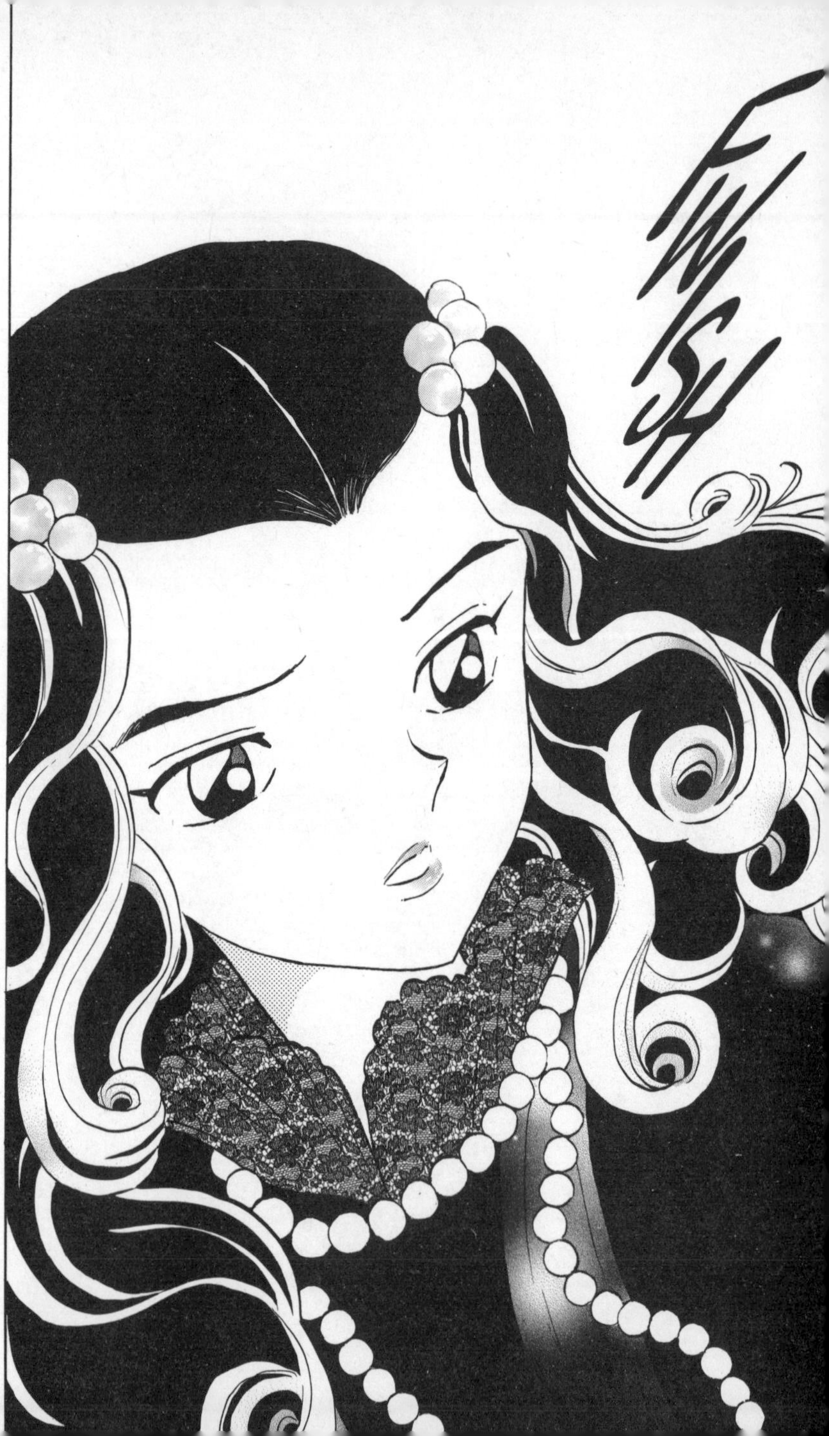
FWISH

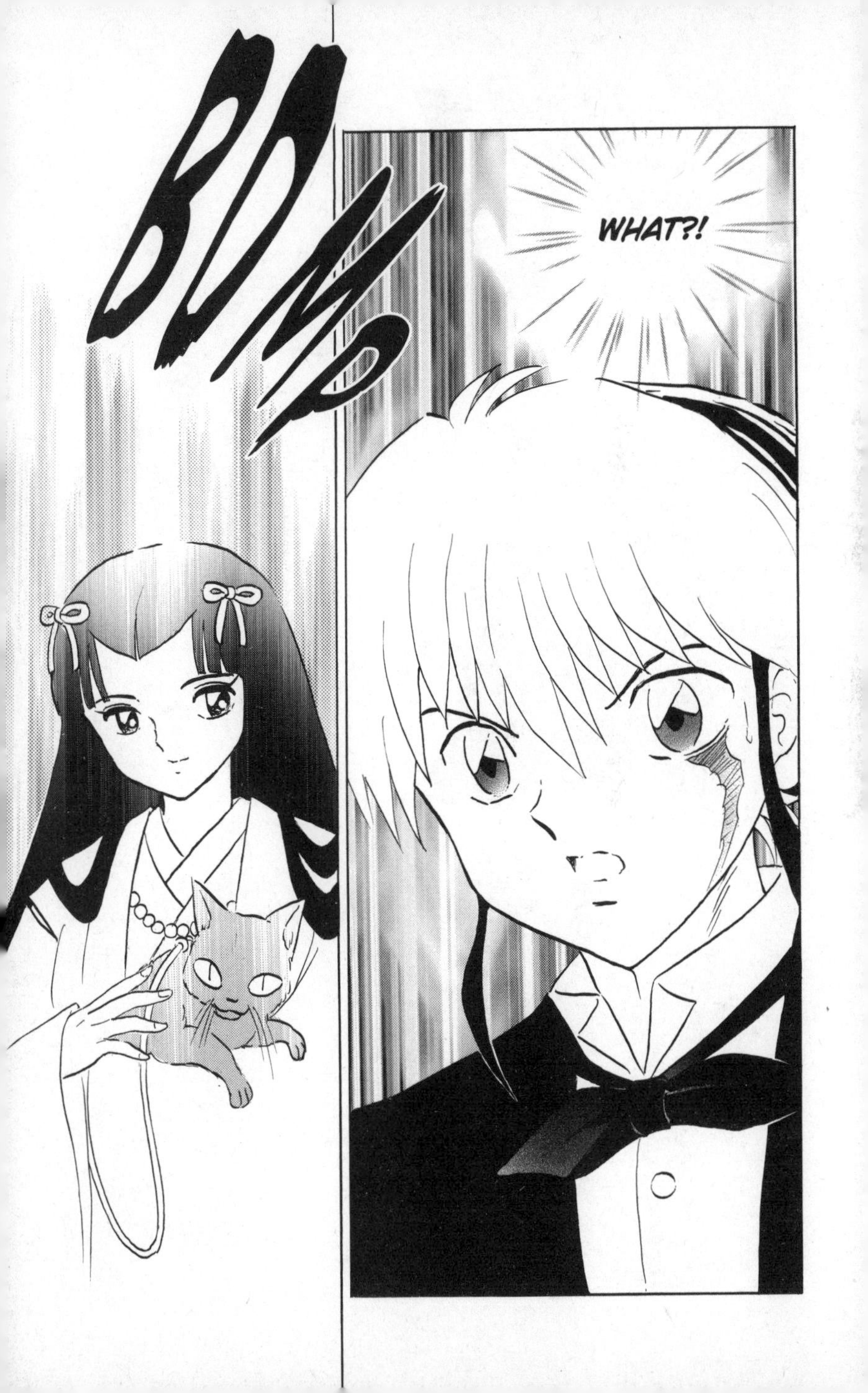
WHAT?!
BOMP

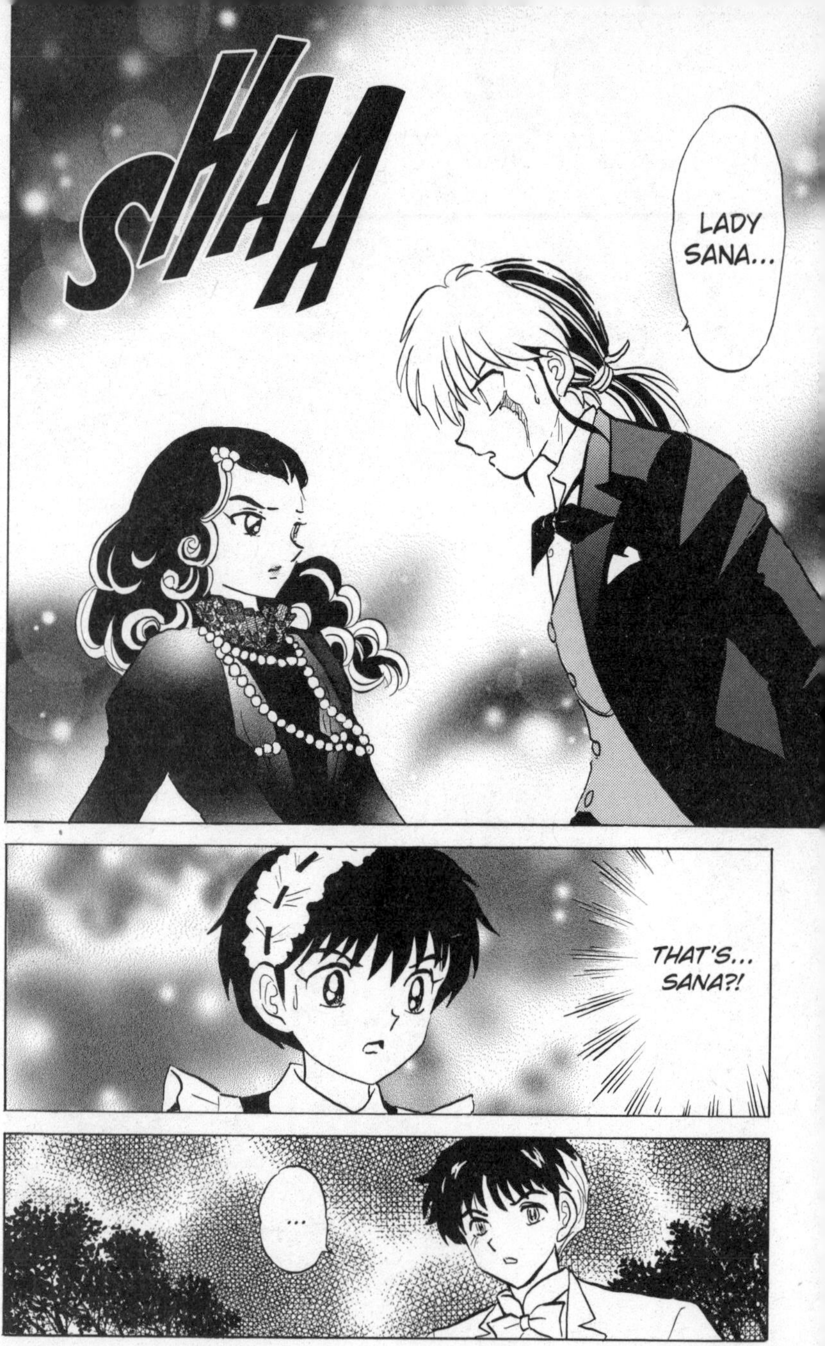
LADY SANA...
SHAA
THAT'S... SANA?!
...

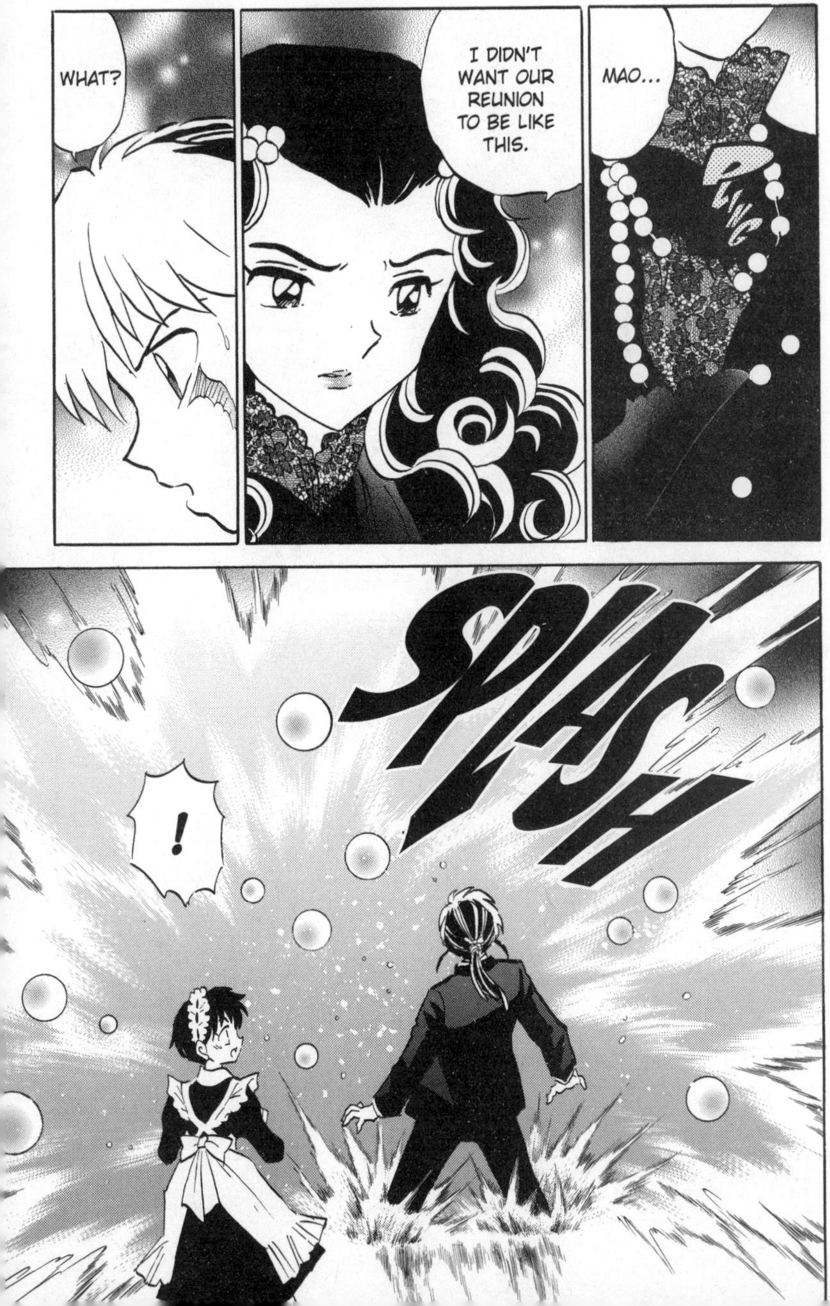
MAO...
CLING
I DIDN'T WANT OUR REUNION TO BE LIKE THIS.
WHAT?
SPLASH
!

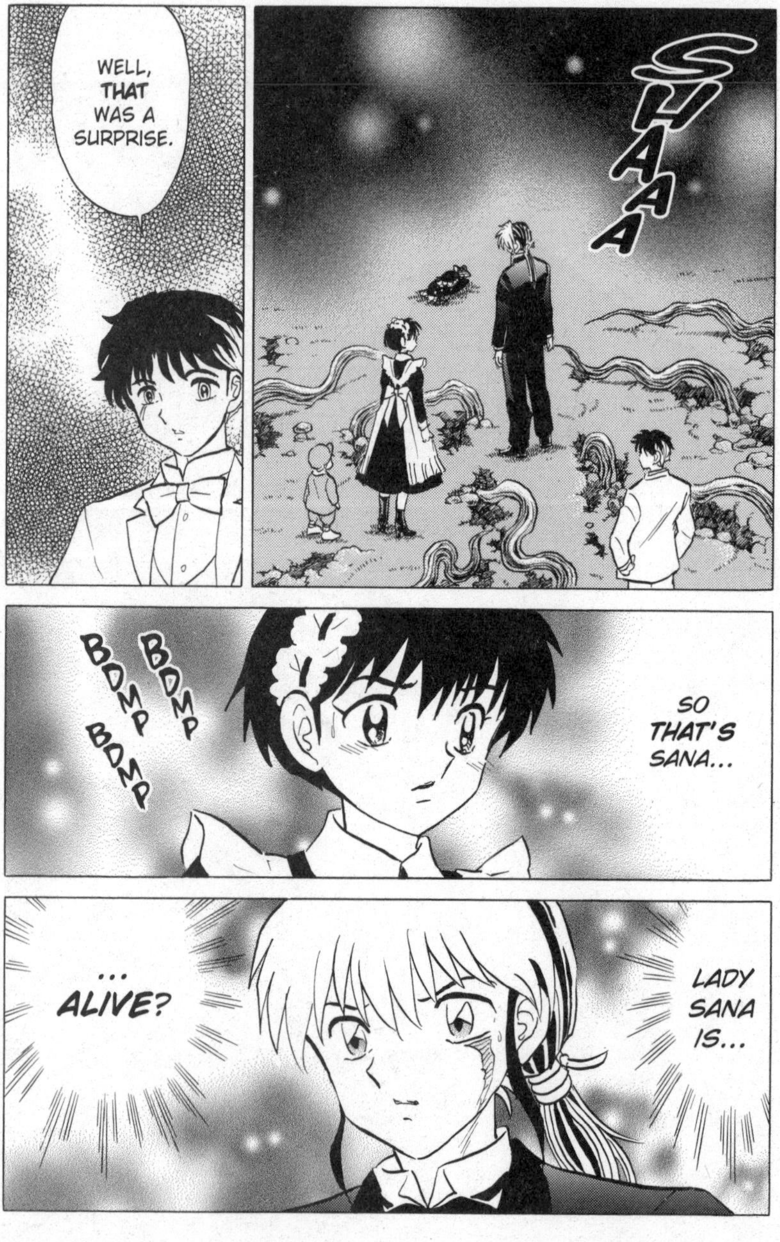
SHAAAA
WELL, THAT WAS A SURPRISE.
SO THAT'S SANA...
BDMP BDMP BDMP
LADY SANA IS...
... ALIVE?

Chapter 9:
Sana's End

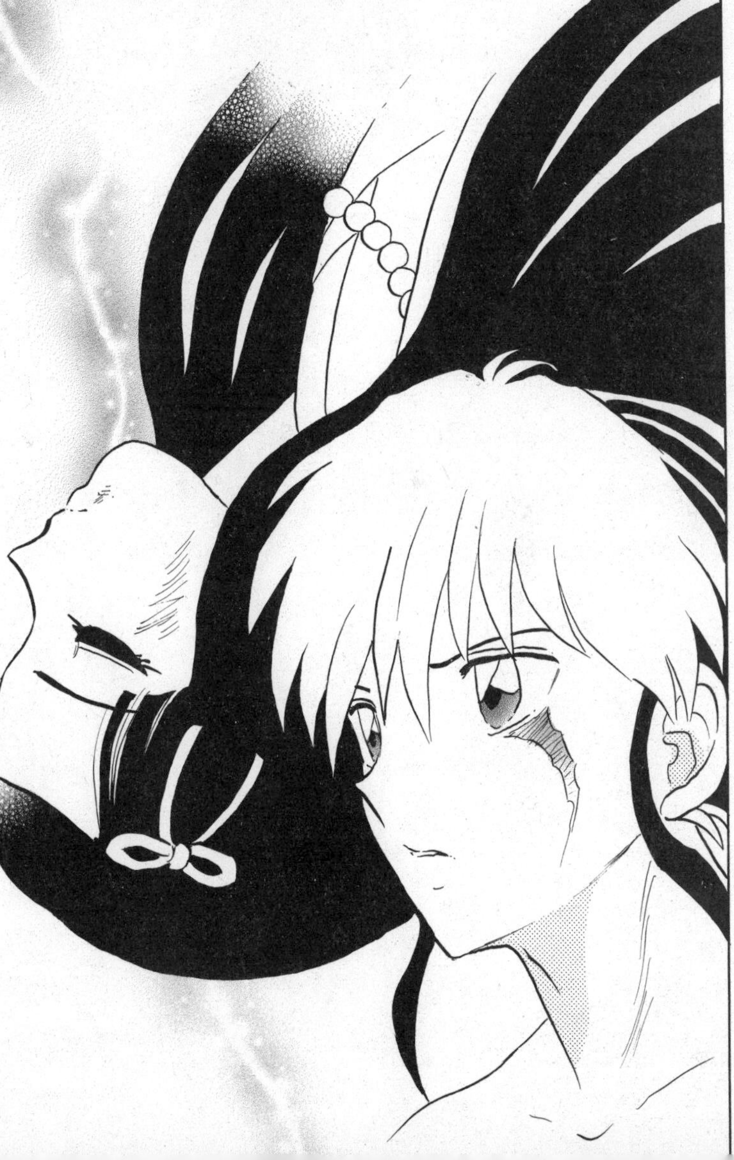

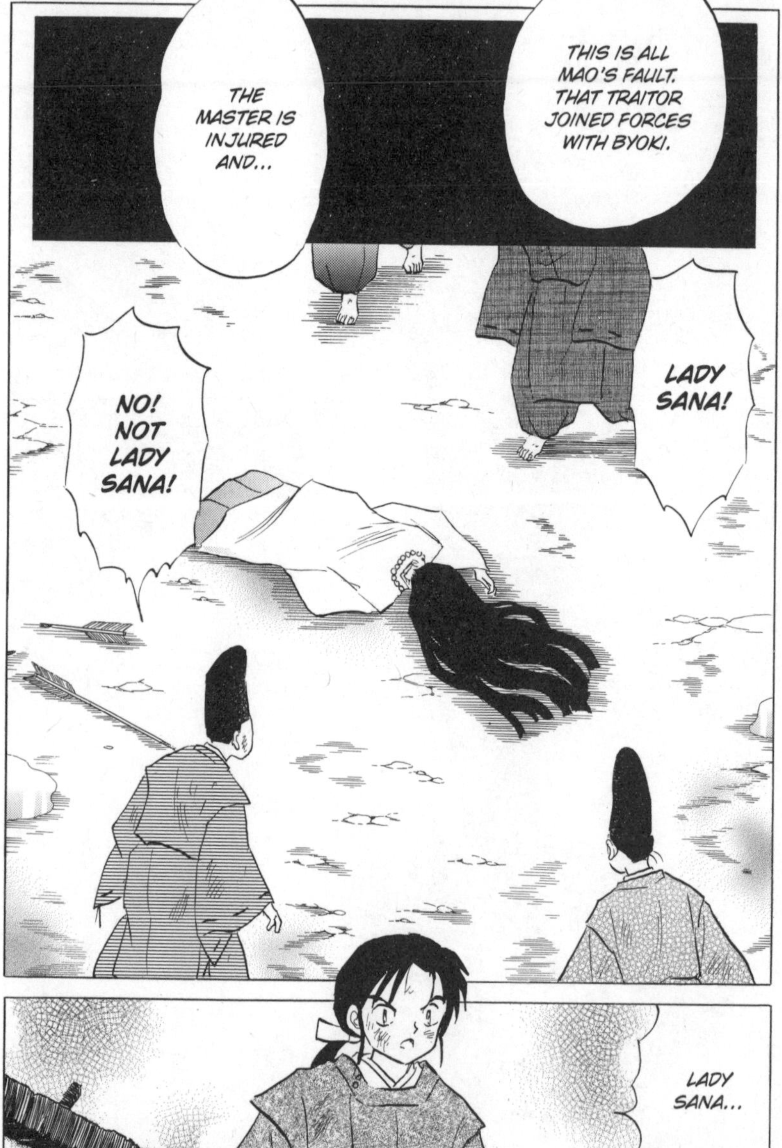
THIS IS ALL MAO'S FAULT. THAT TRAITOR JOINED FORCES WITH BYOKI.
THE MASTER IS INJURED AND...
LADY SANA!
NO! NOT LADY SANA!
LADY SANA...

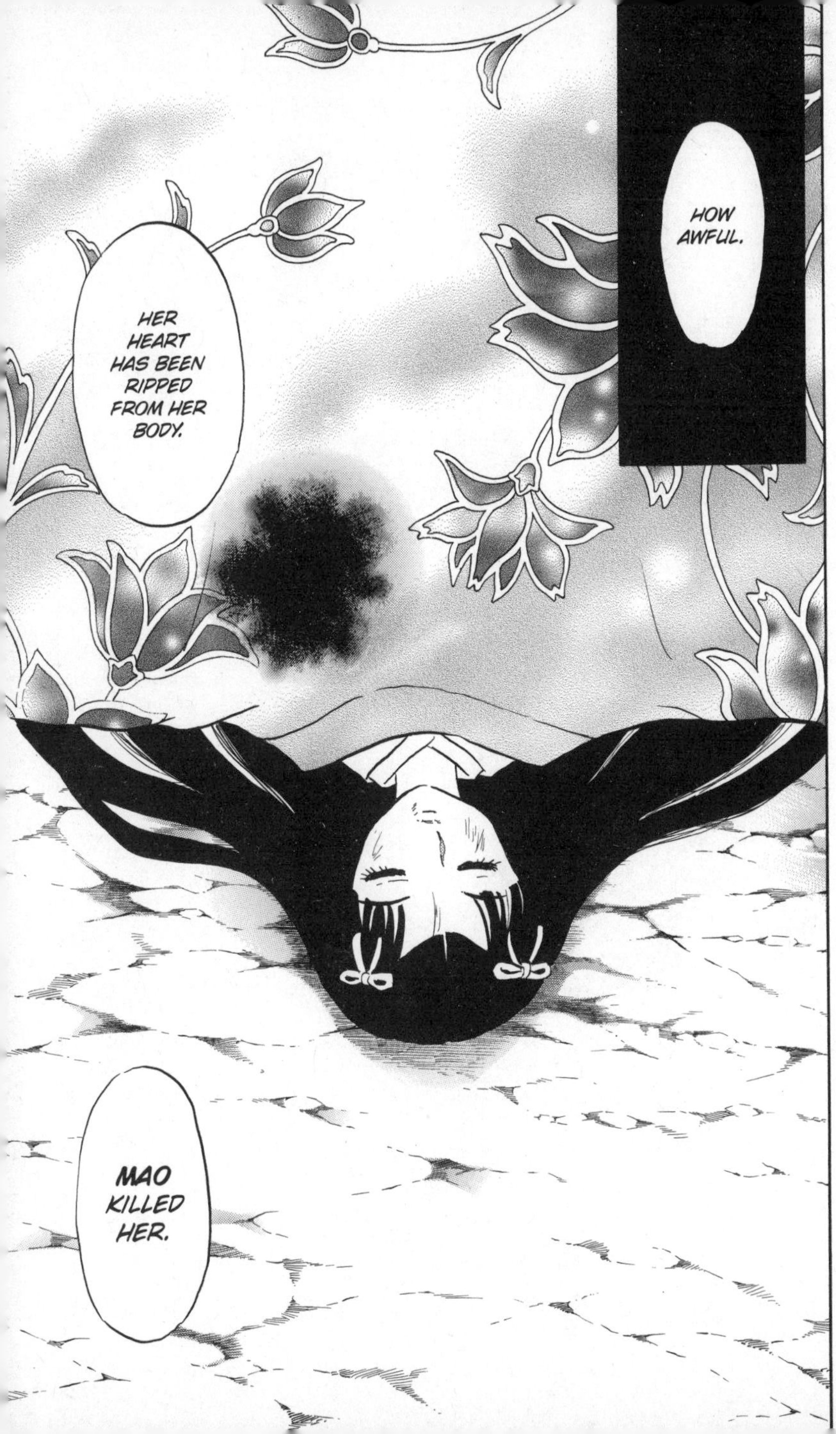
HOW AWFUL.
HER HEART HAS BEEN RIPPED FROM HER BODY.
MAO KILLED HER.

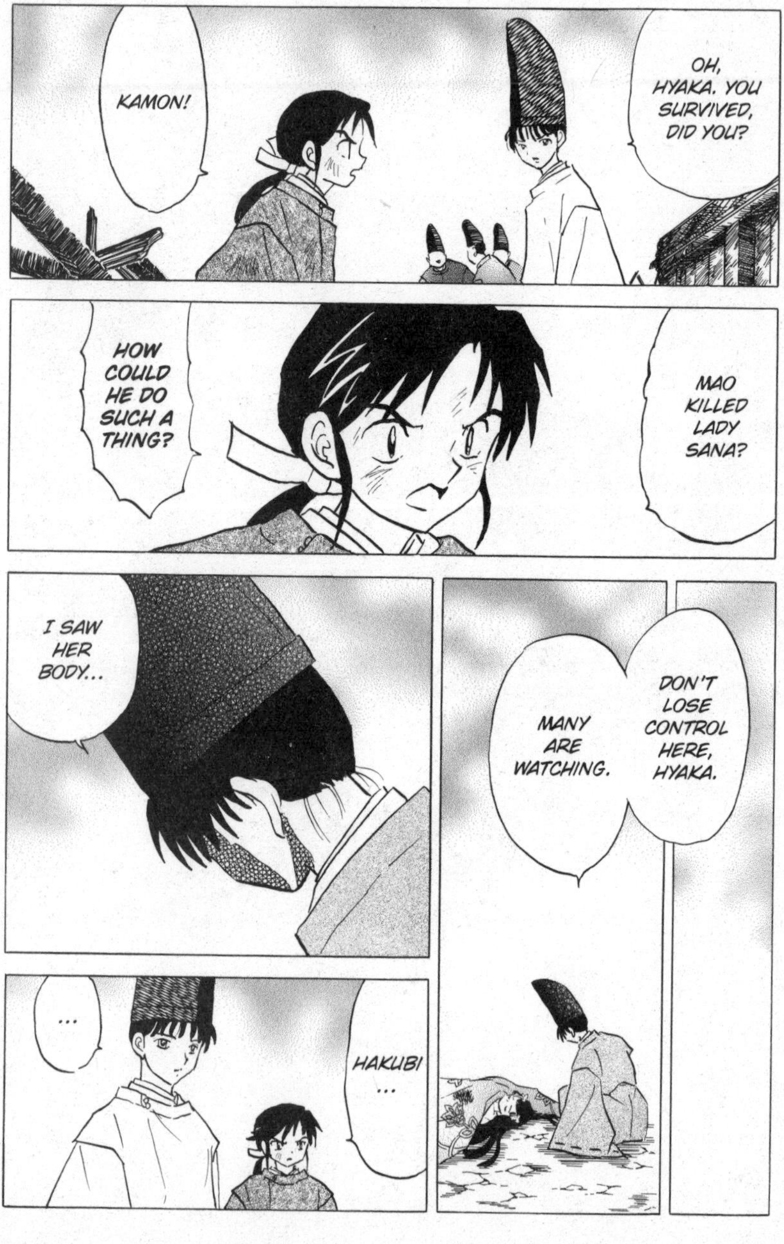

OH, HYAKA. YOU SURVIVED, DID YOU?
KAMON!
MAO KILLED LADY SANA?
HOW COULD HE DO SUCH A THING?
DON'T LOSE CONTROL HERE, HYAKA.
MANY ARE WATCHING.
I SAW HER BODY...
HAKUBI ...
...

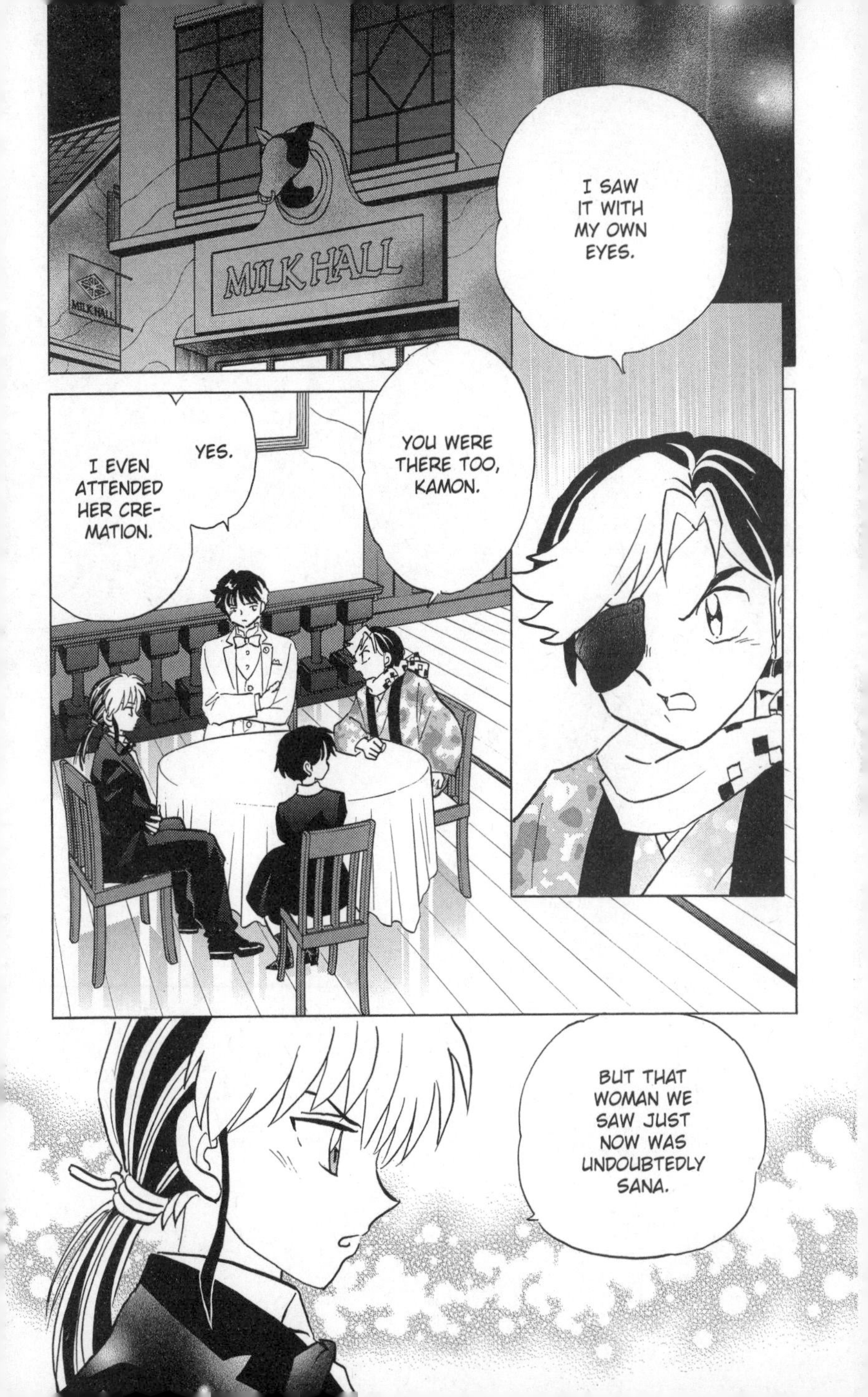
MILK HALL
MILK HALL
I SAW IT WITH MY OWN EYES.
YOU WERE THERE TOO, KAMON.
YES.
I EVEN ATTENDED HER CRE-MATION.
BUT THAT WOMAN WE SAW JUST NOW WAS UNDOUBTEDLY SANA.

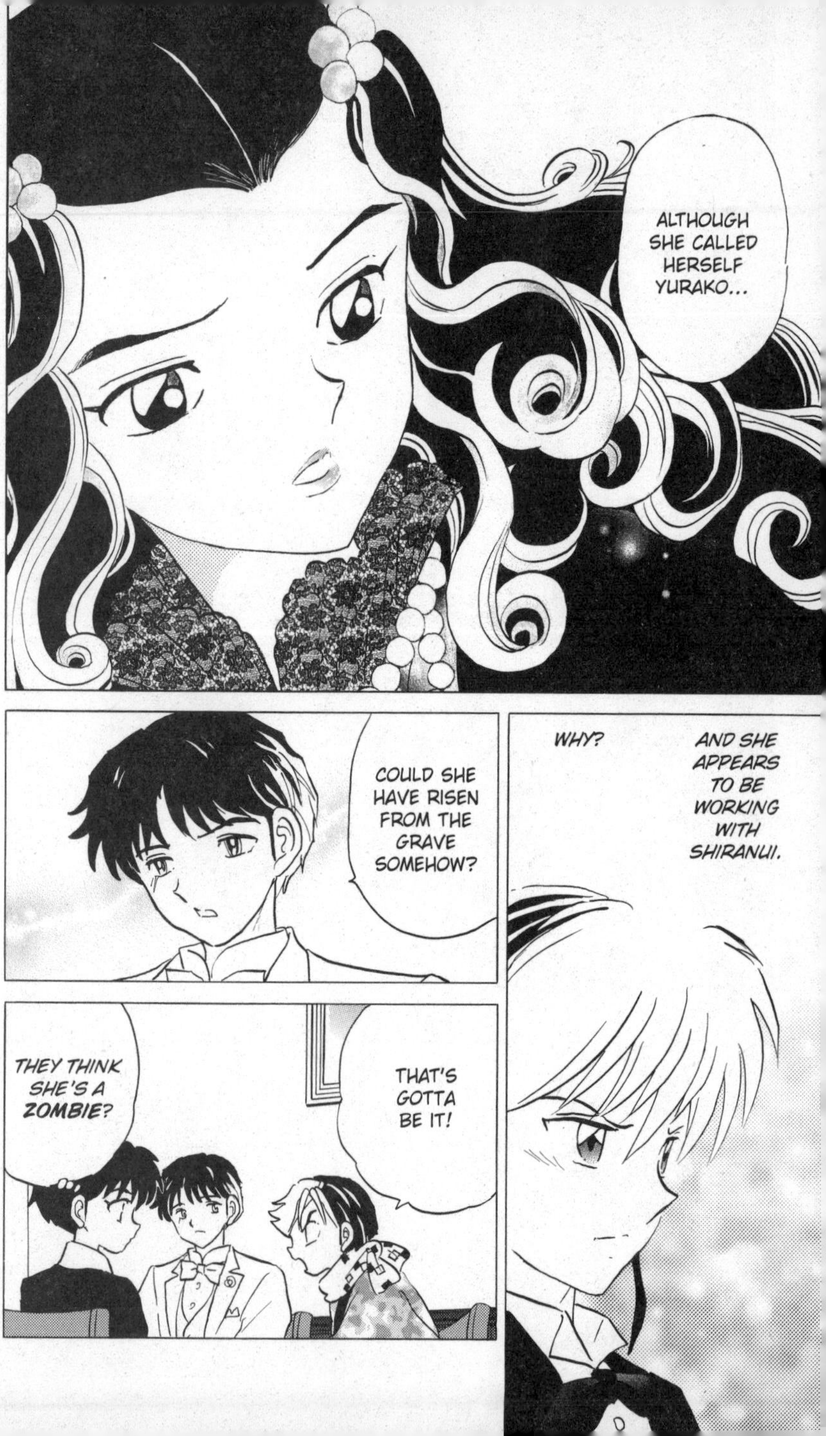
ALTHOUGH SHE CALLED HERSELF YURAKO...
AND SHE APPEARS TO BE WORKING WITH SHIRANUI.
WHY?
COULD SHE HAVE RISEN FROM THE GRAVE SOMEHOW?
THAT'S GOTTA BE IT!
THEY THINK SHE'S A ZOMBIE?

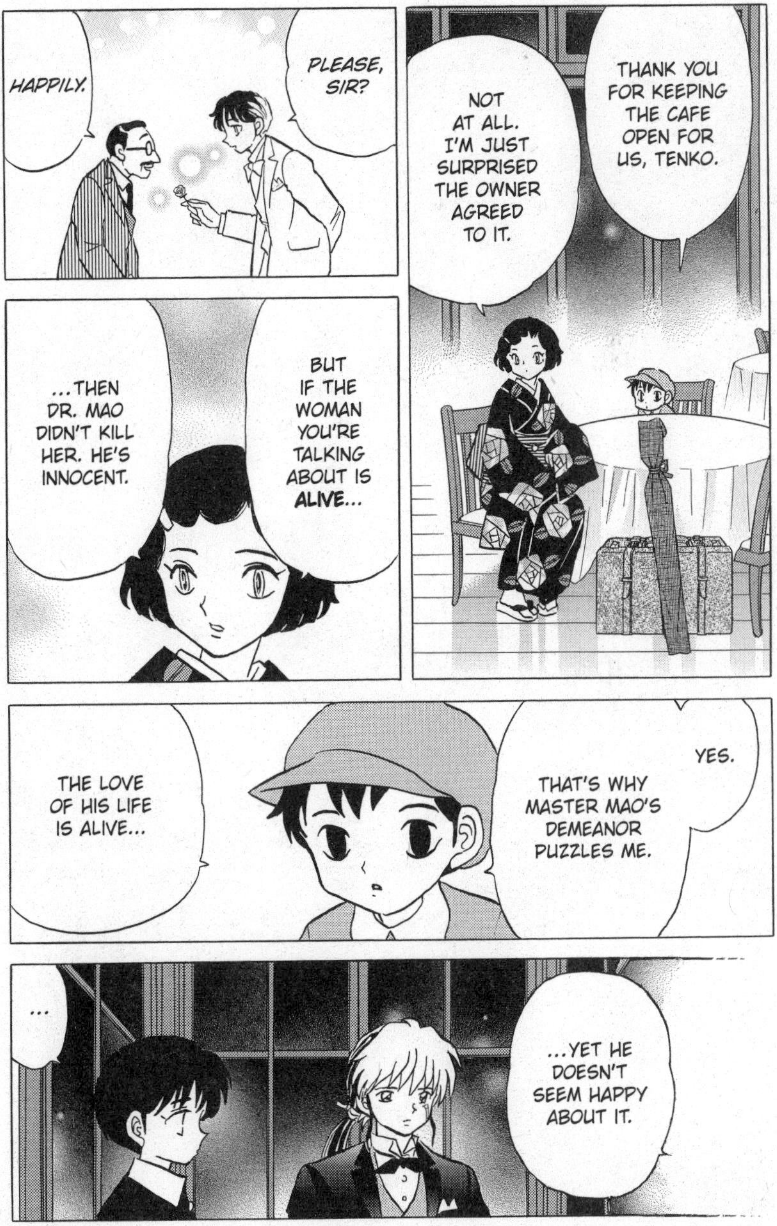
THANK YOU FOR KEEPING THE CAFE OPEN FOR US, TENKO.
NOT AT ALL. I'M JUST SURPRISED THE OWNER AGREED TO IT.
PLEASE, SIR?
HAPPILY.
BUT IF THE WOMAN YOU'RE TALKING ABOUT IS ALIVE...
...THEN DR. MAO DIDN'T KILL HER. HE'S INNOCENT.
YES.
THAT'S WHY MASTER MAO'S DEMEANOR PUZZLES ME.
THE LOVE OF HIS LIFE IS ALIVE...
...YET HE DOESN'T SEEM HAPPY ABOUT IT.
...

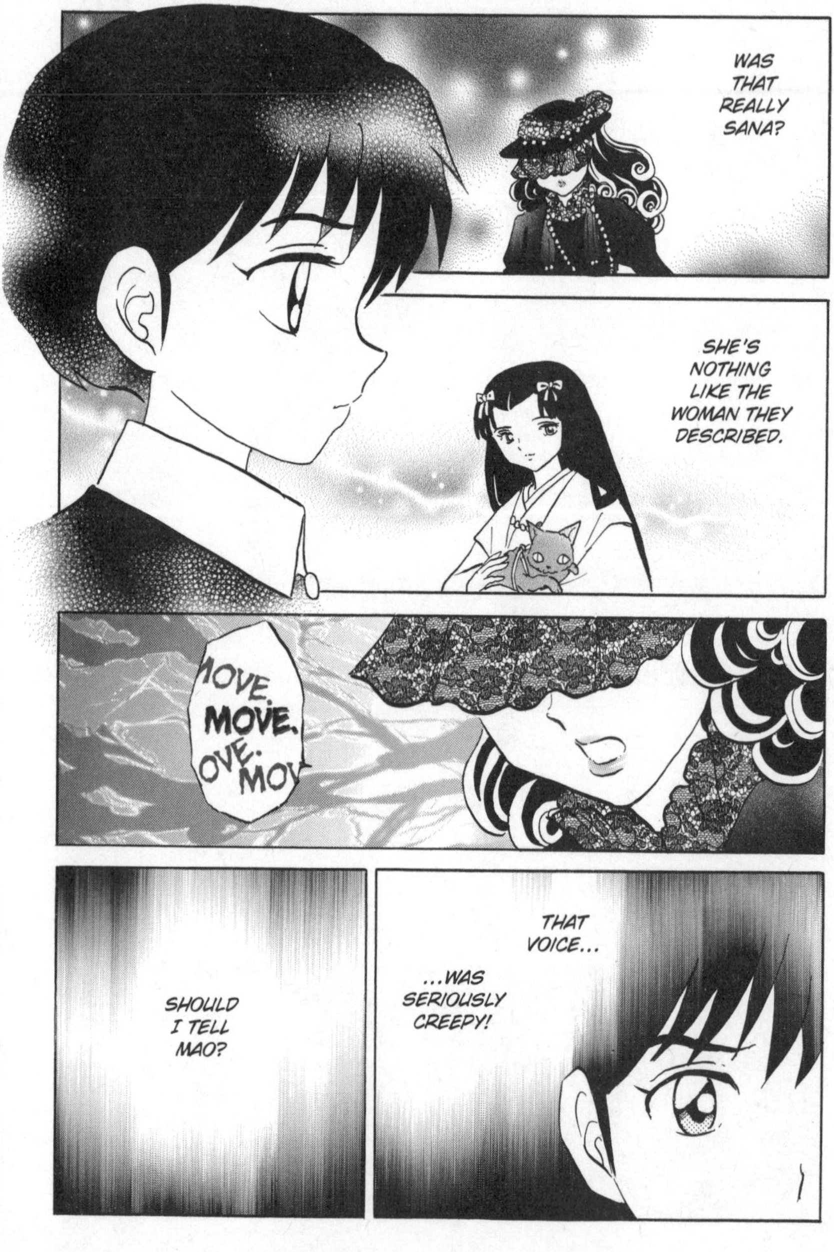
WAS THAT REALLY SANA?
SHE'S NOTHING LIKE THE WOMAN THEY DESCRIBED.
MOVE. MOVE. MOVE. MOVE. MOV
THAT VOICE...
...WAS SERIOUSLY CREEPY!
SHOULD I TELL MAO?

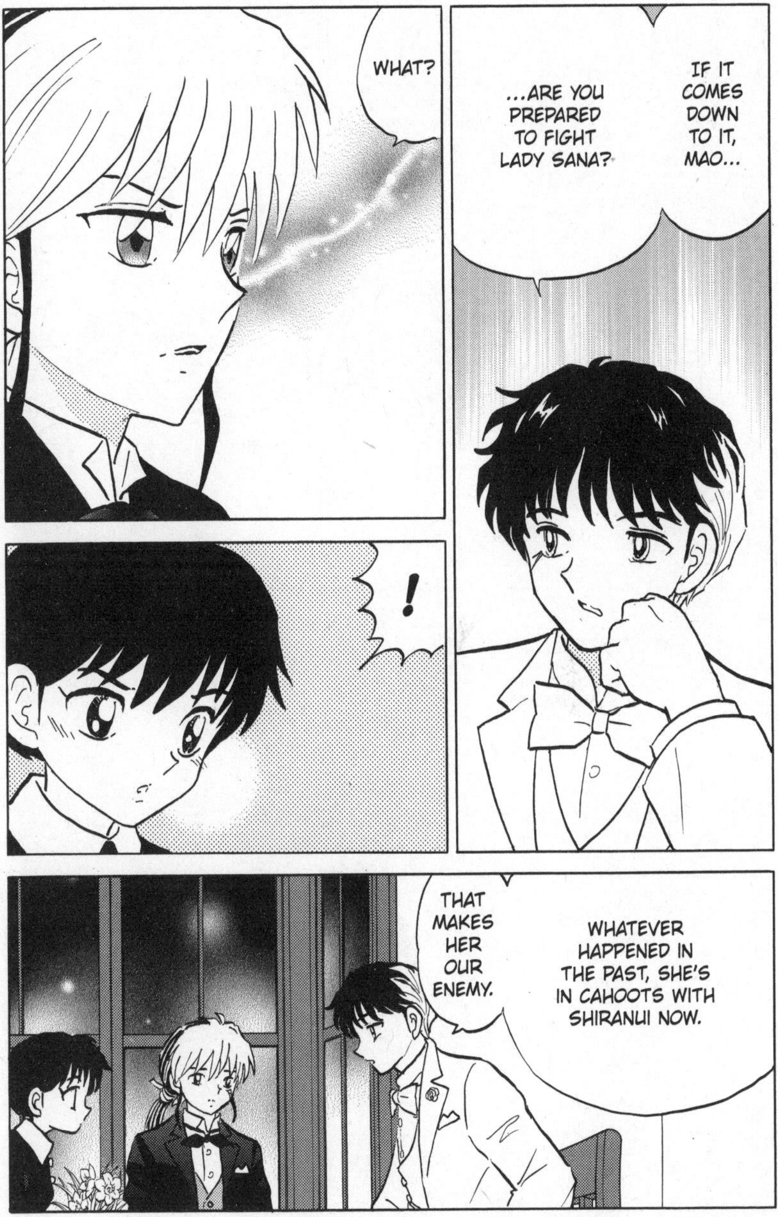
IF IT COMES DOWN TO IT, MAO...
...ARE YOU PREPARED TO FIGHT LADY SANA?
WHAT?
!
WHATEVER HAPPENED IN THE PAST, SHE'S IN CAHOOTS WITH SHIRANUI NOW.
THAT MAKES HER OUR ENEMY.

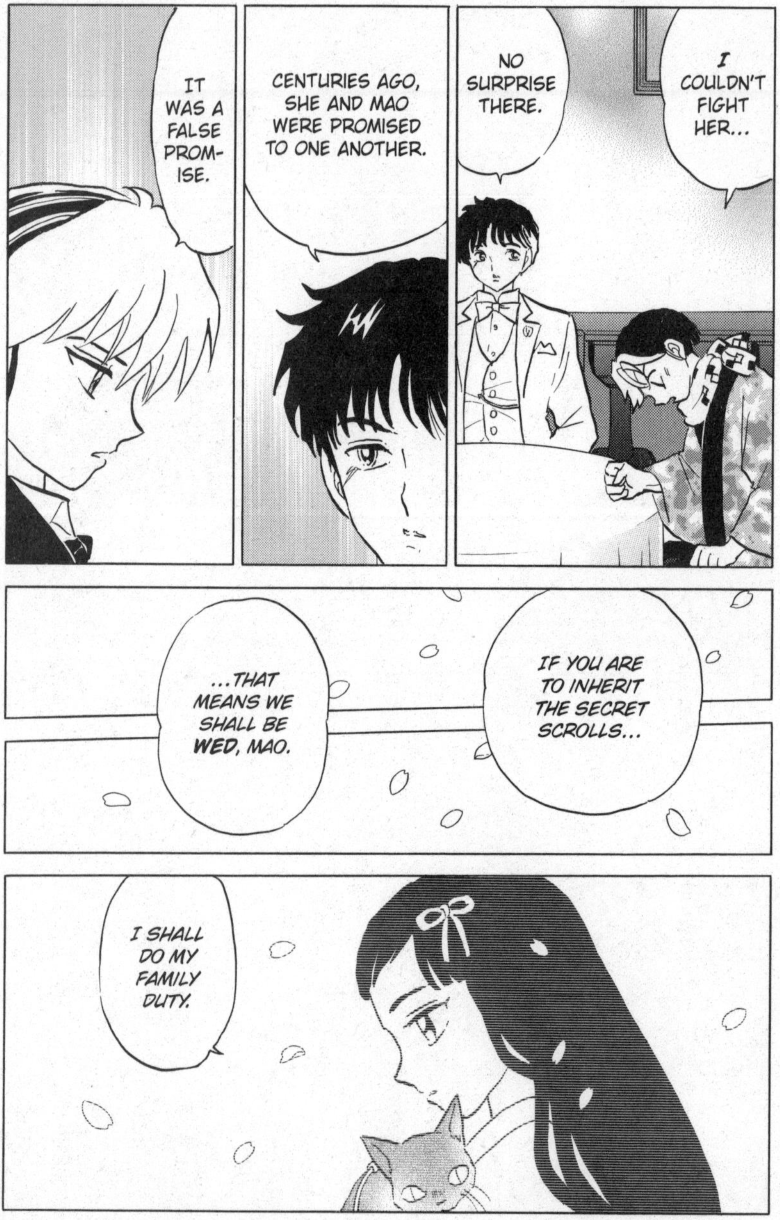
I COULDN'T FIGHT HER...
NO SURPRISE THERE.
CENTURIES AGO, SHE AND MAO WERE PROMISED TO ONE ANOTHER.
IT WAS A FALSE PROM-ISE.
IF YOU ARE TO INHERIT THE SECRET SCROLLS...
...THAT MEANS WE SHALL BE **WED**, MAO.
I SHALL DO MY FAMILY DUTY.

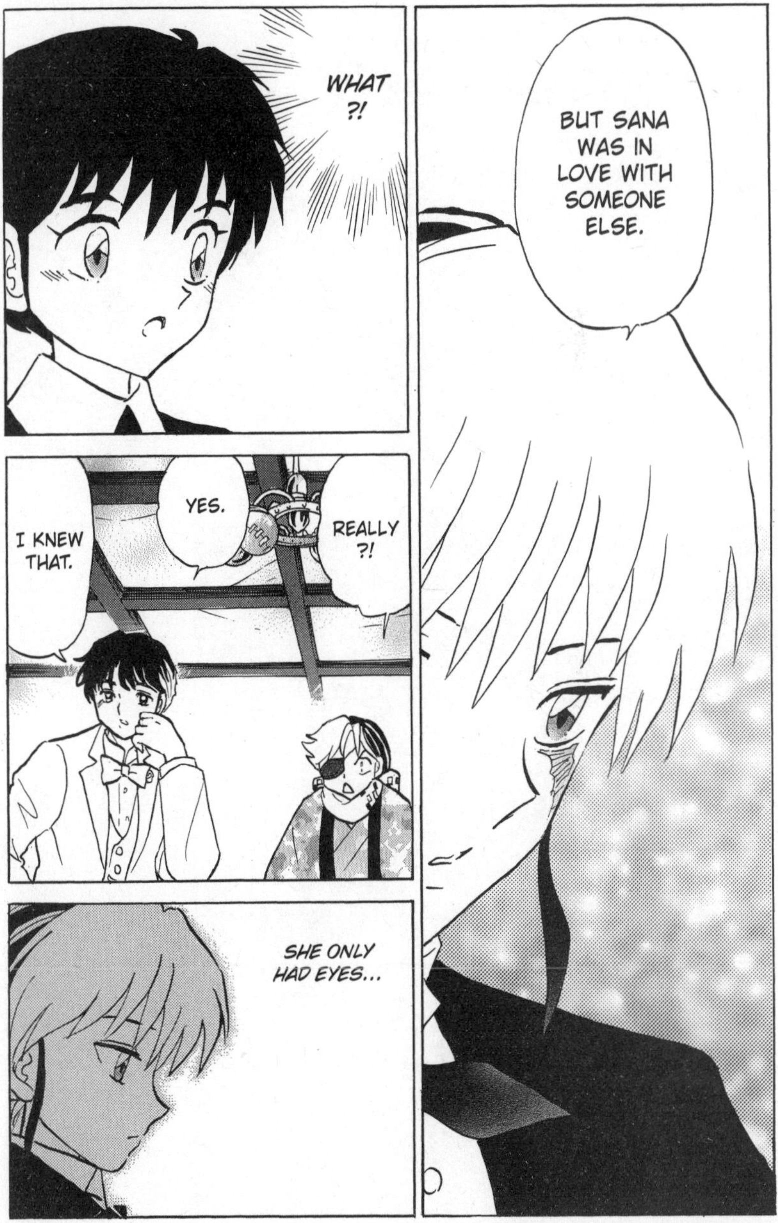
BUT SANA WAS IN LOVE WITH SOMEONE ELSE.
WHAT ?!
REALLY ?!
YES.
I KNEW THAT.
SHE ONLY HAD EYES...

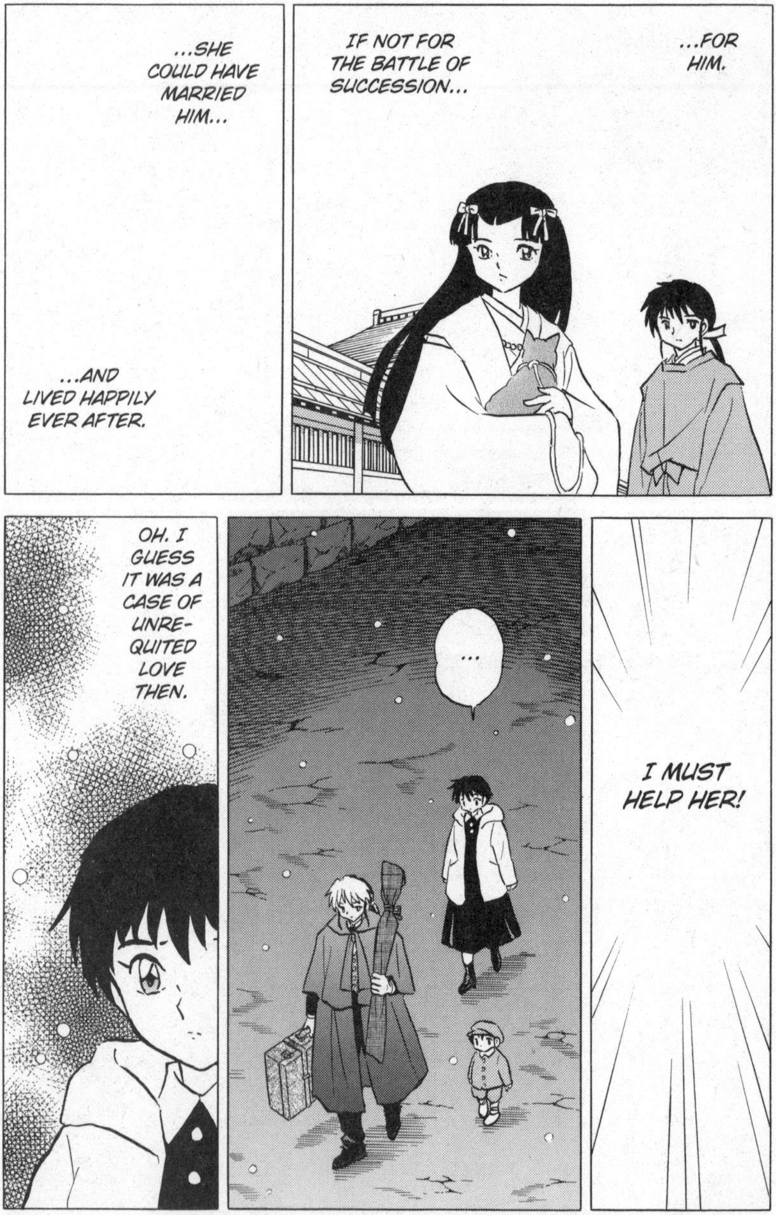
...FOR HIM.
IF NOT FOR THE BATTLE OF SUCCESSION...
...SHE COULD HAVE MARRIED HIM...
...AND LIVED HAPPILY EVER AFTER.
I MUST HELP HER!
...
OH. I GUESS IT WAS A CASE OF UNRE-QUITED LOVE THEN.

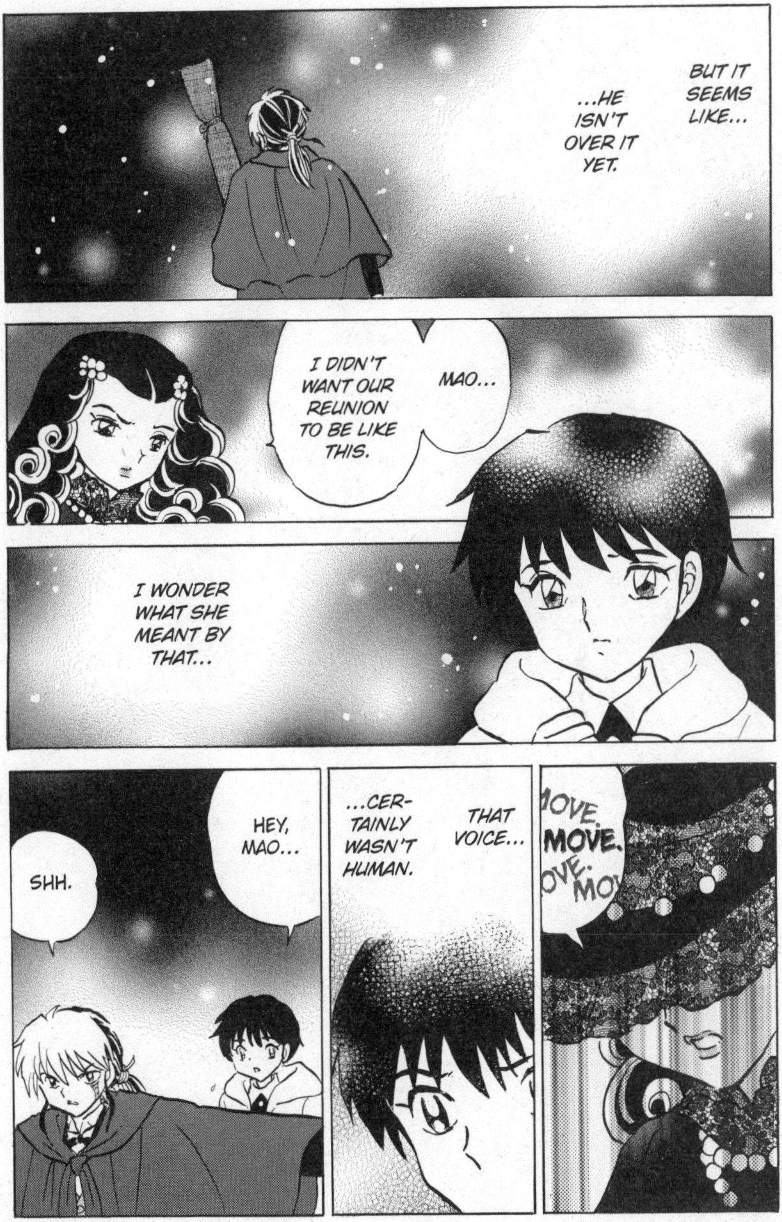
BUT IT SEEMS LIKE...
...HE ISN'T OVER IT YET.
MAO...
I DIDN'T WANT OUR REUNION TO BE LIKE THIS.
I WONDER WHAT SHE MEANT BY THAT...
MOVE.
THAT VOICE...
...CER-TAINLY WASN'T HUMAN.
HEY, MAO...
SHH.

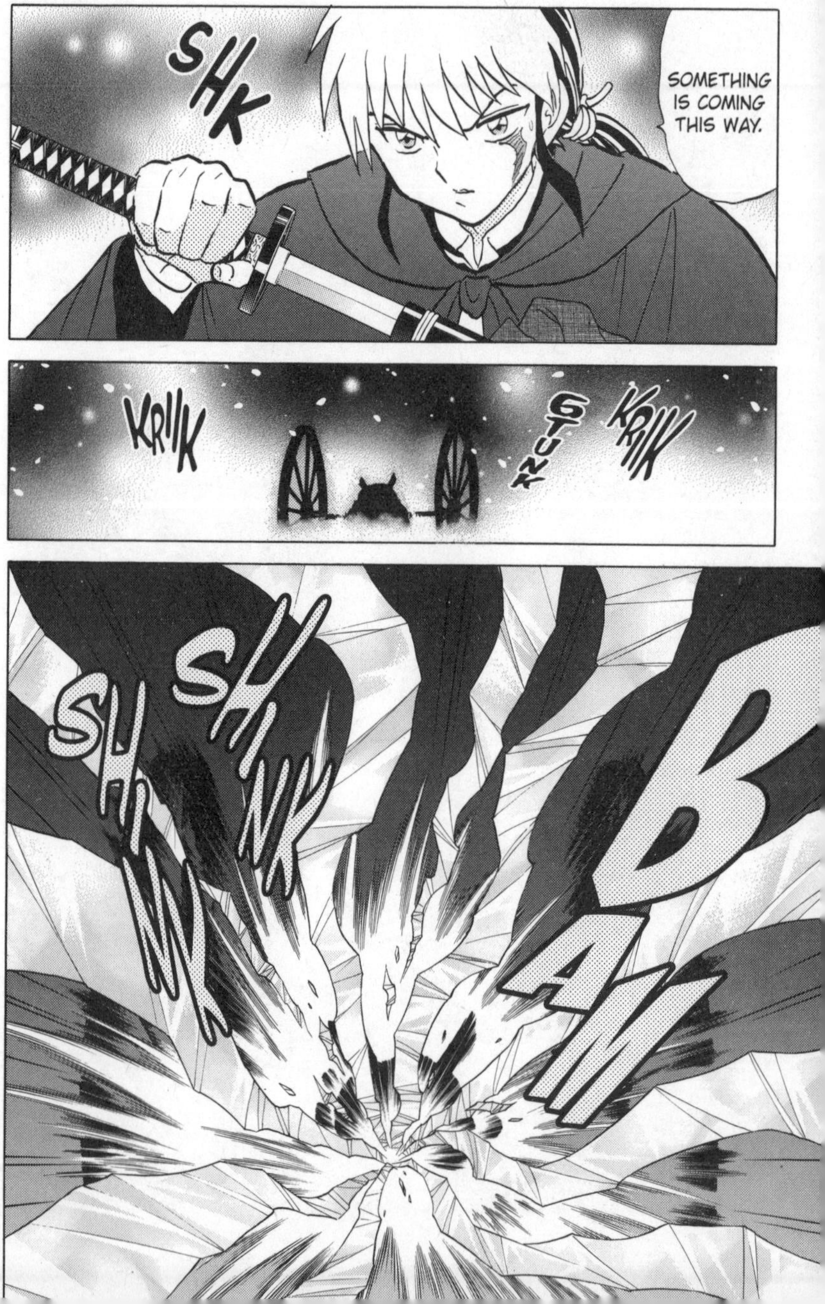
SOMETHING IS COMING THIS WAY.
SHK
KRIIK
STUNK
KRIIK
BAM
SHIIINK
SHIIINK

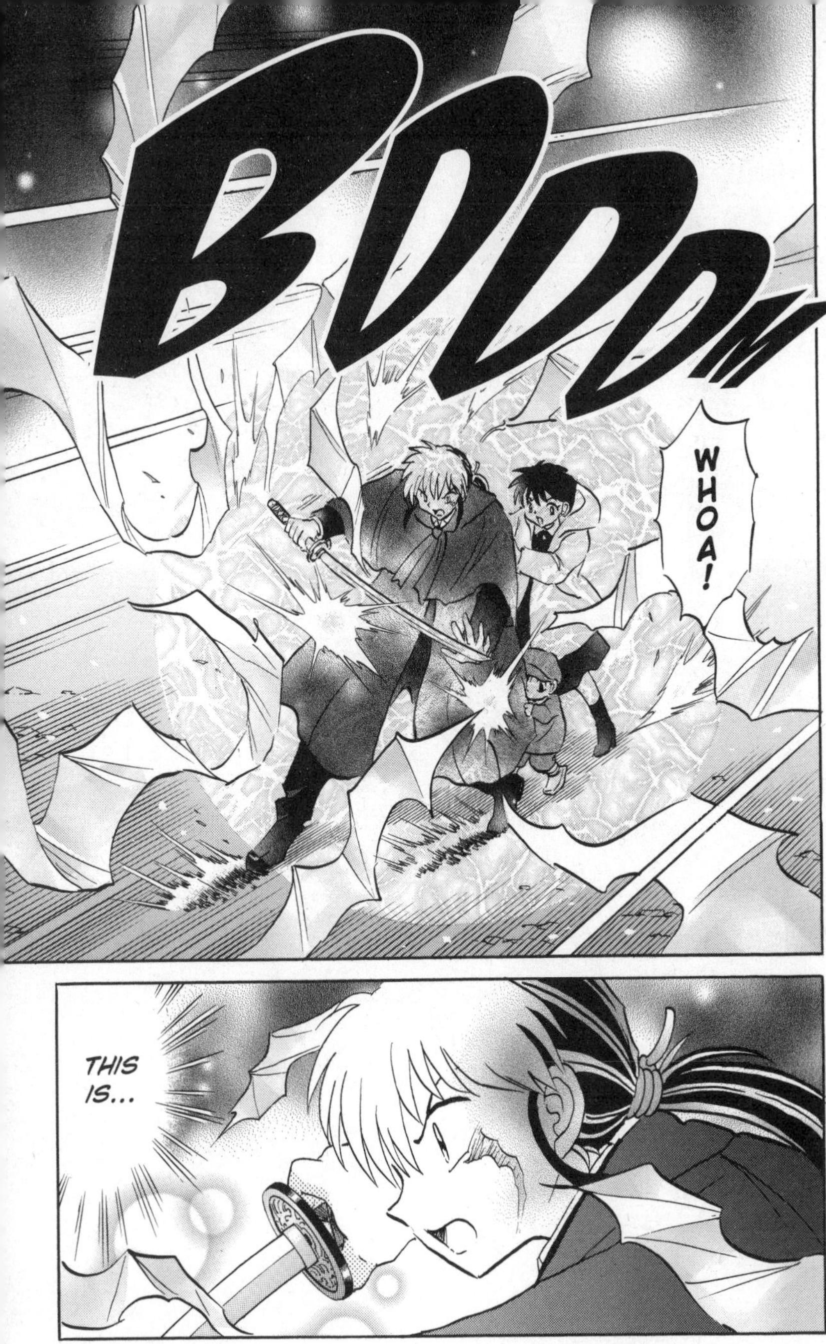
BOOOM
WHOA!
THIS IS...

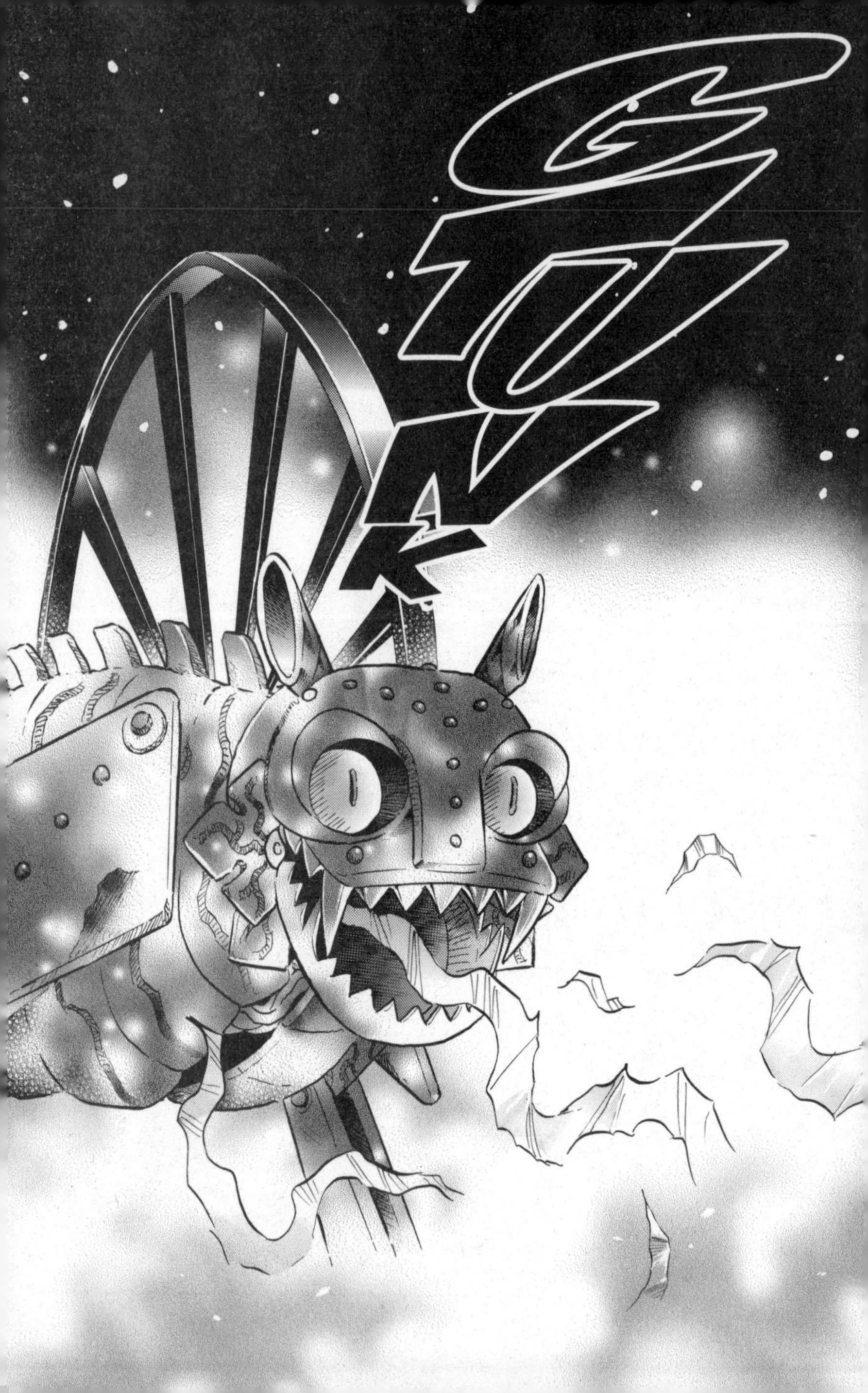
GLUNK

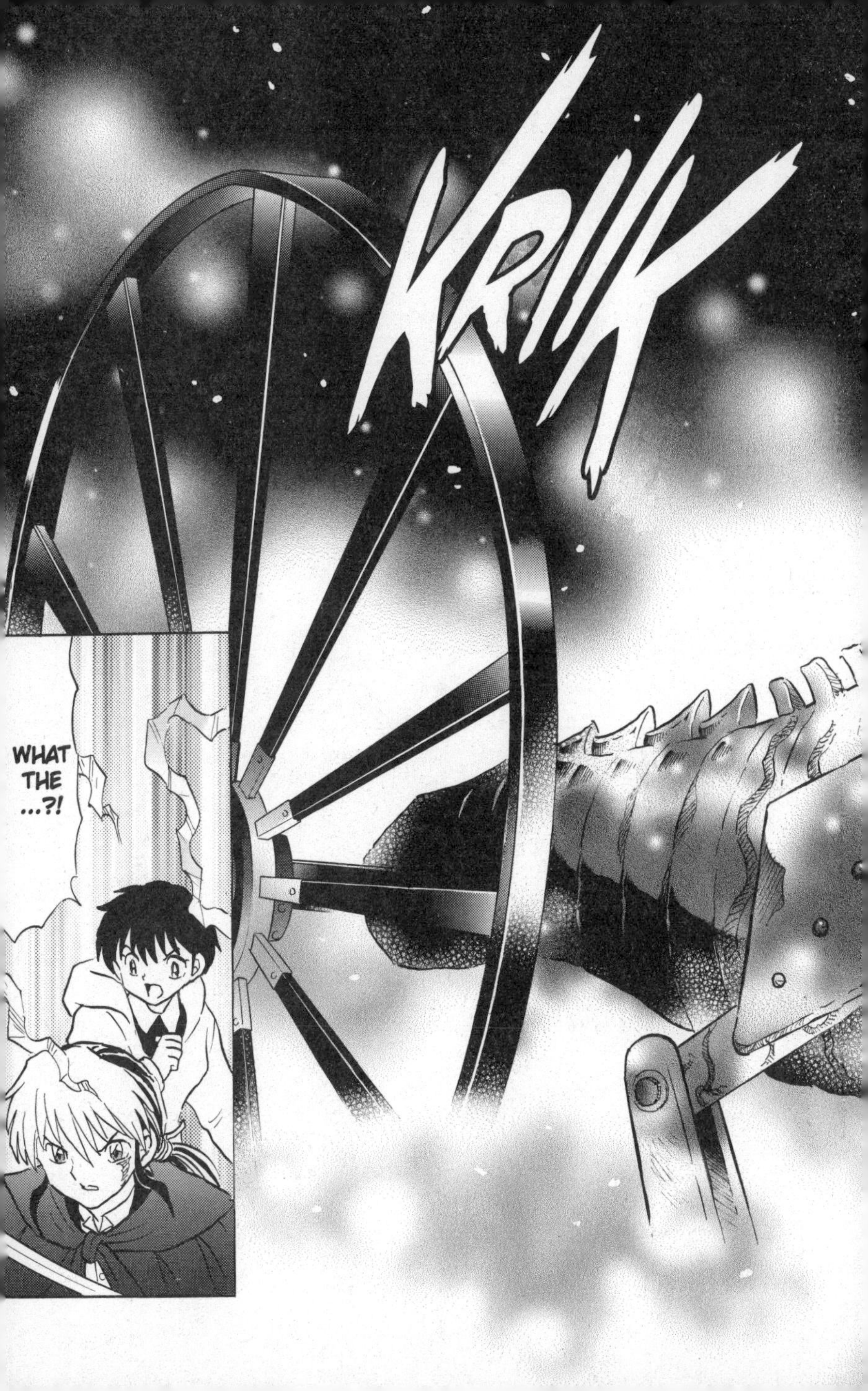
KRIIK
WHAT THE ...?!

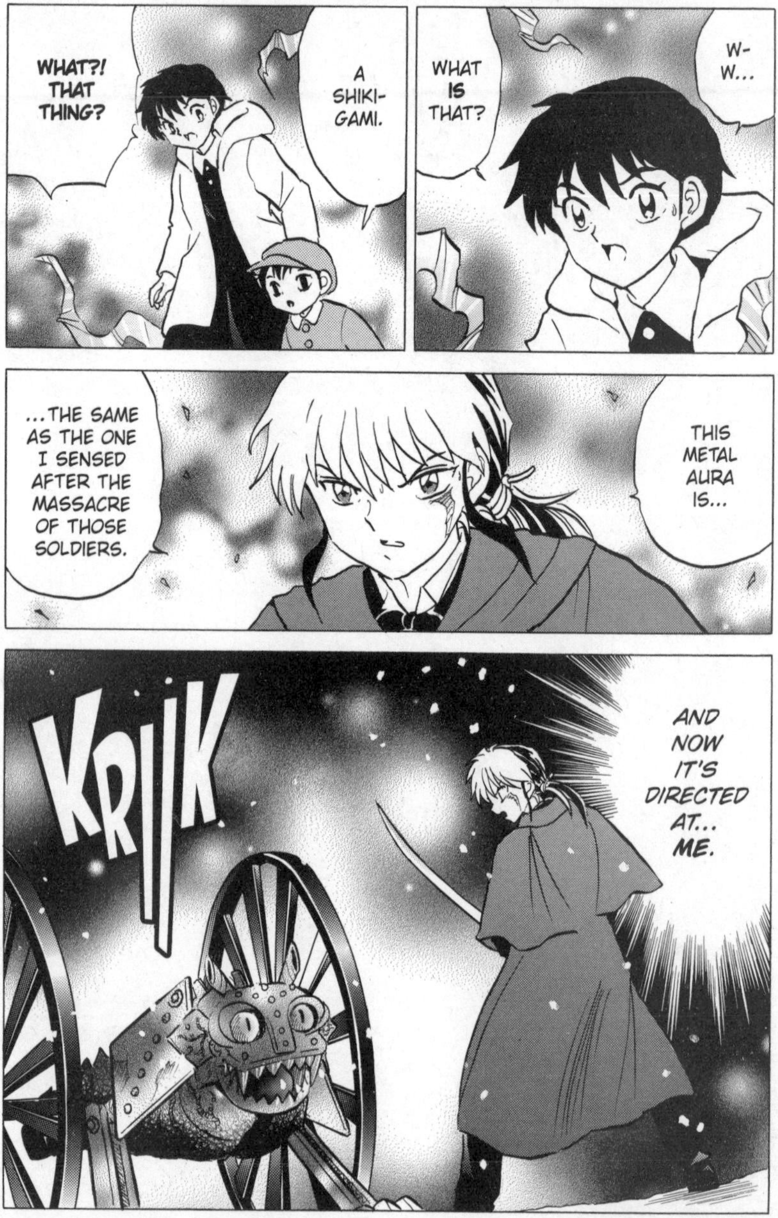
W-W...
WHAT IS THAT?
A SHIKI-GAMI.
WHAT?! THAT THING?
THIS METAL AURA IS...
...THE SAME AS THE ONE I SENSED AFTER THE MASSACRE OF THOSE SOLDIERS.
AND NOW IT'S DIRECTED AT... ME.
KRIIK

Chapter 10:
The Metal Shikigami

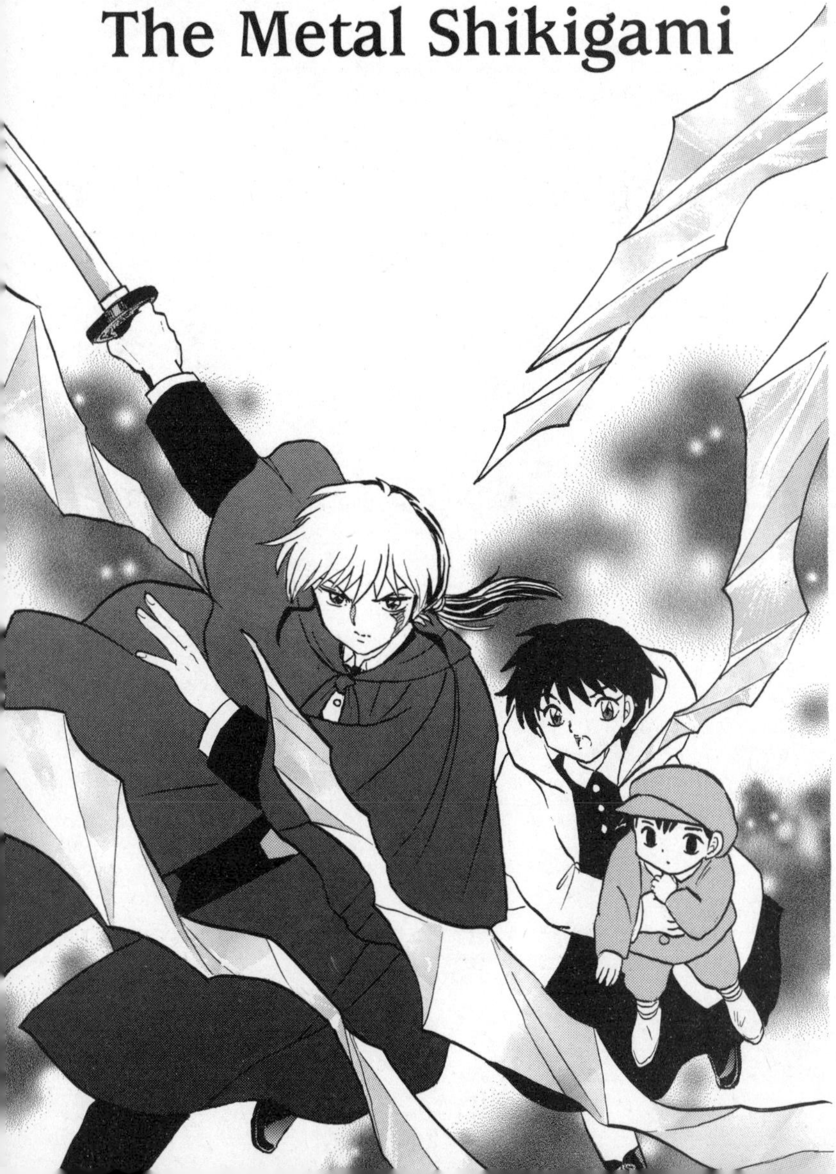

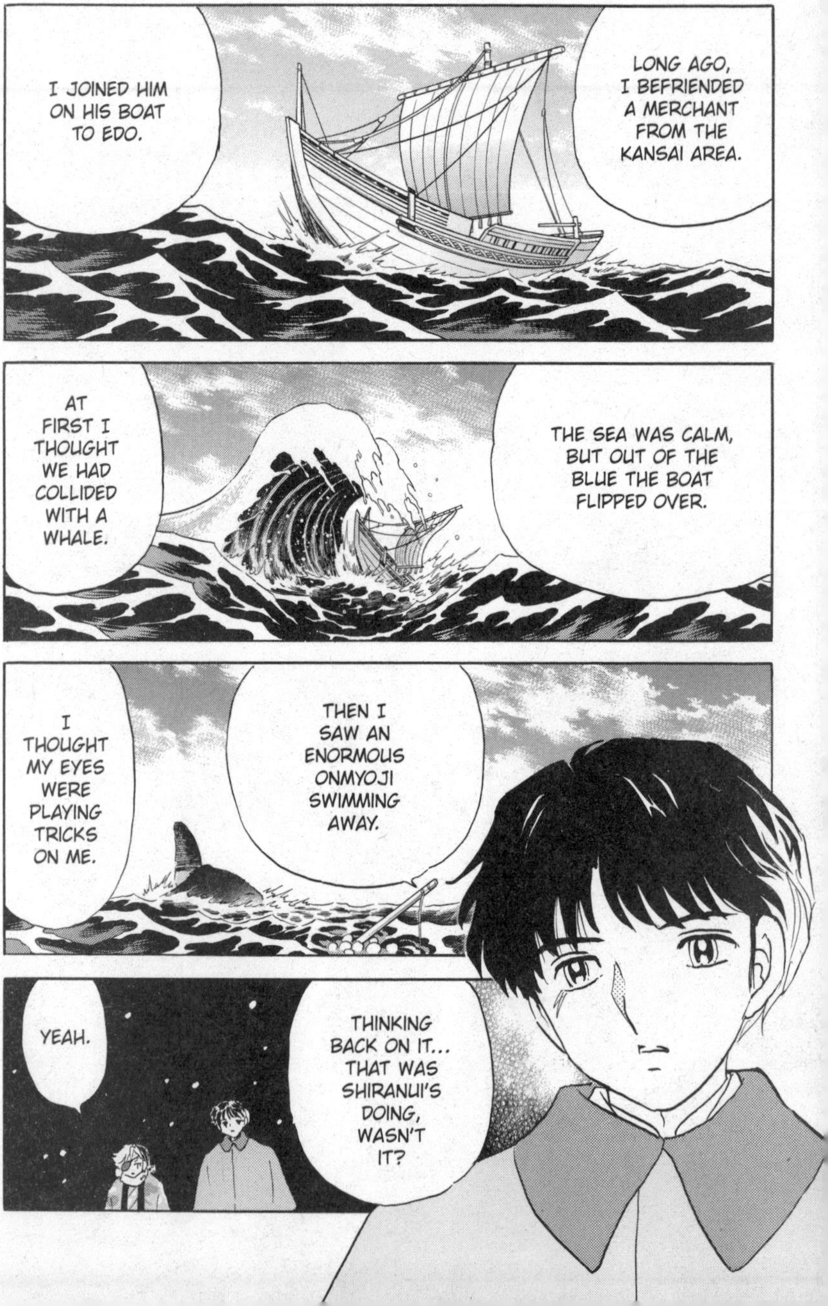
LONG AGO, I BEFRIENDED A MERCHANT FROM THE KANSAI AREA.
I JOINED HIM ON HIS BOAT TO EDO.
THE SEA WAS CALM, BUT OUT OF THE BLUE THE BOAT FLIPPED OVER.
AT FIRST I THOUGHT WE HAD COLLIDED WITH A WHALE.
THEN I SAW AN ENORMOUS ONMYOJI SWIMMING AWAY.
I THOUGHT MY EYES WERE PLAYING TRICKS ON ME.
THINKING BACK ON IT... THAT WAS SHIRANUI'S DOING, WASN'T IT?
YEAH.

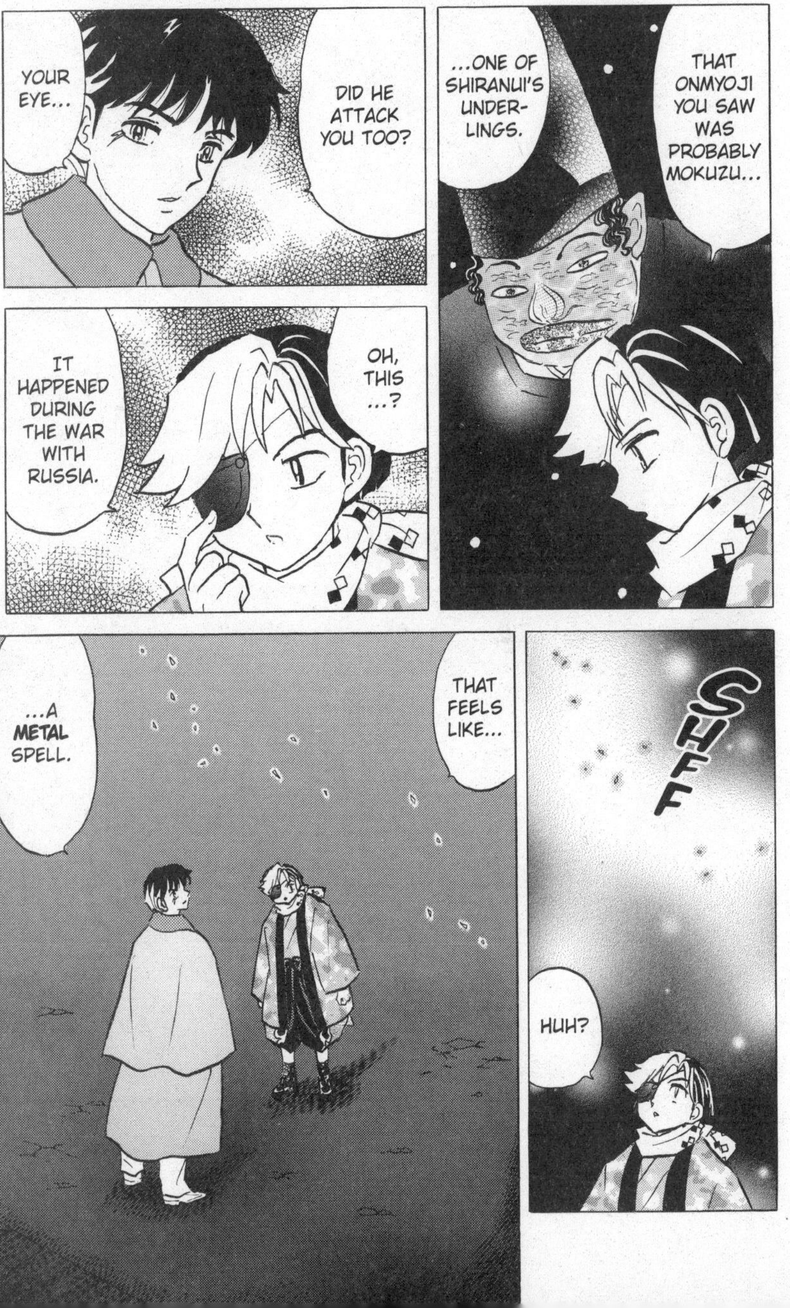
THAT ONMYOJI YOU SAW WAS PROBABLY MOKUZU...
...ONE OF SHIRANUI'S UNDER-LINGS.
YOUR EYE...
DID HE ATTACK YOU TOO?
OH, THIS ...?
IT HAPPENED DURING THE WAR WITH RUSSIA.
SHFF
HUH?
THAT FEELS LIKE...
...A **METAL** SPELL.

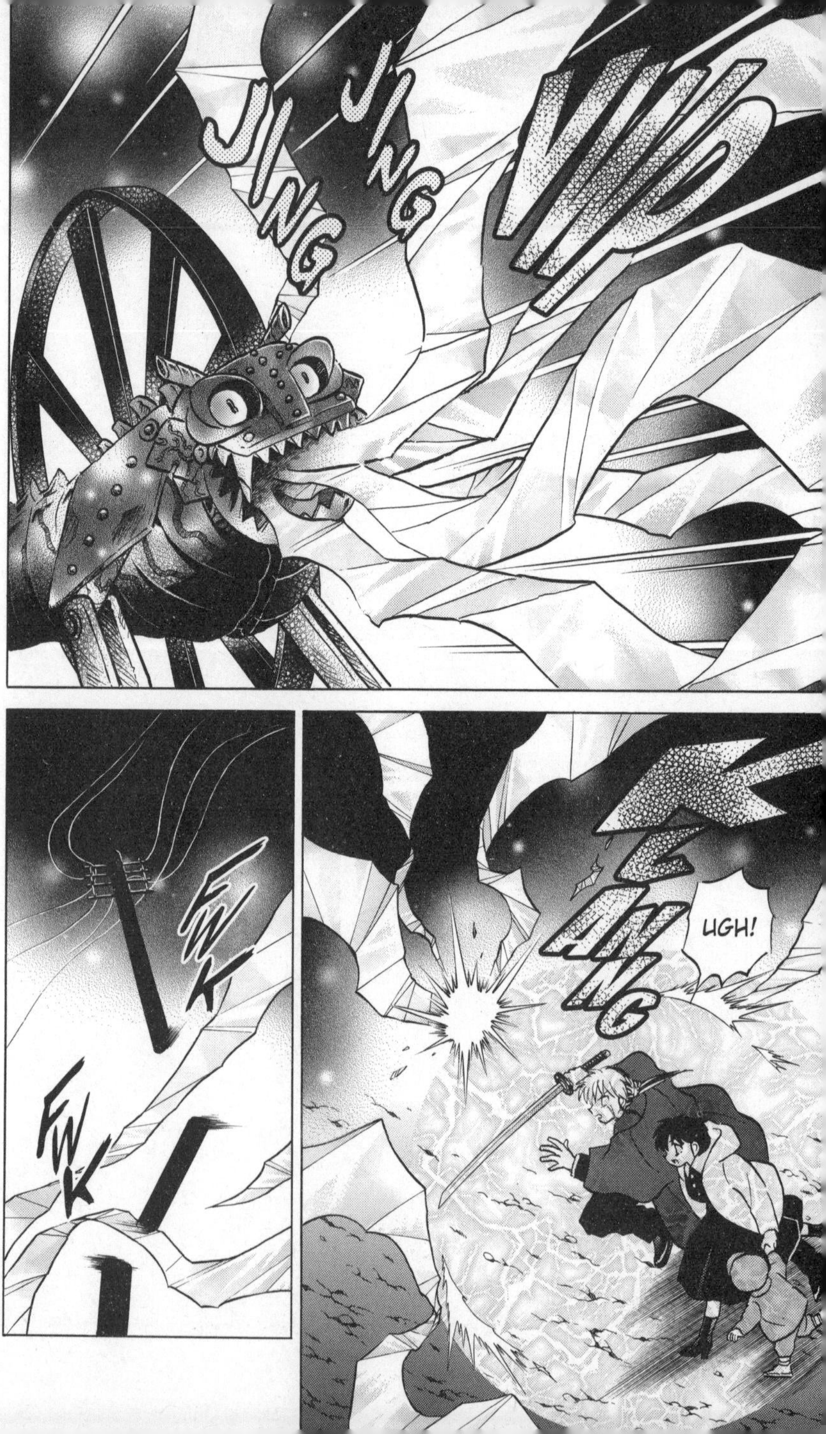
JING JING
VWD
ZWANG
UGH!
FWK
FWK

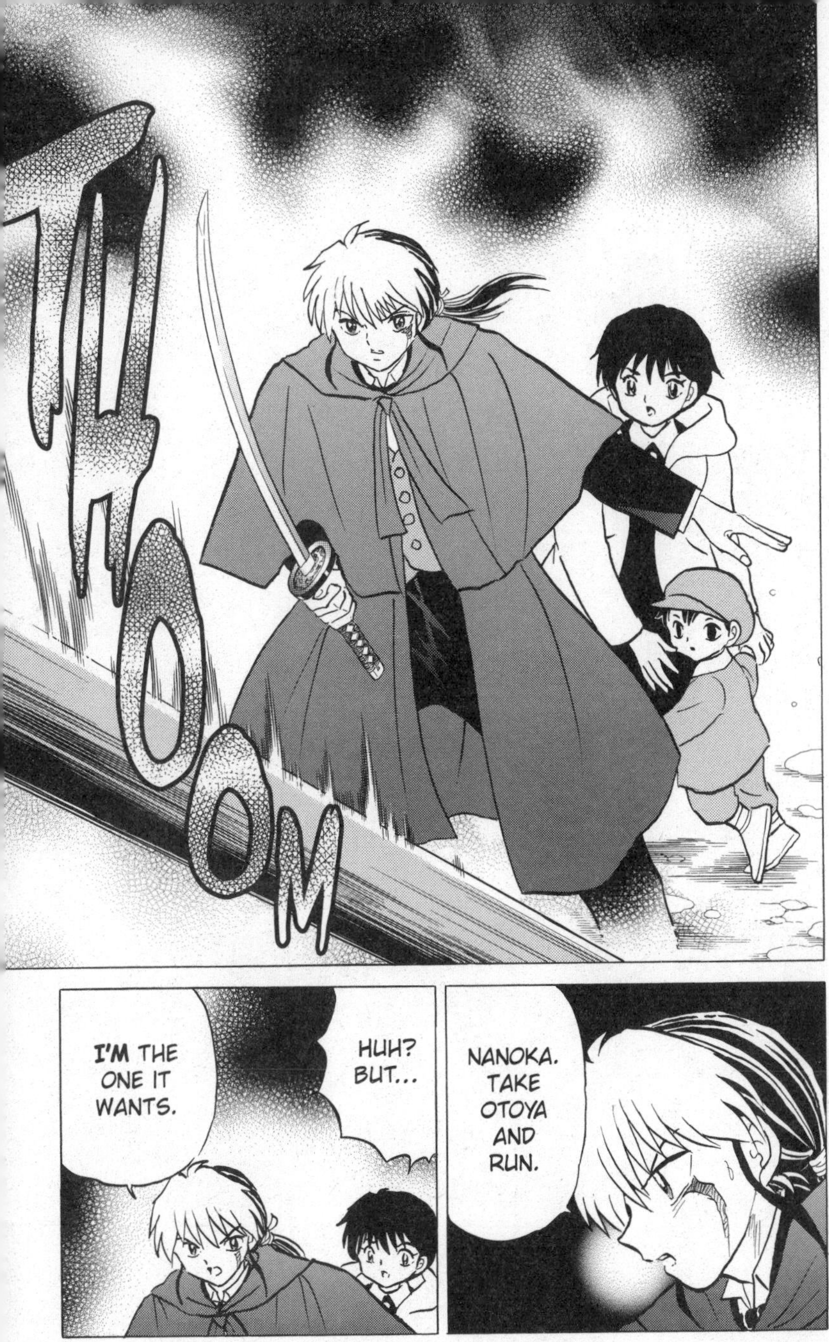
THOOM
NANOKA. TAKE OTOYA AND RUN.
HUH? BUT...
I'M THE ONE IT WANTS.

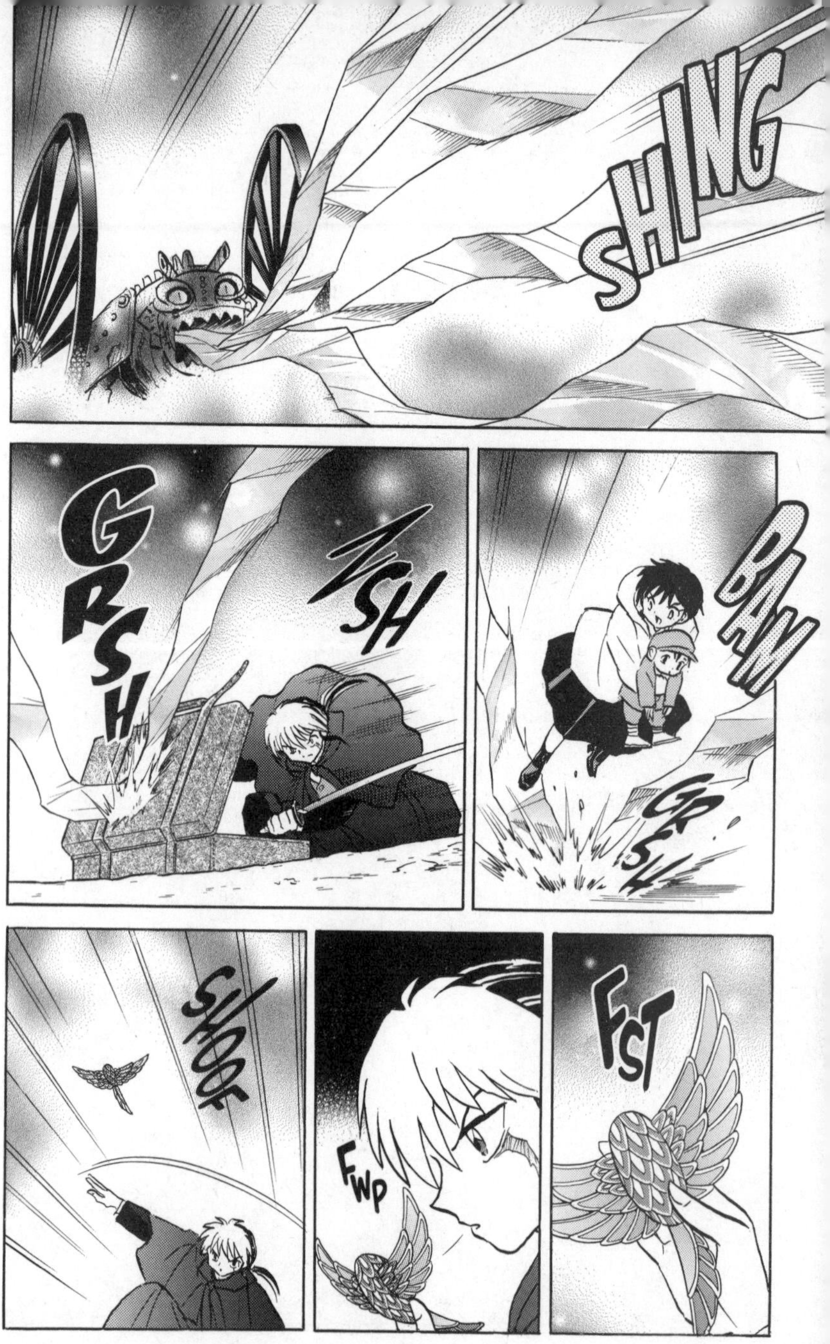
SHING
BAM
GRSH
GRSH
VSH
FST
FWP
SHOOF

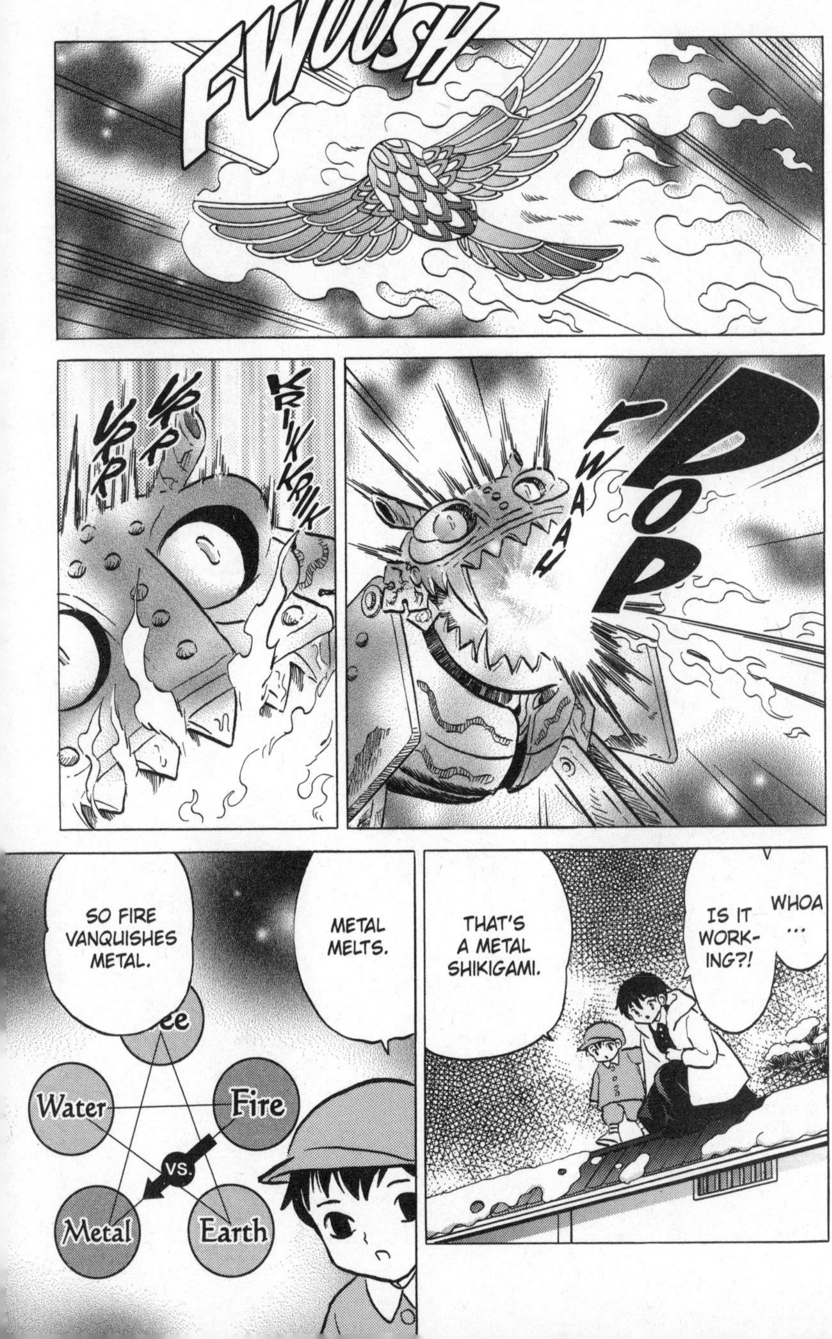
FWOOSH
POP
KWAAH
KRIK KRIK
VRR VRR
WHOA ...
IS IT WORKING?!
THAT'S A METAL SHIKIGAMI.
METAL MELTS.
SO FIRE VANQUISHES METAL.
Water
Fire
VS.
Metal
Earth

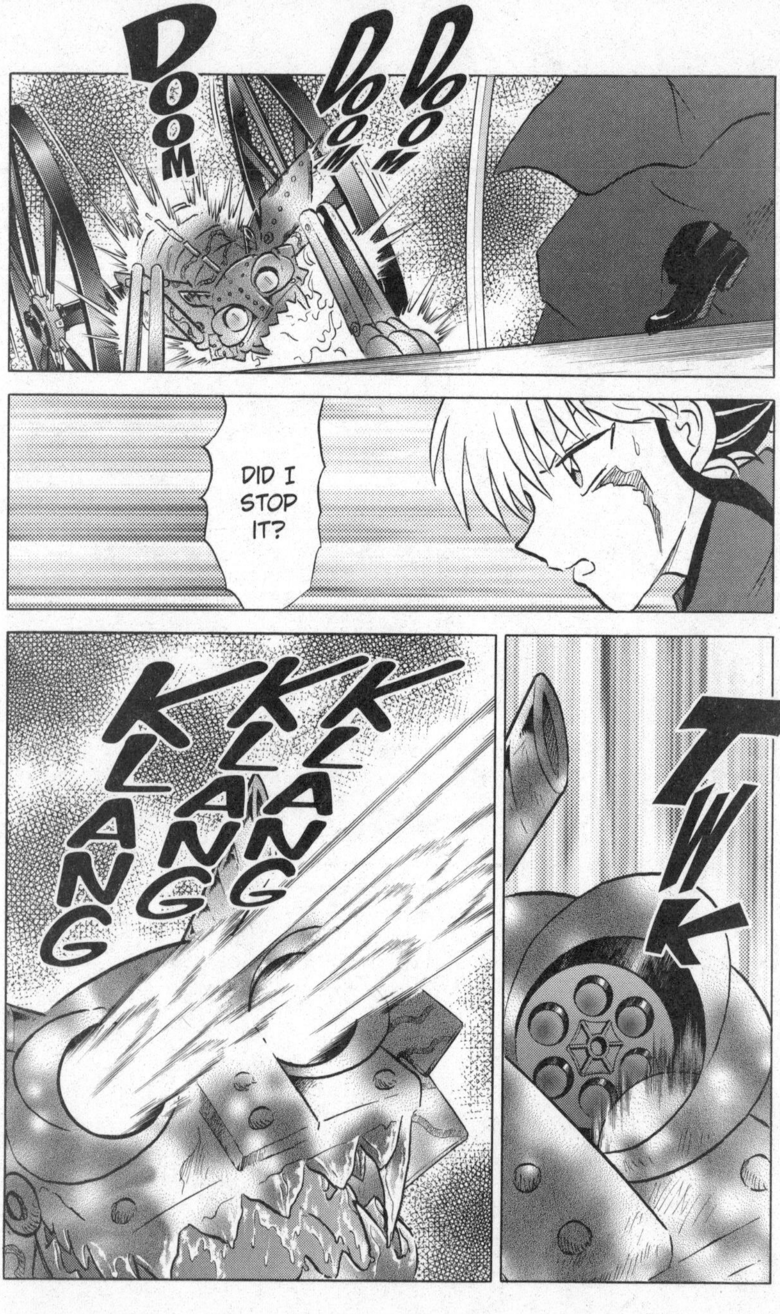
DOOOM
DOOOM
DOOOM
DID I STOP IT?
TWIK
KLANG
KLANG
KLANG

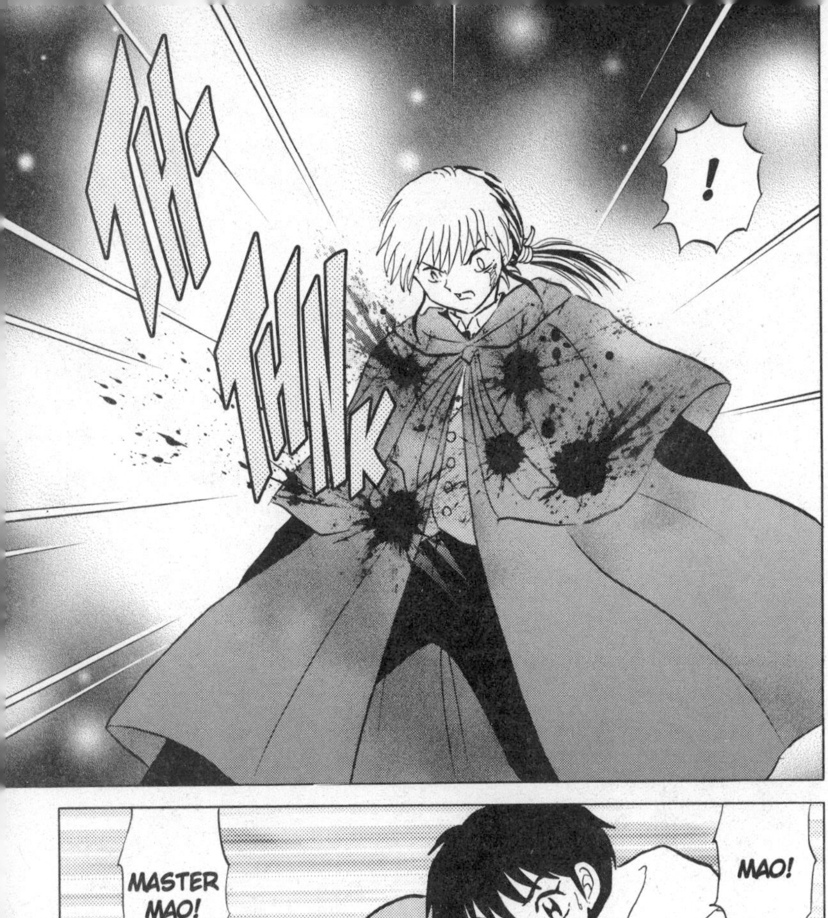
!
THUNK
MAO!
MASTER MAO!

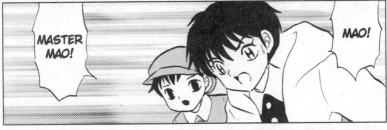

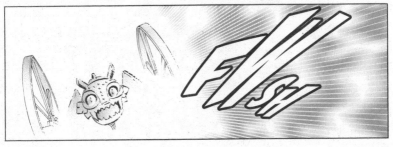

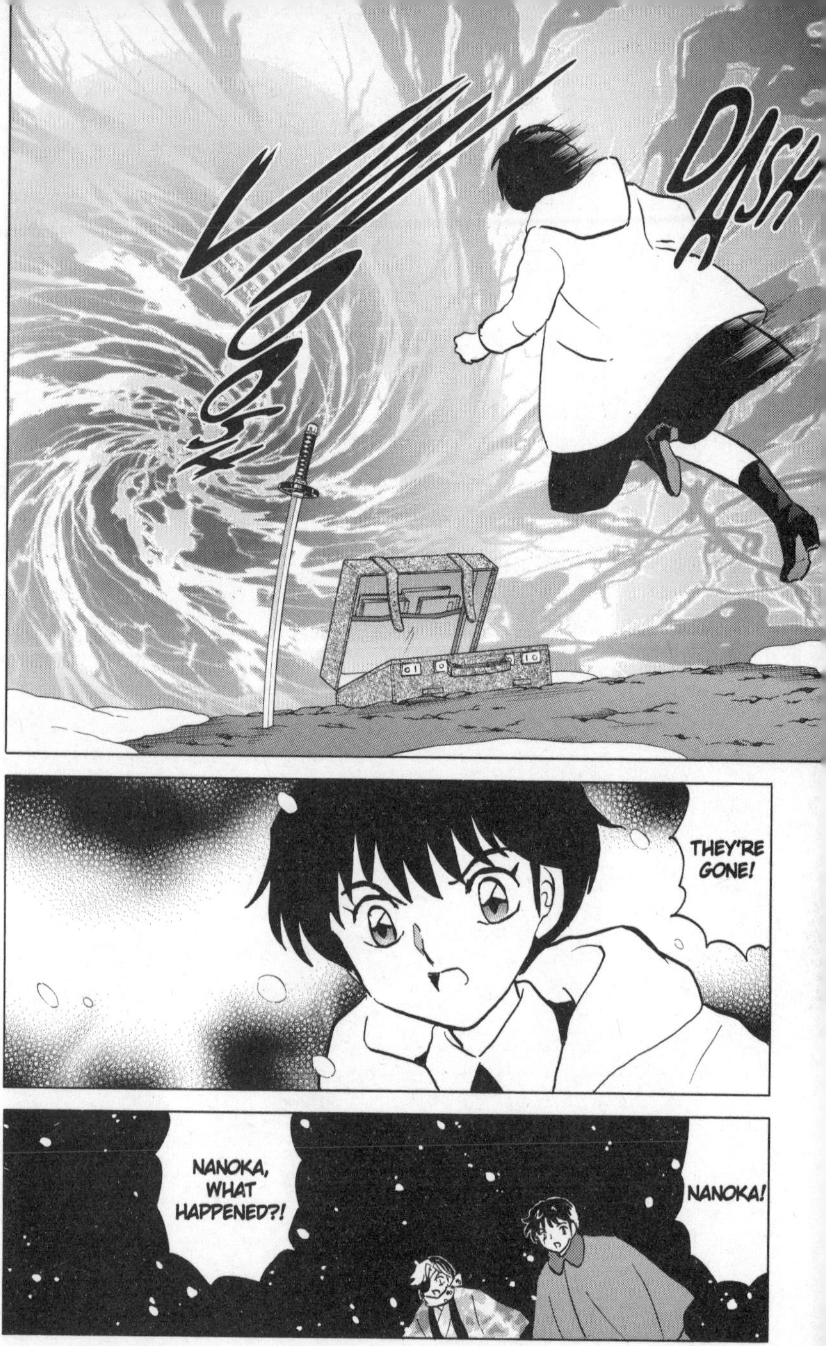
DASH
VWOOSH
THEY'RE GONE!
NANOKA!
NANOKA, WHAT HAPPENED?!

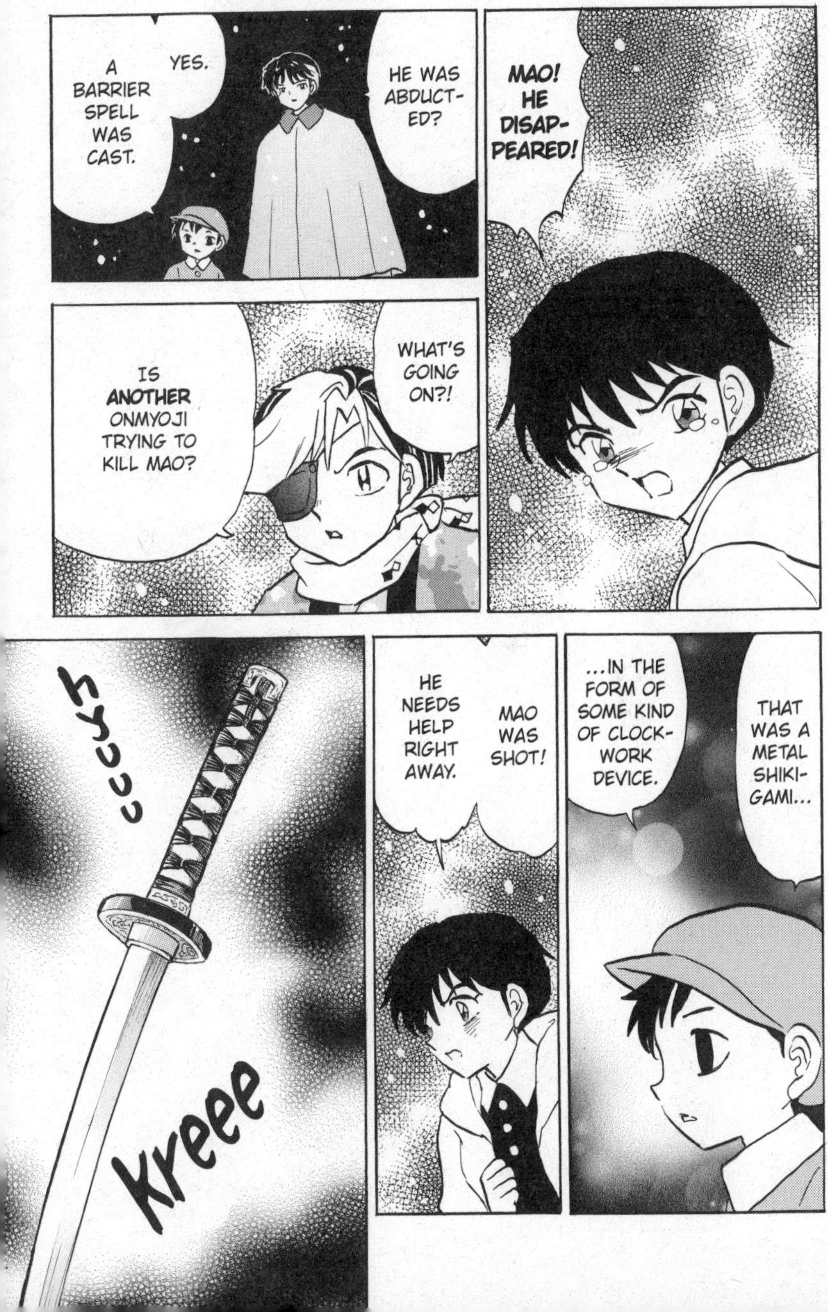
MAO! HE DISAPPEARED!
HE WAS ABDUCTED?
YES.
A BARRIER SPELL WAS CAST.
WHAT'S GOING ON?!
IS ANOTHER ONMYOJI TRYING TO KILL MAO?
THAT WAS A METAL SHIKIGAMI...
...IN THE FORM OF SOME KIND OF CLOCKWORK DEVICE.
MAO WAS SHOT!
HE NEEDS HELP RIGHT AWAY.
Kreee

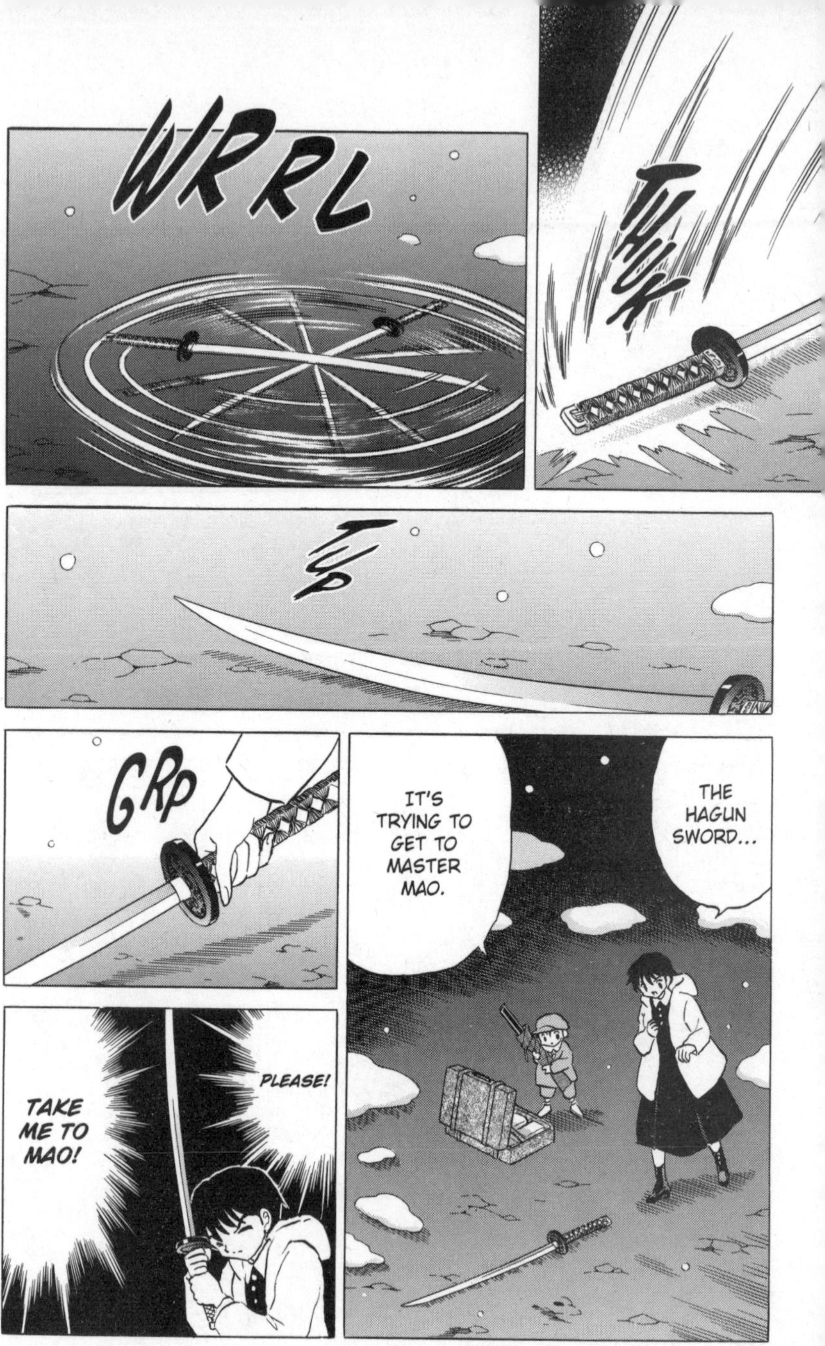
THUK
WRRL
TUP
THE HAGUN SWORD...
IT'S TRYING TO GET TO MASTER MAO.
GRP
PLEASE!
TAKE ME TO MAO!

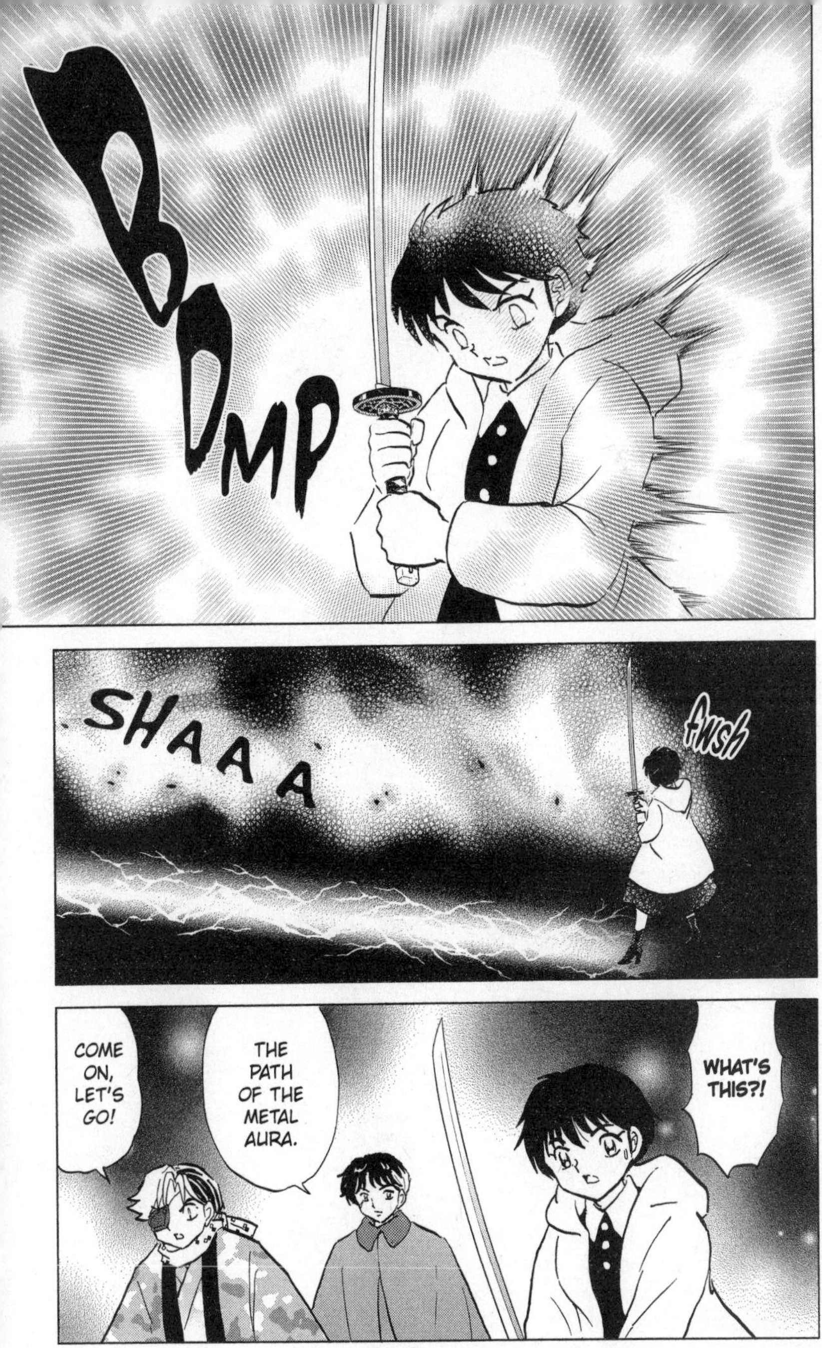
BDOMP
fwsh
SHAAAA
WHAT'S THIS?!
THE PATH OF THE METAL AURA.
COME ON, LET'S GO!

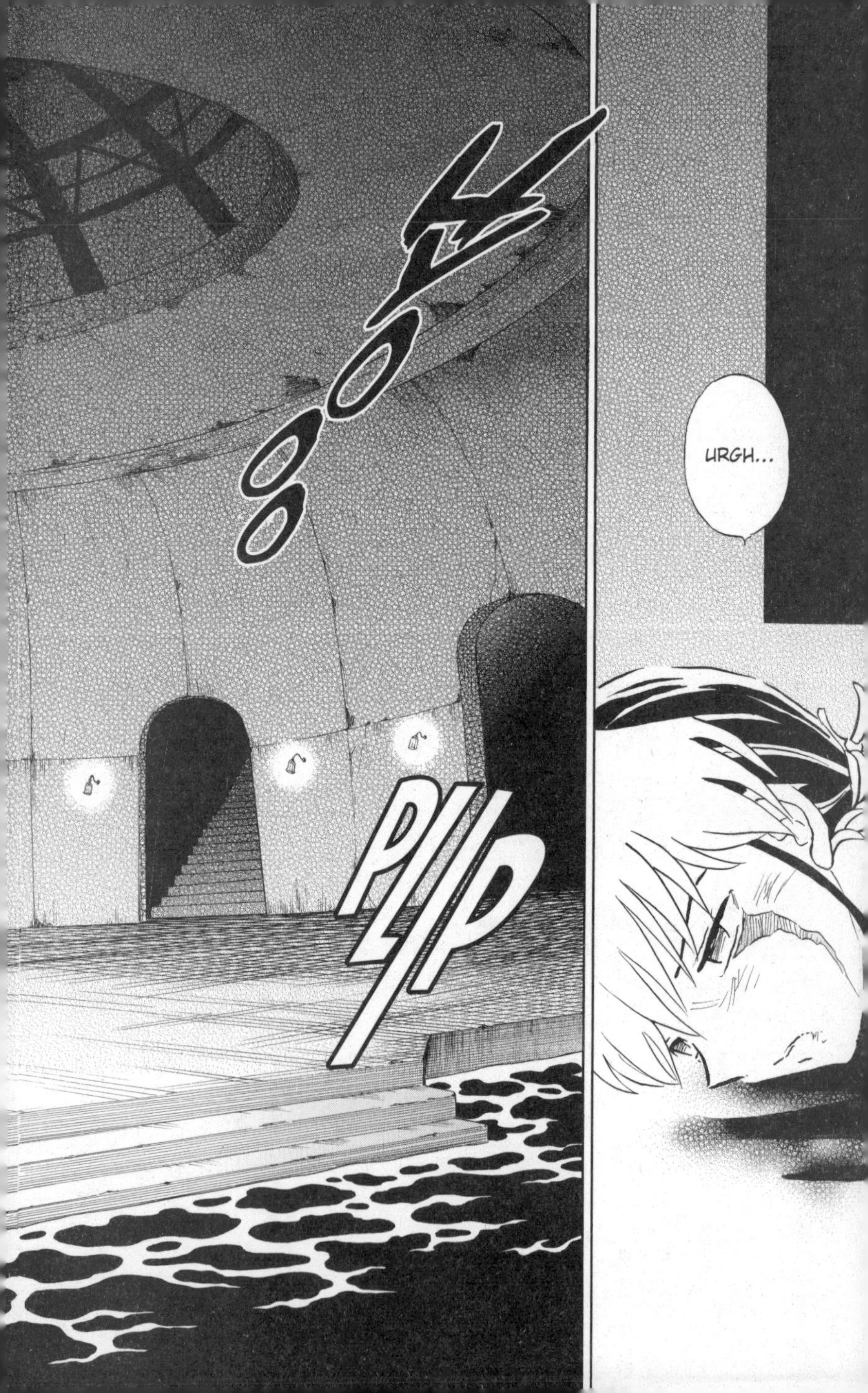
URGH...
WOOO
PLIP

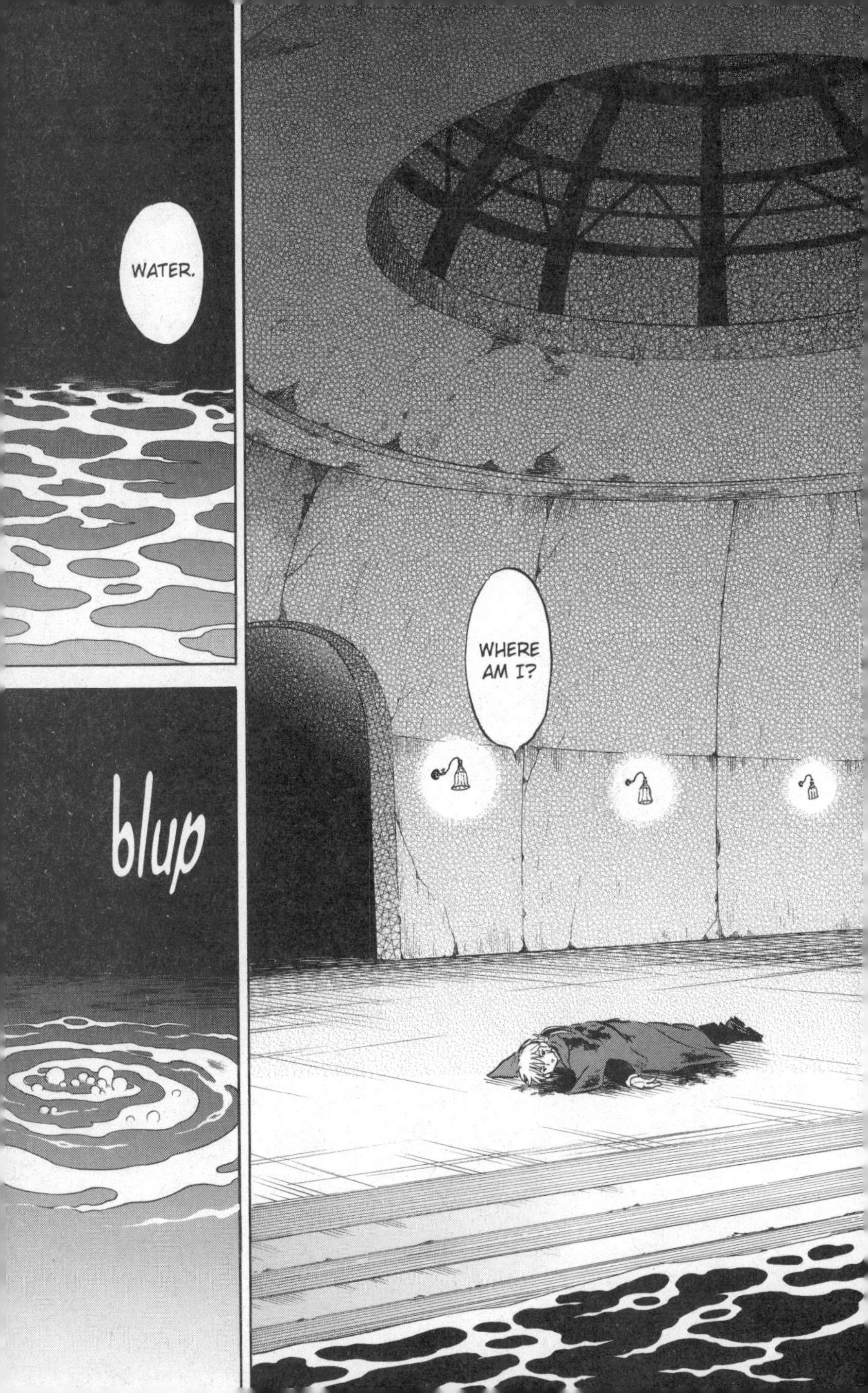
WHERE AM I?
WATER.
blup

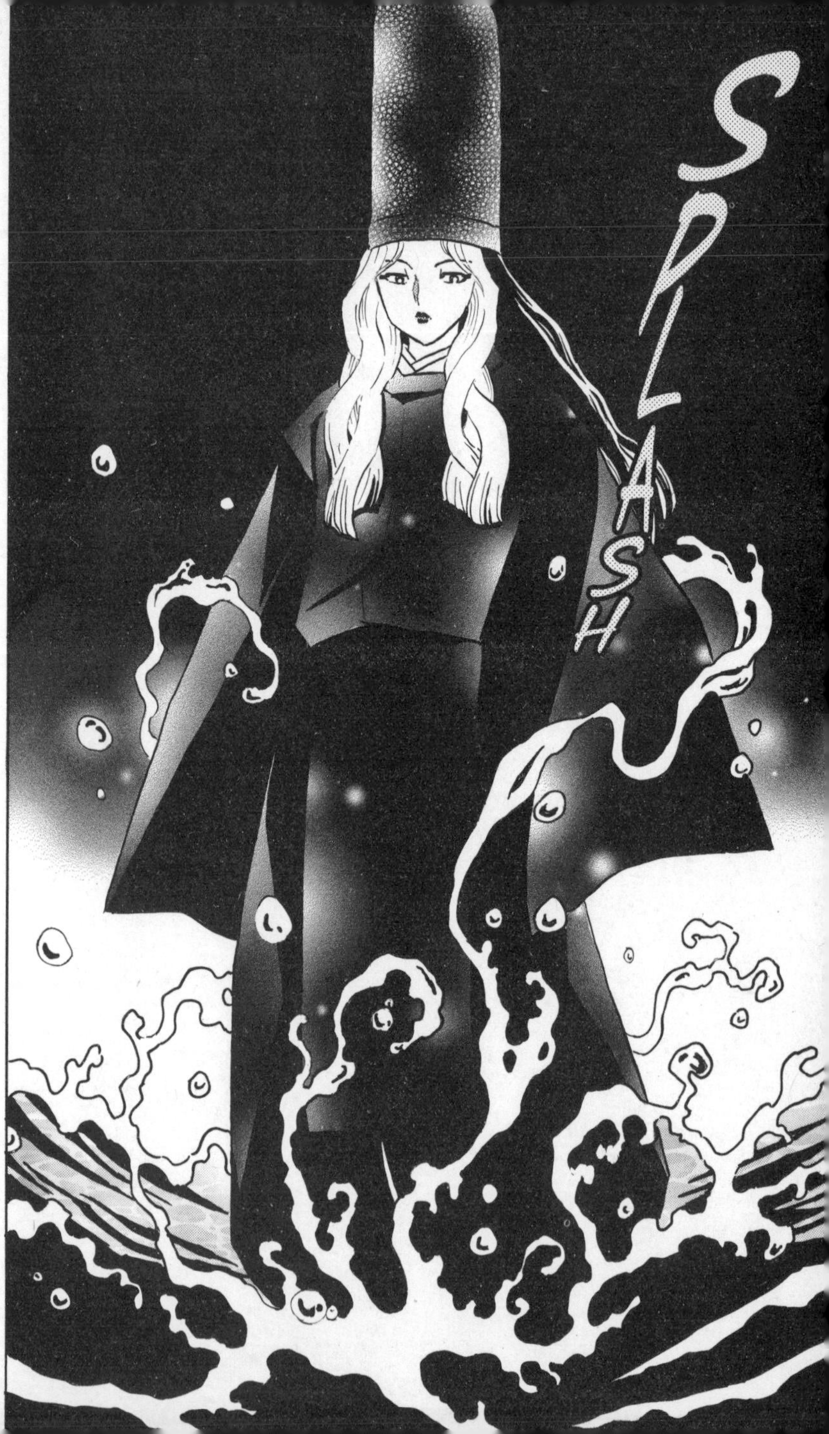
SPLASH

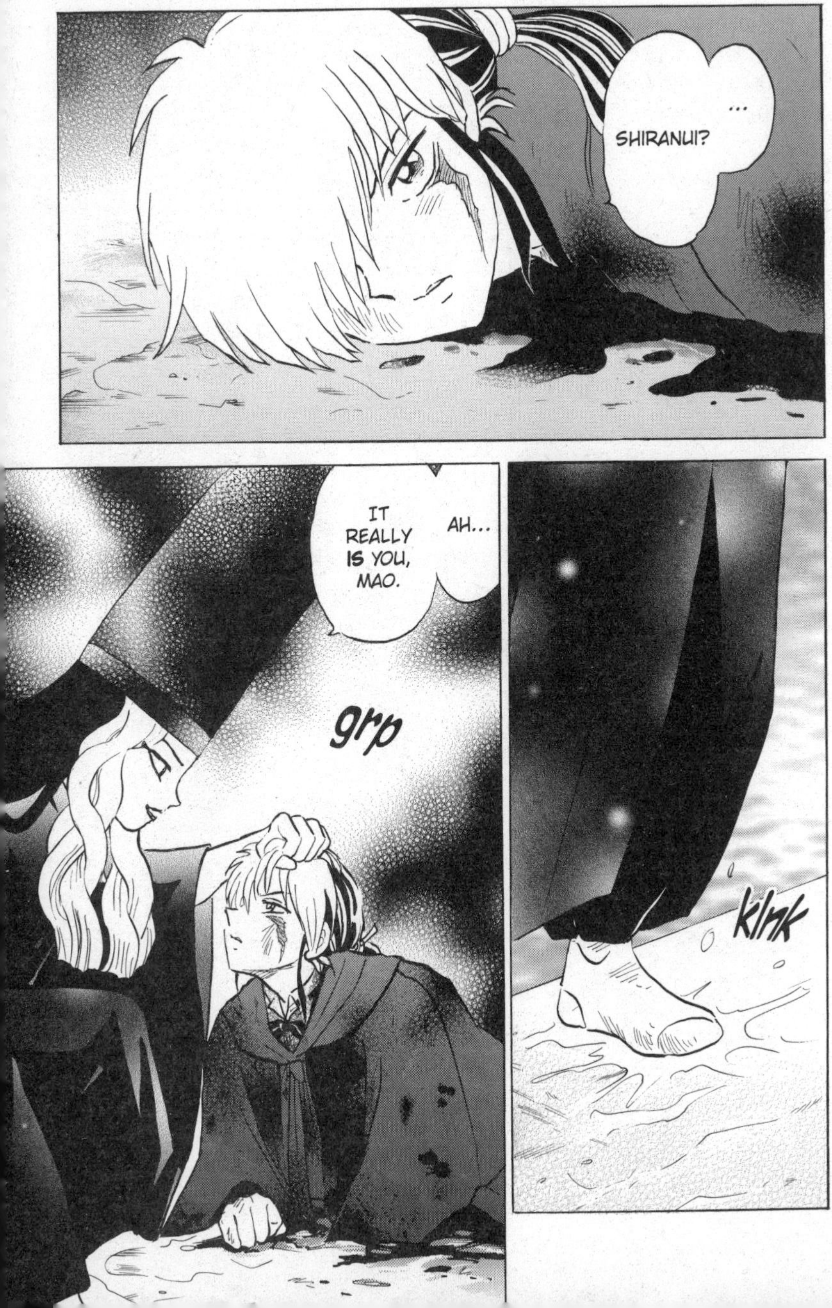

... SHIRANUI?
klink
AH...
IT REALLY **IS** YOU, MAO.
grp

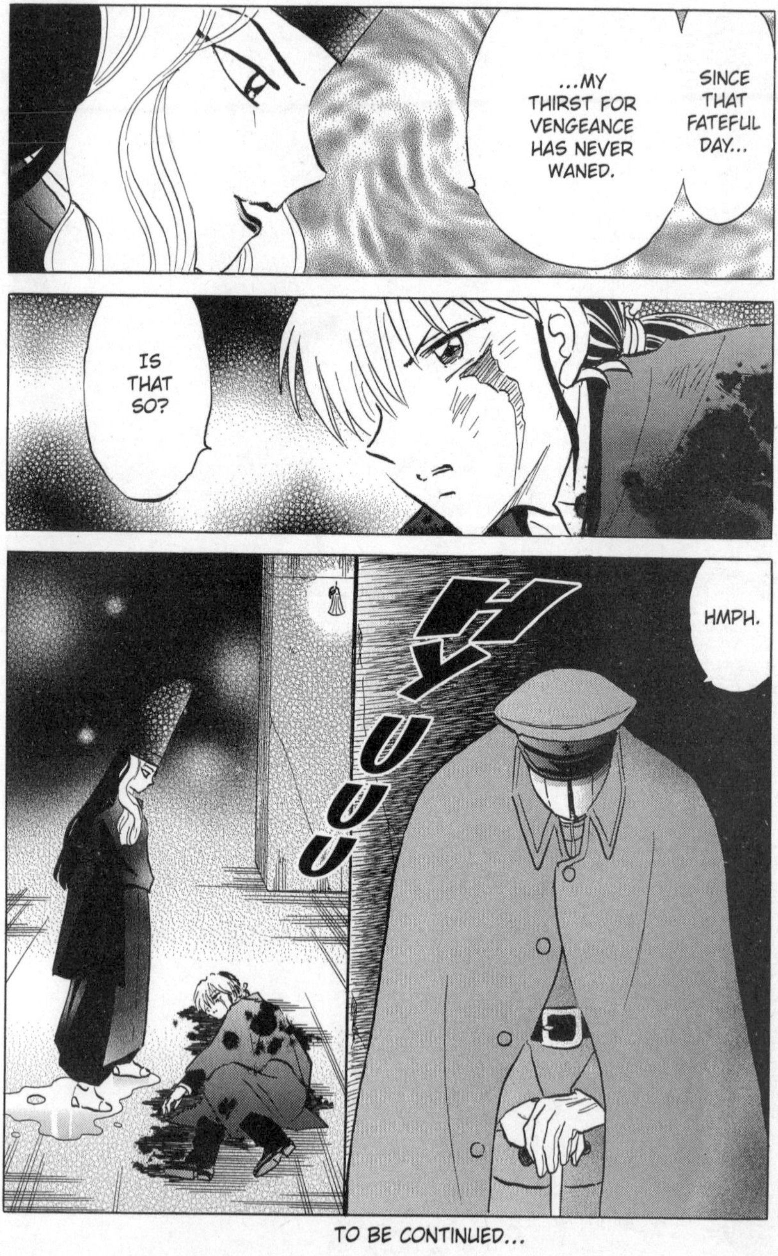
SINCE THAT FATEFUL DAY...
...MY THIRST FOR VENGEANCE HAS NEVER WANED.
IS THAT SO?
HMPH.
HYUUUU

TO BE CONTINUED...

Coming in Volume 6...

The reason for Shiranui's bitter grudge against Mao is revealed. And now he demands that Mao give him the Taizanfukun spell, which has the power to control life spans. But Shiranui isn't the only one who wants it! Then, when the gang floats theories about the origin of Byoki and his powers, Nanoka recruits Shiraha again to help with her research in the present day. Will Shiraha's crush on Nanoka ever be requited, or does she only have cat eyes for Mao? Plus, the story of the attack that left the scar under Mao's eye!

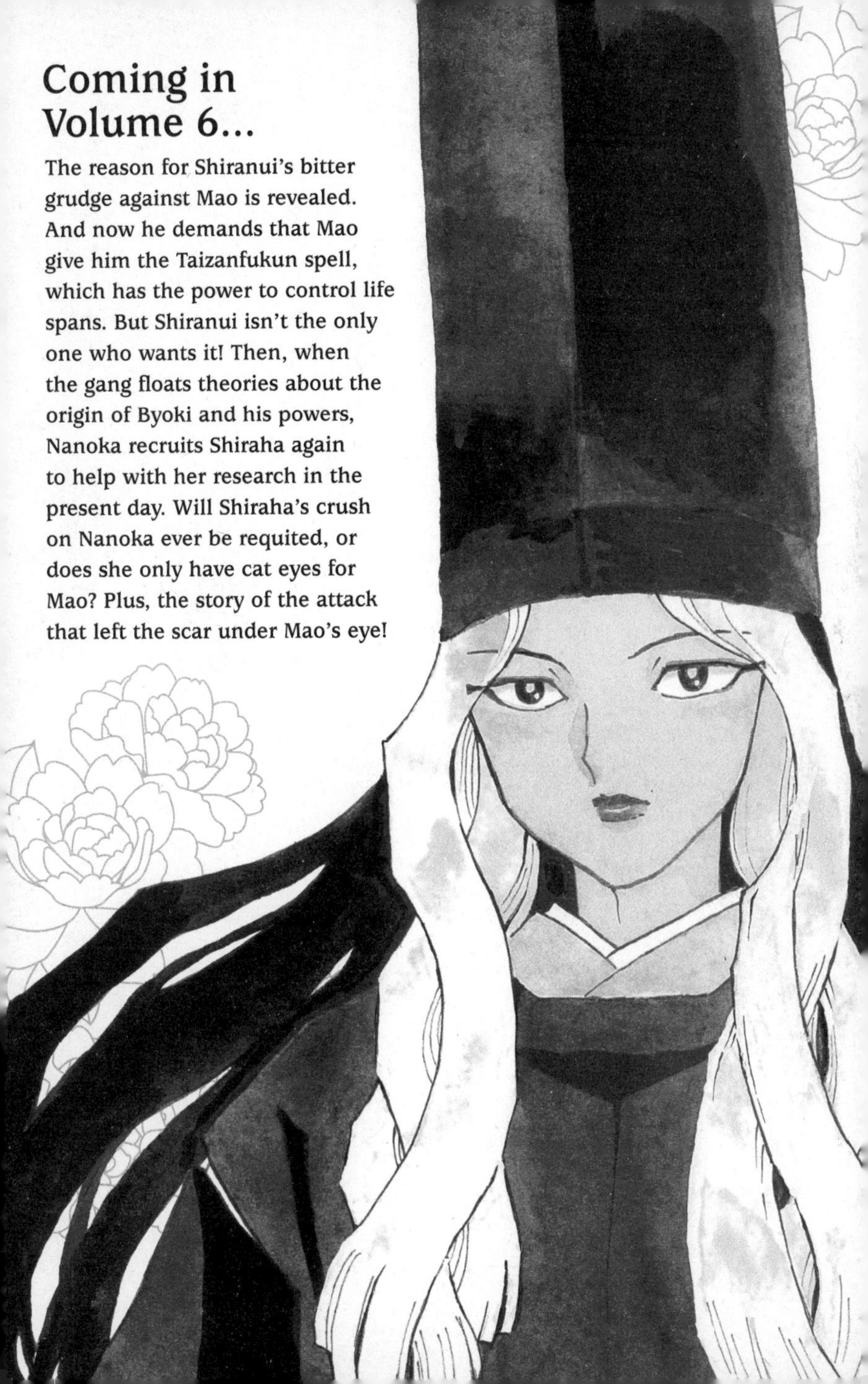

Rumiko Takahashi

The spotlight on Rumiko Takahashi's career began in 1978 when she won an honorable mention in Shogakukan's prestigious New Comic Artist Contest for *Those Selfish Aliens*. Later that same year, her boy-meets-alien comedy series, *Urusei Yatsura*, was serialized in *Weekly Shonen Sunday*. This phenomenally successful manga series was adapted into anime format and spawned a TV series and half a dozen theatrical-release movies, all incredibly popular in their own right. Takahashi followed up the success of her debut series with one blockbuster hit after another—*Maison Ikkoku* ran from 1980 to 1987, *Ranma ½* from 1987 to 1996, and *Inuyasha* from 1996 to 2008. Other notable works include *Mermaid Saga*, *Rumic Theater*, and *One-Pound Gospel*.

Takahashi was inducted into the Will Eisner Comic Awards Hall of Fame in 2018. She won the prestigious Shogakukan Manga Award twice in her career, once for *Urusei Yatsura* in 1981 and the second time for *Inuyasha* in 2002. A majority of the Takahashi canon has been adapted into other media such as anime, live-action TV series, and film. Takahashi's manga, as well as the other formats her work has been adapted into, have continued to delight generations of fans around the world. Distinguished by her wonderfully endearing characters, Takahashi's work adeptly incorporates a wide variety of elements such as comedy, romance, fantasy, and martial arts. While her series are difficult to pin down into one simple genre, the signature style she has created has come to be known as the "Rumic World." Rumiko Takahashi is an artist who truly represents the very best from the world of manga.

MAO

VOLUME 5
Shonen Sunday Edition

STORY AND ART BY
RUMIKO TAKAHASHI

MAO Vol. 5
by Rumiko TAKAHASHI
© 2019 Rumiko TAKAHASHI
All rights reserved.
Original Japanese edition published by SHOGAKUKAN.
English translation rights in the United States of America,
Canada, the United Kingdom, Ireland, Australia, and New
Zealand arranged with SHOGAKUKAN.

Original Cover Design: Chie SATO + Bay Bridge Studio

Translation/Junko Goda
English Adaptation/Shaenon K. Garrity
Touch-up Art & Lettering/Susan Daigle-Leach
Cover & Interior Design/Yukiko Whitley
Editor/Annette Roman

Printed in the U.S.A.

Published by VIZ Media, LLC
P.O. Box 77010
San Francisco, CA 94107

10 9 8 7 6 5 4 3 2 1
First printing, May 2022

viz.com

shonensunday.com

Hey! You're Reading in the Wrong Direction!

This is the end of this graphic novel!

To properly enjoy this VIZ graphic novel, please turn it around and begin reading from right to left. Unlike English, Japanese is read right to left, so Japanese comics are read in reverse order from the way English comics are typically read.

This book has been printed in the original Japanese format in order to preserve the orientation of the original artwork. Have fun with it!

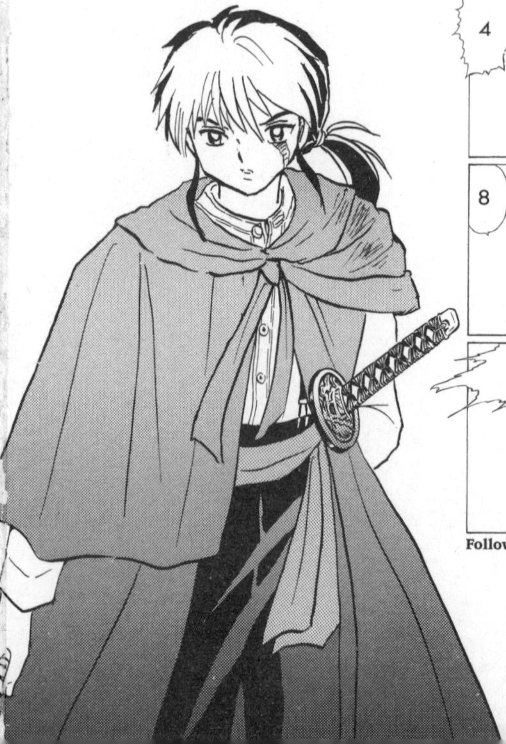

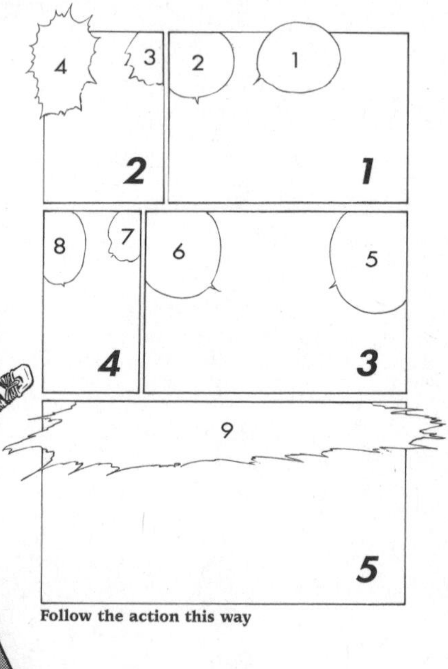
1
2
1
3
4
2
5
6
3
7
8
4
9
5
Follow the action this way